SOCIALISM
FROM BELOW

Hal Draper

SOCIALISM FROM BELOW

Hal Draper

Haymarket Books
Chicago, Illinois

First published in 2001 by Center for Socialist History, Alameda, California
© 2019 Center for Socialist History

This edition published in 2019 by
Haymarket Books
P.O. Box 180165
Chicago, IL 60618
773-583-7884
www.haymarketbooks.org
info@haymarketbooks.org

ISBN: 978-1-60846-792-1

Distributed to the trade in the US through Consortium Book Sales and Dis-
tribution (www.cbsd.com) and internationally through Ingram Publisher
Services International (www.ingramcontent.com).

This book was published with the generous support of Lannan Foundation
and Wallace Action Fund.

Special discounts are available for bulk purchases by organizations and
institutions. Please call 773-583-7884 or email info@haymarketbooks.org
for more information.

Cover photo of students at a mass demonstration on the Left Bank of the
Seine in Paris on June 1, 1968, to protest against President de Gaulle. (AP
Photo). Cover design by Jamie Kerry.

Printed in Canada by union labor.

Library of Congress Cataloging-in-Publication data is available.

10 9 8 7 6 5 4 3 2 1

TABLE OF CONTENTS

Introduction

The essays of Hal Draper collected here fall into three groups. The first section consists of a number of historical studies, most of them published in the socialist journal *New Politics* in the 1960s. All of them illustrate the thesis that he felt was central to understanding the current plight of the socialist movement. In his view, the divisions running through the history of the socialist movement between reformists and revolutionaries, authoritarians and democrats, putschists and gradualists – the divisions and disputes which have provided the categories in terms of which the history of the movement has been written – were secondary. The important distinction was between those socialists who looked for some outside authority which would hand down salvation to the grateful masses from above and those who saw the key to the reform of existing society in the struggle from below for self-emancipation.

This conviction did not arise in a vacuum. It was not the result of quiet contemplation. Hal Draper joined the socialist movement in 1934. It was one year after the triumph of Nazism in Germany. In Russia, the purge trials were just getting under way. The next few years saw the massive revolt of the Spanish working class in defense of democracy and socialism and the betrayal and defeat of that revolt. The decade ended with the signing of the Hitler-Stalin pact.

By the early 1940s there were plenty of prophets, James Burnham is perhaps the best known example, who insisted that hard-headed logic required everyone to accept the victory of the new totalitarian order (their term) as scientifically predetermined, however distasteful that prospect might seem. Capitalism was doomed but so was any democratic alternative to it. Hopefully, this new order would move in a more liberal and humane direction in the course of its development, leaving behind the admittedly somewhat crude and harsh early models built by Hitler, Stalin and Mussolini. Socialism and democracy, however, were definitely dead. Whatever progressive tasks the working class movement might have claimed as its goal were being carried out by the dictators much more expeditiously.

The thirties were, however, a time of popular rebellion as well as of defeat. The successes of Fascism and Stalinism which led some to despair drove others to the left. In the United States, the elementary explosion of labor militancy that gave birth to the CIO was as much a part of the story as was the demagogy of Huey Long or the pro-fascist sympathies of some liberals and leftists.*

---

* See the chapter in this collection titled *Neocorporatists and Neoreformists* for a discussion of such pro-Mussolini and pro-corporatist sympathies. Lincoln Steffens and George Bernard Shaw are just two, rather notorious, examples of the trend.

It was this side of the thirties that had formed Hal Draper's socialism. As one of the leaders of the Student Strike Against War in the mid-thirties, he saw first hand a popular movement which began as an angry revolt against the system turned into a pro-administration, completely respectable, and pretty much dead, organization. In this episode, which Draper describes in some detail in Chapter VIII of this collection, the Communist Party played a prominent role in alliance with liberals and the *right wing* of the socialists in taming the movement. At the time this behavior was explained as a function of the American CP's dependence on Russian foreign policy. But what explained that?

Throughout the Second World War an even more disturbing pattern kept repeating itself. A liberal administration—or, at any rate, an administration supported by practically all liberals and leftists—carried out some of the most reactionary policies the country had seen in the name of "fighting fascism." Japanese-Americans were shipped off to concentration camps for the crime of having the wrong ancestry. Segregation of African-Americans went unquestioned even in the armed forces. Black men were expected to fight and die in the name of a freedom they did not enjoy. The gains won by a militant CIO were systematically dismantled and a no-strike policy rigidly enforced throughout the union movement. Through it all the Communist Party outdid the most rabid of traditional reactionaries in its denunciations of anyone who dared speak out against the militarization of American society.

From the late thirties on this behavior forced large sections of the socialist movement, and its liberal periphery, to reexamine old ideas. Was state ownership *the* defining characteristic of socialism? If so, was Stalinist Russia socialist? And, if that was socialism, who needed it? "New class" theories of Russia proliferated. As the war against Fascism gave way to the Cold War and Stalinism replaced Nazism as the bogeyman whose defeat required the sacrifice of all the values and institutions that were supposedly being defended, this process of reexamination intensified.

Hal Draper, first as a trade union organizer and shipyard worker active, along with his wife Anne, in the rank and file revolt against the no-strike pledge, and then as a socialist journalist and editor of the independent socialist paper *Labor Action*, participated in this process of re-examination. *Labor Action*, in particular, was a major contributor to the discussion. Its articles and editorials had an influence on left socialist opinion both in America and in Europe.

Draper's unique contribution was his emphasis on the global character of what was going on. It was not just in Russia that traditional socialist and democratic values and ideas were being transmuted into something else — even into their opposites. For many, James Burnham again being the prime example, this rethinking led to nothing more than a vulgar anticommunism. Politically, that meant support for the NATO alliance as the lesser evil and a deep pessimism about the possibility of human progress. Theoretically, it led to a shallow fatalism. For Hal Draper, this kind of cold war theorizing represented a failure of intellectual as well as political nerve.

The first selection in this book is the 1968 pamphlet *The Two Souls of Socialism*. It presents the thesis that is the theme of the collection and sums up the political evolution described above. It's political impact on a generation of socialists in the United States and Great Britain has been considerable.

The first section concludes with a debate between Draper and Max Nomad, which appeared in *New Politics* in response to the publication of *The Two Souls of Socialism*. I know of no other contemporary discussion of the meaning and future of socialism which makes it as clear as this debate does that what is at issue is the possibility of democracy in *any* sense.

The second section of this anthology contains articles dealing with the New Left in the 1960s. Hal Draper was one of the very few leftists of his generation who unreservedly endorsed and supported the radicalism of the new generation. His pamphlet, *The Mind of Clark Kerr*, which is included in this selection as Chapter VII, played a key role in clarifying the aims of the Free Speech Movement for the movement itself. It is hard to see how anyone without Draper's politics could have understood just what was going on in the mind of this liberal administrator.

Despite his unqualified support for the New Left's radical rejection of American politics, which is what frightened so many ex-radicals, Draper was well aware of the difficulties faced by a predominantly student radical movement in a country where the working class and the people in general were still quite conservative. The article in this section titled *Free Speech and Political Struggle*, was written as the New Left was beginning to collapse in the face of these difficulties. It, as well as the article *In Defense of the New Radicals*, was not intended merely to point with alarm to some of the problems of the new radicals but to understand the movement and its limitations in the belief that any movement for self-emancipation has to understand itself, including its own weaknesses, if it is to move forward. These articles appeared in the magazines

New Politics and *The Independent Socialist*. The chapter titled *Berkeley: The New Student Revolt* is taken from a section of the paperback book on the Berkeley events published by *Grove Press*.[1]

The last section is a small sampling of Hal Draper's prolific writing in defense of the tradition of Socialism from Below.

I have included in this section three previously unpublished essays which defend Marx's emphasis on the working class as the agent of social change. The first, on the feminism of the early nineteenth century working class socialist James Morrison, is a chapter from an unpublished manuscript on socialist feminism. The second is an edited transcript of a series of talks directed at an audience of New Left students which attempted to disabuse them of their anti-union prejudices. The third is a reexamination of Lenin's writings on party organization.

The last article in this section, and a fitting conclusion to the book, is an early version of what became several chapters in Draper's study of Marx's political theory and activity. It was published in *Socialist Register* and describes the evolution of Marx and Engels from typical "New Leftists" of the 1840s to advocates of socialism from below.

E. Haberkern
November 2000

Chapter I:
The Two Souls of Socialism

" ... I pondered all these things, and how men fight and lose the battle, and the thing that they fought for comes about in spite of their defeat, and when it comes turns out not to be what they meant, and other men have to fight for what they meant under another name ... ."

The Dream of John Ball

Socialism's crisis today is a crisis in the *meaning* of socialism.

For the first time in the history of the world, very likely a majority of its people label themselves "socialist" in one sense or another; but there has never been a time when the label was less informative. The nearest thing to a common content of the various "socialisms" is a negative: anti-capitalism. On the positive side, the range of conflicting and incompatible ideas that call themselves socialist is wider than the spread of ideas within the bourgeois world.

Even anti-capitalism holds less and less as a common factor. In one part of the spectrum, a number of social-democratic parties have virtually eliminated any specifically socialist demands from their programs, promising to maintain private enterprise wherever possible. The most prominent example is the German social-democracy. ("As an idea, a philosophy, and a social movement, socialism in Germany is no longer represented by a political party," sums up D.A. Chalmers' recent book *The Social Democratic Party of Germany*.) These parties have defined socialism out of existence, but the tendency which they have formalized is that of the *entire* reformist social-democracy. In what sense are these parties still "socialist"?

In another part of the world picture, there are the Communist states, whose claim to being "socialist" is based on a negative: the abolition of the capitalist private-profit system, and the fact that the class which rules does not consist of private owners of property. On the positive side, however, the socio-economic system which has replaced capitalism there would not be recognizable to Karl Marx. The state owns the means of production — but who "owns" the state? Certainly not the mass of workers, who are exploited, unfree, and alienated from all levels of social and political control. A new class rules, the bureaucratic bosses; it rules over a collectivist system — a bureaucratic collectivism. Unless statification is mechanically equated with "socialism," in what sense are these societies "socialist"?

These two self-styled socialisms are very different, but they have more in common than they think. The social-democracy has typically dreamed of "socializing" capitalism from above. Its principle has always been that increased state intervention in society and economy is *per se* socialistic. It bears a fatal family resemblance to the Stalinist conception of imposing something called socialism from the top down, and of equating statification with socialism. Both have their roots in the ambiguous history of the socialist idea.

Back to the roots: the following pages propose to investigate the meaning of socialism historically, in a new way. There have always been different "kinds of socialism," and they have customarily been divided into reformist or revolutionary, peaceful or violent, democratic or authoritarian, etc. These divisions exist, but the underlying division is something else. Throughout the history of socialist movements and ideas, the fundamental divide is between *Socialism-From-Above* and *Socialism-From-Below*.

What unites the many different forms of Socialism-from-Above is the conception that socialism (or a reasonable facsimile thereof) must be *handed down* to the grateful masses in one form or another, by a ruling elite which is not subject to their control in fact. The heart of Socialism-from-Below is its view that socialism can be realized only through the self-emancipation of activized masses "from below" in a struggle to take charge of their own destiny, as actors (not merely subjects) on the stage of history. "The emancipation of the working classes must be conquered by the working classes themselves": this is the first sentence in the Rules written for the First International by Marx, and this is the First Principle of his life-work.

It is the conception of Socialism-from-Above which accounts for the acceptance of Communist dictatorship as a form of "socialism." It is the conception of Socialism-from-Above which concentrates social-democratic attention on the parliamentary superstructure of society and on the manipulation of the "commanding heights" of the economy, and which makes them hostile to mass action from below. It is Socialism-from-Above which is the dominant tradition in the development of socialism.

Please note that it is not peculiar to socialism. On the contrary, the yearning for emancipation-from-above is the all-pervading principle through centuries of class society and political oppression. It is the permanent promise held out by every ruling power to keep the people looking upward for protection, instead of to themselves for liberation from the need for protection. The people looked to kings to right the injustices done by lords, to messiahs to overthrow the tyranny of kings. Instead of the bold way of mass action from below, it is always safer and more prudent to find the "good" ruler who will

10

Do the People Good. The pattern of emancipation-from-above goes all the way back in the history of civilization, and had to show up in socialism too. But it is only in the framework of the modern socialist movement that liberation from below could become even a realistic aspiration; within socialism it has come to the fore, but only by fits and starts. The history of socialism can be read as a continual but largely unsuccessful effort to free itself from the old tradition, the tradition of emancipation-from-above.

In the conviction that the current crisis of socialism is intelligible only in terms of this Great Divide in the socialist tradition, we turn to a few examples of the two souls of socialism.

1. Some Socialist "Ancestors"

Karl Kautsky, the leading theoretician of the Second International, began his book on Thomas More with the observation that the two great figures inaugurating the history of socialism are More and Münzer, and that both of them "follow the long line of Socialists, from Lycurgus and Pythagoras to Plato, the Gracchi, Catilina, Christ ..."

This is a very impressive list of early "socialists," and considering his position Kautsky should certainly have been able to recognize a socialist when he saw one. What is most fascinating about this list is the way it falls apart under examination into two quite different groups.

Plutarch's life of Lycurgus led the early socialists to adopt him as the founder of Spartan "communism" — this is why Kautsky lists him. But as described by Plutarch, the Spartan system was based on equal division of land under private ownership; it was in no way socialistic. The "collectivist" feeling one may get from a description of the Spartan regime comes from a different direction: the way of life of the Spartan ruling class itself, which was organized as a permanent disciplined garrison in a state of siege; and to this add the terroristic regime imposed over the helots (slaves). I do not see how a modern socialist can read of the Lycurgan regime without feeling that he is meeting not an ancestor of socialism but a forerunner of fascism. There is quite a difference! but how is it that it did not impress itself on the leading theoretician of social-democracy?

Pythagoras founded an elite order which acted as the political arm of the landed aristocracy against the plebeian-democratic movement; he and his party were finally overthrown and expelled by a popular revolutionary rising.

Kautsky seems to be on the wrong side of the barricades! But besides, inside the Pythagorean order a regime of total authoritarianism and regimentation prevailed. In spite of this, Kautsky chose to regard Pythagoras as a socialist ancestor because of the belief that he organized Pythagoreans practiced communal consumption. Even if this were true (and Kautsky found out later it was not) this would have made the Pythagorean order exactly as communistic as any monastery. Chalk up a second ancestor of totalitarianism on Kautsky's list.

The case of Plato's *Republic* is well-enough known. The sole element of "communism" in his ideal state is the prescription of monastic-communal consumption for the small elite of "Guardians" who constitute the bureaucracy and army; but the surrounding social system is assumed to be private-property-holding, not socialistic. And — here it is again — Plato's state model is government by an aristocratic elite, and his argument stresses that democracy inevitably means the deterioration and ruin of society. Plato's political aim, in fact, was the rehabilitation and purification of the ruling aristocracy in order to *fight* the tide of democracy. To call him a socialist ancestor is to imply a conception of socialism which makes any kind of democratic control irrelevant.

On the other hand, Catilina and the Gracchi had *no* collectivist side. Their names are associated with mass movements of popular-democratic revolt against the Establishment. They were not socialists, to be sure, but they were on the popular side of the class struggle in the ancient world, the side of the people's movement from below. It seems it was all the same to the theoretician of social-democracy.

Here, in the pre-history of our subject, are two kinds of figures ready-made for adoption into the pantheon of the socialist movement. There were the figures with a tinge of (alleged) collectivism, who were yet thorough elitists, authoritarians and anti-democrats; and there were the figures *without* anything collectivistic about them, who were associated with democratic class struggles. There is a collectivist tendency without democracy, and there is a democratic tendency without collectivism *but nothing yet which merges these two currents.*

Not until Thomas Münzer, the leader of the revolutionary left wing of the German Reformation, do we find a suggestion of such a merger; a social movement with communistic ideas (Münzer's) which was also engaged in a deep-going popular-democratic struggle from below. In contrast is precisely Sir Thomas More: the gulf between these two contemporaries goes to the heart of our subject. More's *Utopia* pictures a thoroughly regimented society, more reminiscent of *1984* than of socialist democracy, elitist through and through, even slaveholding, a typical Socialism-from-Above. It is not surprising that, of these two "socialist ancestors" who stand at the threshold of the modern world, one (More) execrated the other and supported the hangmen who did him and his movement to death.

What then is the meaning of socialism when it first came into the world? From the very beginning, it was divided between the two souls of socialism, and there was war between them.

2. The First Modern Socialists

Modern socialism was born in the course of the half century or so that lies between the Great French Revolution and the revolutions of 1848. So was modern democracy. But they were *not* born linked like Siamese twins. They traveled at first along separate lines. When did the two lines first intersect?

Out of the wreckage of the French Revolution rose different kinds of socialism. We will consider three of the most important in the light of our question.

I. *Babeuf.* The first modern socialist movement was that led in the last phase of the French Revolution by Babeuf ("the Conspiracy of the Equals"), conceived as a continuation of revolutionary Jacobinism plus a more consistent social goal: a society of communist equality. This represents the first time in the modern era that the idea of socialism is wedded to the idea of a popular movement—a momentous combination.*

This combination immediately raises a critical question: What exactly in each case is the relationship that is seen between this socialist idea and that popular movement? *This is the key question for socialism for the next 200 years.*

As the Babouvists saw it: The mass movement of the people has failed; the people seem to have turned their backs on the Revolution. But still they suffer, still they need communism: *we* know that. The revolutionary will of the people has been defeated by a conspiracy of the right: what we need is a cabal of the left to re-create the people's movement, to effectuate the revolutionary

---

*Strictly speaking, this combination had been anticipated by Gerald Winstanley and the "True Levelers," the left wing of the English Revolution; but it was forgotten and led to nothing, historically speaking.

will. We must therefore seize power. But the people are no longer ready to seize power. Therefore it is necessary for *us* to seize power in their name, in order to raise the people up to that point. This means a temporary dictatorship, admittedly by a minority; but it will be an Educational Dictatorship, aiming at creating the conditions which will make possible democratic control in the future. (In that sense we are democrats.) This will not be a dictatorship of the people, as was the Commune, let alone of the proletariat; it is frankly a dictatorship *over* the people—with very good intentions.

For most of the next fifty years, the conception of the Educational Dictatorship over the people remains the program of the revolutionary left—through the three B's (Babeuf to Buonarroti to Blanqui) and, with anarchist verbiage added, also Bakunin. The new order will be handed down to the suffering people by the revolutionary band. This typical Socialism-from-Above is the first and most primitive form of revolutionary socialism, but there are still today admirers of Castro and Mao who think it is the last word in revolutionism.

II. *Saint-Simon.* — Emerging from the revolutionary period, a brilliant mind took an entirely different tack. Saint-Simon was impelled by a revulsion *against* revolution, disorder and disturbances. What fascinated him was the potentialities of industry and science.

His vision had nothing to do with anything resembling equality, justice, freedom, the rights of man or allied passions: it looked only to modernization, industrialization, planning, divorced from such considerations. Planned industrialization was the key to the new world, and obviously the people to achieve this were the oligarchies of financiers and businessmen, scientists, technologists, managers. When not appealing to these, he called on Napoleon or his successor Louis XVIII to implement schemes for a royal dictatorship. His schemes varied, but they were all completely authoritarian to the last planned ordinance. A systematic racist and a militant imperialist, he was the furious enemy of the very idea of equality and liberty, which he hated as offspring of the French Revolution.

It was only in the last phase of his life (1825) that, disappointed in the response of the natural elite to do their duty and impose the new modernizing oligarchy, he made a turn toward appealing to the workers down below. The "New Christianity" would be a popular movement, but its role would be simply to convince the powers-that-be to heed the advice of the Saint-Simonian planners. The workers should organize—to petition their capitalists and managerial bosses to take over from the "idle classes."

What then was his relationship between the idea of the Planned Society and the popular movement? The people, the movement, could be useful as a battering-ram— in someone's hands. Saint-Simon's last idea was a movement-from-below *to effectuate a Socialism-from-Above*. But power and control must remain where it has always been—above.

III. *The Utopians.* — A third type of socialism that arose in the post-revolutionary generation was that of the utopian socialists proper— Robert Owen, Charles Fourier, Etienne Cabet, etc. They blueprinted an ideal communal colony, imagined fullblown from the cranium of the Leader, to be financed by the grace of the philanthropic rich under the wing of Benevolent Power.

Owen (in many ways the most sympathetic of the lot) was as categorical as any of them: "This great change ... must and will be accomplished by the rich and powerful. There are no other parties to do it ... it is a waste of time, talent and pecuniary means, for the poor to contend in opposition to the rich and powerful ..." Naturally he was against "class hate," class struggle. Of the many who believe this, few have written so bluntly that the aim of this "socialism" is "to govern or treat all society as the most advanced physicians govern and treat their patients in the best arranged lunatic hospitals," with "forbearance and kindness" for the unfortunates who have "become so through the irrationality and injustice of the present most irrational system of society."

Cabet's society provided for elections, but there could be no free discussion; and a controlled press, systematic indoctrination, and completely regimented uniformity was insisted on as part of the prescription.

For these utopian socialists, what was the relationship between the socialist idea and the popular movement? The latter was the *flock* to be tended by the good shepherd. It must not be supposed that Socialism-from-Above necessarily implies cruelly despotic intentions.

This side of these Socialisms-from-Above is far from outlived. On the contrary, it is so modern that a modern writer like Martin Buber, in *Paths in Utopia*, can perform the remarkable feat of treating the old utopians as is they were great democrats and "libertarians"! This myth is quite widespread, and it points once again to the extraordinary insensitivity of socialist writers and historians to the deep-rooted record of Socialism-from-Above as the dominant component in the two souls of socialism.

3. What Marx Did

Utopianism was elitist and anti-democratic to the core because it was utopian—that is, it looked to the prescription of a prefabricated model, the dreaming-up of a plan to be willed into existence. Above all, it was inherently hostile to the very idea of transforming society from below, by the upsetting intervention of freedom-seeking masses, even where it finally accepted recourse to the instrument of a mass movement for pressure upon the Tops. In the socialist movement as it developed before Marx, nowhere did the line of the Socialist Idea intersect the line of Democracy-from-Below.

This intersection, this synthesis, was the great contribution of Marx: in comparison, the whole content of his *Capital* is secondary. What he fused was revolutionary socialism with revolutionary democracy. This is the heart of Marxism: "This is the Law; all the rest is commentary." The *Communist Manifesto* of 1848 marked the self-consciousness of the first movement (in Engels' words) "whose notion was from the very beginning that the emancipation of the working class must be the act of the working class itself."

The young Marx himself went through the more primitive stage just as the human embryo goes through the gill stage; or to put it differently, one of his first immunizations was achieved by catching the most pervasive disease of all, the illusion of the Savior-Despot. When he was 22, the old kaiser died, and to the hosannahs of the liberals Friedrich Wilhelm IV acceded to the throne amidst expectations of democratic reforms from above. Nothing of the sort happened. Marx never went back to this notion, which has bedeviled all of socialism with its hopes in Savior-Dictators or Savior-Presidents.

Marx entered politics as the crusading editor of a newspaper which was the organ of the extreme left of the liberal democracy of the industrialized Rhineland, and soon became the foremost editorial voice of complete political democracy in Germany. The first article he published was a polemic in favor of the unqualified freedom of the press from all censorship by the state. By the time the imperial government forced his dismissal, he was turning to find out more about the new socialist ideas coming from France. When this leading spokesman of liberal democracy became a socialist, he still regarded the task as the championing of democracy—except that democracy now had a deeper meaning. Marx was the first socialist thinker and leader who came to socialism *through* the struggle for liberal democracy.

In working out the viewpoint which first wedded the new communist idea

16

to the new democratic aspirations, they came into conflict with the existing communist sects such as that of Weitling, who dreamed of a messianic dictatorship. Before they joined the group which became the Communist League (for which they were to write the (*Communist Manifesto*), they stipulated that the organization be changed from an elite conspiracy of the old type into an open propaganda group, that "everything conducive to superstitious authoritarianism be struck out of the rules," that the leading committee be elected by the whole membership as against the tradition of "decisions from above." They won the league over to their new approach, and in a journal issued in 1847 only a few months before the *Communist Manifesto*, the group announced:

> We are not among those communists who are out to destroy personal liberty, who wish to turn the world into one huge barrack or into a gigantic workhouse. There certainly are some communists who, with an easy conscience, refuse to countenance personal liberty and would like to shuffle it out of the world because they consider that it is a hindrance to complete harmony. But we have no desire to exchange freedom for equality. We are convinced ... that in no social order will personal freedom be so assured as in a society based upon communal ownership ... [Let us put] our hands to work in order to establish a democratic state wherein each party would be able by word or in writing to win a majority over to its ideas
> ...

The *Communist Manifesto* which issued out of these discussions proclaimed that the first objective of the revolution was "to win the battle of democracy." When, two years later and after the decline of the 1848 revolutions, the Communist League split, it was in conflict once again with "crude communism" of putschism, which thought to substitute determined bands of revolutionaries for the real mass movement of an enlightened working class. Marx told them:

> The minority ... makes mere will the motive force of the evolution, instead of actual relations. Whereas we say to the workers: "You will have to go through fifteen or twenty or fifty

years of civil wars and international wars, not only in order to change extant conditions, but also in order to change yourselves and to render yourselves fit for political dominion," you, on the other hand, say to the workers: "We must attain to power at once, or else we may just as well go to sleep.

"In order to change yourselves and to render yourselves fit for political dominion": this is Marx's program for the working-class movement, as against both those who say the workers can take power any Sunday, and those who say never. Thus Marxism came into being, in self-conscious struggle against the advocated of the Educational Dictatorship, the Savior-Dictators, the revolutionary elitists, the communist authoritarians, as well as the philanthropic do-gooders and bourgeois liberals. This was *Marx's* Marxism, not the caricatured monstrosity which is painted up with that label by both the Establishment's professoriat, who shudder at Marx's uncompromising spirit of revolutionary opposition to the capitalist status quo, and also by the Stalinists and neo-Stalinists, who must conceal the fact that Marx cut his eyeteeth by making war on *their* type.

"It was Marx who finally fettered the two ideas of Socialism and Democracy together*" because he developed a theory which made the synthesis possible for the first time. The heart of the theory is this proposition: *that there is a social majority which has the interest and motivation to change the system,* and that the aim of socialism can be the education and mobilization of this mass-majority. This is the exploited class, the working class, from which comes the eventual motive-force of revolution. Hence a socialism-from-below is possible, on the basis of a theory which sees the revolutionary potentialities in the broad masses, even if they seem backward at a given time and place. *Capital,* after all, is nothing but the demonstration of the economic basis of this proposition.

It is only some such theory of working-class socialism which makes possible the fusion of revolutionary socialism and revolutionary democracy. We are not arguing at this point our conviction that this faith is justified, but only insisting on the alternative: all socialists or would-be reformers who

---

* The quotation is from H. G. Wells' autobiography. Inventor of some of the grimmest Socialism-from Above utopias in all literature, Wells is here *denouncing* Marx for this historic step.

repudiate it *must* go over to some Socialism-from-Above, whether of the reformist, utopian, bureaucratic, Stalinist, Maoist or Castroite variety. And they do.

Five years before the *Communist Manifesto*, a freshly converted 23-year-old socialist had still written in the old elitist tradition: "We can recruit our ranks from those classes only which have enjoyed a pretty good education; that is, from the universities and from the commercial class ..." The young Engels learned better; but this obsolete wisdom is still with us as ever.

4. The Myth of Anarchist "Libertarianism"

One of the most thoroughgoing authoritarians in the history of radicalism is none other than the "Father of Anarchism," Proudhon, whose name is periodically revived as a great "libertarian" model, because of his industrious repetition of the word liberty and his invocations to "revolution from below."

Some may be willing to pass over his Hitlerite form of anti-Semitism (The Jew is the enemy of humankind. It is necessary to send this race back to Asia, or exterminate it ..."). Or his principled racism in general (he thought it was right for the South to keep American Negroes in slavery, since they were the lowest of inferior races). Or his glorification of war for its own sake (in the exact manner of Mussolini). Or his view that women had no rights ("I deny her every political right and every initiative. For woman liberty and well-being lie solely in marriage, in motherhood, in domestic duties ...") – that is, the *Kinder-Kirche-Kuche* of the Nazis.

But it is not possible to gloss over his violent opposition not only to trade-unionism and the right to strike (even supporting police strikebreaking), but to any and every idea of the right to vote, universal suffrage, popular sovereignty, and the very idea of constitutions. ("All this democracy disgusts me ... What would I not give to sail into this mob with my clenched fists!"). His notes for his ideal society notably include suppression of all other groups, any public meeting by more than 20, any free press, and any elections; in the same notes he looks forward to "a general inquisition" and the condemnation of "several million people" to forced labor – "once the Revolution is made."

Behind all this was a fierce contempt for the masses of people – the necessary foundation of Socialism-from-Above, as its opposite was the groundwork of Marxism. The masses are corrupt and hopeless ("I worship humanity, but I spit on men!"). They are "only savages ... whom it is our duty to civilize, and without making them our sovereign," he wrote to a friend whom he scornfully chided with: "You still believe in the people." Progress can come only from mastery by an elite who take care to give the people no sovereignty.

At one time or another he looked to some ruling despot as the one-man dictator who would bring the Revolution: Louis Bonaparte (he wrote a whole book in 1852 extolling the Emperor as the bearer of Revolution); Prince Jérôme Bonaparte; finally Czar Alexander II ("Do not forget that the despotism of the czar is necessary to civilization").

There was a candidate for the dictator's job closer to home, of course: himself. He elaborated a detailed scheme for a "mutualist" business, cooperative in form, which would spread to take over all business and then the state. In his notes Proudhon put himself down as the Manager in Chief, naturally not subject to the democratic control he so despised. He took care of details in advance: "Draw up a secret program, for all the managers: irrevocable elimination of royalty, democracy, proprietors, religion [and so on]." — "The Managers are the natural representatives of the country. Ministers are only superior Managers or General Directors: as I will be one day ... When we are masters, Religion will be what we want it to be; ditto Education, philosophy, justice, administration and government."

The reader, who may be full of the usual illusions about anarchist "libertarianism," may ask: Was he then insincere about his great love for liberty?

Not at all: it is only necessary to understand what anarchist "liberty" means. Proudhon wrote: "The principle of liberty is that of the Abbey of Thélème [in Rabelais]: do what you want!" and the principle meant: "any man who cannot do what he wants and anything he wants has the right to revolt, even alone, against the government, even if the government were everybody else." *The only man who can enjoy this liberty is a despot;* this is the sense of the brilliant insight by Dostoyevsky's Shigalev: "Starting from unlimited freedom, I arrive at unlimited despotism."

The story is similar with the second "Father of Anarchism," Bakunin, whose schemes for dictatorship and suppression of democratic control are better known than Proudhon's.

The basic reason is the same: Anarchism is not concerned with the creation of democratic control from below, but only with the destruction of "authority" over the individual, including the authority of the most extremely democratic regulation of society that it is possible to imagine. This has been made clear by authoritative anarchist expositors time and again; for example, by George Woodcock: "even were democracy possible, the anarchist would still not support it ... Anarchists do not advocate political freedom. What they advocate is freedom from politics ..." Anarchism is on principle fiercely anti-democratic, since an ideally democratic *authority* is still authority. But since, rejecting democracy, it has no other way of resolving the inevitable disagreements and differences among the inhabitants of Thélème, its unlimited freedom for each uncontrolled individual is indistinguishable from unlimited despotism by such an individual, both in theory and practice.

The great problem of our age is the achievement of *democratic control from below over the vast powers of modern social authority.* Anarchism, which is freest of all with verbiage about something-from-below, rejects this goal. It is the other side of the coin of bureaucratic despotism, with all its values turned inside-out, not the cure or the alternative.

5. Lassalle and State Socialism

The very model of a modern social-democracy, the German Social-Democratic Party, is often represented as having arisen on a Marxist basis. This is a myth, like so much else in extant histories of socialism. The impact of Marx was strong, including on some of the top leaders for a while, but the politics which permeated and finally pervaded the party came mainly from two other sources. One was Lassalle, who founded German socialism as an organized movement (1863); and the other was the British Fabians, who inspired Eduard Bernstein's "revisionism."

Ferdinand Lassalle is the prototype of the *state-socialist* — which means, one who aims to get socialism handed down by the existing state. He was not the first prominent example (that was Louis Blanc), but for him the existing state was the Kaiser's state under Bismarck.

The state, Lassalle told he workers, is something "that will achieve for each one of us what none of us could achieve for himself." Marx taught the exact opposite: that the working class had to achieve its emancipation itself, and abolish the existing state in the course. E. Bernstein was quite right in saying that Lassalle "made a veritable cult" of the state. "The immemorial vestal fire of all civilization, the State, I defend with you against those modern barbarians [the liberal bourgeoisie]," Lassalle told a Prussian court. This is what made

Marx and Lassalle "fundamentally opposed," points out Lassalle's biographer Footman, who lays bare his pro-Prussianism, pro-Prussian nationalism, pro-Prussian imperialism.

Lassalle organized his first German socialist movement as his personal dictatorship. Quite consciously he set about building it as *a mass movement from below to achieve a Socialism-from-Above* (remember Saint-Simon's battering-ram). The aim was to convince Bismarck to hand down concessions—particularly universal suffrage, on which basis a parliamentary movement under Lassalle could become a mass ally of the Bismarckian state in a coalition against the liberal bourgeoisie. To this end Lassalle actually tried to negotiate with the Iron Chancellor. Sending him the dictatorial statutes of his organization as "the constitution of my kingdom which perhaps you will envy me," Lassalle went on:

> But this miniature will not be enough to show how true it is that the working class feels an instinctive inclination towards a dictatorship, if it can first be rightly persuaded that the dictatorship will be exercised in its interests; and how much, despite all republican views—or rather precisely because of them—it would therefore be inclined, as I told you only recently, to look upon the Crown, in opposition to the egoism of bourgeois society, as the natural representative of the social dictatorship, if the Crown for its part could ever make up its mind to the—certainly very improbable—step of striking out a really revolutionary line and transforming itself from the monarchy of the privileged orders into a social and revolutionary people's monarchy.

Although this secret letter was not known at the time, Marx grasped the nature of Lassalleanism perfectly. He told Lassalle to his face that he was a "Bonapartist," and wrote presciently that "His attitude is that of the future workers' dictator." Lassalle's tendency he called "Royal Prussian Government socialism," denouncing his "alliance with absolutist and feudal opponents against the bourgeoisie."

"Instead of the revolutionary process of transformation of society," wrote Marx, Lassalle sees socialism arising "from the 'state aid' that the state gives to the producers' cooperative societies and which the state, not the worker,

22

'calls into being.'" Marx derides this. "But as far as the present cooperative societies are concerned, they are of value *only* insofar as they are the independent creations of the workers and not proteges either of the government or of the bourgeoisie." Here is a classic statement of the meaning of the word *independent* as the keystone of Socialism-from-Below versus state-socialism.

There is an instructive instance of what happens when an American-type academic anti-Marxist runs into this aspect of Marx. Mayo's *Democracy and Marxism* (later revised as *Introduction to Marxist Theory*) handily proves that Marxism is anti-democratic mainly by the simple expedient of defining Marxism as "the Moscow orthodoxy." But at least he seems to have read Marx, and realized that nowhere, in acres of writing and a long life, did Marx evince concern about more power for the state but rather the reverse. Marx, it dawned on him, was not a "statist":

> The popular criticism leveled against Marxism is that it tends to degenerate into a form of 'statism'. At first sight [i.e., reading] the criticism appears wide of the mark, for the virtue of Marx's political theory ... is the entire absence from it of any glorification of the state.

This discovery offers a notable challenge to Marx-critics, who of course know in advance that Marxism *must* glorify the state. Mayo solves the difficulty in two statements: (1) "the statism is implicit in the requirements of total planning ..." (2) Look at Russia. But Marx made no fetish of "total planning." He has so often been denounced (by other Marx-critics) for failing to draw up a blueprint of socialism precisely because he reacted so violently against his predecessors' utopian "plannism" or planning-from-above. "Plannism" is precisely the conception of socialism that Marxism wished to destroy. Socialism must involve planning, but "total planning" does not equal socialism—just as any fool can be a professor but not every professor need be a fool.

6. The Fabian Model

In Germany, behind the figure of Lassalle there shades off a series of "socialisms" moving in an interesting direction.

The so-called Academic Socialists ("Socialists of the Chair," *Kathedersozialisten* — a current of Establishment academics) looked to Bismarck more openly than Lassalle, but their conception of state-socialism was not in principle alien to his. Only, Lassalle embarked on the risky expedient of calling into being a mass movement from below for the purpose — risky because once in motion it might get out of hand, as indeed it did more than once. Bismarck himself did not hesitate to represent his paternalistic economic policies as a kind of socialism, and books got written about "monarchical socialism," "Bismarckian state-socialism," etc. Following further to the right, one comes to the "socialism" of Friedrich List, a proto-Nazi and to those circles where an anti-capitalist form of anti-Semitism (Dühring, A. Wagner, etc.) lays part of the basis for the movement that called itself socialist under Adolf Hitler.

The thread that unites this whole spectrum, through all the differences, is the conception of *socialism as equivalent merely to state intervention in economic and social life*. "Staat, greif zu!" Lassalle called. "State, take hold of things!" — this is the socialism of the whole lot.

This is why Schumpeter is correct in observing what the British equivalent of German state-socialism is — Fabianism, the socialism of Sidney Webb.

The Fabians (more accurately, the Webbians) are, in the history of the socialist idea, that modern socialist current which developed in most complete divorcement from Marxism, the one most alien to Marxism. It was almost chemically-pure social-democratic reformism unalloyed, particularly before the rise of the mass Labor and socialist movement in Britain, which it did not want and did not help to build (despite a common myth to the contrary). It is therefore a very important test, unlike most other reformist currents which paid their tribute to Marxism by adopting some of its language and distorting its substance.

The Fabians, deliberately middle-class in composition and appeal, were not for building any mass movement at all, least of all a Fabian one. They thought of themselves as a small elite of brain-trusts who would permeate the existing institutions of society, influence the real leaders in all spheres Tory or Liberal, and guide social development toward its collectivist goal with the "inevitability of gradualness." Since their conception of socialism was purely in terms of state intervention (national or municipal) and their theory told them that capitalism itself was being collectivized apace every day and had to move in this direction, their function was simply to hasten the process. The Fabian Society was designed in 1884 to be pilot-fish to a shark: at first the shark was the Liberal party; but when the permeation of Liberalism failed miserably, and labor finally organized its own class party despite the Fabians, the pilot fish simply reattached itself.

There is perhaps no other socialist tendency which so systematically and even consciously worked out its theory as a Socialism-from-Above. The nature of this movement was early recognized, though it was later obscured by the merging of Fabianism into the body of Labor reformism. The leading Christian Socialist inside the Fabian Society once attacked Webb as "a bureaucratic Collectivist" (perhaps the first use of that term.) Hilaire Belloc's once-famous book of 1912 on *The Servile State* was largely triggered by the Webb type whose "collectivist ideal" was basically bureaucratic. G.D.H. Cole reminisced: "The Webbs, in those days, used to be fond of saying that everyone who was active in politics was either an 'A' or a 'B' — an anarchist or a bureaucrat — and that they were 'B's' ..."

These characterizations scarcely convey the full flavor of the Webbian collectivism that was Fabianism. It was through-and-through managerial, technocratic, elitist, authoritarian, "plannist." Webb was fond of the term wirepulling almost as a synonym for politics. A Fabian publication wrote that they wished to be "the Jesuits of Socialism." The gospel was Order and Efficiency. The people, who should be treated kindly, were fit to be run only by competent experts. Class struggle, revolution and popular turbulence were insanity. In *Fabianism and the Empire* imperialism was praised and embraced. If ever the socialist movement developed its own bureaucratic collectivism, this was it.

"It may be thought that Socialism is essentially a movement from below, a class movement," wrote a Fabian spokesman, Sidney Ball, to disabuse the reader of this idea; but now socialists "approach the problem from the scientific rather than the popular view; they are middle-class theorists," he boasted, going on to explain that there is "a distinct rupture between the Socialism of the street and the Socialism of the chair."

The sequel is also known, though often glossed over. While Fabianism as a special tendency petered out into the larger stream of Labor Party reformism by 1918, the leading Fabians themselves went in another direction. Both Sidney and Beatrice Webb as well as Bernard Shaw — the top trio — became principled supporters of Stalinist totalitarianism in the 1930's. Even earlier, Shaw, who thought socialism needed a Superman, had found more than one. In turn he embraced Mussolini and Hitler as benevolent despots to hand "socialism" down to the Yahoos, and he was disappointed only that they did not actually abolish capitalism. In 1931 Shaw disclosed, after a visit to Russia, that the Stalin regime was really Fabianism in practice. The Webbs followed to Moscow, and found God. In their *Soviet Communism: A New Civilization,* they proved (right out of Moscow's own documents and Stalin's own claims, industriously researched) that Russia is the greatest democracy in the world; Stalin is no dictator; equality reigns for all; the one-party dictatorship is needed; the Communist Party is a thoroughly democratic elite bringing civilization to the Slavs and Mongols (but not Englishmen); political democracy has failed in the West anyway, and there is no reason why political parties should survive in our age ...

They staunchly supported Stalin through the Moscow purge trials and the Hitler-Stalin Pact without a visible qualm, and died more uncritical pro-Stalinists than can now be found on the Politburo. As Shaw has explained, the Webbs had nothing but scorn for the Russian Revolution itself, but "The Webbs waited until the wreckage and ruin of the change was ended, its mistakes ended, and the Communist state fairly launched." That is, they waited until the revolutionary masses had been straitjacketed, the leaders of the revolution cashiered, the efficient tranquility of dictatorship had settled on the scene, the counter-revolution firmly established; and then they came along to pronounce it the Ideal.

Was this really a gigantic misunderstanding, some incomprehensible blunder? Or were they not right in thinking that this indeed was the "socialism" that matched their ideology, give or take a little blood? The swing of Fabianism from middle-class permeation to Stalinism was the swing of a door that was hinged on Socialism-from-Above.

If we look back at the decades just before the turn of the century that launched Fabianism on the world, another figure looms, the antithesis of Webb: the leading personality of revolutionary socialism in that period, the poet and artist William Morris, who became a socialist and a Marxist in his late forties. Morris's writings on socialism breathe from every pore the spirit of Socialism-from-Below, just as every line of Webb's is the opposite. This is perhaps clearest in his sweeping attacks on Fabianism (for the right reasons); his dislike of the "Marxism" of that British edition of Lassalle, the dictatorial H.M. Hyndman; his denunciations of state-socialism; and his repugnance at the bureaucratic-collectivist utopia of Bellamy's *Looking Backward.* (The last moved him to remark: "If they brigaded *me* into a regiment of workers, I'd just lie on

26

my back and kick.")

Morris's socialist writings are pervaded with his emphasis from every side on class struggle from below, in the present; and as for the socialist future, his *News from Nowhere* was written as the direct antithesis of Bellamy's book. He warned

> that individual men cannot shuffle off the business of life on to the shoulders of an abstraction called the State, but must deal with it in conscious association with each other ... Variety of life is as much of an aim of true communism as equality of condition, and ... nothing but an union of these two will bring about real freedom.

"Even some Socialists," he wrote, "are apt to confuse the cooperative machinery towards which modern life is tending with the essence of Socialism itself." This meant "the danger of the community falling into bureaucracy." Therefore he expressed fear of a "collectivist bureaucracy" lying ahead. Reacting violently against state-socialism and reformism, he fell backwards into anti-parliamentarism but he did not fall into the anarchist trap:

> ... people will have to associate in administration, and sometimes there will be differences of opinion ... What is to be done? Which party is to give way? Our Anarchist friends say that it must not be carried by a majority; in that case, then, it must be carried by a minority. And why? Is there any divine right in a minority?

This goes to the heart of anarchism far more deeply than the common opinion that the trouble with anarchism is that it is over-idealistic.

William Morris versus Sidney Webb: this is one way of summing up the story.

7. The "Revisionist" Facade

Eduard Bernstein, the theoretician of social-democratic "revisionism," took his impulsion that Fabianism, by which he was heavily influenced in his London exile. He did not invent the reformist policy in 1896: he merely became its theoretical spokesman. (The head of the party bureaucracy preferred less theory: "One doesn't say it, one *does* it," he told Bernstein, meaning that the politics of German social-democracy had been gutted of Marxism long before its theoreticians reflected the change.)

But Bernstein did not "revise" Marxism. His role was to uproot it while pretending to prune away withered limbs. The Fabians had not needed to bother with pretense, but in Germany it was not possible to destroy Marxism by a frontal attack. The reversion to Socialism-from-Above ("die alte Scheisse") had to be presented as a "modernization," a "revision."

Essentially, like the Fabians, "revisionism" found its socialism in the inevitable collectivization of capitalism itself; it saw the movement toward socialism as the sum of the collectivist tendencies immanent in capitalism itself; it looked to the "self-socialization" of capitalism from above, through the institutions of the existing state. The equation of *Statification=Socialism* is not the invention of Stalinism; it was systematized by the Fabian-Revisionist-State-socialist current of social-democratic reformism.

Most of the contemporary discoveries which announce that socialism is obsolete, because capitalism no longer really exists, can already be found in Bernstein. It was "absurd" to call Weimar Germany capitalist, he declared, because of the controls exercised over the capitalists; it follows from Bernstein-ism that the Nazi state was even more anti-capitalist, as advertised ...

The transformation of socialism into a bureaucratic collectivism is already implicit in Bernstein's attack on workers' democracy. Denouncing the idea of workers' control of industry, he proceeds to redefine democracy. Is it "government by the people"? Thus the very notion of workers' democracy as a *sine qua non* of socialism is junked, as effectively as by the clever redefinitions of democracy current in the Communist academies. Even political freedom and representative institutions have been defined out: a theoretical result all the more impressive since Bernstein himself was not personally anti-democratic like Lassalle or Shaw. It is the theory of Socialism-from-Above which requires these formulations. *Bernstein is the leading social-democratic theoretician not only of the equation Statification=Socialism, but also of the disjunction of socialism from workers' democracy.*

It was fitting, therefore, that Bernstein should come to the conclusion that Marx's hostility to the state was "anarchistic," and that Lassalle was right in looking to the state for the initiation of socialism. "The administrative body of the visible future can be different from the present-day state only in degree," wrote Bernstein; the "withering away of the state" is nothing but utopianism even under socialism. He, on the contrary, was very practical; for example, as the Kaiser's non-withering state launched itself into the imperialist scramble for colonies, Bernstein promptly came out for colonialism and the White Man's Burden: "only a conditional right of savages to the land occupied by them can be recognized; the higher civilization ultimately can claim a higher right."

Bernstein contrasted his own vision of the road to socialism with that of Marx: Marx's "is the picture of an army. It presses forward, through detours, stands beckoning the desired goal—the state of the future, which can be reached only through a sea, a *red* sea as some have said." In contrast, Bernstein's vision was not red but roseate: the class struggle softens into harmony as a beneficent state gently changes the bourgeoisie into good bureaucrats. *It didn't happen that way*—when the Bernsteinized social-democracy first shot down the revolutionary left in 1919, and then, reinstating the unregenerate bourgeoisie and the military in power, helped to yield Germany into the hands of the fascists.

If Bernstein was the theoretician of the identification of bureaucratic collectivism with socialism, then it was his left-wing opponent in the German movement who became the leading spokesman in the Second international of a revolutionary-democratic Socialism-from-Below. This was Rosa Luxemburg, who so emphatically put her faith and hope in the spontaneous struggle of a free working class that the myth-makers invented for her a "theory of spontaneity" which she never held, a theory in which "spontaneity" is counterposed to "leadership."

In her own movement she fought hard against the "revolutionary" elitists who rediscovered the theory of the Educational Dictatorship over the workers (it is rediscovered in every generation as The Very Latest Thing), and had to write: "Without the conscious will and the conscious action of the majority of the proletariat there can be no socialism ..." —"[We] will never assume governmental authority except through the clear unambiguous will of the vast majority of the German working class ..." And her famous aphorism: "Mistakes committed by a genuinely revolutionary labor movement are much more fruitful and worthwhile historically than the infallibility of the very best Central Committee."

Rosa Luxemburg versus Eduard Bernstein: this is the German chapter of the story.

8. The 100% American Scene

At the wellsprings of American "native socialism," the picture is the same, only more so. If we overlook the imported "German socialism" (Lassallean with Marxist trimmings) of the early Socialist labor party, then the leading figure here is, far and away, Edward Bellamy and his *Looking Backward* (1887). Just before him came the now-forgotten Laurence Gronlund, whose *Cooperative Commonwealth* (1884) was extremely influential in its day, selling 100,000 copies.

is so up-to-date that he does not say he rejects democracy—he merely "redefines" it; as "Administration by the Competent," as against "government by majorities," together with a modest proposal to wipe out representative government as such as well as all parties. All the "people" want, he teaches, is "administration—good administration." They should find "the right leaders," and then be "willing to thrust their whole collective power into their hands." Representative government will be replaced by the plebiscite. He is sure that his scheme will work, he explains, because it works so well for the hierarchy of the Catholic Church. Naturally he rejects the horrible idea of class struggle. The workers are incapable of self-emancipation, and he specifically denounces Marx's famous expression of his First Principle. The Yahoos will be emancipated by an elite of the "competent," drawn from the intelligentsia; and at one point he set out to organize a secret conspiratorial American Socialist Fraternity for students.

Bellamy's socialist utopia in *Looking Backward* is expressly modeled on the army as the ideal pattern of society—regimented, hierarchically ruled by an elite, organized from the top down, with the cozy communion of the beehive as the great end. The story itself pictures the transition as coming through the concentration of society into one big business corporation, a single capitalist: the state. Universal suffrage is abolished; all organizations from below eliminated; decisions are made by administrative technocrats from above. As one of his followers defined this "American socialism": "Its social idea is a perfectly organized industrial system which, by reason of the close interlocking of its wheels, shall work at a minimum of friction with a maximum of wealth and leisure to all."

As in the case of the anarchists, Bellamy's fanciful solution to the basic problem of social organization—how to resolve differences of ideas and interests among men—is the *assumption* that the elite will be superhumanly

30

wise and incapable of injustice (essentially the same as the Stalinist-totalitarian myth of the infallibility of the Party), the point of the assumption being that it makes unnecessary any concern bout democratic control from below. The latter is unthinkable for Bellamy because the masses, the workers, are simply a dangerous monster, the barbarian horde. The Bellamyite movement — which called itself "Nationalism" and originally set out to be both anti-socialist *and* anti-capitalist was systematically organized on a middle-class appeal, like the Fabians.

Here were the overwhelmingly popular educators of the "native" wing of American socialism, whose conceptions echoed through the non-Marxist and anti-Marxist sectors of the socialist movement well into the 20th century, with a resurgence of "Bellamy Clubs" even in the 1930s, when John Dewey eulogized *Looking Backward* as expounding "the American ideal of democracy." Technocracy, which already reveals fascist features openly, was a lineal descendant of this tradition on one side. If one wants to see how thin the line can be between something called socialism and something like fascism, it is instructive to read the monstrous exposition of "socialism" written by the once-famous inventor-scientist and Socialist Party luminary Charles P. Steinmetz. His *America and the New Epoch* (1916) sets down in deadly seriousness exactly the anti-utopia once satirized in a science-fiction novel, in which Congress has been replaced by direct senators from Dupont, General Motors and the other great corporations. Steinmetz, presenting the giant monopolistic corporations (like his own employer, General Electric) as the ultimate in industrial efficiency, proposed to disband the political government in favor of direct rule by the associated corporate monopolists.

Bellamyism started many on the road to socialism, but the road forked. By the turn of the century, American socialism developed the world's most vibrant antithesis to Socialism-from Above in all its forms: Eugene Debs. In 1887 Debs was still at the point of asking none other than John D. Rockefeller to finance the establishment of a socialist utopian colony in a western state; but Debs, whose socialism was forged in the class struggle of a militant labor movement, soon found his true voice.

The heart of "Debsian socialism" was its appeal to, and faith in, the self-activity of the masses from below. Debs' writings and speeches are impregnated with this theme. He often quoted or paraphrased Marx's "First Principle" in his own words: "The great discovery the modern slaves have made is that they themselves their freedom must achieve. This is the secret of their solidarity; the heart of their hope ..." His classic statement is this:

> Too long have the workers of the world waited for some Moses
> to lead them out of bondage. He has not come; he never will
> come. I would not lead you out if I could; for if you could be led
> out, you could be led back again. I would have you make up
> your minds that there is nothing you cannot do for yourselves.

He echoed Marx's words of 1850:

> In the struggle of the working class to free itself from wage
> slavery it cannot be repeated too often that everything depends
> on the working class itself. The simple question is, Can the
> workers fit themselves, by education, organization, cooperation
> and self-imposed discipline, to take control of the productive
> forces and manage industry in the interest of the people and for
> the benefit of society? That is all there is to it.

Can the workers fit themselves ... He was under no starry-eyed illusions
about the working class as it was (or is). But he proposed a different goal than
the elitists whose sole wisdom consists in pointing a finger at the
backwardness of the people now, and in teaching that this must always be so.
As against the faith in elite rule from above, Debs counterposed the directly
contrary notion of the revolutionary *vanguard* (also a minority) whose faith
impels them to advocate a harder road for the majority:

> It is the minorities who have made the history of this world [he
> said in the 1917 anti-war speech for which Wilson's government
> jailed him]. It is the few who have had the courage to take their
> places at the front; who have been true enough to themselves to
> speak the truth that was in them; who have dared oppose the
> established order to things; who have espoused the cause of the
> suffering, struggling poor; who have upheld without regard to
> personal consequences the cause of freedom and righteousness.

This "Debsian socialism" evoked a tremendous response from the heart of
the people, but Debs had no successor as a tribune of revolutionary-democratic

socialism. After the postwar period of radicalization, the Socialist Party became pinkly respectable on the one hand, and the Communist Party became Stalinized on the other. On its side, American liberalism itself had long been undergoing a process of "statification," culminating in the great New Deal illusion of the '30s. The elite vision of a dispensation-from-above under the aegis of the Savior-President attracted a whole strain of liberals to whom the country gentleman in the White House was as Bismarck to Lassalle.

The type had been heralded by Lincoln Steffens, the collectivist liberal who (like Shaw and Georges Sorel) was as attracted to Mussolini as to Moscow, and for the same reasons. Upton Sinclair, quitting the Socialist Party as too "sectarian," launched his "broad" movement to "End Poverty in California," with a manifesto appropriately called *I, Governor of California, and How I Ended Poverty* (probably the only radical manifesto with two I's in the title) on the theme of "Socialism-from-Up-in-Sacramento." One of the typical figures of the time was Stuart Chase, who wove a zigzag course from the reformism of the League for Industrial Democracy to the semi-fascism of Technocracy. There were the Stalinoid intellectuals who managed to sublimate their joint admiration for Roosevelt and Russia by hailing both the NRA and the Moscow Trials. There were signs of the times like Paul Blanshard, who defected from the Socialist Party to Roosevelt on the ground that the New Deal program of "managed capitalism" had taken the initiative in economic change away from the socialists.

The New Deal, often rightly called America's "social-democratic period," was also the liberals' and social-democrats' big fling at Socialism -from-Above, the utopia of Roosevelt's "peoples' monarchy." The illusion of the Rooseveltian "revolution from above" united creeping-socialism, bureaucratic liberalism, Stalinoid elitism, and illusions about both Russian collectivism and collectivized capitalism, in one package.

9. Six Strains of Socialism-from-Above

We have seen that there are several different strains or currents running through Socialism-from-Above they are usually intertwined, but let us separate out some of the more important aspects for a closer look.

(1) *Philanthropism.* —Socialism (or "freedom," or what-have-you) is to be handed down, in order to Do the People Good, by the rich and powerful out

of the kindness of their hearts. As the *Communist Manifesto* put it, with the early utopians like Robert Owen in mind, "Only from the point of view of being the most suffering class does the proletariat exist for them." In gratitude, the downtrodden poor must above all avoid getting rambunctious, and no nonsense about class struggle or self-emancipation. This aspect may be considered a special case of—

(2) *Elitism.*—We have mentioned several cases of this conviction that socialism is the business of a new ruling minority, non-capitalist in nature and therefore guaranteed pure, imposing its own domination either temporarily (for a mere historical era) or even permanently. In either case, this new ruling class is likely to see its goal as an Educational Dictatorship over the masses—to Do Them Good, of course—the dictatorship being exercised by an elite party which suppresses all control from below, or be benevolent despots or Savior-Leaders of some kind, or by Shaw's "Supermen," by eugenic manipulators, by Proudhon's "anarchist" managers or Saint-Simon's technocrats or their more modern equivalents—with up-to-date terms and new verbal screens which can be hailed as fresh social theory as against "nineteenth-century Marxism."

On the other hand, the revolutionary-democratic advocates of Socialism-from-Below have also always been a minority, but the chasm between the elitist approach and the *vanguard* approach is crucial, as we have seen in the case of Debs. For him as for Marx and Luxemburg, the function of the revolutionary vanguard is to impel the mass-majority *to fit themselves to take power in their own name, through their own struggles.* The point is not to deny the critical importance of minorities, but to establish a different relationship between the advanced minority and the more backward mass.

(3) *Plannism.*—The key words are Efficiency, Order, Planning, System—and Regimentation. Socialism is reduced to social-engineering, by a Power above society. Here again, the point is not to deny that effective socialism requires over-all planning (and also that efficiency and order are good things); but the *reduction* of socialism to planned production is an entirely different matter; just as effective democracy requires the right to vote, but the *reduction* of democracy merely to the right to vote once in a while makes it a fraud.

As a matter of fact, it would be important to demonstrate that the separation of planning from democratic control-from-below makes a mockery of planning itself; for the immensely complicated industrial societies of today cannot be effectively planned by an all-powerful central committee's ukases,

34

which inhibit and terrorize the free play of initiative and correction from below. This is indeed the basic contradiction of the new type of exploiting social system represented by Soviet bureaucratic collectivism. But we cannot pursue this subject further here.

The substitution of Plannism for socialism has a long history, quite apart from its embodiment in the Soviet myth at *Statification=Socialism*, a tenet which we have already seen to have been first systematized by social-democratic reformism (Bernstein and the Fabians particularly). During the 1930's the mystique of the "Plan," taken over in part from Soviet propaganda, became prominent in the right wind of the social-democracy, with Henri de Man hailed as its prophet and as successor to Marx. De Man faded from view and is now forgotten because he had the bad judgment to push his Revisionist theories first into corporatism and then into collaboration with the Nazis.

Aside from theoretical constructions, Plannism appears in the socialist movement most frequently embodied in a certain psychological type of radical. To give credit due, one of the first sketches of this type came in Belloc's *The Servile State*, with the Fabians in mind. This type, writes Belloc,

> loves the collectivist ideal in itself ... because it is an ordered and regular form of society. He loves to consider the ideal of a State in which land and capital shall be held by public officials who shall order other men about and so preserve them from the consequences of *their* vice, ignorance and folly. [Belloc writes further:] In him the exploitation of man excites no indignation. Indeed, he is not a type to which indignation or any other lively passion is familiar ... [Belloc's eye is on Sidney Webb here.] ... the prospect of a vast bureaucracy wherein the whole of life shall be scheduled and appointed to certain simple schemes ... gives his small stomach a final satisfaction.

As far as concerns contemporary examples with a pro-Stalinist coloration, examples-a-go go can be found in the pages of Paul Sweezy's magazine *Monthly Review*.

In a 1930 article on the "motive patterns of socialism," written when he still thought he was a Leninist, Max Eastman distinguished this type as centered on "efficiency and intelligent organization ... a veritable passion for a plan ... businesslike organization." For such, he commented, Stalin's Russia has a fascination:

It is a region at least to be apologized for in other lands — certainly not denounced from the standpoint of a mad dream like emancipation of the workers and therewith all mankind. In those who built the Marxian movement and those who organized its victory in Russia, that mad dream was the central motive. They were, as some are prone now to forget, extreme rebels against oppression. Lenin will perhaps stand out, when the commotion about his ideas subsides, as the greatest rebel in history. His major passion was to set men free ... if a single concept must be chosen to summarize the goal of the class struggle as defined in Marxian writings, and especially the writings of Lenin, *human freedom* is the name for it ...

It might be added that more than once Lenin decried the push for total-planning as a "bureaucratic utopia."

There is a subdivision under Plannism which deserves a name too: let us call it Productionism. Of course, everyone is "for" production just as everyone is for Virtue and the Good Life; but for this type, production is the decisive test and end of a society. Russian bureaucratic collectivism is "progressive" because of the statistics of pig-iron production (the same type usually ignores the impressive statistics of increased production under Nazi or Japanese capitalism). It is all right to smash or prevent free trade-unions under Nasser, Castro, Sukarno or Nkrumah because something known as "economic development" is paramount over human rights. This hardboiled viewpoint was, of course, not invented by these "radicals," but by the callous exploiters of labor in the capitalist Industrial Revolution; and the socialist movement came into existence fighting tooth-and-nail against these theoreticians of "progressive" exploitation. On this score too, apologists for modern "leftist" authoritarian regimes tend to consider this hoary doctrine as the newest revelation of sociology.

(4) *"Communionism."* — In his 1930 article Max Eastman called this "the united-brotherhood pattern," of "the gregarian or human-solidarity socialists" — "those yearning with a mixture of religious mysticism and animal gregariousness for human solidarity." It should not be confused with the notion of solidarity in strikes, etc., and not necessarily identified with what is commonly called comradeship in the socialist movement or a "sense of

community" elsewhere. In specific content, as Eastman says, is a "seeking for submersion in a Totality, seeking to lose himself in the bosom of a substitute for God."

Eastman is here pointing to the Communist Party writer Mike Gold; another excellent case is Harry F. Ward, the CP's hardy clerical fellow-traveler, whose books theorize this kind of "oceanic" yearning for the shucking-off of one's individuality. Bellamy's notebooks reveal him as a classic case: he writes about the longing "for absorption into the grand omnipotency of the universe;" his "Religion of Solidarity" reflects his mistrust of the individualism of the personality, his craving to dissolve the Self into communion with Something Greater.

This strain is very prominent in some of the most authoritarian of the Socialisms-from-Above and is not seldom met in milder cases like the philanthropic elitists with Christian Socialist views. Naturally, this kind of "communionist" socialism is always hailed as an "ethical socialism" and praised for holding class struggle in horror; for there must be no conflict inside a beehive. It tends to flatly counterpose "collectivism" to "individualism" (a false opposition from a humanist standpoint), but what it really impugns is *individuality*.

(5) *Permeationism.* — Socialism-from-Above appears in many varieties for the simple reason that there are always many alternatives to the self-mobilization of masses from below; but the cases discussed tend to divide into two families.

One has the perspective of *overthrowing* the present, capitalist hierarchical society in order to replace it with a new, non-capitalist type of hierarchical society based on a new kind of elite ruling class. (These varieties are usually ticketed "revolutionary" in histories of socialism.) The other has the perspective of permeating the centers of power in the existing society in order to metamorphose it — gradually, inevitably — into a stratified collectivism, perhaps molecule by molecule the way wood petrifies into agate. This is the characteristic stigmatum of the reformist, social-democratic varieties of Socialism-from-Above.

The very term permeationism was invented for self-description by what we have already called the "purest" variety of reformism ever seen, Sidney Webb's Fabianism. All social-democratic permeationism is based on a theory of mechanical *inevitability*: the inevitable self-collectivization of capitalism from above, which is equated with socialism. Pressure from below (where considered permissible) can hasten and straighten the process, provided it is kept under control to avoid frightening the self-collectivizers. Hence the social-democratic permeationists are not only willing but anxious to "join the Establishment" as cabin boys or cabinet ministers. Typically the function of their movement-from-below is primarily to blackmail the ruling powers into buying them off with such opportunities for permeation.

The tendency toward the collectivization of capitalism is indeed a reality: as we have seen, it means the bureaucratic collectivization of capitalism. As this process has advanced, the contemporary social-democracy has itself gone through a metamorphosis. Today, the leading theoretician of this neo-reformism, C.A.R. Crosland, denounces as "extremist" the mild statement favoring nationalization which was originally written for the British Labor program by none other than Sidney Webb (with Arthur Henderson)! The number of continental social-democracies that have now purged their programs of all specifically anti-capitalist content — a brand new phenomenon in socialist history — reflects the degree to which the ongoing process of bureaucratic collectivization is accepted as an installment of petrified "socialism."

This is permeationism as grand strategy. It leads, of course, to permeationism as political tactic, a subject we cannot here pursue beyond mentioning its presently most prominent U.S. form: the policy of supporting the Democratic Party and the lib-lab coalition around the "Johnson Consensus," its predecessors and successors.

The distinction between these two "families" of Socialism-from-Above holds for *home grown* socialisms, from Babeuf to Harold Wilson; that is, cases where the social base of the given socialist current is *inside* the national system, be it the labor aristocracy of declasse elements or any other. The case is somewhat different for those "socialisms-from-outside" represented by the contemporary Communist parties, whose strategy and tactics depend in the last analysis on a power base *outside* any of the domestic social strata; that is, on the bureaucratic-collectivist ruling classes in the East.

The Communist Parties have shown themselves uniquely different from any kind of home-grown movement in their capacity to *alternate or combine both* the "revolutionary"-oppositionist and the permeationist tactics to suit their convenience. Thus the American Communist Party could swing from its ultra-left-adventurist "Third Period" of 1928-34 into the ultra-permeationist tactic of the Popular Front period, then back into fire-breathing "revolutionism: during the Hitler-Stalin Pact period, and again, during the ups-and-downs of the Cold War, into various degrees of combination of the two. With the current Communist split along Moscow-Peking lines, the "Khrushchevites" and the Maoists tend each to embody one of the two tactics which formerly alternated.

Frequently, therefore, in domestic policy the official Communist party and the social-democrats tend to converge on the policy of permeationism, though from the angle of a different Socialism-from-Above.

(6) *Socialism-from-Outside.* — The preceding varieties of Socialism-from-Above look to power at the tops of society; now we come to the expectation of succor from the outside.

The flying-saucer cult is a pathological form, messianism a more traditional form, when "outside" means out of this world; but for present purposes "outside" means *outside the social struggle at home.* For the communists of East Europe after World War II, the New Order has to be imported on Russian bayonets; for the German Social-Democrats in exile, liberation of their own people could finally be imagined only by grace of foreign military victory.

The peacetime variety is socialism-by-model-example. This, of course, was the method of the old utopians, who built their model colonies in the American backwoods in order to demonstrate the superiority of their system and convert the unbelievers. Today, it is this substitute for social struggle at home which is increasingly the essential hope of the Communist movement in the West.

The model-example is provided by Russia (or China, for the Maoists); and while it is difficult to make the lot of the Russian proletarians half-attractive to Western workers even with a generous dose of lies, there is more success to be expected from two other approaches:

(a) The relatively privileged position of managerial, bureaucratic and intellectual-flunky elements in the Russian collectivist system can be pointedly contrasted with the situation in the West, where these same elements are subordinated to the owners of capital and manipulators of wealth. At this point the appeal of the Soviet system of stratified economy coincides with the historic appeal of middle-class socialisms, to disgruntled class-elements of intellectuals, technologists, scientists and scientific employees, administrative bureaucrats and organization men of various types, who can most easily identify themselves with a new ruling class based on state power rather than on money power and ownership, and therefore visualize themselves as the new men of power in a non-capitalist but elitist setup.

(b) While the official Communist Parties are required to maintain the facade of orthodoxy in something called "Marxism-Leninism," it is more common that serious theoreticians of neo-Stalinism who are not tied to the party do free themselves from the pretense. One development is the open abandonment of any perspective of victory through social struggle inside the capitalist countries. The "world revolution" is equated simply with the demonstration by the communist states that their system is superior. This has now been put into thesis-form by the two leading theoreticians of neo-Stalinism, Paul Sweezy and Isaac Deutscher.

Baran and Sweezy's *Monopoly Capitalism* (1966) flatly rejects " the answer of traditional Marxist orthodoxy — that the industrial proletariat must eventually rise in revolution against its capitalist oppressors." Same for all the other "outsider" groups of society — unemployed farm workers, ghetto masses, etc.; they cannot "constitute a coherent force in society." This leaves no one; capitalism cannot be effectively challenged from within. What then? Some day, the authors explain on their last page, "perhaps not in the present century," the people will be disillusioned with capitalism "as the world revolution spreads and *as the socialist countries show by their example* that it is possible" to build a rational society. [Emphasis added.] That is all. Thus the Marxist phrases filling the other 366 pages of this essay become simply an incantation like the reading of the Sermon on the Mount at St. Patrick's Cathedral.

The same perspective is presented less bluntly by a more circumlocuitous writer in Deutscher's *The Great Contest*. Deutscher transmits the new Soviet theory "that Western capitalism will succumb not so much — or not directly — because of its own crises and inherent contradictions as because of its inability to match the achievements of socialism [i.e. the Communist states]"; and later on: "It may be said that this has to some extent replaced the Marxist prospect of a permanent social revolution." Here we have a theoretical rationale for what has long been the function of the Communist movement in the West: to act as border guard and shill for the competing, rival establishment in the East. Above all, the perspective of Socialism-from-Below becomes as alien to these professors of bureaucratic collectivism as to the apologists for capitalism in the American academies.

This type of neo-Stalinist ideologist is often critical of the actual Soviet regime — a good example is Deutscher, who remains as far as possible from being an uncritical apologist for Moscow like the official Communists. They must be understood as being *permeationists with respect to bureaucratic-collectivism*. What appears as a "socialism-from-outside" when seen from the capitalist world, becomes a sort of Fabianism when viewed from within the framework of the communist system. Within this context, change-from-above-only is as firm a principle for these theoreticians as it was for Sidney Webb. This was demonstrated *inter alia* by Deutscher's hostile reaction to the East German revolt of 1953 and to the Hungarian revolution of 1956, on the classical ground that such upheavals from below would scare the Soviet establishment away from its course of "liberalization" by the Inevitability of Gradualness.

10. Which Side Are You On?

From the point of view of intellectuals who have a choice of roles to play in the social struggle, the perspective of Socialism-from-Below has historically had little appeal. Even within the framework of the socialist movement it has had few consistent exponents and not many inconsistent ones. Outside the socialist movement, naturally, the standard line is that such ideas are visionary, impractical, unrealistic, "utopian'" idealistic perhaps but quixotic. The mass of people are congenitally stupid, corrupt, apathetic and generally hopeless; and progressive change must come from Superior People rather like (as it happens) the intellectual expressing these sentiments. This is translated theoretically into an Iron Law of Oligarchy or a tinny law of elitism, in one way or another involving a crude theory of inevitability — the inevitability of change-from-above-only.

Without presuming to review in a few words the arguments pro and con for this pervasive view, we can note the social role it plays, as the self-justificatory rite of the elitist. In "normal" times when the masses *are* not moving, the theory simply requires pointing with scorn, while the history of revolution and social upheaval is simply dismissed as obsolete. But the recurrence of revolutionary upheavals and social disturbances, defined precisely by the intrusion onto the historical stage of previous inactive masses and characteristic of periods when basic social change is on the agenda, is just as "normal" in history as the intervening periods of conservatism. When the elitist theorist therefore has to abandon the posture of the scientific observer who is merely *predicting* that the mass of people will always continue quiescent, when he is faced with the opposite reality of a revolutionary mass threatening to subvert the structure of power, he is typically not behindhand

41

in switching over to an entirely different track: denouncing mass intervention from below as evil in itself.

The fact is that the choice between Socialism-from-Above and Socialism-from-Below is, for the intellectual, basically a *moral* choice, whereas for the working masses who have no social alternative it is a matter of necessity. The intellectual may have the option of "joining the Establishment" where the worker does not; the same option holds for the labor leaders, who, as they rise out of their class, likewise confront a choice that did not exist before. The pressure of conformity to the mores of the ruling class, the pressure for bourgeoisification, is stronger in proportion as personal and organizational ties with the ranks below become weak. It is not hard for an intellectual or bureaucratized official to convince himself that permeation of and adaption to the existing power is the smart way to do it, when (as it happens) it also permits sharing in the perquisites of influence and affluence.

It is an ironic fact, therefore, that the "Iron Law of Oligarchy" is ironclad mainly for the intellectual elements from whom it arises. As a social stratum (i.e., apart from exceptional individuals) intellectuals have never been known to rise against established power in anything like the way that the modern working class has done time and again through its relatively brief history. Functioning typically as the ideological flunkies of the established rulers of society, the brain-worker sector of the non-propertied middle classes is yet, at the same time, moved to discontent and disgruntlement by the relationship. Like many another servant, this Admirable Crichton thinks, "I am a better man than my master, and if things were different we would see who should bend the knee." More than every in our day, when the credit of the capitalist system is disintegrating throughout the world, he easily dreams of a form of society in which he can come into his own, in which the Brain and not Hands or Moneybags would dictate; in which he and his similars would be released from the pressure of Property through the elimination of capitalism, and released from the pressure of the more numerous masses through the elimination of democracy.

Nor does he have to dream very far, for existing versions of such a society seem to be before his eyes, in the Eastern collectivisms. Even if he rejects these versions, for various reasons including the Cold War, he can theorize his own version of a "good" kind of bureaucratic collectivism, to be called "Meritocracy" or "managerialism" or "Industrialism" or what-have-you, in the U.S.; or "African Socialism" in Ghana and "Arab Socialism" in Cairo; or

42

various other kinds of socialism in other parts of the world.

The nature of the choice between Socialism-from-Above and Socialism-from Below stands out most starkly in connection with a question on which there is a considerable measure of agreement among liberal, social-democratic and Stalinoid intellectuals today. This is the alleged inevitability of authoritarian dictatorships (benevolent despotisms) in the newly developing states of Africa and Asia particularly—e.g. Nkrumah, Nasser, Sukarno, et al.—dictatorships which crush independent trade unions as well as all political opposition and organize to maximize the exploitation of labor, in order to extract from the hides of the working masses sufficient capital to hasten industrialization at the tempo which the new rulers desire. Thus to an unprecedented degree, "progressive" circles which once would have protested injustice anywhere have become automatic apologists for any authoritarianism which is considered non-capitalist.

Apart from the economic-determinist rationale usually given for this position, there are two aspects of the question which illuminate what is broadly at stake:

(a) The economic argument for dictatorship, purporting to prove the necessity of breakneck industrialization, is undoubtedly very weighty for the new bureaucratic rulers—who meanwhile do not stint their own revenue and aggrandizement—but it is incapable of persuading the worker at the bottom of the heap that he and his family must bow to super-exploitation and super-sweating for some generations ahead, for the sake of a quick accumulation of capital. (In fact, this is why breakneck industrialization requires dictatorial controls.)

The economic-determinist argument is the rationalization of a ruling-class viewpoint; it makes human sense *only* from a ruling-class viewpoint, which of course is always identified with the needs of "society." It makes equally good sense that the workers at the bottom of the heap *must* move to fight this super-exploitation to defend their elementary human dignity and wellbeing. So was it also during the capitalist Industrial Revolution, when the "newly developing states" were in Europe.

It is not a question simply of some technical-economic argument but of sides in a class struggle. The question is: Which side are you on?

(b) It is argued that the mass of people in these countries are too backward to control the society and its government; and this is no doubt true, not only there. But what follows? How does a people or a class become fit to rule in their own name?

Only by fighting to do so. Only by waging their struggle against oppression — oppression by those who tell them they are unfit to govern. Only by fighting for democratic power do they educate themselves and raise themselves up to the level of being able to wield that power. There has never been any other way for any class.

Although we have been considering a particular line of apologia, the two points which emerged do in fact apply all over the world, in every country, advanced or developing, capitalist or Stalinist. When the demonstrations and boycotts of the Southern Negroes threatened to embarrass President Johnson as he faced an election, the question was: *Which side are you on?* When the Hungarian people erupted in revolt against the Russian occupier, the question was: *Which side are you on?* When the Algerian people fought for liberation against the "socialist" government of Guy Mollet, the question was: *Which side are you on?* When Cuba was invaded by Washington's puppets, the question was: *Which side are you on?* and when the Cuban trade unions are taken over by the commissars of the dictatorship, the question is also: *Which side are you on?*

Since the beginning of society, there has been no end of theories "proving" that tyranny is inevitable and that freedom-in-democracy is impossible; there is no more convenient ideology for a ruling class and its intellectual flunkies. These are self-fulfilling predictions, since they remain true only as long as they are taken to be true. In the last analysis, the only way of proving them false is in the struggle itself. That struggle from below has never been stopped by the theories from above, and it has changed the world time and again. To choose any of the forms of Socialism-from-Above is to look back to the old world, to the "old crap." To choose the road of Socialism-from-Below is to affirm the beginning of a new world

Independent Socialist Club 1968

44

Chapter II:
Karl Marx and Simon Bolívar:
A Note on Authoritarian Leadership
In a National-Liberation Movement

1

Contemporary politics is familiar with the moot issue of the justification for authoritarian dictatorships in developing countries, where the economic and political backwardness of the people and society is taken to prove the undesirability of democratic institutions for popular control from below. Generally speaking, there are two schools of apologia: one defending only those authoritarian regimes that orient toward dependence on American power and that protect foreign capital investments with adequate enthusiasm; and the other vindicating only those dictatorships that replace the old property-holding classes with a new class of bureaucratic-collectivist rulers, or seem to be on the way to do so. While the first type of dictatorship automatically becomes a member of the Free World, in Washington's slang, the latter type may adopt a sobriquet like "Communism" or "African Socialism," etc. with appropriate references to a hyphenated or unhyphenated Marxism.

The subject of this study is not the line of argument used to justify "progressive" authoritarianisms today, but only the relation of Marx's views to this question, since his name is so often taken in vain. It is true Marx did not have an opportunity to express an opinion on the regimes of Castro, Nkrumah, Mao, Nasser and their similars; but as it happens, he took up a case which would seem to be a far less disputable example of a "progressive" authoritarian who led a great national-liberation movement. This was Simon Bolívar, the "Liberator" of northern South America.

The case is sharpened by the fact that Marx does not question the progressiveness and legitimacy of that national-independence movement itself; and by the fact that, over a century ago, justification-by-backwardness had a better prima-facie case than in the modern world, which on an international scale is rotten-ripe for socialism from the Marxist point of view.

There is no suggestion that the case is closed by putting Marx's views in evidence; the aim is only to establish the facts in Marx's case, since they have been disputed, as we shall see. We shall also see that Marx's views, controversial over a century ago, were just as controversial only a few years ago when they once more became involved in a large-scale historical hassle in Latin America over Bolívar.

It is not only a matter of Bolívar. It is strange that there are "Marxists" today who think that support to modernizing dictatorships is a new and fresh idea for socialists, dating from about the end of World War II. In point of fact, the socialist movement *began* with the concept of the "educational dictatorship," as I have discussed elsewhere, and nothing could be more natural. There were social struggles in undeveloped countries in Marx's day too; after all, more countries were undeveloped. Indeed, the first underdeveloped countries with which Marx dealt historically were none other than England, France, and Germany, taken when they were faced with the initial tasks of industrializing, under an exploiting ruling class which was yet willy-nilly performing a certain historic role. The most passionate pages in Marx are reserved for denouncing the oppressive forms of capitalist rule in the Industrial Revolution. The political form which often clothed the modernizing function of the bourgeois New Class in underdeveloped France was Bonapartism; and there is no political force which Marx spent more time excoriating.

Still, the case of Bolívar more clearly brings out the then-and-now symmetry of the underlying problem. True, Marx viewed Bolívar as a case of Bonapartism; but here was a Bonapartism which did not arise after a Thermidor, and still less after a whole historical interval like the third Bonaparte; rather, it was integrally involved in the leadership of the ongoing national-liberation movement itself, as in several modern cases.

Let us first establish Marx's views on Bolívar.

2

That Marx looked into Bolívar at all was something of an accident. In 1857 Charles Dana, managing editor of the *New York Tribune*, to which Marx had been contributing since 1851, asked him to collaborate on the projected *New American Cyclopaedia*, mainly on matters of military history, biography and terminology.* Among the generals beginning with the letter B on Dana's list was, for example, Bernadotte, whose biography was half military, half political; and it was as a military leader, no doubt, that Bolívar's name got into this list. Since Engels (ghostwriting for Marx) was already overburdened with the

---

* The *NAC* was edited by George Ripley and Charles A. Dana (New York, Appleton, 1858-63) in 16 volumes. Dana, greatly impressed by the brilliance of the military-affairs articles sent in by Marx though actually written by Engels, excluded Marx from writing on more controversial subjects for the *NAC* because he wanted a bland, objective and impartial tone, and he did not expect Marx to do this successfully on more ideological subjects. The detailed story of Marx's relation to the *NAC* is included in the introduction to my edition of Marx-Engels' collected *Articles in the New American Cyclopaedia*.

strictly military articles, Marx undertook Bolívar himself.

Up to this time there had been no mention of Bolívar in any of Marx's writings or correspondence — therefore no indication he had ever given Bolívar a thought before he started doing research for the article in the British Museum. We know from the Marx-Engels correspondence on the *Cyclopaedia* work that Marx typically started with the articles in the various encyclopedias — English-language, French, and German at least.

Marx came out of this research with a powerful reaction of political hostility against Bolívar. This comes through plainly in the *Cyclopaedia* article, even though it was supposed to be couched in colorlessly impartial language. As was often true with Marx, political hostility also engendered an element of personal hostility; and he injected into the article a systematic disparagement of Bolívar's personal character and abilities, taken over from his anti-Bolívar sources.

We must stress that Marx's article on Bolívar is neither reliable nor important for any information it contains on its subject, about whom there is today much more material available. *It is of great interest only for what it tells us about Marx*, as he reacts politically to what he reads about Bolívar. To be sure, there is an interplay between Marx's reaction and certain facts about Bolívar, which we will explore; but the governing aim is to understand Marx. It is unrewarding to try to correct Marx's extremely overdrawn depreciation of Bolívar's military talents and activities, etc. The article has many biographical details wrong.* But since the source of all this was Marx's *political* evaluation, we are going to concentrate exclusively on the attack against Bolívar as an authoritarian and Bonapartist.

Marx's article[1] on the "Liberator" (the quotation-marks are Marx's too) first establishes his class background, "the creole nobility in Venezuela" of which his family was one of the wealthiest. We are told of his second visit to Europe, where he "was present at Napoleon's coronation as Emperor, in 1804, and at his assumption of the iron crown of Lombardy, in 1805 ." After an account of Bolívar's early career in the war of independence, Marx writes: "Having proclaimed himself 'dictator and liberator of the western provinces of

---

* Including the subject's name, which appears as "Bolivar y Ponte ." Marx obviously did not understand the Spanish surname. Bolivar y Ponte was the name of the subject's father, but his own was Simon Bolívar y Palacios. Even in 1963 the editors of the Marx-Engels *Werke*, Vol. 29, repeat Marx's mistake in their name index.

Venezuela' ... he created 'the order of the liberator', established a choice (i.e. elite) corps of troops under the name of his bodyguard, and surrounded himself with the show of a court ." But "his dictatorship soon proved a military anarchy, leaving the most important affairs in the hands of favorites, who squandered the finances of the country, and then resorted to odious means in order to restore them ."

A little later Marx describes one of the charades common in Bolívar's career, in which the general refuses to continue as dictator but finally "yields" to insistent supporters: "the dictatorship was thus invested with some sort of legal sanction ." He continues to refer to Bolívar as a dictator through the ensuing narration of military events, noting carefully his demand, at the 1816 meeting of his staff just before renewing the war, for "uniting the civil and military power in his person," and, just as carefully, the desire of other independence leaders to confide the civil power to a representative assembly instead. In spite of his promise (as Marx relates) to "assemble a congress, and not meddle with the civil administration," when he entered Barcelona "he proclaimed ... martial law and the union of all powers in his single person ."

When he tells of Bolívar's blood-purge of his rival General Piar (one of the blackest incidents of his career), he mentions that Piar called Bolívar a "Napoleon of the retreat ." He writes that when the national congress of February 1819 was called, "the mere name of (the congress) proved powerful enough to create a new army," thereby contrasting the popular mobilizing appeal of the representative institution against the dampening effects of Bolívar's dictatorial methods.

He continues to concentrate on Bolívar's authoritarian role as opportunity presents itself. The Angostura congress, he recounts, ousted Bolívar's man Zea, and "On receiving this news, Bolívar suddenly marched his foreign legion toward Angostura ... and restored Zea to his dignities. Dr. Roscia, fascinating him with the prospects of centralized power, led him to proclaim the 'republic of Colombia.' .. ."

The Cúcuta congress of 1821 met, and "after Bolívar had again pretended to resign, renewed his powers ." ... "Through his Colombian bodyguard, he swayed the votes of the congress of Lima, which, February 10, 1823, transferred to him the dictatorship, while he secured his re-election as president of Colombia by a new tender of resignation ."

Then the republic of Bolivia was set up: "Here, where (his general) Sucre's bayonets were supreme, Bolívar gave full scope to his propensities for arbitrary power, by introducing the 'Bolivian Code,' an imitation of the *Code Napoléon*. It was his plan to transplant that code from Bolivia to Peru, and from Peru to Colombia — to keep the former states in check by Colombian troops, and the latter by the foreign legion and Peruvian soldiers. By force, mingled with intrigue, he succeeded indeed, for some weeks at least, in fastening his code upon Peru ." But in Colombia a struggle broke out "between the centralists or Bolívarists and the federalists, under which latter name the enemies of military anarchy (i.e. Bolívar's dictatorship) had coalesced with military rivals ." Bolívar used "a pretext for overthrowing the (Colombian) constitution and re-assuming the dictatorship ."

The 1827 congress of Panama had "ostensible object of establishing a new democratic international code," but "What he really aimed at was the erection of the whole of South America into one federative republic, with himself as its dictator ."

But his power was slipping. "The congress of Ocaña, convoked by Bolívar, with a view to modify the constitution in favor of his arbitrary power, was opened March 2, 1828, by an elaborate address, insisting on the necessity of new privileges for the executive ." But Bolívar's opponents walked out. "Under the pressure of his bayonets, popular assemblies ... anew invested him with dictatorial power ." An assassination attempt "allowed him for some time to introduce a sort of military terrorism. He did not, however, lay hands on Santander, although he had participated in the conspiracy, while he put to death General Padilla, whose guilt was not proved at all, but who, as a man of color, was not able to resist ."

The rest is a brief summary of Bolívar's loss of power, and death in 1830.

3

Considering that the article was supposed to be bland and nonpartisan, Marx was clearly presenting an extremely hostile view of Bolívar's authoritarianism by means of selection and emphasis. Through all this, the progressiveness of the struggle for independence itself is not only unquestioned but confidently assumed. The criticism of Bolívar is always fully within the framework of the view that his policy weakened the independence struggle. We have already seen this when Marx contrasted the popular appeal of the revolutionary congress to the negative aspects of Bolívar's dictatorship.

In another place Marx explains that "The further they (Bolívar's forces) advanced, the stronger grew their resources; the cruel excesses of the Spanish acting everywhere as the recruiting sergeants for the army of independence ." He speaks of "the new enthusiasm of the people" over independence, which "turned to dissatisfaction" on account of Bolívar's dictatorship, thus allowing the Spanish to recover. This is the picture at many points in the article. It takes for given the liberation of the Negro slaves as one of the revolutionary forces, though Bolívar is not given his portion of the credit. We may add that another of the *NAC* articles is "Ayacucho," written by Marx and Engels in collaboration, which portrays this decisive battle as a triumph for the independence forces: "Thus the Spanish dominion was definitely destroyed," etc.[2]

Thus, for Marx, Bolívar's Bonapartism is *counterposed* to the interests of the revolution. The issue is clearly not the national struggle but Bolívar's political role in it.

This is the only one of the Marx-Engels articles for the *NAC* which editor Dana questioned, because of its anti-Bolívar leaning. Marx told Engels in a letter of 14 February 1858:

> With regard to a rather long article on 'Bolívar,' Dana furthermore expresses misgivings because it is written in a partisan style, and he asks for my authorities. Of course, I can give them to him, though it is a peculiar demand. As for the partisan style, I did somewhat drop the encyclopedic tone, to be sure. To see the most cowardly, mean and wretched scoundrel decried as Napoleon I was somewhat too absurd. Bolívar is a true Soulouque.

"Soulouque" is only nominally a reference to the Haitian emperor. Marx and other anti-Bonapartists commonly used it as a sobriquet for the third Napoleon. It summarizes Marx's view of Bolívar as a type of Bonapartist dictator.

Marx's article on Bolívar remained virtually unknown until it was republished for the first time, albeit in Russian translation, in the Marx-Engels *Sochineniia*, vol. II, Part 2, (1934). In 1937, it was included in the Communist-published collection *Revolution in Spain*, which also appeared in Spanish as *La Revolucion Española*. There was no editorial comment on Marx's viewpoint. As late as 1951, when the U.S. Communist Party chief W. Z. Foster published his *Outline Political History of the Americas,* Marx's article was quoted favorably.

But this turned out to be the "wrong line" on Latin American history. When the second edition of the *Sochineniia* was published, Vol. 14 (1959) carried a sharp attack on Marx's article, which was also faithfully translated in the East German Marx-Engels *Werke* (vol. 14, 1961). The attack by the Communist editors is couched in the usual terms of "excusing" Marx for not knowing any better in his day. It decries Marx's sources as untrustworthy (which they were indeed), and includes in this decrial also any conception of Bolívar as a "dictator ." Its claims for Bolívar as a "progressive" include this:

> He succeeded in binding together for a while in this struggle the patriotic elements of the Creole landowners ... the bourgeoisie, and the mass of people, including the Indians and Negroes.

And it disposes of Marx as follows:

> Naturally Marx had at that time no other sources at his disposal than the books of the authors mentioned, whose bias was then only little known. It was therefore inevitable that Marx got a one-sided view of Bolívar's personality which was reflected in his essay. The striving of Bolívar's for personal power which was exaggerated in the literature mentioned could not remain without influence on Marx's attitude toward Bolívar ...

The key claim, that "Naturally Marx had at that time no other sources at his disposal" than the anti-Bolívar books he cited, is intended to suggest that Marx's view of Bolívar was merely the result of misinformation, rather than of political opinion. Even if one grants that Marx innocently accepted the "misinformation," this does not change the political meaning of his reaction to this "misinformation ." If you react to the news that the U.S. has dropped an H-bomb on Peking by denouncing Washington, then this is an indicator of your political views, even if it turns out later that the news was misinformation.

Marx reacted to *his* image of Bolívar with a kind of political attack which nowadays is ridiculed not only by Communist *Realpolitiker* but also by a legion of bourgeois "realists," who agree that undeveloped nations need dictators. The conclusion is inescapable that Marx put a human value on democratic freedom which is alien to both of these varieties of "realism."

But as a matter of fact, the Communist editors' claim is quite false. It is not true that "Marx had no other sources at his disposal" etc. it is not true that an anti-Bolívar attitude was prevalent and accepted when Marx wrote his article.

We have already mentioned that, in working on the *NAC* articles, Marx went through the extant encyclopedias—French, German, and English-language. The articles which he read in these encyclopedias were overwhelmingly pro-Bolívar, mainly uncritically so. This can be checked with little trouble in the then current editions of the *Encyclopaedia Americana*, the *Encyclopaedia Brittanica*, the *Penny Encyclopaedia*, the *Encyclopedie du XIX Siècle*, the *Dictionnaire de la Conversation*, the Brockhaus *Conversations-Lexicon*. For all four countries represented here, the picture is unequivocal. It was Marx's article that was out-of-step, and that is exactly why Dana questioned it apprehensively.

As for the Communist editors' claim that modern scholarship disposes of Marx's view of Bolívar's political role, and that Marx "exaggerated" Bolívar's striving for personal power:

A discussion of the state of modern scholarship on Bolívar's dictatorial ambitions is not possible in this article. It is a thorny subject. On the one hand, there is the standard hagiography, or Bolívarolatry, of most Latin American writings on the subject. On the other hand, the polar-opposite view is now represented most prominently by Salvador de Madariaga's devastating job *Bolívar*,[3] whose impact was fatally weakened by its essentially pro-Spanish slant to the point of drawing attention away from its massive documentation. The result was an anti-Madariaga furor which we cannot here untangle.

However, if we limit ourselves to the single question of Bolívar's authoritarianism, the picture is not quite so complicated. The numerous and violent denunciators of Madariaga have had little to say on the facts in *this* respect, preferring either to ignore them or to justify them with fairly common varieties of anti-democratic argumentation.[4] In the light of Madariaga's factual structure, Marx's attack on Bolívar's dictatorial politics suffered only from mildness.

But, because of the *guerra a muerte* around Madariaga, the next section is not based on his work, but on the work which has gained the widest acceptance in Latin-Americanist (not Latin American) circles: Gerhard Masur's *Simon*

Bolívar.[5]

Masur's book is not, and does not pretend to be, impartial. It is frankly *pro-Bolívar*, often openly slanted. Masur frequently surrounds disagreeable facts about Bolívar's authoritarianism with passionate argumentation to justify it. But the point is that he presents many of the facts.

4

Bolívar's politics must be viewed in two periods — before and after the final military victory in 1825 — not because there was really a qualitative change but only because of the nature of the rationalizations. As long as the fighting was going on, Bolívar's dictatorship could be defended as a military necessity, though it was not. After victory, this apologia is not available. Hence the existence of the viewpoint, which was embodied in the Communist editors' attack on Marx, that Bolívar became objectionably authoritarian only in his last years.

Bolívar's first important political pronouncement was the 1812 Manifesto of Cartagena. It marked his first clear demands for highly centralized "strong" government. "Our compatriots," he said, "are not yet capable of exercising their legal rights ." And "government must prove to be formidable and ruthless without regard to law or constitution, until peace is established ." That he meant dictatorship was shown the next year when his forces took Caracas and he openly assumed the dictator's role.

In 1815 his "Letter from Jamaica" strikes the same note on the impossibility of extending democratic rights to the people: "As long as our fellow citizens do not acquire the talents and virtues which distinguish our brothers to the north (the U.S.), a radical democratic system, far from being good for us, will bring ruin upon us. Unfortunately, we do not possess these traits .. ." At this time Bolívar was thinking in terms of a hereditary Senate composed of the wealthy families of the Creole upper classes, with an elected lower chamber based on property qualifications for voting.

At the 1819 Congress of Angostura, Bolívar (according to Masur) already wanted, but did not openly propose, a lifetime presidency, which would control all national power without responsibility to Congress or courts. His speech attacked "absolute democracy" (which meant democracy), and Masur remarks that "his concepts of state were closer to those of Napoleon than to the men of the Terror ." In fact, "Bolívar's ideas approximate those of Napoleon and anticipate something of the fascist system ." He thought in terms of an elite class, "irreconcilable with democratic principles," and Masur points out (what is obvious enough) that to this day South America is ruled by such an elite oligarchy of wealth.

In 1812 the Congress of Cúcuta adopted a constitution too democratic for his taste. It is "Colombia's death knell," he complained. He blamed the "lawyers and ideologists": "In the end," he wrote, "the literati will do so much that they will be outlawed by the Colombia Republic as Plato outlawed the poets of his Republic. These gentlemen think that their opinion is the will of the people, without realizing that in Colombia the people are in the army .. ." (A false statement if taken at face value, the army being very small; what Bolívar meant was that the people who counted were the military.) As for others, "Their only right is to remain passive citizens," he wrote, and again denounced people who wanted a republic like that in the North.

His opportunity to insist on dictatorship came with military success. In 1822, after taking Guayaquil, he deliberately encouraged "anarchy and confusion" (says Masur) so that he might declare himself dictator of the province to save it from anarchy and confusion. He next aimed to be invested as dictator of Colombia. First he demanded an all-powerful presidency for himself: "I am convinced," he wrote, "that Colombia can only be kept in order and well-being by absolute power ." While bitter resistance in Colombia kept him from achieving his goal, he did become Dictator of Peru after victory there in 1823.

When peace came after the battle of Ayacucho at the end of 1825, Bolívar did not reverse his field but pressed more strongly than ever for an authoritarian regime in all the new republics. His goal was committed to paper in the form of the Bolivian Constitution which he wrote himself, and which to the end of his life he proposed for adoption by all the other countries singly and collectively as well as by the projected "Federation of the Andes," his longed-for empire.

"Bolívar's constitution," writes Masur, "restricts the people, as far as possible, from exercising any influence on government; it emulates Napoleon's consular government ." It "admits no form of self-government ." Of the three legislative chambers, the Censors are responsible for "morals" and elected for life. The Tribunes (administrative supervisors) and Senators, once elected by a complicated system, are never freely elected again: the citizens are permitted

54

only to present candidates, from whom each chamber chooses its own successors. The "sun" of this system is the President, who is named for life, and then appoints his own successor, the vice-president, who is also the prime minister—and hereditary.

Masur is moved to write that all this "merely made Bolivia a monarchy without a monarch, with an elected kingship such as the Catholic church and the Holy Roman Empire possessed ." (But the Pope does not designate his own successor.) Bolívar explained: "According to such a procedure, elections would be avoided, elections which are the greatest scourge of republics and which produce only anarchy ." Masur adds: "The other parts of the constitution do not need detailed analysis. Those paragraphs that deal with human rights are short and somewhat vague; those concerning administration are traditional; those which take up the administration of justice are open to question ."

Colombia resisted imposition of the Bolivian system; so did Peru but in August, 1826 Bolívar imposed it there by force. Masur's heart is plainly sore at the telling: "Bolívar was now accustomed to dictatorial power ." In Peru "his position assumed the attributes and prerogatives of a sultanate ." We are reminded that "Bolívar had said on many occasions that South America could be ruled by an astute despot ." To achieve his end, Bolívar more and more allied himself with reactionary clericalism to add the power of the Church to the backing of the wealthy and the landed.

How and why Bolívar failed to achieve the personal dictatorship he sought, in spite of his prestige as "Liberator," is another story; the nub of it is the fierce resistance of the mass of people to his aims. By 1829, when he faced the issue of bullying through to power behind his praetorian legions, he was already a physical wreck for quite different reasons; and he died the following year.

In the light of these facts, Bolívar's drive for personal dictatorship was not in the least "exaggerated" by Marx (contrary to the claim of the Communist editors) nor has modern scholarship contradicted Marx's over-all picture in this respect. On the contrary, of all the encyclopedia accounts of the period which we mentioned, only Marx's corresponds with historical truth—as far as concerns the political issue we have been discussing.

5

The facts are one thing—justificatory rationalizations another. To this day, more than a century after Marx registered his protest against Bolívar's anti-democratic views and goals, what other voice has been willing to make a basic criticism of this authoritarianism, or to counterpose faith in democratic institutions against the dictatorial leader of the independence movement?

From the South American hagiographers who do touch on this issue, there are only the usual justifications.[6] Enrique de Gandía offers a typical statement: The Bolivian Constitution, autocratic to be sure, was "a reflection of the monarchical ideas which were then held by Bolívar, San Martin and the greater part of the sensible (*sic*) people ." But not by the overwhelming majority of the people, not even a century and a half ago. For over a decade, until the mythmakers turned him into a sungod, the masses execrated his name even after his death; for them, only Marx speaks even now.

"Bolívar," writes this apologist, "made a constitution in order to be able to govern energetically and tranquilly ." So says every dictator. But the scheme for the lifetime president, hereditary vice-president and self-perpetuating legislature was a fantasy even in 1826; it could not have kept the people "tranquil" except in their graves.

Vicente Lecuna, the high priest of the Caracas cultists, has only this to say on our subject in his attack on Madariaga's book: "Sr. Madariaga lacks political vision. He does not understand the grandeur of Bolívar's continental ideas for the formation of a great state (*not true of Madariaga*—H.D.), nor the Bolivian Constitution, which was conceived with the idea of giving political stability to his creation ." Stability above all was also the great vision of Hitler's thousand-year Reich. A.F. Brice is cruder: he explains that "democracy" does not require "government of the people by the people" nor by a majority of the people, but only by the "active citizens," not necessarily under universal suffrage. This political principle is propounded for today too.

Carleton Beals' *Eagles of the Andes: South American Struggles for Independence* (Philadelphia, 1963) pays little serious attention to political issues, but the final chapters do not neglect to explain that "There was no basis for democratic or representative government" —the same rationalization that the same author could make for Russia or Cuba today, and just as untrue.

V.A. Belaunde's *Bolívar and the Political Thought of the Spanish American Revolution* (Baltimore, 1938) becomes critical at times of Bolívar's last period;

but the summary in his Preface is a straight-out eulogy of the "originality" of Bolívar's "program of organic, hierarchical and technical democracy" (undefined) as against "individualistic democracy ." He calls it "democratic Caesarism," which has a "unique value" in that it "liberate(s) the political structure from the domination of the will of the individuals," in which respect "Bolívar had an intuition of the real evil in pure democracy .. ."

We have already mentioned that Masur, while presenting a sufficiency of damning facts as a scholar, tries very hard to whitewash Bolívar's dictatorship. (His preface even expresses agreement with "the essence of Bolívar's political credo .") Having made clear that the facts show Bolívar to be an authoritarian, he editorializes his hero into an "authoritarian democrat ." Like Belaunde, he labels the product "democratic Caesarism ." All of these terms are undefined. On the very next page after he has himself said that Bolívar's ideas "anticipate something of the fascist system" (a stronger statement than any we would make), he still finds it possible to write: "He wanted a democracy, but a stable democracy ." (There is nothing in Masur's book that shows Bolívar really wanting any kind of democracy.) On one page he writes, "His will was totalitarian," but (since he never got his will) a couple of pages on he says, "His dictatorship should not be compared to or confused with the abuse of power that characterizes the totalitarian tyrants of our own day ." Which is true as far as it goes: Bolívar's aspirations were Bonapartist, as Marx saw, and one must not be anachronistic.

Masur's summary judgment is: "Bolívar remained dictator, but no one can doubt that this was the only possible solution at the time ." A strange claim: far from being the only possible solution, it is indisputable that Bolívar's dictatorship was no solution at all; it crashed ignominiously. The danger of "anarchy" of which Masur often speaks (he is echoing Bolívar) resulted from the clash between the efforts of the ruling oligarchy to impose oppressive controls on the people, and the struggle of the latter against this oppression. This "anarchy" could be avoided, and the "tranquillity" of Gandia achieved, only if the masses bent their necks without fighting back—always the authoritarian's dream of law and order.

Finally, what about the very model of a modern liberal, Salvador de Madariaga himself? We know, of course, that he takes pains to exhibit Bolívar's dictatorship, as he systematically takes apart the pretenses of the Bolívar cult. But he is *for* it, not against it. He makes clear more than once he believes

Bolívar to have been right in his ambitions: "*Bolívar did want a monocracy; and Bolívar was right*," he says in italics. "Far from yielding to those demagogic notions which have led to compulsory suffrage and to the granting of the vote to the illiterate in his own native land, Bolívar would divide citizens into active and passive .. ." and "had Congress listened to him and granted him his uncrowned kingship and even his hereditary Senate, the new state would have begun its independent life under better auspices ." In fact, Madariaga believes Bolívar was remiss only in *not* pushing boldly for an outright monarchy for himself!

Our Spanish liberal's view of the matter is just about the most openly reactionary of all those we have so far considered. The connection with his over-all thesis is not hard to see, and he virtually makes it himself: "what Bolívar was driving at was the reconstruction of the Spanish Empire without the Spanish king ." If this is so, then in Madariaga's eyes why spill the blood of a continent in order merely to change a crowned monarch for an uncrowned one?[7]

6

Thus Marx remains, to this day, one of the few champions of the democratic aspirations for which the northern South Americans fought *against* their "Liberator." He does not accept the rationalizations for dictatorship, which have not changed much in a century and a half.*We stated at the beginning that we are not here arguing the issue of authoritarianism itself, against those who would ridicule the very idea of counterposing a struggle for democratic rights to the "realistic" dictatorship of Bolívar. But at least we can restate the issue, as follows.

In one corner is Masur's formulation of the justification for authoritarianism which was already well known in Marx's day. Bolívar's dictatorship, says Masur, was "a dictatorship of training — intended to mature

---

* But the biggest gap in Marx's article, in this article, and generally in the literature of Bolívarology, is the lack of attention to the class struggle within the South American camp against the Creole ruling oligarchy which led the revolution. Yet its greatest weight as a historical factor is plain from a multitude of facts in Masur's and Madariaga's work, which remain unexplored — particularly the extreme smallness of the revolution's base among the lower classes and the Indians, who varied mainly from apathetic to pro-Spanish. Very suggestive is Juan Bosch's recent book *Bolívar y la Guerra Social* (Buenos Aires, 1966), especially in putting Bolívar's drive for dictatorship into the context of ruling class interests.

a people that was immature ." This is the notion of the "Educational Dictatorship" which was the most widely accepted idea of the early socialists and communists whom Marx combated.

But nowhere in history do we know of a dictatorship which trained the masses to become "mature" democrats — *except insofar as it "trained" them to fight against it.* Just as there has never been any imperialist domination of a backward people which carried through the well-advertised White Man's Burden of preparing the subjects for self-rule — except insofar as it stimulated the people to organize themselves for revolution. A people do not become "trained" for democracy nor do they "mature," except by their own fight for democracy, *against* the power that tells them it is "training" them — and against the intellectual servitors who apologize for the dictatorship with these arguments.

There seems to be a contradiction: if there is no way for people to become "ready" for democracy except by fighting for democracy, then it follows they must begin fighting for it *before* they are certified to be "ready." And in historical fact, this is the only way in which democracy has advanced in the world. The continuous solution to the contradiction lies in the process of revolution itself. This is a dialectic which will always be jeered at by those mentalities which know how to celebrate revolutionary struggles only after they have been straitjacketed by a new oppressive establishment.

New Politics 1968

Chapter III:

The Fabian and the African
or
How Sidney Webb Became Lord Passfield and Johnstone Kenyatta Became Jomo

Almost everyone knows that Sidney Webb's Fabianism was, if nothing else, practical, constructive, and hardheaded, unlike the revolutionary extremists he held in sovereign contempt. Now there is no better opportunity to be practical, constructive, and hardheaded than as a cabinet minister. In fact, one of the main aims of the Fabian Society was to ensure that socialists would know exactly what to do when they took over the government.

In 1929 the Labor party did take over the government, and Sidney Webb entered the cabinet as Secretary of State for Colonial Affairs. For technical constitutional reasons he had to be raised to the peerage before taking office, becoming Lord Passfield.

It is rather strange that nothing of any importance has ever been written on this decisive test of Mr. Fabian himself — until the recent appearance of an unheralded monograph by Robert G. Gregory, *Sidney Webb and East Africa*.[1] Now we have an examination in depth of Webb's activity as colonial secretary, concentrating on the main problem (outside Palestine) that faced him: Kenya. The picture that emerges, often despite Gregory, gives a fascinating insight into the underlying nature of Fabianism, that is, of the purest variety of socialist reformism ever developed in the history of socialist thought. One aspect of this picture is fairly well known: Webb's almost unquestioning pro-imperialism; but this is not the side we are interested in here.[2] It is something else. When Webb took office, the British policy of White Supremacy in Africa had already gone under various pseudonyms: the Dual Policy, or Multi-Racial Partnership, or Equal Rights à la Cecil Rhodes. Another such term was Native Paramountcy. This Orwellian synonym for White Supremacy was invented under the 1923 Tory government when the Duke of Devonshire was colonial secretary. It was an admonition that "the interests of the African natives must be paramount" in the minds of the white masters, i.e., a rewording of the tired slogan of the White Man's Burden.

After a year in office Webb issued two White Papers on East Africa, in one of which he revived the 1923 term and ordered that "the doctrine of native paramountcy" be applied "without delay." The doctrine was defined by explicitly approving the 1923 formulation of the good duke, together with some additional benevolent banalities. Webb's document insisted on the continuity of imperial policy since 1923 and fully accepted the White Paper of 1927, which had been a fairly plain statement of the "Dual Policy" brand of White Supremacy. This insistence on continuity in policy was implemented by Webb's definition of "right to equal treatment" of races as "right to equal treatment *in accord with their several needs*."

Let us get out of the way, first, any suspicion that Webb expected any new policy to be applied with or without delay. The Kenya government was *de facto* the governor alone, Sir Edward Grigg (later Lord Altrincham). Grigg had a long public record as a virulent White Supremacy imperialist, the kind who could openly say in his opening address as governor: "The base on which the whole pyramid of our civilization in this Colony is reared is native labor," and extol the "white man's burden." He was an admirer of Mussolini and liked to address his public dressed in similar black-and-tan military attire. Just before Webb came in, Grigg had been scheming with Tory officials in Britain to put across a program dear to the white settlers, one not only more ruthless toward the Africans but aimed at loosening even London's reins on their power. (We have here blood-brothers of the French Algerian *colons*, the ultras of Kenya.)

Now the new colonial secretary was not stuck with Grigg, who was going to retire shortly. On the contrary: "Webb, favorably impressed with Grigg and desirous of minimizing change during the transition in governments, persuaded the Governor to accept an additional year of office ."

This may be deemed merely an error in judgment by our hardheaded statesman, especially by change-minimizers. After all, it is the legitimate duty of a gradualist to be gradual, and he might fear lest the shock of replacing a fascist-minded ultra with a less virulent type be too much for the social fabric to bear all at once. But this was not all. Grigg openly and stridently opposed and sabotaged Webb's orders. For example, Webb, who was a benevolent man, wanted an African leader released from jail. Grigg refused. In long diatribes he denounced not only his minister Webb but the government party. "Such criticism by a governor of his Secretary of State was so extraordinary that the officials [in the Colonial Office] were perplexed as to how to word the reply ." Webb did nothing; did not even censure, let alone recall Grigg.

Then there was the episode of the Joint Committee of 1931.

Webb's White Papers on East Africa were unacceptable to the settlers (and Tories) for two reasons. First of all, Webb advocated stricter control from London than the settlers aimed to achieve. Second, the latter objected to the "benevolent" part of Webb's benevolent colonialism: security of land tenure for Africans, not quite so exploitative a taxation schedule, better education, housing, etc. Modest enough, but the whites were in no humanitarian mood. In addition, they were often political reactionaries on principle and were not loth to use any handle against the "socialist government" in office.

Therefore there had to be a fight, and the battleground chosen by Webb himself was the device of a Joint Committee of Parliament. Since he and his government would name the members, this would seem to be a safe move; a hardheaded man would know what to do.

First of all, the government decided that the Committee would consist of 20 members drawn equally from both Houses and from the two leading parties. Fair and square, except for one inconvenience: this meant the appointment of five Labor members of the Lords, and outside of Webb himself *there existed only three.* The scheme therefore handed the Tories a free-and-clear majority of 12 to 8, gratis. Secondly, the chairman naturally had to be either a Laborite or a Tory. It might seem that a Labor government would have no hesitation in doing what a Tory government would have done by reflex: taken the chairmanship for its own man. "But," writes Gregory, "Webb paid too much heed to the opinion of others that the chairman should be a disinterested person. The *Times*, for example, had devoted an editorial to this plea ."

Did then Webb appoint a "disinterested person"? He did not. The chairmanship went to a "strong Conservative," and when he died, to another strong Conservative. The rigging was complete.

The Tory majority had no reluctance to use its control, all the more since it obviously had nothing to fear from Webb. "That the Committee was biased is evident in the record," says Gregory. Webb never uttered a complaint or reproach; but then it is not certain what he would have recognized as bias. For example, in the list of witnesses gotten up by Webb, not a single African was included. "Only because organizations such as the Anti-Slavery Society protested did Webb and the Committee correct this oversight [sic] ." When ultimately three African witnesses from each of the three East African territories did appear before the Committee, they were heard only cursorily and *pro forma*: "Obviously, they were summoned, not because they could furnish important information, but because without them the committee could not claim that it had head the opinions of all communities ."

Of course, no African suspected of an independent attitude was permitted to appear; Webb saw to that. When Africans in Kenya heard that they were to be represented on the committee, the Kikiyu Central Association requested that it be authorized to proceed with the election of the Kikiyu delegates. The local government flatly refused; and ...the association at its own expense finally sent its president Johnstone Kenyatta, and a Kikiyu teacher, Parmenas Mockerie, to appear before the committee. The two were well educated and could speak English fluently. But when they arrived in London, even though examination of witnesses was to continue for many weeks, there were notified that they had arrived too late ... as a last resort, they submitted to the committee a written exposition of their grievances. To their consternation, however, the memorandum was not published as part of the written evidence.

Gregory is moved to comment that this showed "the existence of Kikiyu grievances was scarcely acknowledged by the British government," i.e., the Laborites. One can be sure that the man who called himself Johnstone Kenyatta thought so too.

Not only the African independents were excluded. The prominent Labor men interested in African affairs whom Gregory labels the "humanitarians" — Josiah Wedgwood, Leonard Woolf, Julian Huxley, Norman Leys, W. M. Ross — were regarded as too pro-African by Webb and likewise kept out. Five other "humanitarians" did get before the Committee, but "most witnesses expressed the settlers' viewpoint," says Gregory. Naturally the conclusions in the Committee's report went to the Right; essentially the "Dual Policy" was endorsed with an obeisance to the term "native paramountcy ." Webb never expressed any objection to the report. More outlandish still, he did not think there was anything objectionable about it.

The consequences of labor's failure to make even a gesture in the direction of African interests may well have been decisive for the direction taken by Africa:

> The report of the Joint Committee ... was the final act in a drama of intense controversy that had held the attention of British, African, and Indian audiences for a decade. discouraged by failure and confused by the many definitions of policy, humanitarians ceased to campaign for a change in East Africa. After the disgraceful collapse of their second government, Labor abandoned a radical approach to reform in imperial as well as domestic affairs. For many years the Labor Party avoided all reference to native paramountcy. In 1949, during the third Labor government, the Minister of State for Colonial Affairs, the

Earl of Listowel, assured Conservatives in the House of Lords
that the doctrine was no longer the official policy in East Africa.

What Webb established for the Africans was that none of the whites, not
even the white "socialists," was willing to concede self-government; they
would have to conquer it themselves.

> Convinced that their trust in the British government was
> betrayed, many Africans was betrayed, many Africans in
> subsequent years sought other means to redress their
> grievances. The logical alternative was subterfuge; and the
> causes of Mau Mau ... can be traced to the fluctuations in British
> colonial policy between 1923 and 1931.

It was after this that the man called Johnstone Kenyatta changed his name
to Jomo Kenyatta, and, as secretary of the Kikiyu Central Association, set about
"to rouse the African community into mass protest against the white man's
civilization ."

*

Why?

It is an extraordinarily *extreme* picture, this account of Webb's fatuous
futility as colonial secretary. As mentioned, it is easy to explain it all by Webb's
imperialist mindedness, but while this is a fact, it does not get to the bottom of
the episode. A deeper level of motivation—and incidentally a farther insight
into Fabianism—is suggested from another direction.

To begin with, Gregory insists justly that Webb's policy cannot be blamed
on "bad advisers"; the responsibility was his.

There was, indeed, a party Advisory Committee on International Questions
which concerned itself closely with East Africa, but

> Ironically, it exerted less influence when Labor controlled the
> government than when Labor was in opposition ... because of
> Webb's attitude and an ill-defined party constitution, it had no
> direct connection with the administration. It could not even
> persuade the Secretary of State to attend its meetings.

Leonard Woolf thought Webb was begin misled by Grigg, but his was untrue, says Gregory:

> Through the years, as an opponent of Marxist revolution, Webb
> had directed the Labor Party toward socialism along a course in
> line with his own philosophy, "the inevitability of gradualness
> ." In his opinion the advisory committee had fallen into the
> hands of militant radicals—Buxton, Woolf, Leys, Ross, and
> Wedgwood.

Perhaps needless to say, none of these men was a left-wing socialist, let alone a Marxist or a revolutionary. They were merely relatively militant in advocating redress of African grievances. After a first meeting Webb decided that Ross was "very fanatical ." As we have seen, he did not even permit his party "advisers" to testify before the Joint Committee.

He certainly did not want any advice from Africans themselves. When Kenyatta and Mockerie came to London at considerable expense to present their views in person to the white-sahib Colonial Secretary, they were granted an audience only with one Permanent Under-Secretary "and their conversation with him was disappointing ."

Whom, then, *did* Webb rely on, if we count out Tories, Laborites and Africans?

> While Webb held office, he was accused of being the tool of his
> civil servants. "But that is inevitable," explained Beatrice, who
> was aware of this criticism. "By temperament and training
> Sidney belongs to the Civil Service ." Webb also was attracted
> to his permanent officials because they were neither reactionary,
> as he thought preceding Secretaries of State had been, nor
> radical, like some within his own party.

To be sure, Gregory rightly insists that Webb was not the "tool" of his civil servants, but "These men made suggestions, of course, and their recommendations usually were accepted without question; and they drafted the letters he sent to Grigg and also his main statements of policy ."

Drummond Shiels, his under-secretary in the Colonial Office, wrote in *The Webbs and Their Work*:

It has been asserted that he has dominated by his Civil Servants. This is not accurate, though the effect of the real position may seem to have been somewhat similar. He had spent the first ten years of his career in the Colonial Office and during these impressionable years, he, no doubt, got into a civil service way of looking at things ... Another influence which affected him was his great respect for the individual whom he believed to be an expert. ... He regarded as experts most, if not all, of the senior men in the Colonial Office and was, perhaps, inclined to accept their judgments without always applying the same critical examination which he gave to other matters.

Beatrice Webb wondered in her diary, what the Colonial Office staff thought of Sidney:

A super-civil servant added to the C.O. staff: His main activity is to pick the brains of all and sundry, selecting from or harmonizing conflicting or divergent policies. Not quite all and sundry, by the way! His would-be visitors are censored. "Not desirable that you should see Philby; he has been most troublesome to the office fomenting discontent over there," said his official adviser. And S. did *not* see him. Why not meet him casually in the Fabian office?" said, on behalf of the rebel, who happens to be a Fabian approved by Galton. "Perhaps," replied Sidney, doubtfully. (Oct. 2. He did).

That is a lovely picture painted by Beatrice: the Fabian minister refusing to see a fellow Fabian because his civil-service expert informs him the fellow is a troublemaker... Essentially, Beatrice shared the faith in the permanent government bureaucracy: she had meditated in her diary a few years before that the "civil servants—a fine body of men—[are] I think the most upright and intelligent class in the community ."

Gregory's remark that Webb viewed the permanent officialdom as being neither reactionary nor radical hits the mark. They were not reactionary: that is, they did not (most of them) act as mouthpieces of the white settlers against London. They were not radical: that is, they did not get "fanatical" about African interests. As permanent bureaucrats their concern was maximizing the interests of the State. But what were the interests of the State? These could hardly be viewed except within the framework of white supremacy in Africa, even though the white settlers also had to be kept under control by London. Some day, of course (said the doctrine of the inevitability of Gradualness), the Africans would have more freedom, but for today what was inevitable was white supremacy. Webb settled comfortably into the groove as first among the servants of the State.

The interests of the State also demanded no rude shocks to its stability or prestige among the Lesser Breeds. "The most disappointing of Webb's actions," says Gregory, "was his stand before the Joint Committee," because he took his stand on the parliamentary myth of "continuity of policy ." According to this pretense, the policy of His Majesty's Government had remained unchanged throughout the various White Papers. Before Webb, this "continuity" was also the Tory tradition.

What was the general reason for the myth, and why did Webb fall in with this pattern of apparent parliamentary cretinism? One powerful motivation was the maintenance of the united front of the white sahibs before the native eyes. The whites must not seem to split among themselves because this emboldens the natives to make trouble. If the white masters admit that they sometimes *change* policy, the natives too may get the idea that the policy can be changed ... by other means.

Dr. Norman Leys, the Laborite "humanitarian," wrote after the Labor government's debacle that the Laborites "allowed themselves to be misunderstood. All over East Africa the news has gone that the Labor Government has recanted ." Was it a misunderstanding? Suppose that the Fabian colonial secretary had pushed ahead with a militant "pro-African" policy and had gotten defeated on it; the news "all over East Africa" would have been that there was a deep split between the central government of the white masters in London and the local power of the white settlers. The consequence would have been an earlier spur to African unrest.

The Fabian super-civil servant dreaded this as much as the Duke of Devonshire. Webb yielded to Tory outcries and white settlers' pressure not because he was convinced by their arguments nor because he was a coward, but because he was convinced by their arguments nor because he was a coward, but because he was afraid of the same danger they were afraid of, i.e., stimulating the Africans to take matters into their own hands. Webb differed from the reactionaries wholeheartedly in wishing to control the subject races benevolently, but he did not differ in fearing their tendencies toward self-emancipation. He wanted no more inconvenience from below than did the Kenya whites.

The interests of the State were paramount because this State was itself, by the inevitability of gradualness, being transformed in the direction of collectivism. This transformation depended particularly on "the most intelligent class in the community," the enlightened bureaucracy, with whom Webb felt at one even as against Fabians. While it was in the happy process of being transformed from above, it could not tolerate any disturbances from below that might shake its equilibrium. Hence the rather venomous hostility toward "extremists" Kenyatta and Mockerie, the "fanatics" Ross and Wedgwood, the "militant radicals" Woolf et al. This was the essence of Fabianism at work.

*

Postscript:

It was precisely at this time, while the Labor cabinet was foundering and the colonial secretary was floundering, that Beatrice was discovering the fascinating vision of the Super-Civil-Service State in the totalitarian system under Stalin. By August 24, 1931 when the Labor government fell, she was well on the way. About two weeks before, Bernard Shaw, returned from Russia, had given his Fabian lecture in which he explained that the Russian regime was pure Fabianism, that Stalinism was Webbism plus the new concept of a party-oligarchy. On September 10, Beatrice wrote in her diary: "Am I strong enough to go to Russia so as to give vividness to any line we take? ... For without doubt we are on the side of Russia .. ." On January 4, 1932 she jotted down: "Will she [Russia] become the Mecca? if so it will be the British Fabians who will show the way: not the continental Marxists. A pilgrimage to the Mecca of the equalitarian state led by a few Fabians ... will bring about the world's salvation! Well, well; it is an exhilarating, even an amusing prospect .. ." On May 17 she and Sidney drafted "our hypothetical conclusion prior to our tour," since they already knew what they were going to find in the promised land. In the course of their sojourn in Russia, Sidney would whisper, "See, see, it works, it works ." On their return they devoted their remaining years to consummating a near-total marriage of Fabianism and Stalinism.

Dissent 1960

Chapter IV:
Neo-Corporatists and Neo-Reformists

...the application of joint-stock companies to industry marks a new epoch in the economical life of modern nations ... in joint-stock companies it is not the individuals that are associated, but the capitals. By this contrivance, proprietors have been converted into shareholders, i.e. speculators. The concentration of capital has been accelerated ... A sort of industrial kings have been created, whose power stands in inverse ratio to their responsibility - they being responsible only to the amount of their shares, while disposing of the whole capital of the society - forming a more or less permanent body, while the mass of shareholders is undergoing a constant process of decomposition and renewal, and enabled, by the very disposal of the joint influence and wealth of the society, to bribe its single rebellious members. Beneath this oligarchic Board of Directors is placed a bureaucratic body of the practical managers and agents of the society ... It is the immortal merit of Fourier to have predicted this form of modern industry, under the name of Industrial Feudalism. - Karl Marx, in *N. Y. Daily Tribune*, July 11, 1856.

The replacement of capitalism by a New Order is being discussed, even advocated or at least viewed with kindliness, by some very eminent and respectable thinkers in this country not usually associated with revolutionary ideologies. This trend, or school of thought, seems to have gained steadily in the last few years. Its meaning can best be understood in the context of a wider, a worldwide trend in relation to which it constitutes only one strain or national form.

The wider, international trend is the burgeoning of *bureaucratic-collectivist ideologies* in a broad-spread infiltration of all bourgeois thought today. By "bureaucratic-collectivist" I mean in this connection the ideological reflection or anticipation of a new social order which is neither capitalist nor socialist, but which is based on the control of both economy and government by an elite bureaucracy — forming a new exploitive ruling class — which runs the fused economic-political structure not for the private-profit gains of any individual or groups, but for its own collective aggrandizement in power, prestige, and revenue, by administrative planning-from-above. One premise of this conception is that the totalitarian statified economy developed under Stalinism in Russia, which is today consolidating its power over a good portion of the globe, is one well-developed form of bureaucratic-collectivism.

Whatever the label conferred on this system, however, it is less controversial that key elements characteristic of its structure have, in our own day, already had a massive impact on the capitalist world and its thought. The channels by which this society-wide pressure has been exerted are two related ones. First is provided by the contradictions and difficulties of capitalism itself, the solutions of which point to some type of collectivism and to some form of increased statification, whether under the Great Depression (with the New Deal as carrier) or under the Permanent War Economy of today. Second is the direct impact of the Russian advance-model on the system of the old world, in evoking emulation, triggering analogous patterns, enforcing imitation by the logic of rivalry.

1

The current - within the borders of this larger phenomenon - which this article proposed to investigate shares with all others a common desire to present itself as being "beyond capitalism or socialism ." In a key document to be discussed, W. H. Ferry, of the Center for the Study of Democratic Institutions founded by the Fund for the Republic at Santa Barbara, says for example:

> I think there is something brand new emerging here as well as
> in Europe which is certainly not capitalism. If you wish, you
> can call it socialism. Several of my less friendly critics suggested
> that the new fascism was being proposed here. Naturally, I
> don't agree to that statement.

But what apparently distinguished it from the other, more typical bureaucratic-collectivist currents is its hostility to statification or "statism," which it aspires to replace with a more pluralistic constellation of corporate powers. *Thus it finds itself developing a new corporatism* — which naturally leads right back to bureaucratic statism by a different theoretical route.

A.A. Berle Jr. strikes this keynote in his foreword to the recent book edited by Harvard's E. S. Mason, *The Corporation in Modern Society*, whose several chapters by leading authorities convey many of the leading conceptions of this neo-corporatism. Berle is discussing the "two systems" of modern industrialism, the one in Russia and the "modern corporation" in the U.S. He calls the corporations "these non-Statist collectivisms" and sees them as "suggesting an eventual non-Statist socialization" of profits. In another place Berle says the present system is really "Collectivism" or "non-Statist Socialism," and though (being unafraid of labels) he also calls it "People's Capitalism," he makes clear he believes the social order is traveling beyond capitalism or socialism.[1]

These neo-corporatist ideas have their roots, in the immediate sense, not in a predilection for any of the older and more famous corporatisms which come to mind, but in a reaction to distinctively American conditions, in the soil of the one capitalism left in the world which seems to be a going concern.

One root is a wave of intensified soul-searching about the dominant institution of this capitalism, the corporation. "What Mr. Berle and most of the rest of us are afraid of is that this powerful corporate machine ... seems to be running without any discernible controls," writes Prof. Mason. Why does the system seem to them out of control?

It is certainly not controlled by the famous Invisible Hand of the Market, they agree. A new stage in the concentration of economic power has come into being. In *Power Without Property* Berle has laid great stress on the immense expansion of the fiduciary institutions (pension funds, mutual funds, etc.) and their economic consequences. These funds buy common stocks, i.e. formal shares in the ownership of the economy. They grow and their holdings proliferate. Then –

> A relatively small oligarchy of men operating in the same atmosphere, absorbing the same information, moving in the same circles and in a relatively small world knowing each other dealing with each other, and having more in common than in difference, will hold the reins. These men by hypothesis will have no ownership relation of any sort. They will be, essentially, non-Statist civil servants – unless they abuse their power to make themselves something else.

This, he argues, is creating "a new socio-economic structure," with basic political effects. "Then, the picture will be something like this. A few hundred large pension trust and mutual fund managers (perhaps far fewer than this number) would control, let us say, the hundred largest American industrial concerns ." Again: "In result, the greatest part of American economic enterprise, formerly individualist, has been regrouped and consolidated into a few hundred non-Statist, collective cooperative institutions ."

So, as noted, divorce between men and industrial things is becoming complete.   A Communist revolution could not accomplish that more completely.   Certainly it could not do so with the same finesse.   When a Russian Communist government says to the workers that "the people" own the instruments of production but it will take care of them, it is assigning to its population a passive-receptive position closely comparable to the one we are studying.   The difference lies in the fact that the criteria for reception are different, and that the political State exercised the power factor now gradually but steadily being aggregated under the American system is nonpolitical but equally impersonal fiduciary institutions.

This concentrated power of the fiduciary managers, a stage beyond the "America's Sixty Families" pattern, is only potential: in practice they eschew voting control. Thus, the lack of any control over the corporate managements becomes institutionalized. But whether they exercise their power or not, the result is a small oligarchy of uncontrolled managers, continuously making decisions which have a vital impact on the society as a whole.

2

Berle's next question is: What "legitimates" this uncontrolled corporative power?   Not assignment of this power to the managements by the shareholders. Berle and Means took care of the fiction of shareholder control back in 1932; and even Adler and Kelso's *Capitalist Manifesto* only advocates that the shareholder *should* control, meaning that he does not now.

A second source of "legitimacy" could be the market, if one argues that it is the objective hand of the market which imposes decisions on the managers, not their whims. But our neo-corporatists do not believe this.

What then can legitimate the decisions of management? The solution of government control arises, of course, but to our subjects this means "state control," which means "statism" which means socialism, communism, totalitarianism, Sovietism and other unthinkable things. In general, they are in a flight from statism under the impress of the Russian horrible example. They grope for an alternative.

What then? Beardsley Ruml has suggested an appointed-trustee system: the Board of Directors co-opts a special member to act as "trustee" for a given interest-group (the company's customers, or suppliers, or employees, or the "community," etc.) protecting its interest against the board. I cite this mainly to illustrate what "groping" means.

The next grope is cited not only because it is Berle's but because it gives a proper sense of the hopelessness of the effort. This is the feudal analogy presented by Berle in *The 20th Century Capitalist Revolution* (1954), a much misunderstood book which does *not* present a Luce-type celebration of our economic system. In his strange chapter on "The Conscience of the King and the Corporation," Berle is trying to answer the question: How have absolute, uncontrolled powers been curbed in the past, not by upheavals from below but by organic dispensations from above? - for perhaps this will also apply to the absolute, uncontrolled power which is our present problem. He finds an answer in the medieval Curia Regis. Any man could throw himself before the king's feet and get justice dispensed on the spot by the kings' conscience. The custom became institutionalized. Hence the beginning of equity courts and (one gathers, in this Berlean history) eventually other democratic counterpoises to the absolute power. "It is here suggested," Berle concludes, "that a somewhat similar phenomenon is slowly looming up in the corporate field through the mists that hide us from the history of the next generation ."

The legitimation, therefore, is immanent in the historical process itself. The important thing, he is saying, is not whether the king's rule was legitimate but that this *was* the way the new system arose.

The approach stirs a reminiscence. It is our American school's analogue of the standard Stalinist "historical" justification of *its* absolute power: totalitarianism and terror are passing phenomena preparatory to a glorious morrow, mere flecks on the wave of the future. If it is dressed in feudal terms, this is partly because Berle has long been fascinated by the virtues of feudal society. (Compare his rather amazing paean of praise to medieval institutions, over 20 years ago in *New Directions in the New World*.) But this nostalgia for feudalism is not confined to Berle. In reaction to monolithic-statism, feudalism begins to appear "pluralistic," which in contemporary sociological jargon is high praise. Its integration of the individual in pre-capitalist community relationships looks good as against the alienation of man under capitalism. The feeling crops up especially in the neo-corporatists, as they view the "feudal" pattern of a society where overweening social power lumps up in a number of huge agglomerations, with a relatively small number of corporations lording it over their own "baronies," each one with vassals dangling after, like the auto dealers after the Big Three of Detroit.[2]

3

Berle's announcement in *The 20th Century Capitalist Revolution* that the big corporation not only has a soul but also a conscience was subjected to a good deal of understandable ribbing, even before those General Electric executives went to jail; but this discovery of the corporate conscience should be considered only one form of another grope, not yet examined. This is the proposal for the Statesmen-Managers. If the decisions made, without control, by the big corporation executives are so vital for society, these executives must be more than glorified shopkeepers.

Their decisive job cannot be simply to further the interests of the corporation, maximize profits, etc., with primary responsibility to the owners. They must train themselves to think in social terms, in terms of the impact of their decisions on the bigger world outside; in short, to be Statesmen rather than parochially profit-minded businessmen. This becomes also a solution, or part of a solution, to the problem of legitimacy. It may be soul-quaking to think that the fate of our whole society is in the hands of corporate overlords whose nearsighted eyes are fixed only on the shortest way to money-grubbing, but it is heartening to think that this fate is taken care of by Experts who, having proved their managerial skill in the rough-and-tumble of business, now blossom out as broadgauged Social Thinkers too. This is the meaning of the refrain in Philip Selznick's recent *Leadership in Administration*: "The executive becomes a statesman as he makes the transition from administrative management to institutional leadership ." The theme can also be found in some of the contributions to the Mason book.

In this approach, then, the new irresponsibility of the uncontrolled Institutional Leaders is no longer a thing to view with alarm but rather a necessary precondition to freeing them from the petty, distorting influences of short-range, profit-maximizing considerations.

In this context we get demonstrations (which once would have sounded like muckraking) of how our corporate barons are indeed making the vital decisions politically and socially, as well as economically: how the oil companies determine our foreign policy; how General Dynamics decides strategy in the struggle for the world, etc. The objection, of course, is not that this is done but that it is too often done by executives who are not also Statesmen.

But this line is inherently dangerous, as Mason points out:

> If equity rather than profits is the corporate objective, one of the
> traditional distinctions between the private and public sectors
> disappears. If equity is the primary desideratum, it may well be
> asked why duly constituted public authority is not as good an
> instrument for dispensing equity as self-perpetuating corporate
> managements?

And Eugene V. Rostow warns that this trend invites the response that it is
men elected to advance the general welfare who should make the decisions
rather than uncontrolled oligarchs. But this implies *democratic control* of the
decision-making apparatus, and democracy is the only way out which our neo-
corporatists reject with unquestioning uncertainty.

4

Neo-corporatism presents itself, first of all, as another attempt to answer
the problem of legitimacy. But this problem, after all, is only the current way
in which its posers formulate to themselves the basic question of the
underpinnings of the whole social system. Real solutions are bound to lie in
radical, i.e., systemic, changes.

The outline of such a change appears under the name of "Constitutionaliz-
ing the Corporation" in the deliberations (already mentioned) of the Center for
the Study of Democratic Institutions led by W. H. Ferry.[3] Ferry began with a
number of complaints about the present system which could once have been
part and parcel of a socialist propaganda pamphlet: against over-concentration
of wealth, the "paradoxes and contradictions" of contemporary capitalism,
alienation, the myth of the "self-regulating economy," the "greed of the
affluent," economic individualism, "the messiness of the present economic
arrangements," etc. This leads on to formulations favoring "a political
economy based on the purposive use of law, politics, and government on
behalf of the common good," "the primacy of politics" for "the rational control
of our economic affairs," "bringing the economic order under political
guidance," and so on.

These phrases seem to give the primacy to *political* power over the
corporate power, subordinating the latter to the former, i.e. installing "statism,"
in the terminology previously referred to. This general "socialistic" approach
gave way to something else as the discussions at the Center advanced, with the

participation of an impressive panel of eminent thinkers: Robert Hutchins, Berle, Scott Buchanan, Reinhold Niebuhr, I. I. Rabi, J. C. Murray, Walter Millis, and others. At a month-long meeting — a sort of enlarged plenum — of the Center held last summer, Ferry presented a programmatic paper for discussion by the group.

The concrete idea that emerged is the foundling of a new political order on a "commonwealth of corporations." Ferry proposed (after raising the question of a "fourth branch of government" for economic questions):

> A less dramatic form of constitutionalization might be the formation by statute of a commonwealth of corporations, an "association of free, self-governing nations ." This would call for federal charters, or "constitutions," which would recognize the autonomy of the member-corporations but charge them collectively with specific powers and responsibilities ... Along some such route might also come the legitimacy that Berle believes the modern corporation is seeking. Establishing a commonwealth or federation of corporations would necessitate, for example, a review of corporate charters.

He explains further:

> ...we keep on thinking in the very limited terms of nationalization or non-nationalization, private ownership or national ownership. It is quite possible, for example, to give a good deal more authority and responsibility to corporations ... I am looking for a legal order to enclose and to make coherent what is being done in this country by the corporations.

And he stresses several times that his vision means "a new and different type of state," "something new, a qualitatively different way of looking at the economy ."

Father Murray, the Jesuit member of the panel of consultants, who took a prominent part in the discussions, thereupon spoke the following, not at all antagonistically:

I know that you have expressly disclaimed that what you wish is socialism, and quite rightly, especially in the classic definition. It doesn't seem to me that that is what you wish. However, the tendency of your paper is to install intervention of a sort that is referred to technically as the corporative state. I don't mean the corporative state of the fascist sort, which was frankly totalitarian ... [Murray explains he means the corporative state as invented by "some German economists and political thinkers" as an alternative to both capitalism and socialism.] You seem to be aiming at something of the same sort. You seem to want an integration of the economic processes and political processes, if you will, or a constitutionalization of it. The net effect would be radically new.*

5

This observation by Father Murray, which was not a criticism, ties up with the views of another Jesuit social thinker who had recently published on the question. This is Father Harbrecht, whose brochure *Toward the Paraproprietal Society* (1960) had appeared with a laudatory introduction by none other than Berle.

Harbrecht's thesis is that our social system is turning into a system of property tenure which is neither socialism nor really capitalism. His analysis starts at the same place as Berle's discussion of the fiduciary institutions and the new stage of divorcement between property and power. In this new order "beyond property," inevitably "the economic power that is growing in the institutions is being drawn, or shunted away, from the generality of the people ." The result has "striking parallels" with feudal institutions, which also "began with a separation of control from the ownership of productive property." Today corporations correspond to the Great Domains of the baronial principalities. "A man's place in medieval society was determined by

---

* It should be remembered that the Catholic Church officially has its own program for a sort of corporatism (also called "industry council plan," etc.), a very elastic one: it has been interpreted into anything from Mussolini's fascist corporations to mere labor-management committees. Father Murray can therefore raise the question of corporatism more objectively than most.

his place in the domain. Today men are bound to their corporations ... the present-day corporate managers are like the vassals of the great domains. They have control, but not ownership of great wealth, yet their tenure in power is in fact limited by their continuing ability to perform a service ."

Thus Father Harbrecht in his own book. It is easy to see why it delighted Berle. For Harbrecht, this process of "feudalization" of the corporate-political structure is his own version of the Wave of the Future.

Now we learn from Father Murray (in the Center discussion) that Harbrecht made a criticism of Ferry's paper. He found that Ferry wants to go too far with "the *politization* of the economic process" — that is, the imposition of outside political (state) controls *over* the corporations (the baronial powers), whereas Harbrecht sees the increased power as going *to* the corporations.

Faced with the explicit posing of this question, Ferry denied that Harbrecht's criticism applied to his position: "I do not accept the criticism. *I will accept Father Harbrecht's own proposal for imposing larger responsibilities on corporations* ." (Emphasis added.)

The distinction is very important for our purposes. What is being worked out here is not simply more of the familiar liberal-collectivist trend toward increased statification, a line running from Croly through the New Deal and on to Schlesinger and others today. This, as Berle likes to stress, is an attempt at a "non-statist" alternative: the assignment of political power not *over* the corporate bodies of the economy but *to* them.

6

The Center consultant who has developed a more clearly thought-out program of corporatism, perhaps thereby inspiring Ferry, is Scott Buchanan. Buchanan was a leader of the Wallace Progressive Party in 1948; I do not know what his politics became after that, but when he published his *Essay in Politics* in 1953, the preface explained that it was based on conversations in 1947 which led most of the participants to join the Wallace movement the following year. The 1953 book presents essentially the same views he has now.

In a 1959 discussion at the Center, Buchanan criticized Ferry along the same lines as Harbrecht: for wanting to give too much power to the government instead of giving more powers to the corporations. But the government, he argued, "is obviously incapable of dealing with the big economic, military, and other problems that arise ... When you turn this all over to the government as

is done in Sweden, you get a very dull, not necessarily stupid, kind of society,"
So—

> What I am thinking of, as some of you are guessing, is that you
> don't hand such a function over to the government - the
> national government. You hand over this function to a new
> kind of corporation which is chartered to determine its own
> function and legalize its own operation - a self-governing body.
> This might be some federal scheme. You would not have one
> national economic corporation. You would have 200 or 500
> corporations, or whatever they are, and some kind of congress
> of corporations that would deal with political-economic matters
> through legal means.

The corporation, said Buchanan, should "think about itself in terms of the
rule of the law":

> This would mean that the corporation think of itself literally as
> a government, as Berle has put it often enough, and try to
> constitutionalize itself in some way. This doesn't necessarily
> mean that we should impose a democratic dogma on it. It
> means that the corporation, if it isn't going to be democratic,
> should say it is not going to be and find a mode of operation
> that will discharge its responsibilities and be efficient in its own
> operation.

This is laudably clear: not democracy but efficiency. In another brochure
issued by the Center in 1958, Buchanan ties up a number of things in the olio:

> The Marxist used to speak vividly, if not too accurately, about
> the concentration of capital and the expropriation of the worker.
> If the dialectic is still working, he ought now to point out the
> next stage or moment when the labor union applies for
> corporate membership in the big corporation whose directors
> grant annual tenure and salaries, pensions, and the power of
> veto on the policy of the corporation instead of the right to
> strike. As a result, the corporation is a government by and with

the consent of the workers as well as the stockholders. As Adolf Berle puts it in "The 20th Century Capitalist Revolution," creeping socialism has become galloping capitalism, and, we might add, corporate communism, free-world variety.

It is not surprising to find him adding that Russia has gone ahead to entrust its economy to "three separate but coordinated giant corporations" and "The other socialist countries have invented other forms to meet their needs. It is not to be supposed that we are lacking in inventive imagination ."

The final chapter of his 1953 book even presents some modest details of a New order in which the corporations have taken on certain sovereign powers making the corporate structure autonomous and coordinate with the government. (Example: the N.A.M. becomes the "sponsor" of the Federal Trade Commission.) There is a separate House "representing managers, engineers, and workmen ." The same corporations which "moderate socialists mark for nationalization" are in this scheme to be given wide self-governing "powers and privileges ." The "chronic civil war between labor and the corporation" will be eliminated. The "three giant corporations" of the Soviet system (which are the Trade Unions, Soviet, and Consumers Cooperatives!) "should be intelligible to us as a kind of preview of ourselves if we continue to increase our corporate development in the same way in the future as we have in the past ..." The vision is global: "incorporated trading companies, making cartel treaties in the twentieth century, could become the United States of the World .."

7

Buchanan is the most unreserved of our neo-corporatists, but Berle is recognized as their leading theoretician. Berle, as far as I know, has not put it as bluntly as some others, and I am not certain how far he would go. He is, to be sure, entirely uninhibited in describing the present system as corporate collectivism. He militantly insists on labeling it collectivism as often as possible - "true collectivism," etc. - and since he also quite calmly describes the corporate system as "an automatic self-perpetuating oligarchy," we need not suppose he has any illusion that we are living under a *democratic* collectivism. Nor does he think there is an unbridgeable gulf between this system and the bureaucratic-collectivist system on the other side of the Iron Curtain:

> The private property system in production ... has almost
> vanished in the vast area of American economy dominated by
> this system. Instead we have something which differs from the
> Russian or socialist system mainly in its philosophical content.

Nor, for this matter, is he even exercised about democratic controls over this spreading collectivism. One of the troubles with liberals, he writes, is that

> ... they thought of ownership by "the people" as something real,
> whereas a moment's thinking would make it clear that "the
> people" was an abstraction. Its reality meant some sort of
> bureaucratic management.

And if bureaucratic management is inevitable, it should be efficient bureaucratic management. The oligarchic methods of the corporation "work remarkably well" and "Conventional stereotypes of 'democratic procedure' are not particularly useful in dealing with this problem ."

"Public consensus" is counterposed to "public opinion ." The important difference, of course, is that "public opinion" can finally be ascertained only by the conventional stereotypes of democratic procedure. But public consensus? This is the body of "unstated premises" lying behind the superficialities of public opinion. It does not emanate from the people, that abstraction; nor merely from the business community. Where then? Here is the answer: from "the conclusions of careful university professors, the reasoned opinions of specialists, the statements of responsible journalists, and at times the solid pronouncements of respected politicians ." These constitute "the real tribunal to which the American system is finally accountable," and it is their consensus which confers legitimacy upon the system.

So the bureaucratic nature of this corporate collectivism - which by Orwellian rules he sometimes calls "the reality of economic democracy in the United States" - does not give him pause. It would indeed take a riotous imagination to equip the new corporate order with the aforesaid "conventional stereotypes" of democracy. In his good society, "organizations in each industry and inter-industry" - like the Iron and Steel Institute, which is properly "not Statist" - can be encouraged to "synchronize or harmonize" their planning, with the assistance of "relief from some of the rigidities of the antitrust laws ."

Like Buchanan, he sees that "in any long view the American and Soviet systems would seem to be converging rather than diverging .. ." For here too "power centralizes itself around a politico-economic instead of a governmental institution," the politico-economic institution on this side being the corporation. He is as enthusiastically in favor of cartels as Buchanan, with a similar vision of a corporate world government:

> In point of surprising fact, the large American corporations in certain fields have more nearly achieved a stable and working world government than has yet been achieved by any other institution. The outstanding illustration is the case of the oil industry.

For Berle, corporatism is the American surrogate for socialism. Socialism, he writes, was the instrument of the 20th century revolution in many countries, but "In the United States, the chief instrument has proved to be the modern giant corporation." If the corporations "do not assume community responsibilities, government must step in and American life will become increasingly statist ." The corporation's powers are in fact "held in trust for the entire community ."

> The choice of corporate managements [he writes in the chapter "Corporate Capitalism and 'The City of God,'" in The Twentieth Century Capitalist Revolution] is not whether so great a power shall cease to exist; they can merely determine whether they will serve as the nuclei of its organization or pass it over to someone else, probably the modern state ... It seems that, in diverse ways, we are nibbling at the edges of a vast, dangerous and fascinating piece of thinking.

Vast, dangerous and fascinating it is, and Berle is nibbling.

8

In discussions of corporatism, the word corporation is more often than not used in more than one sense. The broader and earlier sense is any body (of people) corporate, whose association for some purpose is recognized; the narrower sense is the business corporation. The "corporations" of Italian Fascist theory were, however, not business corporations nor joint-stock companies, but associations of labor and capital assigned a given role in society. Corporatist ideologies have not necessarily begun with the business corporation; but as we have seen, our own neo-corporatists do begin this way. While beginning this way, however, do they go on to a broader conception of corporatism?

The bridge from the narrower to the broader sense is constituted by the question of who are the "members" of a corporation.

Once you entertain the idea of turning the corporation into a sovereign power, of turning autonomous political powers over to it in some fashion, you must bethink yourself that it will not do to confer this boon simply on the Board of Directors. The base must be widened to receive the weight. The corporation must be more inclusive, if it is to be turned into a political community or the base for one. We do not want to strengthen management at the expense of labor - no, we are all liberals and believe that labor must be treated equally. The solution is plainly to integrate labor *into* the corporation ... on an equal basis, naturally ... In a number of steps presented as expanding the "membership" of the corporation, the business corporation of today becomes the politically autonomous body of corporatist theory. Basic is the unity of all classes inside the confining forms of the corporate structure.

Buchanan has it all laid out: he wants "a highly structured corporation in which the union would be a part of the structure ." Not only investors and managers but "creditors, workers and buyers" should all get "explicit status as members or citizens of these governments [corporations] ." Hutchins opines it is labor itself, not the union as such, which should be included in the structure of the corporation, since the idea "does not necessarily involve the maintenance of a national union of any kind ." We have seen that in Father Harbrecht's wave of the future, "men are bound to their corporations ."

In the Mason tome, Prof. Abram Chayes of Harvard elaborates a "more spacious" conception of "membership" of the corporation: "Among the groups now conceived as outside the charmed circle of corporate membership, but which ought to be brought within it, the most important and readily identifiable is its work-force ." Does this mean worker representation in its managing board? Apparently not, however. Still, something has to be done about the present sad state of affairs in which labor and management "are

85

made to appear as hostile antagonists in a kind of legalized class-warfare ."
(The reference is to ordinary collective bargaining.) By bringing the labor force
into the corporation, negotiations become merely an act of adjusting common
relations. Chayes is arguing that class collaboration, as against class struggle,
entails the corporatist principle as the method of tying up two now-warring
constituencies into a single constituency.

For Frank Tannenbaum in *A Philosophy of Labor,* the unions must save the
corporation by endowing it with "a moral role in the world, not merely an
economic one ." "In some way the corporation and its labor force must become
one corporate group and cease to be a house divided and seemingly at war."
*In that one of his many, and not always consistent, books in which he comes
closest to a kind of corporatism, Peter Drucker also naturally turns up with the
notion that the trade union must be made an institutional part of the corporate
structure. This is in his *The New Society* (1949), written under the impress of the
British Labor government. A man who thinks in managerial terms from first
to last, Drucker views the trade-union leader as just another type of manager,
who, like the corporation executive, has a responsibility not to his
organization's members but to the Organization as such. Integration of the
union will also help to make the government of the corporation "legitimate,"
he argues.

Interesting is the context of Drucker's approach to corporatism in this book.
Generally speaking Drucker is a militant conservative, and in his other books
he is usually a fervent apologist for the corporation and its managers as a going
concern. Here, however, Drucker has a remarkable section on "Democratic
Socialism," plainly meaning mainly the ongoing British Labor regime, in which
he *defends* it against American misunderstanding - in his own way. His own
way is the corporatist way.

He announces that capitalism has failed at least outside our own charmed
country, that the New Society will be (naturally) "beyond capitalism and
socialism," and insofar as he concretizes this vision, it is in terms echoing what
we have already considered. The modern industrial enterprise is already

---

* In 1921 (*The Labor Movement,* N.Y.). Tannenbaum was for the revolutionary mission of
the working class and socialism, and friendly to something he called the "dictatorship
of the proletariat," but it is interesting to see how, even then, this revolutionism was
based on as reactionary and anti-humanistic a version of the organicist theory of society
as I have ever seen and was combined with insistence on the outlawry of strikes and the
excommunication from society of strikers.

"collective," it is a "governmental institution"; it is, however, "independent of the State in its origin as well as in its function. It is an organ of Society rather than one of the state ... There is not one prime mover in our society but at least two: State and enterprise ." The investor (shareholder) deserves no special rights in the corporation; the thing to do is to put the de-facto situation on a legalized basis, so that the sovereign control of the corporation by its managers is institutionalized.

From here Drucker naturally goes over to the question of how to broaden the corporate structure in line with its broader role: we get an echo of Ruml's trustee-tribunes. We get the theory of the convergence of the capitalist corporation with the Russian system, a characteristic accompaniment.* And we also get the already mentioned integration of the trade unions into the "membership" of the broadened corporation, which is now ready to fulfill its bigger tasks.

9

Our neo-corporatist school consists of liberals, not conservatives or reactionaries.

The people of the Santa Barbara Center are in general conscious liberals, as evidenced by their output on other questions like war and nuclear disarmament, civil liberties and civil rights, etc. Berle is a certified liberal, being a leader of the New York Liberal Party. Buchanan was what I am accustomed to call a Stalinoid-liberal, and probably still is. Drucker, the conservative proved the rule, as explained, in the book in which he approached corporatism. Tannenbaum is an ex-socialist; and so on.

The trend is cropping out of the bureaucratic-collectivist side of today's liberalism. It is not the only outcropping; the dominant one is still what Berle would call "statist ." But it is an especially interesting outcropping.

These are not the first liberals to discover corporatism. The famous German liberal capitalist Walter Rathenau embodied it in the new social order outlined

---

* This theory of convergence and its popularity deserves an article by itself. One of the most amazing examples is *Industrialism and Industrial Man*, by Clark Kerr and three colleagues (Harvard, 1960), which paints the coming New Order as an authoritarian society ("a new slavery") extrapolated almost entirely from the convergence of a bureaucratized capitalism with a somewhat mellowed Stalinism. The authors insist this is the wave of the future to be accepted without vain "moral indignation ."

in his book *In Days to Come,* written during the First World War. In 1947 John Fisher in *Harper's* (he was then one of its editors and is now editor-in-chief) offered a well developed program of corporatism as platform for the revival of liberalism, very similar to Buchanan's finished product. In return for this dispensation, "In a few peculiarly vital industries, however, labor might have to forego its right to strike: and in return it would have to receive a special standing and special privileges comparable to those of the civil service ." Rightists, he admitted, "might try to convert it into a corporative state ."

Probably more significant are the views of the liberal whose economics is the bridge between liberalism and Laborism, J. M. Keynes. In *The End of Laissez Faire* (1926) Keynes advocated a status for corporations as "semi-autonomous bodies within the State":

> I propose a return, it may be said, towards medieval conceptions of separate autonomies. But, in England at any rate, corporations are a mode of government which has never ceased to be important...

> But more interesting than these is the trend of Joint Stock Institutions, when they have reached a certain age and size, to approximate to the status of public corporations rather than that of individualistic private enterprise. One of the most interesting and unnoticed developments of recent decades has been the tendency of big enterprise to socialize itself...

> ...The battle of Socialism against unlimited private profit is being won in detail hour by hour ... It is true that many big undertakings ... still need to be semi-socialized ... We must take full advantage of the natural tendencies of the day, and we must probably prefer semi-autonomous corporations to organs of the Central Government ...

Note that views similar to those which are American school *counterposes* to socialism are here offered as socialistic. To confound the picture further, the reader has no doubt been aware that corporatism is most notorious as a fascist ideology. Well, then, is corporatism liberal, socialist, or fascist? Or are there three distinct kinds of corporatism? When a liberal adopts corporatism, is he

88

falling for a fascist theory or is he rescuing this theory from the fascists? Where, in short, does this neo-corporatism fit in?

10

The difficulty arises because corporatism is thought of as being a fascist theory. It became so, of course; we shall see how. But historically it arises as a *socialist* idea, and as such it has a far from negligible past. Its liberal incarnation, which we have been observing, is only an extension of this phenomenon.

Its main appeal to socialist thought, as to Berle, was as a framework for the radical reform-from-above of capitalist society through what were thought of as "non-statist" or non-political channels. It looked to a transformation of society not through a struggle for political power but through the assignment of social powers to autonomous economic bodies. (This in fact is the basic definition of corporatism in whatever form it presents itself.)

Some elements usually associated with corporatism go back very far in pre-Marxist socialist thought, particularly a beehive-view of society as an organic whole of which the human individual is only a cell (organicism) and a related "communitarian" outlook. But these are by no means peculiar to corporatism, being common in all forms of socialism-from-above. Fourier's phalanx, Cabet's Icaria and Robert Owen's model factory can also be taken as ancestors, but these utopian socialisms, of course, saw their autonomous economic bodies as infiltrators on the margin of society rather than commanders in the center.

The first prophet of a full-fledged corporatism was Saint-Simon—not a utopian and not really a socialist—who was fertile in schemes for the radical reform-from-above of society through autonomous economic and social bodies which would dispense with "politics" and rule by direct administration, under the benevolent control of financiers, businessmen, scientists, and technicians. In Saint-Simon labor and capital were institutionally amalgamated not only in theory but in terminology: the very term "workers" meant primarily the capitalists who carried on productive work as distinct from the "idlers" of the old ruling class. (Derivative trends in bourgeois thought stem from Saint-Simon's disciple, Comte, and the schools of sociology basically inspired by him; *vide* Durkheim.)

The conception of a new order built along the lines of a corporate society was one element in Edward Bellamy's version of socialism. Bellamy's system, though mainly modeled after military organization, explained the great change in terms of pushing the corporate development to its final conclusion, "the one great corporation in which all other corporations were absorbed ."

Perhaps the classic statement of "socialist" corporatism was expounded by Charles P. Steinmetz, prominent socialist in his day as well as eminent scientist. In his *America and the New Epoch* (1916) "socialism" is a society where the giant corporations, like his employer General Electric, literally rule directly, having eschewed profit and embraced the goal of sheer efficiency.

But the most massive corporatist element in the development of socialist thought was injected by syndicalism. The basic conception of the re-organization of society through (presumably) non-political but autonomous economic bodies was here the distinctive content of the movement.

Here corporatism diverged in two quite different directions. Saint-Simon, Bellamy's *Looking Backward*, and Steinmetz were almost purely authoritarian, not to say totalitarian. But syndicalism, like socialism as a whole, was a movement with two souls.

One was a socialism-from-below which looked toward the organization of democratic control of governmental authority through workers' control; the other was a thoroughly anti-democratic, elitist and "administered" view of the new order which was associated with the anarchist element in anarcho-syndicalism.* The former strain later dissolved itself into the general socialist movement and early revolutionary Communist movement, where its positive outcome was represented in such tendencies as guild-socialism and acceptance of a workers-council basis for a new type of democratic state. (These can still be termed "corporative," if one absolutely insists, insofar as they look to the assignment of power in society to "occupationally" determined bodies, although these bodies were not "economic" but thoroughly political.)

The latter strain flowed into the later bureaucratic-collectivist ideologies of corporatism, the ones to which that term actually became attached. In the heartland of the syndicalist movement, pre-1914 France, this current in syndicalism was documented in the book which most bluntly concretized the syndicalist new order: Pataud and Pouget's *Comment Nous Ferons la Revolution* (1909). When syndicalism traveled north to England, its anarchist element

---

* I am aware that this passing remark flies in the face of the myth of anarchist "libertarianism" and "anti-authoritarianism ." I have dealt with this legend in Vol. 4 of *Karl Marx's Theory of Revolution*, published by Monthly Review Press.

tended to dissolve out, leaving guild-socialism as a deposit; but when it traveled south to Italy, it was anarcho-syndicalism and Georges Sorel's protofascist reading of syndicalism which expanded.

Now it was this latter wing or current of syndicalism which transformed itself organically into the "black socialist" wing of Italian Fascism, and which thereby created what we know as the corporatism of the fascist ideology. Its architects were Enrico Corradini, Edmondo Rossoni, and other syndicalists-turned-fascist, plus D'Annunzio-type nationalists-turned-syndicalist like Alfredo Rocco and Dino Grandi. Corporatism was the *serious* ideology only of this "socialist" face of fascism. As is well known, though Mussolini later adopted it officially it remained an empty facade for purely social-demagogic purposes.*

In German fascism too, within the Nazi movement, it was the assigned manipulators of the "Labor Front" who played with it and it was the *serious* ideology only of the "black socialist" wing. Strasser developed it into a view of a new corporate order called "state feudalism," with a chamber of corporations, etc. Here it was not even officially adopted for demagogic purposes; the Hitler regime rejected it.

We see, then, that corporatism enters the fascist world not *as* a fascist ideology but as a socialistic idea, indeed as *the* program to transform fascism into socialism. In this role corporatism is a direct and organic outgrowth of that one of the "two souls of socialism" which I have called socialism-from-above.

Once having arisen in this way, fascist corporatism had a powerful reactive impact on the socialist movement itself. It attracted - sucked out toward itself, so to speak - precisely those socialist currents which felt their kinship to it. In the case of the Marquet group in the French Socialist Party and the Mosley group in the British Labor Party, wings of the socialist movement split off to become fascist themselves. But more significant were the currents which were attracted specifically by corporatism *without* going over to fascism.

A hand of ideological sympathy to the Strasser wing of Nazism was stretched out by the not-insignificant tendency in the Social-Democracy led by

---

* For the benefit of Berle, it should be emphasized that even if the corporative structure had ever been realized, it would not and could not have been "non-statist" in any meaningful sense. The state power would still have been omnipotent, however dressed up. The "non-statist" illusion about corporatism is analogous to the "non-political" illusion of its ancestor syndicalism, which was thoroughly political.

the German-Czech social-democrat Wenzel Jaksch. Bernard Shaw, the no. 2 architect of Fabianism, was enthusiastically pro-Mussolini before he became even more enthusiastically pro-Stalinist; in a sober lecture before the Fabian Society in 1933 he described the Italian corporate-state plan and added, addressing Il Duce in the name of Fabianism:

> I say "Hear, hear! More power to your elbow ." That is
> precisely what the Fabian Society wants to have done ...
> Although we are all in favor of the corporative state,
> nevertheless it will not really be a corporative state until the
> corporations own the land in which they are working ...

In Belgium, the socialist party leader Henri de Man, who had made a great if now forgotten reputation as a "revisionist" offering a theoretical alternative to Marxism within the socialist movement, wrote *Corporatisme et Socialisme* in 1935 and later became virtually a Nazi collaborator. Lincoln Steffens—I list him here rather than as a liberal; the distinction becomes terminological—glowed with ardor for both Mussolini and the application of the corporative idea to the U.S. Without throwing him into the very same bag, I would also suggest a look at Leon Blum's introduction to the French edition of Burnham's *Managerial Revolution*.

Corporatism was also an element in the ideological jumble of the New Deal, but my impression is that it was more prominent in non-socialistic New Dealers like Hugh Johnson than in the radical wing, who tended to be overweeningly "statist ."

11

This identification of corporatism as a *socialist* current - as one of the strains in the history of socialism-from-above - rather than as an idea necessarily connoting fascism, is the first key to understanding the burgeoning of new corporatist ideologies today. But now widen the focus on this picture:

"Socialism-from-above" did not arise from socialism. It was and is merely the form taken within the framework of socialism - the intrusion *into* socialism - of what is in fact all-pervasive in the entire history of man's aspirations for the good society and a better life. This is true everywhere, in all times, and in all ideological guises. It is the expectation of emancipation or reform from some powers-that-be who will hand down the new world to a grateful people, rather than the liberating struggle of the people themselves, associated from below, to win and control the good society for themselves. It is the octroyal principle, which is still dominant as always, versus the revolutionary-democratic principle, which during most of man's history could be nothing but a phantasm and which could become a realistic aspiration *only* within the framework of socialism. What is distinctive about socialism is not its dominant "socialism-from-above" wing, for this is dominant everywhere, but the fact that it and it alone could generate the ever-arising and so-far-defeated movements for emancipation-from-below.

Reform-from-above, under the economic and political impulsions of a period when the dominant social system is decaying, characteristically takes the form of a bureaucratic-collectivist ideology. Corporatism is one of the bureaucratic-collectivist ideologies which arises. It arises quite inescapably both inside and outside the socialist movement. What we have examined in the case of the American school, in a country with a tiny socialist movement, is its rise in circles outside the socialist movement. But in most countries of the world, ideologists like Berle, Buchanan, Ferry, *et al.* would not be outside the broad socialist movement; they are social-democratic types. Their ideology would arise within the framework of socialism and take on a socialistic coloration and vocabulary, instead of taking care to couch itself in non-socialist or even anti-socialist terms. This American development is an anomaly in that it produces a corporatism stripped of any socialist dress.

But this means that if we look abroad, we should expect to see its analogues *with* a socialist dress. And we do plainly enough; in fact, the picture is gratifyingly simplified when we find that both sides recognize their affinity.

The British co-thinker of our American school is C.A.R. Crosland, the leading theoretician of the right (Gaitsekll) wing of the British Labor Party. He, in turn, is the apostle of a new "revisionism" (his term) for which he claims most of the European social-democracies.

Prof. Mason appeals to Crosland's book *The Future of Socialism* for British evidence that "the form of ownership of large enterprise is irrelevant" and that the large corporation is fundamentally the same whether private in the U.S. (where it is called capitalism) or public as in Britain (where it is called an installment of socialism). If this is so, then the transplantation of Crosland revisionism to the private "corporate collectivism" of the U.S. produces a resultant ideology similar to the neo-corporatism we have been discussing.

Prof. Rostow states his understanding of Crosland-Gaitskellism in terms of the American problem as follows: "In England, socialists say that the managers have already socialized capitalism, so that it is no longer necessary to invoke the cumbersome formality of public ownership of the means of production ." By the same token - this is Rostow's point - the managers may also be said to have already socialized capitalism in the U.S. Thus Crosland equals Berle plus a difference in latitude and longitude.

The chapter in Mason's book on the British corporation was, in fact, assigned to Crosland himself, as collaborator with the American authors. Crosland winds up this essay by quoting the 1957 thesis of the Labor Party, *Industry and Society*, in which the anti-nationalization view was established: "The Labor party recognizes that, under increasingly professional managements, large firms are as a whole serving the nation well ." This is why nationalization is unnecessary, according to Crosland. It follows that the big corporations, under even more professional managements, are serving the U.S. at least as well if not better.

Industry and Society was the official theoretical exposition of this revisionism; and especially because it was a formal "resolution" and not simply an article, it is interesting to see, in "motto" form at the head of a chapter, not a quotation from Marx but one from Berle's *20th Century Capitalist Revolution*. Quoted also is the Drucker of *The New Society*. This is symbolic of a fact. The line of analysis in *Industry and Society* is essentially Berlean.

If W. H. Ferry proposes a corporatist program for the U.S., he himself at any rate sees no great difference between this and the views of the Swedish social-democrat Gunnar Myrdal, or with the British and New Zealand welfare-states. Scott Buchanan says he wants to see his ideas worked out by a Fabian Society.

12

It is this relationship, mutually recognized, between American neo-corporatism and the new post-war trend of European social-democratic reformism which helps to explain both. I refer to the trend toward the repudiation of public or social ownership (*not* merely nationalization) as an important part of the socialist program. Crosland (*Encounter*, March, 1960) chortles that "nearly all the European socialist parties" have gone this way.

But this is not traditional or historical social-democratic reformism in economic program, any more than Molletism in France has been traditional reformism in politics. The qualitative transformation that has taken place was pointed up when Crosland denounced "the extremist phraseology of the Party's formal aims" in its constitution regarding nationalization, and demanded that it be rewritten. This phraseology, now "extremist," was written in by Sidney Webb and Arthur Henderson.

Why is this neo-reformism engaged in a precipitous flight away from public ownership? First it should be seen as analogue to Berle's evolution from New Deal "statism" to his new enthusiasm for "non-Statist collectivism," which we have discussed. The line of thought goes like this

Public ownership is no longer necessary for the gradual reform of capitalism into socialism because capitalism is socializing itself in other forms. The transference of power in the corporations to socially responsible managers means that the forms of private property are no longer incompatible with our ends. Socialization will now go forward with the inevitability of gradualism in these new corporate forms. Public ownership can now be stored away in the cellar of our program because the development of the new corporate collectivism is adequately doing the job which the socialist movement once thought it was called on to perform ."

What is accepted as the road to "socialism" is the ongoing process of bureaucratic- collectivization of the capitalist world. This neo-reformism of the European social-democrats and the neo-corporatism of our American liberal school are analogous forms of one type of bureaucratic-collectivist ideology.

New Politics 1962

Chapter V:
The New Social-Democratic Reformism

The thesis of this article is that the ideology of the dominant wing of the European social-democracy has, since the end of World War II, visibly become something different from the traditional reformism of the Second International; it has entered a new stage and demands a new analysis, a tentative sketch of which is offered here.

"New" is always relative, of course; there is no doubt that the new ideology is an organic outgrowth of the old, as it claims to be; but it continues so far along the lines implicit in the old that a qualitative change must be registered.

By traditional reformism I mean the political ideology which assumed clearest self-consciousness in the form of Fabianism in England and Bernstein's "revisionism" in Germany. It looked to the gradual transformation, or metamorphosis, of capitalism into socialism by an inherent process working out through patchwork changes, however minute but cumulative in effect, which would eventually mean that capitalism itself grows into socialism, without any visible break in the continuum of change. Capitalism would not be "abolished," let alone "overthrown"; it would *become* socialism. The movement toward socialism was simply the sum of collectivist tendencies immanent in the present system. Reformism's perspective was the inevitable collectivization of capitalism itself, its self-socialization from above, rather than its change by action from below.

Hence the reformists' equation was: *collectivized capitalism equals socialism*. To the extent that statification was one important form of such collectivization, though not the only one, they had a second equation: *statification equals socialism*. (There is a generation of socialists today who associate this formula only with the Stalinist ideology: this deprives the old reformists of their proper historical credit.) The reformists, both Fabian and Bernstein varieties, left little room for the idea that workers' democracy, in the sense of some type of democratic control of production from below, was a *sine qua non* of socialism.

Before 1914 the lively conflict in the Second International between the revisionists and the "orthodox Marxists" was in large part fought out over ideology; in practice, it is notorious that there was considerable agreement on what to do from day to day (except in crises). Ignoring what this reflected about the "orthodox," I point out only that today, on the contrary, what has been conspicuously new about the new reformists has in many cases been their *practice*, above all.

The most spectacular case has been the practice of the Socialist Party of France under Guy Mollet, undoubtedly one of the blackest chapters in the history of the international socialist movement. On August 4, 1914 the German

Social-Democrats made history by voting for the Kaiser's war credits; and the Second International collapsed. That was traditional reformism. But let us imagine that instead of simply going along with the patriotic current, a Social-Democratic government had been in charge of the famous "rape of Belgium," and moreover had modernized it with concentration camps, torture of prisoners, organized massacres. ... This gets nearer the difference between Philip Scheidemann, who was an old-fashioned type, and the modern Guy Mollet, who as Premier of France and leader of the French Socialists, stubbornly carried on the "dirty war" against Algerian liberation, by a regime and by methods which revolted even half-decent French liberals, not to speak of Senator John F. Kennedy.

The Molletist regime organized - not tolerated; it *organized* - a brutal fascist-like repression in Algeria, not under the personal direction of some reactionary assigned to do the dirty job while the government held its nose and pretended not to look, but under the personal direction of a close "socialist comrade" of Mollet's acting as his political right hand man and obdurately defended by him. This social-democratic regime organized McCarthy-like crackdowns on dissidents within France; the leading McCarthyite was Mollet himself. Naturally it also brought about a whole series of expulsions from the SP itself. The most noted expulsion was not of a left-winger but of an old-line reformist, André Philippe; and the most vicious expulsions and persecutions were directed against the young socialists and student socialists.

This led to a rather unusual type of split in the Party, precipitated not only by the Algerian policy but more immediately by Mollet's role in bringing de Gaulle into power.

The break was not a left-right split, though of course all leftist elements went along with the new Party formed (Parti Socialiste Autonome, now merged into the present Parti Socialiste Unifié). What characterized the leaders of the minority that split, such as Depreux and Mayer, was that they were largely *traditional* reformists, who could not live with Molletism.

Finally, the Mollet party produced another startling phenomenon: a proto-fascist wing, around the figures of Lacoste and Lejeune—a wing so seen not simply by Mollet's opponents in the party but even by *Le Monde*.

Nothing like the Mollet phenomenon can be ascribed to the practice of the reborn German Social-Democracy; here we point first to an ideological development. After the death of Kurt Schumacher and with growing Cold War prosperity in Germany, the German party moved simply to dump *socialism* from its program. Now I do not want to get this statement involved in a terminological dispute over the word, for of course the new reformists maintain stoutly that what they propose is still "socialism." What is important for present purposes is the safe statement that what was dumped from the new reformist program was that which the *traditional* reformists would have accepted as elementary socialism. They eliminate all connection between socialism and *any* conception of advance toward the social ownership of the means of production; they make protection of private enterprise one of the key features of the new reformism's economic policy on the same grounds as they make allowance for any state interference with private enterprise.[1]

Since the formalization of its new politics in the Bad Godesberg program of 1959, the German party under the practical leadership of Willy Brandt, has deliberately set out to become as indistinguishable in political program as possible from Adenauer's Christian Democrats, on the model of the American two-party bi-partisan system. Only incidental to this has been its throttling of elements in the party aspiring to anti-war action or its suppression of the socialist student organization.

The change in Germany has been the most noteworthy but not the only one, nor the first, among the Western European social-democracies. The Austrian Socialist Party disembarrassed itself of socialism in its new program in 1958. This party has been in a permanent government-sharing coalition with the Catholic party (People's party) since 1945: a whole generation has never seen a wholly independent action by its socialist party. Here, in a sense which the old social-democracy never knew, the social-democrats have integrated their whole party existence with the state structure. It probably also has, incidentally, the most bureaucratized and monolithic party structure in the International.[2]

Here and there, another question about these parties forces itself on the attention: unusual social composition. The traditional social-democracy was not only indisputably a workers' party, but also (what is not always the same thing) *the* party of the working class in the country. It still is in West Germany, Austria, and other countries as far as mass membership is concerned. But in the two countries where the Communist Party has mass workers' support and membership, France and Italy, where therefore the social-democratic leadership is relatively freed of the social weight of the working class, and where those workers who do stay with it in spite of all tend to be a self-selected kind, visible internal social changes have taken place.

It has been reported that one quarter of the membership of Mollet's SP are state employees (petty functionaries in nationalized industry, government bureaus, municipal offices, etc.)[3] Shortly before he died Marceau Pivert described to me how the Mollet party leadership had finally succeeded in winning a majority in the traditionally left-wing Paris region of the party: he detailed it in terms of the mobilization of the functionaries concentrated in Paris, who were or became members of the SP, as against the traditional working-class population of the party region who were predominantly "Pivertists." In Italy, Saragat's Social-Democratic party is notoriously lacking in working-class support. Virtually the entire working class of the country is divided between the Communist Party and the Socialist Party led by Nenni (the latter also containing the *traditional*-reformist wing of the movement) with a more conservative labor wing adhering to the Christian Democrats.*

This aspect of Mollet's French party, combined with its extreme political record, has more than once caused a big question mark to be placed over its basic character. It was put perhaps most directly by Maurice Dufour in Pivert's *Correspondence Socialiste International* (March 1958 — i.e., at the lowest depth of Molletism):

> Certain passages of Djilas's book [*The New Class*] give food for thought. Let us put the question brutally: has not the French Socialist Party become the nursery of this new class? The French nationalizations supply a valuable example: the heads of the nationalized enterprises, many of whom hold a party card, behave like the old bosses: same attitudes, the same reactions. Perhaps there is this difference: the new bosses claim to be of the proletariat! So, the French SP has not colonized the bourgeois state; the other way round is nearer the truth.

Along with the other statifications desired by the reformists, the reformist party itself gets statified. ...

All of this is intended to raise the same question about the new European social-democratic reformism which I have already raised in *New Politics* about

---

* Although the Saragat party is in my opinion one of the most extreme examples of reformism, I have not discussed it here because, frankly, I do not know how it can be documented. My own view was formed in the course of considerable discussion in Italy in 1957-58 with both Saragatists and others.

certain currents in American liberalism: viz., relationship to the burgeoning of various types of *bureaucratic-collectivist ideologies*. To repeat briefly: "By 'bureaucratic-collectivist' I mean in this connection the ideological reflection or anticipation of a new social order ... which is based on the control of both economy and government by an elite bureaucracy - forming a new exploitive ruling class - which runs the fused economic-political structure not for the private-profit gains of any individual or groups, but for its own collective aggrandizement in power, prestige, and revenue, by administrative planning-from-above ." This entails the view that the particular type of totalitarian statified economy developed under Stalinism in Russia, and now elsewhere, is only *one* form of bureaucratic collectivism. We are concerned with others.

I have reviewed some phenomena of the post-war social-democracy only in order to indicate, inconclusively at this point, how the question of the *bureaucratic-collectivization of social-democratic reformism* is posed not only by the writings of certain reformist theoreticians, but also in life, in the political arena. The rest of this article will be devoted to analyzing, from this standpoint, the theoretical formulations of the new reformism by its leading ideologue, who otherwise might too easily be written off.

C.A.R. Crosland, the British Labor Party M.P. has systematically set out to formulate the ideology of the new reformism (which he calls "revisionism"); in doing it, he has set himself forth as the theoretical champion of the continental social-democracies, which he counterposes to the "extremist" British; and the continental social-democrats, insofar as they are interested in theoretics, perforce look upon him in this light. It is interesting that when an International Socialist Conference of reformist theoreticians, mainly from the Low Countries, met in Holland in early 1960 to discuss the new social-democratic programs, Crosland was the only Briton present; and, in his introduction to its published papers, J. M. den Uyl (of the Netherlands) cold think of only two books which "might be regarded as a renewing of socialist theory" - Crosland's *Future of Socialism* and Jules Moch's *Confrontations*.*

---

* Moch's book is pretty much a standard rehearsal of reformist tunes with Gallic bravura; it has about as much relation to Moch's actual hatchet-wielding operations as Mollet's Minister of Interior as the Declaration of Independence has to the activities of the D.A.R. The papers presented in this conference, including Crosland's on "Economic Backgrounds," were published in a little pamphlet entitled *Orientation--Socialism Today and Tomorrow*, Part 1, (Amsterdam, 1959); and a report of the conference, including two interventions by Crosland, was published under the same title, Part 2 (Amsterdam, 1960).

Crosland has this further distinction, as compared with his "revisionist" friends and co-thinkers like (say) Douglas Jay or Roy Jenkins: he has gone farthest in putting the new politics bluntly, frankly and uninhibitedly. For all these reasons, it is from him that we can best learn what is happening.

Nothing in the following discussion is intended to refute Crosland's views; the sole aim is to exhibit their internal logic.

The first distinctive feature of Crosland's "revisionism" is its enthusiastic satisfaction with the social system which others call Western capitalism. He was of course delighted with the Labor Party's Gaitskellite statement in 1958 that "under increasingly professional managements, large firms are as a whole serving the nation well ." In the essay which he contributed to *The Corporation in Modern Society* (ed. E. S. Mason) he used this for all it was worth as his peroration. But this is mild. For as lyrical and uncritical an account of the operation of the present economic system as one can find anywhere left of Nelson Rockefeller, one must read Crosland's paper at the Dutch conference, keeping in mind that he is presumably not writing only about Britain:

There is no shadow over permanent full employment; "even Right-Wing governments" will maintain it without question; there is "a general feeling of contentment;" standard of living has risen gratifyingly especially for the poorer; the benefits of the system are distributed "more equally and more justly"; there is no "suffering from oppression or capitalist exploitation"; the employers have in good part assumed "the social responsibilities of industry"; "feelings of social justice" are now a big problem only among "socialist idealists," not the people. And:

> Aggressive individualism gives way to a suave and sophisticated sociability; and the traditional capitalist ruthlessness is replaced by a belief in modern, enlightened methods of personnel management. Large-scale industry has become humanized...

Much more of this, and *that's all; there is no other side; there are no other aspects to the economic picture.*

A comparison with the Bernsteinians, such as Crosland insists on, would be entirely beside the point. The traditional "revisionists" were mild, pinkish, tepid *critics* of the system; Crosland is one of the most eulogistic defenders of

The New Social-Democratic Reformism

the system known to economic science today. It gives pause.

One of the more unusual aspects of Crosland's lack of inhibition about justifying virtually everything about the economic status quo is his insistence on fiercely defending even the advertising industry, as it exists not only in Britain but also in the U.S., against the kind of far-from-basic strictures made by (say) Vance Packard's books. He counterposes the hoary myth of "consumer sovereignty." The present set-up permits the consumer "libertarian judgments" because the individual decides for himself what he wants and registers his opinion by buying it... "[4]

I am trying to underline that there is something new here. All previous differences among socialists have been over differing degrees and forms of *hostility* to the economic system. Crosland is the first socialist theoretician in history, as far as I know, to take his stand on *complete identification with the going system*. Insofar as this is accepted as socialism at all, there could scarcely be any more finished exemplar of a socialism-from-above.

It should not be supposed that Crosland's contentment with the economic system is simply founded on the character of the British situation, where the Labor movement and Labor governments have had a special impact. Another one of Crosland's sides that brings one up sharp is his insistence on specifically extending his eulogies to the U.S. He sometimes verges on representing the United States as being the country nearest the socialist ideal, with the possible exception of Sweden. "In the U.S.A. the Trade Unions have invaded the prerogatives of management in such a way that we might almost speak of industrial democracy there," he said in Holland. After claiming that in Britain the trade unions "remain effective masters of the industrial scene" even under the Tories, he has the amazing fortitude to add the note: "This is increasingly true in the U.S. also ." The leaders of the AFL-CIO will be glad to learn about their master over "the citadels of capitalist power ."[5] But then they will be happy to know, also, that Crosland considers the American labor movement a model in another respect:

> Workers who take managerial posts are not condemned as traitors to their class. Trade Union leaders are not thought to be in danger of contamination if they have large cars, and smoke cigars, and draw huge salaries. The Unions are not thought guilty of treachery if they cooperate with management to boost sales or raise productivity, or even accept a wage-cut to save a

firm from bankruptcy ...[6]

Lucky American workers to have such modern type leaders! Crosland should explain why these American paragons, shored up by their huge salaries and rejoicing in mastery over the citadels of capitalist power, have not been able to get even a feeble medicare program, let alone socialized medicine.

It is inevitable that Crosland should enthuse also over the "convergence of political attitudes" of the contending parties both in the U.S. and England; i.e., in the U.S., the absence of political differences between the Democrats and Republicans. He specifically complements the "mature, educated voter" in the U.S. for making his choice in the 1960 election "on the basis of such issues as ... simply the complacency of the existing [Eisenhower] regime."

We, not the Tories, have the right to claim American society for our own, says Crosland:

> It is in fact a complete illusion that British Conservatives really want a mobile equal-opportunity society on the American pattern... Their true ideology is poles apart from the restless, egalitarian ideology of contemporary America. This indeed comes much closer, though this is not always understood in England, to the egalitarian ideas of the Left than to the more static, conservative instincts of the Right.[7]

Crosland, of course, would be a heartfelt charter-member of the club which is now raising a banner with a strange device paraphrased from Earl Browder's old slogan: "Americanism Is Twentieth-Century Socialism!" In the United States, he finds, "there is little trace of a elite psychology," a claim which can be understood - not accepted but just understood - if we assume that Crosland is thinking only of the peculiar British forms of institutionalized status symbols such as the "public" schools and accent-snobbery.

Crosland not only identifies himself with the going economic system, but also strives heroically to identify himself as completely as possible with all of American bourgeois society - viz., the only society left on earth where capitalism is still entirely self-confident and feels the bloom of health. There are, of course, far more numerous elements in British society with which one *can* identify, and in that country various positive features can be ascribed to the impact of the socialist movement; but in the United States this interpretation is impossible. Crosland draws the inevitable conclusion: he would *not* be a socialist in the United States; or, in other words, there is no need for a socialist movement in this blessed land - not even a "revisionist" one. This seems to be the plain sense of his rather tortuous statement that in the U.S.

> ... a Leftist, who was a socialist in Britain, would be much less concerned to promote more social equality of material welfare, of which plenty exists already, than with reforms lying outside the field of socialist-capitalist controversy...[8]

At this point we get a peculiar inversion of the Bernsteinian "revisionism" of which Crosland thinks he is merely the continuator. Bernstein became notorious for saying, "The movement is everything, the goal nothing ." Crosland now envisions the full transformation of the U.S. into a socialist society, apparently, without any socialists at work, without any socialist *movement* at all. As far as I know, he is (another record) the first socialist theoretician in history to have stared this thought in the face. What it sets down without any equivocation is, for one thing, the perspective of socialization-from-above in fullblown form. The system is going to have to socialize itself, for sure.

For another thing, this makes it *very* difficult for Crosland to have American disciples, since their first duty on agreeing with him fully is to commit hari-kari (politically speaking). As a matter of fact, this is more or less what has happened periodically in the later history of American socialism: there has been little or no room for reformist socialism to take root, and rightwing developments have tended to propel themselves, in the course of finding self-awareness, outside the socialist movement.

However, the system with which Crosland identifies himself is no longer to be called "capitalism," naturally; it is a new and better one. At his most definite, he dates this after the Second World War; when - he is a little more vague, it is something that is in process of happening, or is "almost" true. It would be unprofitable to make anything of his varying formulations, for the underlying thought is both clear enough and inevitable for him: capitalism effectively no longer exists.

Now it is very important to understand that he is not and cannot be merely talking about "Socialist Britain." He must apply this just as much not only to the U.S., as we have seen, but also to Western Europe, since it is the theoretical basis of his prescriptions for the new "revisionism," and since it is the continental social-democracies that have taken up this new "revisionism" most favorably. Croslandism, therefore, must literally claim that Adenauer's Germany and de Gaulle's France have also left capitalism behind in their ascent to the new progressive order, but I am not aware that Crosland has ever specifically faced this picture.

The theoretical dilemma is deepgoing: the German Social-Democratic Party is perhaps his favorite party and there is no question about his admiration for its "post capitalist" politics; but if post-war Germany abolished capitalism, this happy event actually took place *under the aegis of a right-wing government, which was being roundly denounced by the Social-Democracy all the time the "revolution" was going on.* If, in the U.S., he looks forward to the full blossoming of a "socialism" without any socialist movement, in Germany he implicitly sees the abolition of capitalism by a right-wing government with the socialists in opposition.*

It is no part of this article's restricted task to discuss the way in which he "abolishes" capitalism from today's world. It has to do with a demonstration that there is no special connection between capitalism and profit (production for profit, profit system, or what-have-you), nor anything to do with the ownership of the means of production. His simplest approach was in his contribution to *New Fabian Essays*,[9] where it was done by *defining* capitalism as laissez-faire, right through the '30s.[10] I do not comprehend how he could do this without being hooted out of at least the Fabian Society; but at any rate it is clear that if capitalism means laissez-faire, then it certainly was abolished, if it ever existed at all. But then this happened long before Attlee and Gaitskell's administrations, and so even in England we find Crosland's theory (but not Crosland) detaching the demise of capitalism from the device of socialism.[11]

Even in the same book, his latest, in which he has most thoroughly

---

* In passing I want to point out the close analogy between Crosland's theoretical dilemma and that of the "orthodox Trotskyists" after the war. If Russia is a "workers' state" because its economy is nationalized (statified), then the new East European states must have also become workers' states as statification became complete. Now this "social revolution" must have taken place, at the time, behind the backs of the Trotskyists, who registered the fact of the "revolution" only some time later, after a good deal of puzzlement. They thus invented the category of a social revolution which creates a workers' state not only without a visible revolution but without a revolutionary party and without the support or even the participation of the working class. In fact, the current theory of neo-Trotskyism is entirely based on this theory of the bureaucratic revolution-from-above, which is no easier to swallow than Adenauer's revolution-from-above.

"abolished" capitalism, statements like this keep creeping in "Post-war full employment appeared to demonstrate that capitalism had solved its inner contradictions ."[12] Now it is very difficult for a system which has been abolished to solve contradictions; but Crosland does not mind admitting the existence of capitalism if he can say something nice about it. His way of being nice to the system involves being very contemptuous of the men whom the old-fashioned leftists, in their deplorable dogmatism, consider to be the business rulers. Referring to the very summits of business power in both the U.S. and Britain, Crosland scorns them as "*impotent*" where yesterday's Morgans and Rockefellers used to have overweening power. Directly referring to the "organization men of Shell and I. C. I. [the British chemical trust]" Crosland informs us that they are only "jelly-fish where their predecessors were masterful ... slaves to their public relations departments, constantly nervous ... Suburban ... Apologetic .. ."[13]

At any rate this system, which seems to superficial people to be run on the economic side by the impotent jellyfish slaves, is not the old capitalism; and Crosland does not label it socialism as yet. It is merely a new, progressive social order in which all our economic problems have been essentially solved. Crosland once played with the problem of giving it a name: shall it be "the Welfare State, the Mixed Economy, the Managerial State, Progressive Capitalism, Fair Dealism, State Capitalism, the First Stage of Socialism," he asked? "Differences of opinion about the right nomenclature will partly reflect merely ideological differences," he mused. To show how true this is, he chose a name which reflected uninhibitedly the nature of his ideological inclination: *Statism*.[14]

He was not unaware of the tactical embarrassment:

> The name is ugly, and has too unfavorable a ring. But the most fundamental change from capitalism is the change from laissez-faire to state control, and it is well to have a name which spotlights this crucial change.

Given the triumph of the new progressive social order Statism (if we may continue to use the label properly understood), what is left of the socialist program, and why is something to be called "socialism" still to be pursued at all?

Crosland admits that Statism already puts into effect "a very large part of [socialism's] traditional programme" and himself asks "what (if anything) there is of socialism which statism does not already give ." Of the 1951 Frankfurt programmatic declaration of the re-established Socialist International, he says, "Now what is significant about this declaration is that socialism, as here defined, already largely obtains under statism "[15]. In five different writings from this date (1952) on, Crosland has listed what is left of socialism in his view. The five different formulations pretty much add up to the same thing,* though there is difference in detail. For convenience only, I take up this briefest version, from an article in *Confluence* (Summer 1958). It has four items:

(1) ..". altering, not the structure of society in our own country, but the balance of wealth and privilege between advanced and backward countries ." - There is no indication why this is so specifically socialistic, in his opinion, that Statism cannot do it handily, particularly the U.S. variety. In any case the crux is the negative clause.

(2) More welfare, to take care of "residual social distress," by which means (he explains) "the misfortunes of small or exceptional groups" like backward children rather than "large categories," no problems existing about the latter. There is no indication why the wonderfully progressive society of Statism would not be sufficient to clean up these corners. (Besides, in his 1960 pamphlet *Can Labor Win?* Crosland rendered the judgment that "full employment and the Welfare State" are now obsolete as issues.)

(3) Getting rid of the special British "obvious social stratifications," especially the elite educational system peculiar to the island. - This is so far from being a distinctively socialist issue that, as Crosland often stresses quite rightly, it does not even exist in other countries.

(4) "A number of socio-cultural reforms" such as an amelioration of divorce laws, abortion laws, sex-perversion laws, urban sprawl, censorship, amount of art patronage, and the like.

"It is therefore an illusion to suppose, so far as Great Britain is concerned, that the advent of the full-employment Welfare State has denuded the Left of

---

* The main exception is the point in his earliest version[16] emphasizing the need "to give the worker a sense of participation" to change "the general tone and atmosphere in industry ." True, this came to things like "joint consultation schemes" even then, but the question itself ceased to have any importance in his later versions. Completely lacking in all versions is any recognition of peace and an anti-war foreign policy as a socialist issue at all. This points to a whole sector of the new reformists' ideology which this article does not discuss.

"It is for these reasons that the leadership must come from the Left," he continues. No substantial increase in standard of living can be expected for five years. "There can thus be no loosening of belts," since "total consumption ... must be rigidly restrained if the necessary home and foreign investment is to be secured ."

The whole program of the new reformism would, then, follow for Crosland even if there were no question of socialism - even if he were not a socialist - since only such a policy could persuade the workers to accept the rigid restraints contemplated. It should be stressed that Crosland wants to *persuade* them; he is an English democrat, not a totalitarian. If this were not true, we would be dealing with a different variety of bureaucratic-statist mentality; but with this not unimportant difference, we have above another member of that family of ideologies in which a kind of anti-capitalism is assigned the role of reconciling a working class to a regime of rigid restraint.

The program left for socialism, which we have already discussed, will not (he concedes) "arouse the same emotions, or evoke the same degree of devoted and militant mass support" as before; this is inevitable. "Some people view this decline in political passion [note the word!] with concern ." But Crosland makes clear he is not one of these; he is unperturbed by the prospect that the people should be even more uninvolved than before in their own destinies, that fewer should participate in politics as subjects rather than mere objects. The main danger which he does see in this development underlines the point: this danger is simply that the situation may lead to lack of "a sufficient cadre of active recruits of high quality to man all the necessary full-time and part-time positions in national and local government and the party organizations ." That is, *the* danger is lack of competent functionaries.

"Nor is there any sign of a dangerous degree of apathy amongst the electorate as a whole, he claims. All that has happened has "merely diminished the degree of mass emotional excitement [note the words!] attaching to the political struggle and reduced the numbers, though not necessarily the quality, of the minority of political activists and intellectuals ." The first is a healthy sign, he asserts. And he now has worked himself to the following:

The second also, in my view, is not an unhealthy development, though many politically-minded intellectuals find it so. Looking back on the nineteen-thirties, the extent to which the intelligentsia then concentrated on and was obsessed by political as opposed to artistic or cultural goals, although entirely

109

natural and proper in the context of the time, was greater that would normally be desirable. *We do not necessarily want a busy, bustling society in which everyone is politically active* and suspends his evenings in group discussion and feels responsible for all the burdens of the world. [Emphasis added.]

No, the cadre of high functionaries will take care of these things for us ... *Back to apathy!*

Some other remarks in Crosland become less odd. He goes distinctly out of his way to deny that socialists should be concerned as such with the problem of *bureaucratism:*

> ...the issue of managerial and bureaucratic power ... has little to do either with socialism, which historically has been concerned only with the economic power of private business, or with capitalism.[17]

Now it is true that historically socialism did not use to be concerned with the issue by and large; *hinc illae lacrimae.* One would imagine, however, that more recent history has made it impossible for the question to be fobbed off. Three pages later comes this after discussing the Webbs:

> Permeation has more than done its job. Today we are all incipient bureaucrats and practical administrators. We have all, so to speak, been trained at the L. S. E., are familiar with Blue Books and White Papers, and know our way around Whitehall.

He has a program for the cadre of functionaries and incipient bureaucrats - some modest proposals for the further bureaucratization of the Labor Party apparatus:

(1) Direct representation on the party National Committee for the parliamentary party - the MPs, who already have too much autonomous power. (It is this group, for example, that now elects the Party Leader, not the party.)

(2) "More staff at much higher salaries" at party headquarters.

(3) This point requires attention: Crosland has been complaining that the Labor Party's image is *too* working-class; it should reflect an all-class People's Party. The MPs too should be even more representative of "all social classes" than now. Hence, to implement this, "we need first more young Trade Union

MPs, drawn partly from the newer industries and occupations and *representing the emergent social groups discussed above .. ."* At first blush there appears to be a contradiction when he complains of an overly working-class composition and then proposes "young Trade Union MPs" to remedy the imbalance. We must understand that he does *not* mean working-class candidates. By "young Trade Union MPs" he means new rising union functionaries, aspiring bureaucrats, the professional manager types for which he frequently calls in other places; and he looks on these as representing a New Class, or New Class elements.

Then there is a point calling for public-relations experts to be hired by the party; and more attention to youth, since youth give "a more classless air ." (He does not mention that the party leadership regularly expels young socialist leaders and whole organizations, even periodically dissolving the youth affiliate, since the youth tend to be too left.)

The demand for putting the movement into the hands of professional managers - the accent is on "professional" - is one of the most frequent notes in Crosland's proposals. He denounces "the snobbish anti-professionalism which permeates so much of our national life ." His remedy for the ills of the Co-operative Movement is: higher salaries for the managers; more university personnel; less "interference with management by elected lay boards," and a stronger, more professional national leadership - a platform which has the indubitable characteristic of being single-minded - and he attacks the Movement's "supposed interests" of "equality and democracy" which stand in the way of these changes.

Although he tends to lean heavily on "equality" when putting together definitions of socialism that will exclude social ownership, he cannot be accused of being passionate on the subject of equality of reward. He is in fact a loud advocate of bigger and better rewards for managers, in the interest of "efficiency ." He attacks the New Left because they want to bear hard on "those [inequalities] which derive from personal effort," referring to the managers who really run the corporations, whereas he wants to bear hard on "those which derive from inheritance ." His approach is first to minimize the size of top management rewards in private industry. Then he argues that outsize rewards for managers are inevitable in any economic system.

The proof to which he appeals is the "very high bureaucratic and managerial rewards even in the closed societies of the Communist bloc ." He is not attacking this, you understand; he is accepting it as natural and proper. "The process," he explains, "began with Stalin's famous speech in 1931 in

111

which he denounced 'equity-mongering' and called for a new attitude of 'solicitude' towards the intelligentsia. .. ." Even though the trend has been "partially reversed" under Khrushchev, "the goal is by no means egalitarian ."

Did this perhaps develop under Stalin because of the fact of dictatorship? This is not adequate explanation, he argues: Lenin was wrong and Stalin was right—

> For the original impetus towards inequality came not from political motives of tyranny or self-aggrandizement, but from the harsh *economic* necessities of the First Five-Year Plan. Lenin thought that with large-scale production the functions of management "have become so simplified and can be reduced to such simple operations ... that they can be easily performed by every literate person, can quite easily be performed for ordinary 'workmen's wages,' and can (and must) be stripped of every shadow of privilege, of every semblance of 'official grandeur.'" Stalin found otherwise; and *the extreme inequalities of the Stalin era represented a hardheaded economic policy designed to remedy the desperate scarcity of managerial and technical personnel* ... [Emphasis is added but the history is Crosland's.]

There has been a change under Khrushchev, true—

> But the Soviet rulers continue to believe that substantial differentials are a necessary condition of rapid growth; and in particular they attach a central importance to the creative role of management in fostering growth. *In view of their actual growth-rate, it is hard to say they are wrong.* [Emphasis added.][18]

One rubs one's eyes: so Stalin was right after all. If it was right for him to institute these policies under Harsh Economic Necessities, then is it easy to say he was wrong in also instituting the only political policies which could make the Russian people accept these harsh necessities—i.e., the Stalinist terror? Don't misunderstand: Crosland himself is a democrat and a humane Englishman; it is a good thing he did not personally face Stalin's harsh necessity.

We have seen that, to Crosland, bureaucratism is not a socialist concern. We can now add that there is little room left in his scheme for workers' control or workers' democracy in industry. Crosland does not reject the idea *in toto*; after all there are always the joint consultation schemes. An article by him on this subject comes out unusually pointless (he does usually *say* something), with a conclusion about leaving the question to sociologists for research.

However, the major relationship between Crosland's program and this question does not appear in his explicit discussions. It emerges from the nature of his proposals for the extension of public ownership, in those instances where he is willing to consider such steps. He is for government share-buying:

> ...the object is not to acquire *particular* capital assets with a view to their control; it is *generally* to increase the area of public ownership. There is therefore no need for the compulsory purchase of entire firms or industries; it is sufficient to extend public investment in any direction ... Indeed, it would be a positive nuisance to be saddled with control...[19]

What stands out about this method of extending "public ownership" is that it is the one which guarantees completely leaving all management rights and relations undisturbed. It is designed to leave the same bosses in control no matter what level of "public ownership" is thereby reached. Crosland is utilizing the well-known split between share-ownership and management control to *introduce the same schism between public ownership and public control.* His program for "extension of public ownership" is at the same time a program for maintenance of managers' control.

If we find heavily bureaucratic-collectivized notions informing the new social-democracy of Crosland, we need not be surprised to find that he is willing to go along with the increasingly popular theory of the *convergence* of Western society with the bureaucratic collectivism of the East. This has not played a big role in Crosland's writing up to now, but it is interesting that it makes its appearance in the last chapter of his last book. Douglas Jay plays it bigger[20].

Now the perspective of convergence of the two societies does not make any sense within the framework of Crosland's *rhetoric*. If we in the West are already in a new, progressive, advancing social order, with *more* democracy and equality than ever, and more coming, then even if Crosland swallows the tales about the coming liberalization and democratization of Russia, the picture that results is not of convergence but of a slow catching-up at the best. The real theorists of "convergence" mean, as they must, that a collectivized capitalism gets bureaucratized while a Stalinist-type bureaucratic collectivism gets "liberalized"; the two systems move in each other's direction.

Now this is what is actually happening not only with Crosland's "Statism" but also with the social-democratic theory *about what is happening*. Hence Crosland as well as Jay can in fact accept the reality of "convergence" perspective which makes no sense at all in terms of their theory.

It is the historical function of the new social-democratic reformism to act as the ideological formulation of one of the main processes in the bureaucratic collectivization of capitalism and its society. This is the reality behind what Crosland calls the "new progressive social order" —just as, analogously, a finished form of totalitarian bureaucratic collectivism is the reality behind the vaunted "victory of socialism in one-fifth of the globe ."

New Politics 1963

Chapter VI:
The 'Socialism' that Died
An Obituary for Maynard Krueger

It certainly cannot be said that Maynard Krueger has slunk out of the Socialist Party in the dark of night. He has heralded his departure from the SP with almost as much fanfare as if he were a former managing editor of the *Daily Worker* resigning from the Communist Party, although the bourgeois press has not cooperated on as big a scale. He saw fit to announce his resignation to a Town Hall audience in Chicago, in the first place, and now he has written his "I Confess" or "Twelve Years in a Quandary" for the columns of the magazine *The Progressive* (August 1952).

We consider his article "Is Socialism Dead in America?" of great interest, though not for the reasons which he himself would assign. You will rarely find quite as flatfooted and explicit a presentation of the kind of "socialism" he describes—the kind of "socialism" which he has held, the kind he maintains he still holds, the kind which (with whatever admixture and hedging) has been typical of the Norman Thomas school of socialism, the kind which is now dead or dying and in turn is in process of being the death of the Socialist Party itself as now constituted.

The kind of "socialism" he presents here is no individual aberration of Krueger's. Krueger was national chairman of the SP from 1942 to 1946 and has been a national leader of the party over two decades. In addition, I can testify personally that his ideas are a typical strain in the ideology of the SP. Things are tough all over for the American socialist movement, as we have said before, but it is this *conception of socialism* which is leaving the SP with no role to play and no reason for existence.

The crisis of socialism and socialist ideas today, brought on by the aftermath of the Second World War and the rise of Stalinism against the background of the decay of world capitalism, has pinpointed one fact without possibility of dispute: The basic question for socialists is precisely this one of the *conception of socialism*, or rather it is this which lies behind all the important questions of the movement. It is so when one considers the caricature of socialism which the Stalinists parade, when one considers the socialism of the Fourth International Trotskyists, and it is also so in the case of the Socialist Party's socialism.

This is what makes Professor Krueger's balance sheet interesting.

No, socialism is not dead, says Maynard Krueger. In fact, he finds more of it than ever in the United States.

Here is his statement, which says more about his conception of socialism than if he had muddled things up by trying to get highly theoretical. The italics and emphasis are his very own:

> Ideas and values which are socialist in character are more generally accepted by the public than they were 20 years ago. They manifest themselves in many accepted government policies, and in some which are increasingly popular but are not yet accepted. *There is more socialism in the Republican platform of 1952 than in the program of the first New Deal Democratic administrative,* which was sufficient to pull away to FDR about three-fourths of the 1932 Socialist vote ."

This is itself enough to suggest the idea. What conception of socialism can this socialistic professor have had? He is quite explicit about it, and let us present his own words at greater length since, as we mentioned, we will not again very soon have a chance to see such a chemically pure case.

In one place the increase of "socialist" elements is equated with "the practical business of increasing social controls where they ought to be increased ." In another, he argues that "No administration will allow unemployment to rise above five million without taking remedial steps which will involve increased social controls." The statement itself is probably true; the point is that he makes clear that *this* is what he means by the march of "socialism" in the United States.

Here are some other typical statements which clearly present what is involved in the trend toward "socialism":

> When the control units become very large, neither the consumer nor labor nor management is willing to leave the wage-price-profit relationship exempt from social control through public policy. That relationship, and the rate and allocation of investment are the heart of economic planning.
>
> A third factor making for increased public, as against private, decision-making is the impact of recurrent crises in foreign affairs. In each such crisis, there is an assertion of the primacy of a public interest over private, and a corresponding increase in the area of public control over the economy. ...

116

> Now, if it is true that social decision-making has been
> increasing, and if it can be expected to continue to increase... I
> want to raise this question: *What, then, should socialists be doing
> in a time like this? ...*

Elsewhere he lists some "forms of social enterprise," i.e., forms of enterprise
with *socialistic* elements. The list includes, of course, government enterprise
like the post office and TVA, but it also includes: "the non-governmental,
formally private, functionally socialized non-profit enterprise, such as the
cooperative, *The Progressive* [the magazine], or the University of Chicago
[where Krueger teaches political economy to defenseless students] ."

He adds that there are also "additional hybrid forms," which means that
the above are unhybridized, or pure-bred, "socialistic" elements.

It is quite plain, then, that Krueger equates tendencies toward socialism
with any tendency toward increased state controls. Any state control
whatsoever, any intervention of the state in making economic decisions, is an
installment of "socialism ." The two concepts are completely — 100 per
cent — identical throughout his discussion. Thus the extent of "socialism" is to
be measured:

> In the context of current political controversy, it is no longer
> possible to use the term socialism to mean a society in which *all*
> economic decision-making is collective or public. Nor can the
> word capitalism mean an economy in which *all* economic
> decisions are made by private enterprises seeking the Holy Grail
> of the profit margin ." These, he goes on to say, are the extreme
> poles, neither habitable. What is possible is only a more or less
> mixed economy, the "socialistic" elements in the mixture being
> those where the decision-making is "collective," i.e., statified.

Note that, for Krueger, it is not decisive to ask the question" state control
for what purpose?" or "state control by whom?" No doubt these questions are
of concern to him, but not for the purpose of determining the basic "socialistic"
content.

Even a professor of political economy at the University of Chicago knows,
of course, that the concessions to statism made by the Republicans are matters
of state intervention in the economy for the purpose of ensuring the stability

of the profit system and private enterprise in the commanding heights of the system. He probably even knows that the same is true for New Dealism and Fair Dealism, in different degrees and with different methods.

It is not decisive for him because on the basis of his concept of socialism, it is the capitalists who are themselves compelled to bring in the "socialistic" elements, thereby changing their own system. This kind of "socialism" is not the consequence of working-class (or, if you wish, "people's") struggle; capitalism itself grows into socialism with the inevitability of gradualism:

> Thus, while it is proper to say that the TVA is a socialist element in the economy, it is improper to assume that the sponsors or the administrators of TVA are necessarily socialists. It has been clearly demonstrated in rare and honorable cases that the administrator of a capitalist enterprise need not be politically a capitalist, and may, indeed, be a socialist.
>
> The National Association of Manufacturers and the American Medical Association are wrong when they say the New Deal and Fair Deal are socialist. They are right when they say that both Deals increased the amount of socialism in the United States. They are almost entirely wrong when they say that New Dealers and Fair Dealers are socialists for such use of terminology makes it necessary to say that Senator Robert Taft is a socialist when he intermittently favors federal aid to education or public housing.

All this could be further discussed by showing the complete identity between this view and that of the very crudest varieties of social-democratic reformist gradualism that have ever been expounded. It might even be useful to do this in view of Krueger's apparent impression that, in presenting his concepts, he is doing some "fresh new thinking ."

What is pitiable and ironic about Krueger's political thinking processes is that he actually goes out of his way to complain that "the [SP] party socialists have done less thinking in five years than is manifested in any two issues of *The Progressive* ." This may point to a truth about the state of political thought in the SP, which has never been strong on any kind of socialist thinking, even though we may draw the line at the claims for *The Progressive*; but is Krueger at all aware that, whether he is wrong or right, he is repeating in unsubtle forms some of the stalest and oldest reformist notions that ever gathered moss in the Second International? We suspect that he does not.

He is not alone in that. Anyone who wishes can find enough specimens of the type who stridently demand "bold new approaches" to socialist problems and decry "sterile repetitions of traditional views" – which is very fine in itself – only to reveal at the first positive statement that what they themselves may wish to substitute for the "old" *socialist* views are much older *non-socialist* views, or that they want to substitute for "hoary" Marxist ideas are much hoarier and superannuated non-Marxist views.

There is even danger, because of such characters, that the very term "fresh new thinking," which burbles from their pens so casually and so ignorantly, will come to take on a derisive connotation in spite of the indisputable fact that original rethinking on socialist problems is indeed an important need of the movement.

But, without going back to the ancestors of Krueger's kind of socialism, its nature can be highlighted in terms of present political realities. He himself indicates one.

His concept of socialism is precisely that of the Taftites, Eisenhower, and their ilk who speak of the "creeping socialism" of the Fair Deal. His very mode of disclaimer illustrates it beyond question. Whatever their public sloganizing may seem to say, most – or at least the more intelligent – of the above-mentioned gang do not really think that Truman is a socialist, himself. But when they point to the "creeping socialism" which is endangering their system, Krueger agrees with them (with the value-signs reversed). What he is agreeing about, with these saurian anti-Fair Dealers, is exactly their conception of socialism.

But, on the basis of this essential agreement, some other agreements follow. *Because* the saurians view "socialism" as synonymous with increased state control and intervention in the economy; *they* quite properly go on to equate both with – Stalinism and fascism.

And they are entirely right, once you grant their underlying conception.

The kind of "socialism" which Krueger expounds ("fresh thinking") is the kind of "socialism" which exists under the Kremlin's heel. It is the "socialism" of the Stalinist system.

The biggest mistake the reader can make at this point, I think, is to regard this as a far-fetched analogy. On the contrary, it is *the* fundamental key to explain the political behavior of the whole tendency of Stalinist sympathizers and Stalinoid liberals — whose illusions about Stalinist Russia are based on this equation of complete statification with progress and socialism. Needless to say, but less important, it is made explicit in the present degenerate ideology of the official-Trotskyists, who therefore demand the "defense of the Soviet Union ."

But Krueger is not a Stalinist or any kind of Stalinoid? Of course not; he is a good American patriot. We are pointing to a basic common ground between the Kruegers and (say) the I.F. Stones, not to their identity. Krueger would no doubt point to the question of democracy to distinguish his "socialism" from that of Moscow; and that much would be all to the good; but this criterion, for him, would be completely unrelated to, and inconsistent with, his basic views on the nature of socialism.

Similarly, the saurian-Republican view on "creeping socialism" logically identifies the tendency of statism with fascism. And do not Krueger's formulations also do that? Read them over again and see how many of his statements would apply even more to fascism than to the Fair Deal.

We have made quite a grand amalgam here. It is not for the purpose of "smearing" Krueger with references to unsavory political movements. Still less is it for the purpose of obscuring the differences between reformism, Taftism, Stalinism, fascism, Trotskyism, etc. We are concerned, for present purposes, only with one concept which visibly runs through all of these ideologies, provides a common starting point from which they diverge.

It is common to all of them because it flows from an over-all and all-pervasive tendency in economic and social development: the tendency toward the statification of economy, the bureaucratization of social and economic life. It is a tendency thrown up by the intensified disintegration of world capitalism in our epoch, side by side with the bureaucratic-collectivist expansionism of the Russian system.

This tendency toward state intervention and control will not be turned back or turned off. The great issue of our epoch, which is to be resolved in social struggle, is whether this will continue to be imposed from above by reactionary ruling classes, for the subjection of the people, or utilized and given a progressive social content by the people from below. Whether society's need for collectivization will be satisfied in bureaucratic forms by the existing reactionary classes, capitalist and Stalinist; or whether society will be collectivized in the interests of the working people and by their struggle *against* the exploiters.

It is only the second which represents the road to socialism and which defines

120

its content today. It is also only this approach which permits a consistent and meaningful rejection of Stalinism on democratic ground.

When Krueger identifies the bureaucratization of capitalism with "socialistic" tendencies, he gives himself more than enough reason to take the political step he has announced. For this kind of "socialism," certainly, no socialist movement is necessary! For this kind of "socialism," certainly, one must look to the powers-that-be that are willy-nilly carrying through the trends demanded by the needs of capitalism, and these are to be found in the Republican party and even more in the Democratic Party.

The process is not very welcome to the capitalist agents themselves; for it *does* change their cherished system, even though *not* in the direction of socialism. They hold back, they take the necessary steps reluctantly, incompletely, sometimes unwittingly, they zig-zag in their course, trying to go back whenever a step backward on the road looks possible; as in all of historical development there is no one-to-one correspondence between the inherent tendencies pushed forward by social needs and the day-to-day maneuverings of shortsighted politicians yielding to a multitude of unequal pressures.

In a real sense, people like Krueger (using him only as an example before us) can become a much more conscious "vanguard" element in this trend toward the bureaucratization of capitalism than even the "legitimate" representatives of capitalism themselves, who are men with nostalgic though outmoded reservations about the past. The governmental woods are crawling with ex-socialists and ex-radicals like him who think they are working for historic progress as they idealize the bureaucratic tendencies of capitalism.

This, in fact, is what they mean by "continuing to work for socialism" even though they spit on their socialist past, break with its ideas and ideals, and scorn its movement. Krueger, like so many others who went down the chute before him, also promises to remain an exponent of socialism "in the liberal-labor coalition" which he looks to, "in or just outside the Democratic Party ." It is not his sincerity we doubt. He *will* continue to work for his kind of "socialism. " And — now that he has at least found "political realism," "an effective arena," and the other soul-satisfying formulations for the abandonment of the struggle for a socialist democracy — if he finds himself *acting* like any other non-saurian capitalist apologist, there will not even be reason for him to see an essential contradiction between his past and his future.

Labor Action 1952

121

Chapter VII:
The Mind of Clark Kerr

With his book *The Uses of the University* (Harvard, 1963), Clark Kerr, President of the University of California, became the outstanding theoretician and proponent of a particular view of the university. It is true that his foreword claims that the views put forward do not constitute "approval" or "defense" but only "analysis" and "description." He is only "describing" the Wave of the Future (he uses this term), and all realistic people must bow and accept it, like it or not.

Kerr, like many others, has perhaps forgotten that the very phrase comes from the 1940 book by Anne Lindbergh, *The Wave of the Future*, which presented the thesis that fascism or some type of totalitarianism was inevitably coming. She did not argue that this fascism be approved but only that it must be accepted. This was the identical approach also of James Burnham's *Managerial Revolution*.

The new type of "multiversity," Kerr writes, "is an imperative rather than a reasoned choice ." You cannot argue with an imperative. It is not Kerr's methodology to say, "This is what I think should be done ." He represents himself simply as the interpreter of inexorable "reality ." He is, so to speak, the Administrator of History informing us how to act in conformity with its Rules.

What is beyond question is that Kerr does present a "vision of the end," and that he tells us it *must* be accepted, just like any other ruling of the Administration. What is his vision?

In the first place, Kerr presents the university as an institution which is, and will be, increasingly indistinguishable from any other business enterprise in our industrial society. The reader is likely to think, at first, that this is only a metaphor: "the university's invisible product, knowledge," or "the university is being called upon to produce knowledge as never before ." But Kerr means it literally:

> The production, distribution, and consumption of 'knowledge' in all its forms is said to account for 29 percent of gross national product ... and 'knowledge production' is growing at about twice the rate of the rest of the economy. ... What the railroads did for the second half of this century may be done for the second half of this century by the knowledge industry: that is, to serve as the focal point for national growth.

Naturally, there is a kernel of truth in this language; but can Kerr mean literally that his "multiversity" must become increasingly like a factory and its professors reshaped as businessmen? Consider this:

The university and segments of industry are becoming more
alike. As the university becomes tied into the world of work,
the professor--at least in the natural and some of the social
sciences--takes on the characteristics of an entrepreneur. ...The
two worlds are merging physically and psychologically.

The university, Kerr quotes, is "inside a general social fabric of a given era
." He rejects with justified contempt the Cloister and Ivory Tower approach.
He points out that American universities are more "intertwined with their
surrounding societies" than the European:

When "the borders of the campus are the boundaries of our
state," the lines dividing what is internal from what is external
become quite blurred; taking the campus to the state brings the
state to the campus.

But do not think that Kerr is here thinking of (say) CORE picketing of the
Bank of America, on the ground that if Finance takes problems to the campus,
then the campus will be moved (by inexorable History) to take up certain
problems of Finance.

Indeed, Kerr even writes the following in this connection: "Today the
campus is being drawn to the city hall and the state capitol as never before ."
This was true in the Bay Area especially in 1960: the campus was drawn to the
San Francisco City Hall, and a platoon of police tried to liquidate History by
washing them down the steps. But it is not likely that Kerr was thinking of *this*
brilliant confirmation of his thesis, for his next sentences are these:

The politicians need new ideas to meet the new problems; the
agencies need expert advice on how to handle the old. The
professor can supply both.

He is thinking, of course, of the role of the university in providing
intellectual servicemen for the ruling powers--not students, but professors,
who are not barred from "mounting" *their* interventions into the political and
social action of society.

The campus and society are undergoing a somewhat reluctant
and cautious merger, already well advanced. M.I.T., is at least

> as much related to industry and government as Iowa State ever
> was to agriculture

It is a *good* thing to be related to the industrial and grower interests and to the state and Kerr reiterates and insists on the term "merger":

> The university is being called upon ... to respond to the
> expanding claims of national service; to merge its activity with
> industry as never before; to adapt to and re-channel new
> intellectual currents.

To become "a truly American university," what are the "new intellectual currents" which we must adapt to? It turns out, at bottom, to involve a large amount of currency, indeed, but less intellectuality. The new current, the "vast transformation," the Wave of the Future to which the university must adapt is the impact of the new mass of government money (federal grants) pouring out of Washington "beginning with World War II," under the stimulation of the Cold War, the space race, Sputnik, the concurrently stimulated concern with health programs, etc. And: "The multiversity has demonstrated how adaptive it can be to new opportunities for creativity; how responsive to money .. ."

Not just money: Big Money. Kerr has a very useful section, highly recommended for reading, on the essence of this vast transformation ." "The major universities were enlisted in national defense ... as never before ... 'the government contract became a new type of federalism.'" He is illuminating on what we should call the *statification* of the university in the Cold War. "Currently, federal support has become a major factor in the total performance of many universities .. ." There has been "a hundred-fold increase in twenty years" in higher education's revenue from government; and the two-thirds of this sum devoted to research projects in or affiliated to universities went to "relatively few" universities, accounting for 75% of all university expenditures on research and 15% of total university budgets.

These are stupendous figures, truly. This is what we get; what do we give away for it? Kerr draws the consequences — which, remember, we must all accept as inevitable:

> The federal agencies will exercise increasingly specific controls
> and the universities dependent on this new standard of living
> will accept these controls. The universities themselves will have

to exercise more stringent controls by centralizing authority, particularly through the audit process. In a few situations, self restraint has not been enough restraint; as one result, greater external restrain will be imposed in most situations.

Writing these lines took moral courage, for, as is obvious, this is precisely the charge which the Goldwaterites have thrown at federal money in education, against the indignant denial of the liberals. Kerr is saying that it is true and must be accepted, because, he says, the nation and the universities are "stronger" as a result. It is at this point that, to the distinguished audience listening to these lectures at Harvard, he made the following cogent point about the consequences of taking certain kinds of money, in the form of a limerick:

> *There was a young lady from Kent*
> *Who said that she knew what it meant*
> *When men took her to dine,*
> *Gave her cocktails and wine;*
> *She knew what it meant — but she went.*

And he follows with this comment: "I am not so sure that the universities and their presidents always knew what it meant; but one thing is certain — they went ."

Now in turn I am not sure whether I can plainly state, in an article intended as reading for the whole family, just what Kerr seems to be calling his fellow presidents; but at least one thing is clear. In all this Kerr himself is *not* striking the pose of the innocent maiden who is in danger of being bowled over by a fast line and losing Virtue unawares.

In fact, we had better drop this Kerr line of metaphor altogether, because the image which he does try to project is a different one. It is that of the toughminded bureaucrat, a term Kerr likes.

Please do not think this term is a cussword or a brickbat; you will be selling Kerr short. He likes it.

Discussing the role of the university president today, as distinct from the old days of the campus autocrat, he writes:

Instead of the not always so agreeable autocracy, there is now the usually benevolent bureaucracy, as in so much of the rest of the world. Instead of the Captain of Erudition or even David Riesman's 'staff sergeant,' there is the Captain of the Bureaucracy who is sometimes a galley slave on his own ship ...

And he is gratified that the "multiversity" has emerged from the phase of "intuitive imbalance" into that of "bureaucratic balance ." Mainly he is intent on emphasizing that the Coming Men in the new university-factory are *not* the scholars (either humanist or scientist), *not* the teachers, *not* the faculty, but that its "practitioners" are "chiefly the administrators, who now number many of the faculty among them, and the leadership groups in society at large ."

Administrators—and "leadership groups in society at large": it may be somewhat clearer now what Kerr means by "merging" the university with "society," i.e., with what party of "society." The multiversity, writes Kerr, is no longer to be thought of as an "organism," as Abraham Felxner once did:

It is more a mechanism—a series of processes producing a series of results—a mechanism held together by administrative rules and powered by money.

Now another difference between an organism and a mechanism is that a mechanism is always controlled by a superior power outside. This points up the inaccuracy of Kerr's constant use of the term "merger": a mechanism does not "merge" with its controller. The kind of "merger" that Kerr is celebrating is the "merger" of a horse and rider.

He quotes Nevins: the main strain for the growing multiversity is "not in finding the teachers, but expert administrators," and he propounds the theorem that the multiversity president is now "mostly a mediator." This brings us to Kerr's vision of himself, not as an individual but as the Multiversity President; and it is a poignant one.

The mediator, whether in government or industry or labor relations or domestic quarrels, is always subject to some abuse. He wins few clear-cut victories; he must aim more at avoiding the worst than seizing the best. He must find satisfaction in being *equally* distasteful to each of his constituencies ...

And so should the student constituency be harsh on him if it finds him distasteful in chopping a piece here and there off student rights? After all, they must think of how distasteful he is to some of the Regents who believe it is the will of inexorable History that all dissenters be thrown in the clink immediately; they must think of the abuse he invites when he explains (in effect): *No, we can't do it that way; we have to be liberal* — and proceeds to chip (not chop) off a liberal piece. Isn't it realistic to understand that the difference between the "liberal" bureaucrat and the reactionary is the difference between Chip or Chop?

We have pointed out that there seemed to be a wide gap between Kerr's published theory about the "merger" of the university and "society," and his moves toward restricting student involvement in political and social action off-campus. On the one hand he tells us we must accept the integration of the university with the state and industry in this Cold War (in fact, with what has been called the Military-Industrial Complex) and must erase the boundary lines; on the other hand, he tries to muzzle and rein student activity on campus which tends to step beyond the boundary line — which, as his administration puts it, "mounts" political and social action off-campus — while at the same time other "constituencies" in the university community are lauded for doing just that.

This contradiction is not due to muddleheadedness. Behind it is a clear consistency, which appears as soon as we make explicit the assumption which permeates Kerr's book.

This is: The use of the university, or the role of the multiversity, is to have a relationship to the present power structure, in this businessman's society of ours, which is similar to that of any other industrial enterprise. There are railroads and steel mills and supermarkets and sausage factories — and there are also the Knowledge Factories, whose function is to service all the others and the State.

We are here to serve the Powers that rule society: this is the meaning of Kerr's reiterations that the university is merging with society. But now, suppose you have "nonconformists" and "extremists" who *also* want to move outside the obsolete boundary line, *but as dissident or radical critics and adversaries, not as intellectual flunkies?*

Obviously, this is not the same thing. The contradiction disappears. It is not "society" that the multiversity must merge with: it is the *"leadership groups in society,"* which, to the mind of the Captain of the Bureaucracy, are identical with "society." Kerr virtually says as much, in a revealing sneer at "nonconformists":

> A few of the "nonconformists" have another kind of revolt [than one against the faculty] in mind. They seek, instead, to turn the university, on the Latin American or Japanese models, into a fortress from which they can sally forth with impunity to make their attacks on society.

A whole thesis on the Bureaucratic Mind could be derived from a dissection of this last sentence alone, but here we are interested only in one facet of the gem. As we know, it is honorific for the good professors of the University of California`s Giannini Foundation and the Division of Agricultural Sciences to sally forth with their apologias for the growers' bracero program. But when CORE students sally forth to picket the Bank of America or, perhaps worse, William Knowland's *Oakland Tribune*, this is an attack on—

The Giannini financial empire of the Bank of America? Or Knowland?

No, they are "attacks on *society*."

There is more to Kerr's theory of "society." It is given in a passage in which he deprecates the "guild view" of the university which is held by some faculty members, because it stands for self-determination and for resistance against the administration and the trustees ." In opposition to this deplorable Resistance view, he advances (*fasten your seat belts*) nothing less than—

> ...the socialist view, for service to society which the administration and the trustees represent.

"We are all socialists now," said a Tory long ago. "We are socialists," say the Russian despots now, the Nasser bureaucrats, the Indian nationalists, and some other demagogues. It is interesting to see these varied characters reach for the word "socialist" when they need a good looking label for their wares. But don't buy it. What Kerr is selling under the label is the old mildewed article: that "society" is represented by the capitalist Establishment, its bureaucrats, agents, and braintrusters.

It is true we have been told that the multiversity president must be many-faced, but at this point we must ask whether there isn't a limit. A man who conscientiously tries to face in *this* "many directions at once" faces an occupational hazard: the risk of eventually forgetting where the boundary line is between a soft-soaping mediator and an academic confidence-man. It is only a risk, to be sure, like silicosis for coalminers, but it is well to be forewarned.

Behind Kerr's vision of the university-factory is a broad-gauged world-view, a view of a Brave New World (his term) or Orwellian 1984 toward which all this is headed. What we have discussed so far is, according to him, only the "managerial revolution" of society at large as applied to the campus world. There is a larger picture, of which we have examined only one corner.

Kerr described the coming New Order in 1960 in *Industrialism and Industrial Man.*

It is a remarkable work, which failed to get the attention it deserves.

This methodology we have already seen: Kerr is presenting the Wave of the Future, which must be accepted as the imperative of history. It is roughly a variant of Burnhamism, with "bureaucrats" and "managers" interchangeable. We have space here for only a summary of its leading ideas. While no element is new, the whole is presented with frankness unusual nowadays:

(1) The New Order will result (is resulting) from the presently ongoing *convergence* of the two dominant systems: a capitalism which is becoming more and more authoritarian and bureaucratic, along the road toward Russian totalitarianism; and a Russian Communist system which has softened up and become somewhat milder; the two merging somewhere in-between into an undifferentiated "Industrialism." The imperative is the force of industrialization; it is the road of progress.

(2) It is refreshing to note that Kerr wastes no space on ritualistic obeisances to democracy. There is no pretense, no lip-service. It simply is not in the picture. The reader must remember that this does not mean Kerr dislikes democracy, any more than Anne Lindbergh approved of fascism, or Von Papen of Hitler. In the shadow of the New Order, you do not approve, you merely have to *accept.*

(3) *Statism*: the leviathan State has taken over; it has expanded everywhere. It is "omnipresent." (There is no mention of TV eyes in the glades, but "Big Brother" is in the book.) The State will never "wither away" as Marx utopianly

---

* Kerr is the chief author of this work, listed first, with joint authors J.T. Dunlop, Frederick Harbison and C.A. Myers (Harvard University Press). An Oxford paperback edition has appeared this year, with some parts shortened or condensed; a cursory examination indicates that some of the frank passages, but not all, have been left out. This discussion is based on the original work.

predicted, Kerr assures us.

(4) *Full-blown bureaucratic (or managerial) elitism*: The progressive and socially decisive elements are only "the managers, private and public," with their technicians and professionals. "Turning Marx on his head, they are the 'vanguard' of the future ." Kerr bluntly defines the elements he is addressing: "In particular, we hope to speak to the intellectuals, the managers, the government officials and labor leaders [another species of bureaucrats, to Kerr] who today and tomorrow will run their countries .. ." There is no pretense of a role for "the people" other than as the working cattle who are to be herded by the manager-bureaucrats.

With this theoretical equipment, Kerr comes to the last chapter, "The Road Ahead," in which his perspective of "a new slavery" is sketched: Here is a quick run-down:

There is a convergence toward one-party-ism in form or fact. "The age of ideology fades ." "Industrial society must be administered; ...The benevolent political bureaucracy and the benevolent economic oligarchy are matched with the tolerant mass ." "Parliamentary life may appear increasingly decadent and political parties merely additional bureaucracies. ...Not only all dictatorships but also all democracies are 'guided' [a term for authoritarian] ." "The elites become less differentiated ... all wear grey flannel suits ." Professional managers run the economy: "Economic enterprise is always basically authoritarian under the necessity of getting things done ... Authority must be concentrated .. ." The managers "will be bureaucratic managers, if private, the managerial bureaucrats, if public ." "Class warfare will be forgotten and in its place will be the bureaucratic contest ... memos will flow instead of blood ." An individual will identify as "the member of a guild," not of a class or plant community. The individual will be neither an independent man nor a human ant, but something between. As a worker, "he will be subjected to great conformity," regimented by the productive process, and will accept this "as an immutable fact. The state, the manager, the occupational association are all disciplinary agents ."

There will be a certain "freedom" in a certain sense (if not democracy). "Politically he can be given some influence. Society has achieved consensus and it is perhaps less necessary for Big Brother to exercise political control. Nor in this Brave New World need genetic and chemical means be employed to avoid revolt. There will not be any revolt, anyway, except little bureaucratic revolts that can be handled piecemeal ." [Has anyone before actually written down such an orgiastic dream of the Bureaucrat's Paradise?

Where will the freedom lie? Maybe, muses Kerr, "in the leisure of individuals ." "Along with the bureaucratic conservatism of economic and political life may well go a New Bohemianism in the other aspects of life and partly as a reaction to the confining nature of the productive side of society ... The economic system may be highly ordered and the political system barren ideologically; but the social and recreational and cultural aspects of life diverse and changing ... The new slavery to technology may bring a new dedication to diversity and individuality ."

Hence this comforting conclusion, offering a glimmer of cheer: "The new slavery and the new freedom go hand in hand ."

In this Kerrian future, the alienation of man is raised to clinical heights: if this society "can be said to have a split personality, then the individual in this society will lead a split life too .. ." (Since ideology has faded, the only "ism" will be schizoidism.)

There is a good deal more, but this sample will have to do. Now a natural question arises: Won't people fight *against* the coming of this monster-bureaucratic state, no matter how cogently it is alleged to be inevitable? Won't there be protest, opposition, struggle—from people who take seriously exhortations to stand up for democracy, given (say) at commencement exercises? What about all the people who are now supposed to be eager to defend the American Way of Life by sternly sacrificing to pay for H-bombs, Polaris missiles, and Livermore research programs?

Will there not be troublemakers who will say: *"Is it for this that we have to sacrifice? Is this why we have to fortify even the moon? Is this why we have to spend more for an Atlas missile than for all cancer research? Is it the right to this future that we are asked to defend by our statesmen, pundits, editors, and (on most occasions) even university presidents?"*

Nonsense, says Kerr. There will be no protest. That's *out.*

There will be no protest, Kerr wrote. From whom could it come? The intellectuals? Here is how he deals with them:

> The intellectuals (including the university students) are a particularly volatile element ... capable of extreme reactions to objective situations—more extreme than any group in society. They are by nature irresponsible, in the sense that they have no continuing commitment to any single institution or

philosophical outlook and they are not fully answerable for consequences. They are, as a result, never fully trusted by anybody, including themselves.

In all likelihood, dear reader, you did not read this carefully enough. Did you notice that the entire tradition of humanistic and democratic educational philosophy has been contemptuously tossed into the famous garbage can of history? It teaches "irresponsibility"; you cannot trust people brought up that way ...

How does the Bureaucratic Manager or the Managerial Bureaucrat deal with these untrustworthy irresponsibles? Kerr is concerned about this problem because today we have a war of ideas, and ideas are spun by intellectuals:

> Consequently, it is important who best attracts or captures the intellectuals and who uses [sic] them most effectively, for they may be a tool as well as a source of danger.

There are the alternative roles of the intellectual in the careen world: *tool* or *danger*. It is a notorious dichotomy, celebrated in the literature of totalitarianism. But we need not go abroad to translate it. If we apply the Kerr method of extrapolation, we get this: Everybody must be either on the FBI informer rolls or on the Subversive List. ... Remember that you do not have to approve this; you are expected only to accept it.

Will there be protest from the ranks of the workers' movements? No, says Kerr: *vieux jeu*. In the New Order, labor is controlled in institutions hierarchically set up. "One of the central traits is the inevitable and eternal separation of industrial men into managers and the managed ." Not only inevitable: *eternal*! There are few men since St. Peter who have thrust their Vision so far. ...

But Kerr's confidence in his no-protest prediction derives from undeniable models:

> Today men know more about how to control protest, as well as how to suppress it in its more organized forms—the Soviet Union has industrialized and China is industrializing without organized strikes. A controlled labor movement has become more common.

It is no part of our present task to pause on the scandalous puerility of this view of the history of protest in Russia and China, where literally millions of human beings had to be destroyed in the process of "controlling protest ." We wish only to remind that on October 2, 1964, there was an army of almost one thousand police called onto campus — to "control protest" by students — by the man who wrote these lines in cold blood.

Obviously we are, in these few pages, able only to exhibit Kerr's views, not refute them; we do not pretend otherwise. Many of the elements therein are rife in academic elitist circles in more or less attenuated form, more or less "underground," or else formulated in "minced" and allusive terms, instead of with Kerr's candor, which is the main contribution of his work.

But Kerr's candor is partly due to the device which we have already mentioned several times, and to which we must now return in a different way. This is his posture as the detached, uninvolved historian of the future, registering his vision of Eternity, and as above approval-or-disapproval as the Recording Angel.

There is an extraordinarily serious question here of intellectual responsibility. *By adding a single sentence, Kerr's book would become the work of a proto-fascist ideologue.* But, of course, this he is not; he is a sort of liberal; he really does *not* approve, and so the single sentence is not there.

Yet, he is not detached and uninvolved. There is another basis for judgment than approval-or-disapproval.

By 1932 the pressure of (what we now know to be) the impending assumption of power by Hitler in Germany was enormous. The Nazis and their conscious tools were, as is well known, yelling at full cry that their victory was in the cards, that heads would roll, and that all realistic people must jump on their bandwagon. What now should we think of a professor, *not* a Nazi tool, who at this juncture announced that, in his utterly scientific opinion, the triumph of the Nazis was indeed written in the scrolls of history and must be accepted (not approved)?

This is itself a political act. It is also, of course, a self-fulfilling prophecy. It is a blow struck to bring the event predicted. But is it not also a scientific opinion? No, it is not, because there is no historical "science" so reliable as to make an opinion on this subject more than an estimate of probability and tendency. We have a right to make a value-judgment on political acts, even when they result from self-delusion (like most evil political acts, including those of the Nazis). There is no academic right to grease the road to fascism in the name of "scientific" detachment.

Whenever the Juggernaut of Power starts rolling, there always are, and always will be, the servitors and retainers who will run before, crying: *It cometh! Bow down, bow down, before the God!* The men who perform this function have done more than made a choice of what to believe; they also have made a choice on how to act. We have the right to make a moral, as well as a social, judgment of the *act*, even apart from the accuracy of the announcement.

But there is a bit more involved in Kerr's book.

We present our views, says the introduction, to aid understanding of this moment in history—"and possibly, as an assistance to some of those who would guide this moment to its next stage .. ."

With this statement the author strikes a different note. It is not detached and uninvolved; he is seeking to *assist* the transformation toward the New Slavery. It is because he really does approve after all? No. It is because he is simply in the intellectual habit of servicing whatever is in the works anyway, because he has no other mode of being than that of the bureaucratic assistant of whatever Power is rolling. It may be a slip, but only in the sense that underneath the cap and gown peers out the retainer's livery.

There is another passage that gives pause. It is not merely the repeated statements, in the introduction, that he has changed his former views: "We unlearned many things .. ." "We changed our program .. ." "Many of our original convictions turned into nothing but once-held prejudices ." The last remark is followed by this meditation on the critical question of state control of labor:

"Free trade unions" under some conditions become no more than Communist unions sabotaging efforts at economic development. Should they be that free? Completely free trade unions are sometimes not possible or desirable at certain stages in the industrialization drive. ... The 'free worker', in our sense, cannot exist in some social systems; in others he might exist, but to his detriment. ... The 'heavy hand of the state' over trade unions and enterprises may be the only substitute, at times, for the 'invisible hand' of market competition which we have so long preferred. And some generals, in some situations, may be by far the best leaders of an industrializing nation, all doctrine of civilian control of the military to the contrary.

Kerr is speaking here of changed views, not new cables from the Future or recent changes in the nature of Eternity. His changed views concern, in a word, *democracy.* He continues:

> Thus we came to be much more conscious of the significance of time and place in the evaluation of some judgments, and of all slogans. [Slogans like democracy?] The whole world cannot be like the United States or the Soviet Union, or India, and one should not be morally indignant about it.

But may one be politically indignant about despotism at any time and place? or just indignant? Is this advice offered only to well-fed political scientists, or is it also relevant to the human beings who are starving and suffering under the despotisms which are declared inevitable? Or let us try this one on the platitude-machine: Since not everybody can be like Clark Kerr, why should Clark Kerr get morally indignant at the rebellious students who did not behave according to his lights?

Now, perhaps this injunction against moral (or other) indignation at despotism an authoritarianism is also to be regarded as a detached and uninvolved report on eternal verities. We do not think so. The issuance of this injunction against moral indignation is itself a moral choice on Kerr's part. The Compleat Bureaucrat does not approve of moral indignation or of political protest and struggle, not because he is cruel and unfeeling, but simply because these phenomena do not file neatly; they cannot be efficiently punched onto IBM cards; they upset routine; they raise non-regulation questions; they cannot be budgeted for in advance; they are refractory to manipulation.

The Compleat Bureaucrat does not believe that protest and struggle really exist even when they explode under his nose: since all this has been ruled out by the historical imperative, he ascribes it to a "Maoist-Castroite" plot. He tries to meet it first by facing in many directions at once, and then, when this gyration naturally lands him on his face, by blowing the whistle for the cops.

Clark Kerr believes that the student's relationship to the Administration bureaucracy can be only that of a tool or a danger. This is also a self-fulfilling prophecy. A university president's very belief of this sort tends to *force* students into one or the other camp.

It is easy enough to become a tool. There are all kinds of tools, and they can come without head, teeth, or point. On the other hand, there is danger in becoming a danger. Which will it be?

Everyone must choose, and it is a matter of life or death: life as an independent human being, or death as a man.

Independent Socialist Club 1964

136

Chapter VIII:
The Student Movement of the Thirties:
A Political History

Most of the references one hears to the student movement of the thirties, and most published references too, are quite wrong in one basic respect: they speak as if "the thirties" represented a single, homogeneous period for the student movement. But the biggest single fact about the history of this movement is that it went through a sweeping change in spirit, methods, and politics, which changed its face completely in mid~course. The present sketch will concern itself mainly with that transformation. [1]

1.

This movement was newborn in 1931; it was not the continuator of a previously existing one. During the twenties there had been a small movement around a magazine called The New Student, but it had never created much of a stir. The "Lost Generation"reflected in F. Scott Fitzgerald's novels was (as he wrote in one of them)"a new generation ... grown up to find all gods dead, all wars fought, all faiths in men shaken ."The rebels too reflected the malaise of the society they rebelled against, as is so often true. The New Student thought that what was needed was a revolt in"manners and morals"; youth had to save the broken-down old world; some kind of change was necessary, something had to be done;"spiritually, this is an age of ruin and nausea." By 1923-24 there were a number of campus battles; but by 1924-25 "normalcy" and prosperity were returning, and The New Student's interests turned amorphously toward moral indignation with such phenomena as the growing "gigantism" of the universities, the evils of commercialized education, and the "quality of life." With increasing depoliticalization, the movement decayed into Menckenism, particularly enamored of Mencken's derision of bourgeois society from an elitist standpoint — one which was as contemptuous of the mass of people as it was of the "booboisie." By 1927 the magazine was confessing that "Where we used to dream of new faith and new communities developing out of colleges and flowering through a thankful country, now the main hope is that students will be less bored by lecturing.. ." And by 1928 it was through. For the bulk of students, what reigned supreme were the three"f"s — football, fraternities, and sex.

Then in 1929 the bottom fell out. It seemed as if the bottom had fallen out of the whole economic system. For there was no natural famine, no devastating war, no plague: it was as if the social machine simply broke inside and had ground to a halt. There was something referred to as "overproduction," which meant that too much wealth had been produced; and since there was too much wealth, millions were unemployed, factories were shut down, and breadlines grew. Apple sellers became a street sight; vaudeville entertainers sang "Buddy, Can You Spare a Dime "? The bodies of financial magnates rained down from upper stories of Wall Street executive suites; and other tycoons, like Charles M. Schwab, were convinced that the Social Revolution was just around the corner.

The social group hardest hit by the depression was the youth. In 1930, the census figure for unemployed of all ages was 3,187,647, and about one-fourth of these were in the fifteen to twenty-four age range. (According to other estimates, over one-third). As of January, 1935, there were 2,876,800 youths between sixteen and twenty-four years of age who were on relief; and this was about 14 per cent of the total for this age group. In 1938, one out of every five youths in the labor market was either totally unemployed or on work relief (not counting those working only part-time). This was the youth problem of the thirties: "unemployment for between 20 per cent and 30 per cent of all youth; scanty education for the great bulk of youth from families in the lower-income brackets; and an extreme intensification of all problems for Negro youth. Youth made up more than its share of the one-third of a nation ill-clothed, ill-housed and ill-fed ."[2]

For this "Locked-Out Generation," the prospects of the student youth were correspondingly dim.

In 1935 one college president told a student assembly that the 150,000 students with degrees were emerging into a world which did not want them. A Columbia University official said: "the social order is unable to absorb those who are annually graduated from our colleges and professional schools ." (This was often true even for the highest-ranking men.) Another well-known educational institution, the U.S. Army, was getting a stream of college graduates at its Whitehall Street recruiting station in New York, and the New York *Post* explained that the attraction was "grub, prosaic grub ." In 1934, the year I was graduated, it was estimated that one-third of the previous graduating class had been able to obtain no employment at all, and that another third had gotten jobs for which they had no interest, talent, or training. One college journal addressed an editorial to the graduating class headed "Into the Wasteland ." There was an "Ode to Higher Education," of which one variation went like this:

> I sing in praise of college,
> Of M.A.'s and Ph.D.'s,
> But in pursuit of knowledge
> We are starving by degrees.

All this meant two other things, too: first, it was increasingly difficult to work one's way through college; and second, retrenchment in educational budgets reduced the opportunity for other students to go to college. A Harper's article of 1935 said: "In many respects, the post-1929 college graduate is the American tragedy. He is all dressed up with no place to go...." A whole section of the American middle class was being declassed; and the student movement was in part a result of this declassment.

2.

The student movement that arose was initiated and launched by two radical youth groups, working separately: the Young Socialists and the Young Communists. This fact determined its whole history. Let us begin with the Socialist wing.

There had been a socialist student organization in existence since 1905, when Jack London, Upton Sinclair, and others formed the Intercollegiate Socialist Society. The I.S.S. later became the League for Industrial Democracy, an adult organization which maintained an intercollegiate department. But after the First World War, the college section of the LID was small and amounted to very little during the 1920s. It was only with the onset of the depression that it began to grow. Two years after the stock market crash the LID's annual student conference, held at Union Theological Seminary on the theme of "Guiding the Revolution," assembled 200 representatives from 44 colleges. In the presidential election of 1932 the Socialist candidate was Norman Thomas, whose campaign drew in a considerable number of students (including myself) and helped to build the LID's student organization.

By December, 1932 the college arm of the LID — at this point called the Intercollegiate Student Council — was chafing at being merely a department of an adult organization; and it was also facing competition from the Communists, as we shall see. Reorganization as an autonomous Student League for Industrial Democracy (SLID) gave it its own structure and a more independent life, but it never achieved independence in one respect: financially. The adult LID continued to pay its officers, whom it had originally appointed, and these remained, as before, Joseph P. Lash and Molly Yard. Lash, a graduate of The City College of New York in his early twenties, remained on as executive secretary of the SLID, and later of the American Student Union, right through the thirties, with Miss Yard as his first lieutenant.

Both were. members of the Socialist party. Lash also became editor of the SLID's new magazine, first called *Revolt* but quickly toned down to the *Student Outlook*.

It must be explained that the SLID was an amalgam of two fairly different kinds of socialist students: the "Yipsels"and the "LID types ." The "LID types" were essentially liberal social-democratic in their approach to politics, and sometimes not very political at all; they often tended to be colored by pacifist, Christian socialist views, and not infrequently were more liberalistic than socialistic. A young man at Swarthmore named Clark Kerr could fit into the SLID chapter there. In their own way, both Lash and Molly Yard were "LID types ."

Numerically more important than the "LID types" were the student members of the Young Peoples Socialist League (YPSL — youth section of the Socialist party), commonly called "Yipsels ." In the larger cities, where there were substantial young socialist groups, the Yipsels tended to dominate the SLID chapters, especially in New York City. (As student director of the New York organization of YPSL for several years, I was largely concerned with mobilizing Yipsels to help build the SLID chapters in the city).

It is important to understand that, by and large, at this time, the young Socialists constituted the left wing of a Socialist party which was itself rapidly going left throughout this period. The YPSL leaders, and an overwhelming majority of its membership, considered themselves to be revolutionary socialists, and, far from being influenced by the Communists in this regard, were utterly contemptuous of them, especially when the communist movement swung right after 1935. The Socialist party also swung sharply left in the thirties, though not enough to please the Yipsels. By 1935, as a result of the increased radicalization of its members and the influx of younger, more militant recruits, the party's extreme right wing (the "Old Guard") walked out. Later that year, the party accepted into its ranks the whole Trotskyist group (Workers Party, with its youth group, the Spartacus Youth league, many of whom were already active in the student movement). Both the loss and the gain served to shift the balance of politics in the party even more to the left — until the latter part of 1937 when another split took place in the party along left-right lines, with the large majority of the youth organization going along with the left wing.

As long as the tone of the student movement remained militant, i.e., up to 1935, the tension implicit in the coexistence of these two socialist strains within

140

the SLID. occasioned little or no hostility. Besides, particular SLID chapters were usually either Yipsel-dominated or else "LID-ish," and went their own ways in practice, as "hards"and "softs," respectively. It was only with the rightward turn in 1935 that a clash developed.

3.

The other source of the student movement came from the Communist students, and eventuated in the building of the National Student League. This part of the story is usually represented under the heading, "Communist Conspiracy Decides to Capture the College Campuses," etc. What actually happened is a good deal more interesting and more complex. Both for this initatory period and for the later turns and changing course of t he student movement's leadership, it is indispensable to understand the coeval turns of the Communist Party line, which constitute the background. On the basis of this background, the story of what happened to the student movement is as clear as crystal; without this background, it is an insoluble mystery.

bbbIn 1929 the Communist International had launched all of its parties into what it baptized the "Third Period," a period of wildly ultra-left and ultra-sectarian policies. The motivation came from the needs of the Russian regime. Having already liquidated the Trotskyist left opposition, the Stalin dictatorship now consolidated itself by turning against the Bukharin "right wing," and was driving hard toward the crystallization of the new Stalinist society in the image of the new ruling class. Internally, the turn toward mass bureaucratic collectivization of the land meant the adoption of terroristic policies toward the peasantry, and a rigidification of the party leadership's autocracy in all aspects of life.

Translated into terms of the satellite parties' tactics, the results was lunatic-fringe politics. (Maoist China, together with its faithful Maoist parties in other countries, is going through a sort of modified "Third Period"development today, for analogous reasons). The revolution was officially announced to be just around the corner. Roosevelt was a fascist. The A.F. of L. and all of its trade unions were fascist, and the party line was to split the unions to form dual "Red" unions, like the National Miners Union. The socialists were another kind of fascists, called "social-fascists ." There was nothing more important than to destroy their organizations, and no united front with them was permissible — except something called "the United Front from Below," which meant that"honest"socialist rank-and-filers were called on to support Communist activities in defiance of their own "social-fascist"leaders. Of all socialists, the leftwing socialists were the worst "social-fascists"of all. Party organizations were oriented toward underground secrecy whether necessary or no, and discipline was conceived in military terms.

The "Third Period" line was still going strong as official policy in 1931 and 1932, when the student movement got started. In 1933 the Communist International was giving signs of softening the line; by 1934 it was clearly on the way out; and in 1935 the decisive flip-flop took place when the Franco-Soviet military assistance pact was signed in may. (The French Communist Party began voting for war budgets and militarization, and the line spread to other countries immediately). Later that year, the new Popular Front line was formally inaugurated at the Seventh Congress of the Comintern.

The Popular Front line meant a 180-degree swing in Communist policy from ultra-left to ultra-right. It, like the preceding course, was decisively motivated by Moscow's orientation in foreign policy. Having helped to stymie resistance to Hitler's seizure of power, the Kremlin now took fright at the Nazis' threats of a holy war against Communism. The widest possible military alliance against Germany, in anticipation of World War II, became the crash-program objective, to which all other considerations were subordinated. To push this perspective, the American Communist Party, like others, spared no effort to convince Washington and the American power structure that Moscow, together with the Communist parties it kept in tow, was no longer a Red Menace, no longer even interested in revolution. That, in fact, it could be depended on as a respectable defender of the status quo — as long as America participated in a system of "collective security" (world bloc) against the danger from Hitler's Germany that might conceivably serve to "defend the Soviet Union" from attack from that quarter. All pretense at prosecuting a Leninist class-struggle policy was sold out in exchange for wooing the government into a foreign policy satisfactory to Moscow, naturally under anti-Nazi slogans.

Before the Popular Front period was over, nothing was too extreme for the Communist Party to use to destroy its image as a Red Menace, including the dissolution of the party itself into a "Communist Political Association ." Every bit of radical language in the Communists' program and propaganda was carefully translated into vague liberalese or unceremoniously abandoned or repudiated. The slogan became "Communism is Twentieth Century Americanism," and quotations from Marx and Lenin gave way to passages

142

from Jefferson or Franklin or folksy evocations of Abraham Lincoln. President Roosevelt was transmogrified from a sinister fascist into a People's Hero, and every good Communist became the most fanatical New Dealer within ten miles. Communist front organizations were hastily re-tailored to the new style: for example, the "anti-imperialist" American League Against War and Fascism became the pro "collective-security" American League for Peace and Democracy.

Not all of this happened at once. For example, by early 1936 when the Communist Party nominated Earl Browder for President, the new line had not yet completely crystallized, but by fall it was clear that the party was advocating a vote for Roosevelt. Since Browder continued formally to run, the Communist press of September-October, 1936 presented one of the weirdest pictures in its checkered history.

While the Communist Party was moving all the way right with bewildering speed, the Socialist party, as we have seen, was steadily going left. In 1936, for example, the Socialist party adopted statements against the danger of imperialist war and for a revolutionary transformation of American capitalism which marked an extreme leftward point for the movement, with the approval even of Norman Thomas. (Incidentally, Thomas was no longer a "fascist" or "social-fascist" in Communist treatment. He was now more likely to be denounced as an ultra-left adventuristic Trotskyite). The YPSL was one of the important ingredients in the leftward pressure within the Socialist party, and pushed for more. Politically speaking, the Socialists and Communists crossed each other, going in opposite directions.

During the first part of the Popular Front period (1935-36), the obsessive concern of the Communist Party was for "unity" with the Socialists in any way whatsoever. (This too was and internationalization of the Communist parties' course in Europe, where unity with the mass social-democratic parties could bring the desired respectability). But by 1937-38 the Communists passed beyond this stage to wooing the real powers of the Establishment, from the Democratic party machines to the National Association of Manufacturers, about whom Browder made unctuous speeches "holding out the hand of friendship" to the "progressive capitalists" who understood the Menace of Hitlerism. Popular Front changed to "Democratic Front" and then to "National Front," as also in Europe where the Italian Communists reached the point of offering common cause with Mussolini's "good" fascists as against the bad Nazi fascists.

This part of the story came to an end with the Hitler-Stalin Pact of 1939, which gave the green light to the Nazis' launching of the Second World War. The nature of the Communists' concern with the menace of Hitlerism was adequately demonstrated when Molotov announced that "fascism is a matter of taste ." But this was politically inconceivable to the student movement that was built during the "Third Period" and Popular Front days.

4.

We can now return to the year 1931, when the student movement was beginning to stir. This was still in the murky depths of the fantastic "Third Period" line of the communist movement; and naturally the Young Communist League (YCL) was a tiny organization. The YCL's leadership, typified by Gil Green, had been handpicked for woodenheaded docility to the party line, now that every slightly critical element had been driven out as a "Trotskyite" or "Lovestoneite ."

This leadership had no interest in orienting toward the organization of students, who were "petty-bourgeois" by definition and unstable intellectuals by occupation (just the kind who had caused so much trouble in the recent factional splits and expulsions). The "Third Period" dogma was that Communists were interested only in "proletarians," although the interest was not reciprocal, and the YCL leaders flatly feared intellectuals, with whom they could not cope in any discussion of their own phantasmagorical politics.

It can be flatly stated that the YCL did not initiate the organization of the National Student League (NSL) and did not want it. Yet it is also true that the NSL was formed by communist students. That these two statements are both true is a testimonial to the misleading simplism of the "conspiracy" theory of radical history.

In New York, where it got started, there were two hostile groups of communist students. The YCL hardliners, in agreement with their leaders, simply went to school and then hurried away to do their stint for the party of the international Workers Order or one of the other party fronts. The other group, consisting of some YCL'ers and a number of Communist sympathizers and fellow-travelers, held to a "student orientation"; that is, they believed in the possibility and utility of Communist organization of students on campus, in the teeth of the party line.

It was the latter group which initiated the New York Student League (

144

predecessor of the National Student League), while the YCL leadership remained cold to the enterprise but did not prohibit the participation of YCL members in it. It was not until 1933 that the leaders went over wholeheartedly to the "student orientation," in part because of the salient success it had scored in making student Communists through the NSL's activities, and in part because (as we have mentioned) the "Third Period" line was already thawing by this time. By 1934 if not before, there was a complete rapprochement between the strategy and tactics of the YCL faction and the course of the NSL leaders; in fact, in this year the YCL inaugurated a comparable project of its own in the shape of the American Youth Congress.

The only teacher prominent in the organization of the National Student League was a young economics instructor at Columbia named Donald Henderson, who became the NSL's first executive secretary. When the university refused to renew his contract, a student strike on campus made the case a cause celebre. (He later threw himself into work for the Communist dominated Farm Equipment Workers Union, which absorbed his energies until his death).

The NSL was one of the most successful of the Communist-led movements of the thirties, and it was also one of the most competently led. Among its top leaders were Joseph Starobin, Joseph Cohen (Joseph Clark), James Wechsler — all of New York — and, from the West Coast, Serril Gerber and Celeste Strack. In general, they were more imaginative and less muscle-bound in style than the cliche-ridden hacks who presided over other Communist Party enterprises in the earlier years; in a real sense the NSL pioneered the Popular Front pattern which, after 1935, paid off so well for the communist movement.

One of the first attention-drawing actions of the NSL was its sponsorship of a student delegation to Harlan County, Kentucky, where a desperate miners' strike was taking place, under the aegis of the National Miners Union, against brutal conditions and "legal" terror. The students were turned back from Harlan County by armed intimidation — in a manner somewhat reminiscent of what happened in the sixties to the Freedom Riders in the South. This was not the only attempt by student leaders to link the student movement with the labor movement (as their ideology demanded) but no other case garnered so much notice.

Then in 1932 came the Reed Harris case. Harris, the crusading liberal editor of the Columbia *Spectator*, ran stories exposing the bad conditions in the campus dining hall with regard to the preparation of food and treatment of student waiters. He was clumsily expelled, in the course of a series of events which highlighted the high-handedness and hypocrisy of the Columbia administration. (There have been some parallels since then). This was the administration of Nicholas Murray Butler — "Nicholas Miraculous Butler," he was called — who was widely thought to have his eyes fixed on tenancy in the White House rather than Morningside Heights. Harris' expulsion precipitated a sort of small-scale free speech movement, with thousands of students coming out in a one-day strike to manifest their indignant protest. The result was mainly a victory; Harris was reinstated, although he had first to make some concessions. The affair was a boost to the NSL, which had organized and led it, and to the student movement in general, particularly in New York City.

The arrival of the Roosevelt administration in 1933 had the effect of heightening political consciousness among the students, as it also did among the general population. A "National Conference of Students in Politics," sponsored by the SLID, took advantage of and reflected this development. The NSL participated in it too, as did the student divisions of the YMCA and YWCA, student Christian associations, and some student service groups. There was a substantial list of eminent professors who allowed their names to be used as sponsors: Charles Beard, Morris R. Cohen, Jerome Davis, John Dewey, and Reinhold Niebuhr. Politicians on the list included Norman Thomas, Philip La Follette, and two senators. It was typical of such gatherings that, although there was a large number of liberals present, it was the Socialists and Communists whose discussions (and disputes) dominated the proceedings, not (in this case) by manipulation but simply because the liberals had nothing distinctive to say. They tended to follow in the wake of the radicals, who set the ideological tone.

5.

Perhaps the greatest impetus to the student movement came from the war question. There is no question but that there has never been a generation of youth more concerned about the danger of war than this one. Their attitude toward this danger was unmistakable: some of the polls and surveys showed a depth of opposition among large masses of youth which was unprecedented. In 1933 a sampling of 920 Columbia students included 31 per cent who considered themselves absolute pacifists — almost one-third; another 52 per cent stated they would bear arms only if the country were invaded; only 8 per cent said they were willing to fight for the United States under any circumstances. A national poll showed 39 per cent who said they would not participate in any war, and another 33 per cent who would do so only if the United States were invaded.

The students obviously did not share the attitude of some of their mentors, like the Fordham dean who denounced student anti-war activity with these words: "They are making fools of themselves.... What war are they worrying about anyway?"

The mounting consciousness of the danger of war crystallized politically around the "Oxford Pledge," an English import. In February, 1933 the Oxford Union, following a debate, had passed a resolution which announced that under no circumstances would they "fight for King and country ." This was adopted by a vote of 273 to 153 ; when Randolph Churchill made a motion at the next meeting to expunge this offense to patriotism, the pledge was sustained by an even higher vote, 750 to 175. The sentiment was echoed at other English universities, including Leicester, Manchester, and Cambridge.

In the United States the Oxford Pledge, while retaining the name, was quickly translated into American as a refusal "to support the United States government in any war it may conduct." For the next period the Oxford Pledge was the platform of the student anti-war movement.

It will be noted that the American version does not say quite the same thing as the Oxford version of the Oxford Pledge. The difference was deliberate. It was formulated here by student leaders who, both Socialist and Communist, regarded themselves as Marxists and did not want to make the pledge a statement of absolute pacifism — a viewpoint which was virtually nonexistent among the Communist leaders of the NSL and infrequent in the leadership of the SLID nationally or locally. Hence the American pledge was pointedly not worded to read as a refusal "to support any war which the U.S. government might conduct ." Instead, it was politically directed against support of the government in any war.

In 1934 the two radical student organizations launched what seemed to many at first a rather wild idea, but which turned out to be the most successful single action of the movement: a "Student Strike Against War." The date was set to commemorate the entrance of the United States into the World War, and it took place on April 13, 1934. It was actually only a "demonstration strike," scheduled for one hour, from 11 :00 to noon, but it did call on all students to "walk out" of their classrooms. (This was intended literally; students were

147

asked not to cut classes but to go to their scheduled class and leave with as many others as possible).

At this point the political orbits of the Socialist and Communist students were at perigee. The Communists had already pulled out of the "revolutionary" buffoonery of the "Third Period" but had not yet entered on the complete abandonment of revolutionary tactics which was going to characterize the Popular Front period. On their side, not only the YPSL but even the Socialist party itself had adopted resolutions on the war question which were thoroughly revolutionary-socialist in content and phraseology (in fact, this was one of the main reasons why its "Old Guard" right wing split away). If, as we have said, the Socialists and Communists were crossing each other as they went in opposite political directions, it was during the period from 1934 to the middle of 1935 that they were closest.

There was therefore little difficulty in achieving complete NSL–SLID cooperation in the organization of the first student anti-war strike. To the surprise of its sponsors, it also achieved a considerable measure of success, especially in its public impact. In spite of a barrage of threats and pressure from administrations, about 25,000 students participated in 1934. To be sure, about 15,000 of these were in New York City — and of these, in turn, nearly half were probably accounted for by the three city colleges, City College of New York (CCNY), Brooklyn College, and Hunter. At other campuses the number was not impressive as yet, but the public sat up and took notice. Attempts to intimidate the student strikers at CCNY, Harvard, and Johns Hopkins added to the headlines.

The number of participants took a big jump on April 12 of the following year. The second Student Strike Against War in 1935 — focused, like the first, on the Oxford Pledge — drew about 150,000 students nationally, according to the student organizations. This claim was probably not much exaggerated provided one notes the qualification that not all of these 150,000 actually participated in a "strike," that is, a walk-out from classes. In some places a more usual form of demonstration or meeting was substituted.

The figures were still highest in New York City, with Brooklyn College easily leading again with 6,000; CCNY and Columbia each had 3,500 out. Philadelphia did well, with 3,000 at the University of Pennsylvania and 2,500 at Temple. In. the Middle West, the biggest strikes took place at the Universities .of Chicago, Minnesota, and Wisconsin. On the West Coast, Berkeley came in, at 4,000, with the second largest demonstration in the country; but even

148

Stanford had 1,500. This time the movement was nationwide: there was some kind of manifestation on over 130 campuses in all regions of the country, including nearly 20 in the South.

This was a great shot in the arm for the student movement, but the fact is that this image of a national mass movement had been projected by the work of comparatively small groups of radical students. To take the example of my own campus, Brooklyn College, which had seen the largest strike in the country for both years: there were probably about thirty active members each in both the SLID and NSL chapters, give or take another dozen. If about 95 per cent of the student body came out on the strike, in the face of administration threats of disciplinary action and the violent opposition of the student newspaper, this was an index not to the size of the *direct* organizational influence of either group but rather to the climate of social and political opinion among the students generally. I doubt whether there was at any time during this period a number of student-movement activists greater than there are today (1965), though there are two important qualifications to be added: the total student population in the universities and colleges was much smaller then and the student readerships insisted on more compact and efficient organization than is common today. The main difference was in the times.

6.

The years 1934-35 were not only those in which the Communists and Socialists came closest together politically, but also those in which the Communists, having abandoned the doctrine that Socialists were "social fascists," started going all-out for "unity" with those whom it had so recently stigmatized. On the student field, the NSL started proposing unity with the SLID in 1934. With cooperation in two student strikes behind them, and increasing cooperation in other projects, the SLID began to look favorably upon the proposal. By 1935, as their own line toward "unity" blossomed internationally, the Communists seemed ready to make almost any concession to get agreement. Within the SLID, the left-wing YPSL also was favorable to merger, feeling that in a united student movement their own politics would have a larger field to operate in. Another source of pressure toward merger was the growth of the NSL, which threatened to overshadow the SLID.

In June the national executive committee of the SLID voted for fusion, and the unity convention was held during Christmas week in Columbus, Ohio. The new organization formed there was called the American Student Union.

There was a considerable bloc of previously unaffiliated liberals at this convention, but, as before, they played no independent role. The agreements, disputes, and discussions emanated from the Socialist and Communist blocs. By this time, not only the Franco-Soviet Pact but also the speeches and documents of the Seventh Congress of the Comintern had begun to make clear the direction of the Popular Front policy. The entire international Communist movement, including the American party with its usual automatism, had already by this time abandoned its anti-war policy and, in all countries earmarked for the anti-German alliance, was headed in the direction of classic jingoism. Soon there were going to be no more shrill "patriots" than the Communists.

The NSL line had not yet been overtly affected. Even though, outside the student field, the Young Communist League had dutifully made clear that the Oxford Pledge was now obsolete, the leaders of the NSL formally stated that the Oxford Pledge would be maintained, in answer to a challenge from the Socialists. In fact the process of coordinating the student movement with the new Communist pro-war line was going to take two years, up to the Vassar convention of the ASU at Christmas time 1937, whereas elsewhere Communist-dominated organizations were able to carry out the flip-flop in weeks or months. The difference was due entirely to the bitter fight made against this turn by the Yipsel forces-in the SLID.

At the fusion convention, therefore, all was not sweetness and light, as might have been the case if the merger had taken place a few months earlier. One sticky question was the attitude of the ASU toward the Russian regime. In a compromise, a resolution referred to the Soviet Union only as an example of a "non-imperialist" nation whose "peace policy" deserved support—a formulation which was then satisfactory to the leftwing Socialists too. Another problem, the relationship of the ASU to the Communist front organization which then still called itself the American League Against War and Fascism, was settled by an agreement not to affiliate with any such body except by a three-quarters vote of the national committee.

The main dispute took place over the question of war policy. In line with the preconvention pledge of the NSL leadership, the Oxford Pledge was re-endorsed, by a vote of 244-49 (the 49 were liberals who agreed with the new Communist line of "collective security"and had no reason to weasel over it). But when the Socialist bloc introduced a resolution which included the idea

150

that the Oxford Pledge would still be applicable even if the United States were aligned with Russia in the war-for-democracy toward which the Communists now looked, this was defeated 155-193 by the combined votes of the Communists and pro-collective-security liberals against the Socialist left wing. But this was still only a negative action, as compared with the later complete endorsement of American foreign policy when the ASU came under unchallenged Communist domination.

The leadership of the new organization was divided according to preconvention agreement. Three "LID types" became national officers: Lash as executive secretary, George Edwards as national chairman, and Molly Yard as treasurer. NSL'ers took the posts of high school chairman, field secretary, and editor f the magazine (Student Advocate). The national committee was divided into three blocs, with an equal number named by the SLID and NSL, leaving a number of seats for "unaffiliated liberals ." There was only one hitch in these proceedings: the morning of the vote, the YCL faction decided that they would not accept one name on the SLID list — mine — in spite of the previous agreement that each of the merging organizations would name its own people to the national committee. The infuriated SLID'ers informed them that this would explode the agreement, and the YCL finally backed down, muttering darkly about the "disruptive" role I had played by presenting the Socialist anti-war resolution on the Oxford Pledge

7.

The typical issues on which the student movement fought and around which it organized were mainly the following six, given roughly in order of importance:

(1) Anti-war activity and opposition ROTC.

(2) Violations of academic freedom and student rights on campus.

(3) Issues involving economic aid to students (tuition fees, free textbooks, etc.).

(4) Reform of college administrations, particularly changes in the boards of trustees who ruled the campuses.

(5) Aid to the labor movement.

(6) Anti-fascist activity — which could be concretized only now and then, as when a delegation of Italian Fascist student leaders were welcomed at CCNY by the administration in one way and by the student body in another.

There were, of course, the usual cries of alarm from all quarters as the student movement grew and impressed the public mind with the fact that something was happening in the colleges. The pulp writer H. Bedford-Jones — emulating Calvin Coolidge's 1921 article, "Are the Reds Stalking Our College Women?" — published an article in *Liberty* under the pen name of J. G. Shaw, asking "Will the Communists Get Our Girls in College?," purporting to explain the terrible dangers to which his daughter had been subjected by sinister Red conspirators. The following week the *New Masses* headlined a reply, "My Father Is a Liar!," by Nancy Bedford-Jones, the daughter, who shortly thereafter atoned for her sins by marrying Lash.

A recurrent image of the student movement of the thirties as "ideological" rather than "activist" needs qualification. It certainly was "ideological," being under the thorough leadership of Communists and Socialists, but it was also at least as "activist" as campus radicals today; the difference was that it did not counterpose one to the other. Probably all wings would have agreed on the following statement from the SLID's *Blueprints for Action – A Handbook for Student Revolutionists:* "The radical movement has too many sideline commentators; the great need is for participants. Besides, action is one of the best ways of getting clarification ."

But the second period of the student movement was now beginning, in which the highly ideological leadership of the Communist students made a turn toward "de-ideologizing" and depoliticalizing the movement in line with their new orientation. The "non-ideological" mask that was to be adopted was incompatible even with ideology in a liberal form. What was beginning was the cant of speaking in the name of "The Students," whose aspirations and most secret thoughts always somehow coincided with the latest pronouncements of the YCL. Already before the ASU merger convention, the NSL Organizer (organizational bulletin) for December, 1935 had inveighed against the belief that the new student organization would be "radical": "For what purpose is the Union formed? We say, simply, to protect our welfare, to advance our interests, to give us strength. Then why do some NSL'ers still view the Union in terms of the "radical," " liberal," "liberal-radical" etc. students in their particular schools? Is it not because these NSL'ers see the Union primarily in terms of vague "social problems," political discussions, etc., and not in terms of student problems, campus issues"[3]. This dichotomy between "social problems" and "student problems, campus issues" was a fraudulent one, for the approach of the NSL — as of the SLID — had been to direct activity and education to bridging the gap between the two, showing the connection between campus issues and broader social problems, and the relevance of society-wide radical solutions to student life. What the NSL–YCL line was now demanding was the dropping of an overtly radical approach to both social problems and campus issues, in the interest of maximum unity of all men of good will for an anti-German alliance.

This was acted out most obviously in the student antiwar actions of 1936 and 1937. There were two influences at work now, only one of which was the new Communist line against militancy. The other was that many of the campus administrations sharply changed their tone. Instead of denouncing the strike and threatening draconic punishment, they rolled with the punch and tried to clinch. They offered auditorium facilities, called off classes for the hour, and proposed to make it all official: only, of course, "why should it be called a strike, since you aren't really striking against us, are you "? And "anti-war"is so negative: why not "for peace "? Increasingly, "Peace Assemblies"replaced the anti-war strikes, and, swathed in respectability, the students listened to peaceful rhetoric in the same pews where they were accustomed to hearing commencement addresses.

The Communists eagerly accepted every such offer by administrations, and the statistics of participants rose mightily, as whole campuses went through the motions of a "Peace Assembly ." There were strikes of the 1934-35 variety, and evocations of the Oxford Pledge, mainly in those places where the 'eft-wing Socialists dominated the ASU chapter. Liberal students in the ASU followed in the wake of the Communist line, which suited them to a T; in fact, they could feel, with justice, that it was the Communist line which had come over to them, not the other way around. By 1937 the guts had been taken out of what had once been the Student Strike Against War.

At the Christmas 1936 convention of the ASU, the time was not yet propitious to unload the Oxford Pledge formally, as was shown by the fact that a YPSL–sponsored resolution attacking the collective-security (pro-war) line lost by only thirty-seven votes. What did happen, however, was that the two "LID types" who had become ASU national officers, Lash and Yard, went over to the Popular Front and collective-security line and became staunch fellow-travelers of the Communist bloc. At a Socialist caucus meeting during the convention itself, a furious denunciation of these two was the main feature, and in effect the national staff of the ASU became monolithic.

During 1937 pro-war feeling in the country grew apace. The New Deal moved more openly toward interventionism, as Roosevelt came out in October with his "Quarantine the Aggressor" speech. The Socialist anti-war minority in the ASU had a harder row to hoe. By the end of 1937 the Communists, in bloc with Lash, were in position to dump the last vestiges of the student movement's militant politics and anti-war activity. At the convention, a well-organized Socialist bloc of delegates carried on a last-ditch fight to save the Oxford Pledge but lost, 282-108. By the 1938 convention, with the Socialist left wing out, the complete Popular-Frontization of the organization bore fruit: the Roosevelt administration finally gave its official blessing to the ASU, in a letter of greetings to the convention from the President; the convention also got messages from the mayor of New York and its Board of Higher Education, from the president of CCNY, from the women's director of the Democratic National Committee, and other notables. The student movement was now completely respectable, completely pro-administration, and completely emasculated.

The new atmosphere that enveloped the ASU can be gathered, in part, from the following comment by a friend of the movement, Bruce Bliven,.writing in the New Republic for January 11, 1939 on the convention that had just taken place:

> Their enthusiasm reached its peak at the Jamboree in the huge jai-alai auditorium of the Hippodrome (seating capacity 4500) which was filled to its loftiest tier. There were a quintet of white-flanneled cheer leaders, a swing band, and shaggers doing the Campus Stomp ("everybody's doing it, ASU'ing it") — confetti. There were ASU feathers and buttons, a brief musical comedy by the Mob Theater and pretty ushers in academic caps and gowns. All the trappings of a big-game rally were present and the difference was that they were cheering, not the Crimson to beat the Blue, but Democracy to beat Reaction. To me, it bordered just alongside the phoney.[4]

It was phoney, of course, whatever one might think of football rally exercises. This was making like Joe College according to the detailed instructions of the YCL Organizer on "How to Be American ."

Later on in 1939 there was a second excellent example of what had happened. This one is directly from the Young Communist League Bulletin at

154

the University of Wisconsin: "Some people have the idea that a YCL'er is politically minded, that nothing outside of politics means anything. Gosh, no. They have a few simple problems. There is the problem of getting good men on the baseball team this spring, of opposition from other ping-pong teams, of dating girls, etc. We go to shows, parties, dances, and all that. In short, the YCL and its members are no different from other people except that we believe in dialectical materialism as the solution to all problems." [5]

This is what the student movement had become. The last chapter was written after September, 1939. After four years of eviscerating the student anti-war movement for the sake of the grand alliance against Nazism, the Second World War was inaugurated with the Hitler–Stalin Pact. The Communist leaders of the ASU ground all gears into reverse, and some of the passengers got shaken out, particularly Lash, who really believed what he had been saying about collective security. At the Christmas 1939 convention, the rug was pulled from under the "innocents ." The Communists held it in iron control, rolling up huge majorities even on procedural questions whenever necessary. A motion condemning the Soviet attack on Finland was defeated 322-49. It was announced that the war was "imperialist," and ASU propaganda echoed the slogan that "The Yanks Are Not Coming ." A motion for a national membership referendum on this line was overwhelmingly turned down. Lash was replaced in the executive secretary's office by the YCL apparatus-man, Bert Witt. At the 1940 convention there was no opposition at all—also no cheerleaders, confetti, or shaggers; the major speakers were Communists or fellow-travelers. But by this time it scarcely mattered, for the ASU was a shell. When the line changed again, after the German attack on Russia, and the Communists became shrill patriots again, it was too late to save the student movement even in its Popular Front form. The student movement was dead.

8.

This is not the place to attempt a full assessment of the impact of the student movement of the thirties, but a word must be said about one type of assessment that has been published. This latter is based on the fact, which I have stressed in connection with the anti-war strike, that there was always a great disparity between the number who actually joined any of the radical student organizations and the larger number who could be moved into action by this small vanguard. Two writers on the subject have operated with the statistics in a manner which is a model of how not to understand social movements.

One is Robert W. Iversen who, in his The *Communists and the Schools*, makes a characteristic remark. When the alumni of CCNY were disturbed by the college's "red" reputation — "The Alumni Association reassured them in 1936 that only 1 per cent of the students belonged to radical organizations. But unfortunately, the 99 per cent possessed few of the gifts for publicity that seemed the peculiar talent of the dedicated few.[6]

This reduction of the radical students' appeal to a "peculiar talent" for clever publicity makes a mystery where there was none. It would be hard to explain how assiduous reading of Marx and Lenin gave rise to this gift. But the radical students at CCNY needed no Madison Avenue gifts when they had a college president like Frederick B. Robinson, a president who could personally make an umbrella-swinging physical attack on a student protest meeting (1933); who first insisted on subjecting the student body to a college reception for an official delegation of Italian Fascist students, and then reacted to the hissing of his guests with an uncontrolled outburst of "Guttersnipes!"(1934). These were only two of his more dramatic exploits, guaranteed equally to make headlines and to convince unaligned students that they had to take a stand. (CCNY blossomed with lapel buttons reading "I Am a Guttersnipe").

Even without such cooperation by administrations gifted with a peculiar talent for alienating their students — especially under the pressure of conservative forces off-campus — Iversen's dichotomy between the "1 per cent" and the "99 per cent"is a basic misunderstanding of the relationship of forces. Around the 1 per cent who actually joined a radical student group were concentric rings of influence, embracing different portions of the student body as different forms of commitment were demanded. For every one who joined there were perhaps two who agreed in the main with what the student movement was trying to do, but who did not join, either for lack of time to devote to such activity of for other reasons which did them less credit. There was another circle of students who were ready to support most of the campaigns or actions which the student organizations might launch on a given issue, such as defense of students victimized by the administration. It was probably most inclusive during the annual antiwar actions, whether in the form of the anti-war strike or the "peace assembly ."

Even outside the widest of these concentric circles, if we consider the students who never participated in any dissenting form of activity at all, it would be an error to suppose that all of them were hostile to the student movement and needed only adequate talents for publicity to make this hostility felt. The general social disillusionment with the status quo, with "The System," conditioned many of them, if only because it put them on the defensive before the self-confident radicals. It deprived them of that capacity to feel that "all radicals must be kooks," which is characteristic of a social system sure of itself.

The picture, then, is far more complex than a "1 per cent" versus a "99 per cent," and it was through this complexity that the organized student movement made itself felt as a relatively small vanguard which, from time to time, could put much larger masses into motion.

Iversen's handling of statistics reflects a profound ignorance of what was going on at the time. Thus he writes:

> In 1941, a careful attempt was made to assess the extent of communism among the students of Brooklyn College and City College during he previous five years. The most reliable index was found to be the communist vote in student elections. Thus, at the peak of Communist power in 1938, 1,002 votes were cast in a Brooklyn College straw ballet. Of this number, 280 were cast for the Communist candidate. Several things may be concluded from this: first, since the total college enrollment was over 10,000, the political indifference of the vast majority of students was virtually monumental, with the Communists comprising less than 3 per cent of the total student body. The figures do show, however, that about one-third of the students who were politically conscious enough to vote at all voted Communist.[7]

What is left entirely out of the picture is the fact that in 1938, after some years of intensive Communist propaganda identifying the Popular Front line with euphoric enthusiasm for the New Deal, and particularly in 1938 when Roosevelt was obviously steering an interventionist course, there were far more Communist sympathizers and fellow-travelers who voted for the New Deal candidates than there were Communist Party members who registered their vote for the ceremonial candidates put up by the party. It would be impossible to pick a year which would be worse than 1938 for determining pro-Communist sympathies on the basis of casting a ballot for the party's candidates.

Iversen's passage continues as follows, with a second case: "At City College, the situation was somewhat different. In a straw vote held during the presidential campaign of 1940, there were only 126 Communist votes out of a total of 2,656. The enrollment at City was about 6,000. City College thus reveals...".[8] But it does not matter what Iversen thinks it reveals, since he seems to be unconcerned about, and does not mention, the fact that this straw poll took place after one year of the Nazi-Soviet pact. The Communist power was now an ally of Hitler—especially in the eyes of a City College student body with a very high proportion of Jewish students. By this time the Communist Party itself was staggering, and especially its sympathizers were falling away in droves. The marked difference between Brooklyn College in 1938 and City College in 1940 depends on the background politics, not on the place.

However, Iversen's subject, the influence of Communists in the colleges, is only a part of the larger problem of the relation of the student movement to the campus. A similar approach is taken, in a more impressionistic fashion, by Murray Kempton in a book about the thirties, *Part of Our Time*, which makes some remarks about the student movement in its last chapter.

Kempton recalls that in *Harper's* of August, 1931, just before the student movement blossomed before the public, Harold J. Laski had published an article whose title asked: "Why Don't Your Young People Care?"The question, asserts Kempton, "was not materially less valid"at the fever pitch of the student movement in 1937 than it had been in 1931, and he cites statistics to indicate this:

> At the height of its uproar, the ASU had only twelve thousand members and claimed another eight thousand who hadn't paid their dues but were otherwise totally committed. The Young Communist League had fewer than five thousand student members at any one time. As the thirties wore on, the Young People's Socialist League, the heroic and historic Yipsels, fell below one thousand members* and the Young Trotskyites below five hundred.

Yet the few persons in those last three organizations made most

---

* But this was true only after the split in the socialist movement which took place toward the end of 1937. For 1935-37, which is the "fever-pitch" Kempton is presumably considering, the YPSL probably had a couple of thousand members or more.

of the history of student rebellion in the thirties. In 1937, as an instance, young Communists, young Socialists, and one young Trotskyite constituted eighteen of the thirty members of the National Executive Committee of the American Student Union; and all its national officers were either Socialists or Communists. There were close to four million high school and college students in the United States in 1937; the myth of their radical impulse was created, at the very most, by fifteen thousand persons. It has been said that these fifteen thousand set the tone for the American campus in the thirties, in which case they did it by default. A tone set by three-tenths of one per cent of a community can hardly, after all, be described as a tone [9]

The problem of how a "tone" is set by the relationship between a small minority of activists and a larger mass of sympathetic or impressionable students is, as I have already discussed, more complex than such statistics can express. However, Kempton's tendentiousness is manifested by his use of the figure "four million high school and college students ." No one has ever claimed that the student movement set the tone in the high schools; it was remarkable enough that fairly active movements of high school students were built during the thirties, at least in New York and Chicago. It is a question, therefore, of about a million and a quarter college students; and even here we must remember that most institutions of higher education, especially the small freshwater colleges, denominational schools, and vocational-technical institutions in nonurban areas, remained little affected by the swirl of events — any events. Nor need it be claimed that the student movement set the tone at, say, Harvard if the totality of university life is thereby meant. In fact, the same point could quite legitimately be made even about what was probably the most highly politicalized college in the country, Brooklyn College, during the time I was chairman of its SLID chapter as well as in the subsequent years. The large majority of students devoted themselves to studying and getting their sheepskins and pursuing their personal lives just as if there were no student movement, but even while doing so they could not help absorbing the climate of ideas which pervaded the political life of the campus as a part of the larger society. Now, the tone which was set by the small vanguard of student activists was precisely this political tone, through all of the concentric circles which

159

I have described.

Here is a final example, from Kempton, of how easy it is to get three mistakes into three sentences: "What history there is asserts that in 1937 half a million American college students took an oath never to support this government in any war. The Selective Service Act came three and one-half years later; fewer than one hundred men refused to register under it as a matter of principle. By 1943, just 1,400 young men of all sorts had gone to prison for ideological or ethical defiance of the draft law. And half of those were Jehovah's Witnesses...."[10]

In the first place, the Oxford Pledge was not an oath to become a conscientious objector, as I have explained. With few exceptions, the Socialists and Communists who led the student movement were vigorously and articulately opposed to conscientious objection as a policy (the *right* to conscientious objection is another matter), and did not advocate that revolutionary students go to jail rather than accept the draft. Second, it is not true, nor was it claimed, that "half a million American college students" took the Oxford Pledge in 1937. That figure is for total participants in the various "peace assemblies" or other anti-war demonstrations that took place in 1937. And, as has been related, by this time the Oxford Pledge had been dumped in practice by the ASU leadership and most chapters, preparatory to being officially dumped at the Christmas conventions. This already suggests the third and most important error. Kempton writes as if the student movement rejected the coming war until it came, and then the movement collapsed. Like Iversen, he ignores the fact that the student movement had been turned into a political instrument for preparing youth to accept the war as a crusade against fascism, years before the test came.

The student movement was one of the first casualties of the Second World War, but its impact was not ended. For the next couple of decades at least, wherever anything was stirring in the labor movement or in liberal campaigns, wherever there was action for progressive causes or voices were raised in dissent from the Establishment, there one was sure to find alumni of this student movement, who had gotten their political education and organizational training and experience in the American Student Union or the Student League for Industrial Democracy or the National Student League. The history we have sketched is that of one of the most important educational institutions of twentieth. century America.

From As We Saw the Thirties
University of Illinois Press 1967

Chapter IX:
Is There a Socialism From Below?

1. A Reply to Hal Draper: Max Nomad

Hal Draper's "Two Souls of Socialism" is a laudable attempt to unmask what he calls "Socialism from Above," because all the variants of this kind of socialism mean only one thing: the substitution of a neo-bourgeoisie of office-holders and managers for the old bourgeoisie of property-owners. However, he has devoted his efforts to a great delusion when, to those neo-bourgeois gospels, he tried to oppose what he calls "Socialism from Below ." For, alas, there never was, there never could be such a thing. To be sure, there are passages in Marx's writings which, according to H.D., are supposed to point to the assumption that his teacher's was the truly democratic, the truly proletarian, the truly anti-bourgeois article. However, it may not be amiss to remind the eager disciple of another passage from the same sage's writings to the effect that "a distinction is to be made between what a man thinks of himself and says, and what he really is and does ."

Was Marx, during the German Revolution of 1848, a revolutionist "from below" when, after joining the German Democratic Party, he avoided any mention of the labor movement in his *Neue Rheinische Zeitung?* Was Engels, his intellectual twin, a socialist "from below" when at the same time, apparently in order to appease the bourgeoisie, he disapproved of the formation of labor unions in his industrial home town, Barmen?

Was Marx a socialist "from below" when, in his *Eighteenth Brumaire*, he called Blanqui "the real leader of the proletarian party" while, in reality, that "party consisted almost exclusively of impecunious students, journalists and other declassés aiming at what Blanqui called a "Parisian dictatorship" — an obviously non-democratic regime of an educated elite? Was Marx a socialist "from below" when, in 1850, he joined the Universal Society of Revolutionary Communists, a super-conspirative body composed exclusively of top leaders?

Was Marx a socialist "from below" when in 1848 — though a fullfledged Marxist, he *justified* the rule of the four million Hungarians (Magyars), over eight million Slavs and Rumanians on the ground that the Hungarians "had more vitality and energy?" Was Marx much better than the unspeakable racist Proudhon when he wrote contemptuously about Jews, Scandinavians, "niggers" (yes, niggers), "Croats, Czechs, and similar scum?" Or when he wrote that it was *no* "misfortune that glorious California has been wrenched from the lazy Mexicans who did not know what to do with it ." (The wording and the sources of all these scandalous utterances are given in Kautsky's *Sozialisten und Krieg*, in Heinrich Cunow's *Partei-Zusammenbruch?* and in Max

Nomad's *Apostles of Revolution* (hard-cover edition). I am mentioning all this because what is sauce for Proudhon is also sauce for Marx.

Was Marx a democratic socialist "from below" when, in the well-known letter to his friend Wedemeyer (dated March 5, 1852), he insisted that "the class struggle leads necessarily to the dictatorship of the proletariat" and that this dictatorship itself is only a transition to the abolition of all classes and to a classless society?" There are those who, to be fair to Marx, try to explain that, in using the term "dictatorship," he actually meant "rule" or democratic rule. But why did he have to use that unsavory term if he actually meant democracy? And is it wrong to assume that in coining the term "dictatorship of the proletariat," Marx may have been inspired by Blanqui's elitist "Parisian dictatorship?" For wasn't Blanqui, in Marx's opinion, a "leader of the proletarian party?"

To be sure there are passages in Marx's writings showing that, in later years, their author was in favor of democratic, parliamentary methods in such countries as the United States, England, and Holland (his speech at The Hague in 1872). This, shall we say, "menshevik" attitude was, however, counterbalanced three years later by an outright "bolshevik" passage in his *Critique of the Gotha Program* (1875) in which he clearly stated that during "the political transition period [between the capitalist and communist society] ... the state can be nothing else than the revolutionary dictatorship of the proletariat ." True, he may have had in mind only the semi-absolutist regimes like Germany and ultra-reactionary post-Commune France, which could be overcome only by a violent revolution as a result of which the Socialists might assume dictatorial power, once attained, would abandon its tendency to remain permanent.

Did Marx attempt to refute the famous passage in Bakunin's *Statism and Anarchy* which contained the prophetic prediction that Marx's "proletarian dictatorship" would really be a dictatorship of office-holders and engineers? It is beside the point that Bakunin's "invisible dictatorship" would have amounted to the same thing. Marx's marginal remark "reverie" was hardly a refutation.

Was Engels a socialist "from below" when he attacked as a "*Studenten-Revolte*" the radical opposition of the *Jungen* to the official leadership of the German Social-Democratic Party, which, after the repeal of the anti-socialist laws in 1890, was turning more and more respectable?

To prove that Marx's was a "socialism from below" H.D. insists on his

162

hostility to "statism" and on the famous "withering away of the state ." But isn't it more realistic to assume that Marx's anti-statism was primarily a defense mechanism against the competition on the part of Proudhon's and, later, Bakunin's followers whose denunciations of the state were quite popular at the time? Didn't the *Communist Manifesto*, in Chapter II, say that "the proletariat will use its political domination for the purpose of ... centralizing all means of production *in the hands of the state*" (emphasis added); and further: "Centralization of credit in the hands of the state through a National Bank with state capital and exclusive monopoly"; "centralization of the transport system in the hands of the state"; "organization of industrial armies especially for agriculture ." If this is not statism in the "best" Lenin-Trotsky-Stalin tradition, then what is it? Marx and Engels may have changed their vocabulary later, but the essence remained the same. To be sure, the state will have to cease to be a state after a period of "transition"; but what interests those alive is not the nebulous "higher phase" but the very unromantic *transition* period during which the better paid office-holders and managers will establish a "new class" benevolently ruling a "classless" and therefore "stateless" society.

As evidence of Marx's "socialism from below," H.D. quotes that passage of Marx's polemic against the conspiratorial putschists of the Willich-Schapper faction, which says that the workers "would have to go through fifteen, or twenty, or fifty years of civil wars and international wars not only in order to change extant conditions, but also in order to change yourselves and to render yourselves fit for political dominion ." H.D. repeats with emphasis the words *"in order to change yourselves and to render yourselves fit for political dominion ."* He does not realize that all the tragedy of the uneducated, horny-handed underdog is epitomized in this passage. For two roads are offered to the workers: (1) that of Willich-Schapper (in our times, it is that of Lenin and Trotsky) which means the seizure of power by an elitist group of educated déclassés who will establish a dictatorship over the proletariat as they did in Russia; or (2) that of gradualism, which means the postponement of their "emancipation" to the Greek calends. For the assumption that the uneducated, horny-handed manual workers might attain their intellectual fitness for their "dominion," including the management of the industrial fabric, while they are still struggling against the exploiting capitalists, is the sheerest illusion. Now, after a century of struggles for better wages, the enormous majority of the workers still constitutes an ignorant mass of near-illiterate, racist-minded tabloid readers, interested in nothing but sports, crime news, and movies, and absolutely unable to understand what is really going on in this complicated world.

To be sure, there are among the workers exceptionally gifted individuals, such as the Bevins, the Bevans, the Thorezes, the Reuthers, the Meanys, and the Krushchevs, who are able to acquire an education above that of the average workers. But is that upstart elite of ex-horny-handed trade union officials and party leaders interested in the "emancipation" of the workers? One may just as well expect salvation from upstart workers who become capitalists. It is a well-known fact that in all countries these self-taught ex-workers are either part of the middle class (or even upper middle class) satisfied with the capitalist system; or, as is the case in the underdeveloped countries, part of the present or future "new class" of totalitarian or simply dictatorial office-holders and managers.

Confronted by this problem, the syndicalists, who aspired to represent "socialism from below" par excellence, at first propounded the idea that, prior to the "expropriating general strike," the workers would have to *study* how to manage the industrial fabric—lest they remain subjected to the rule of bourgeois engineers and managers. Needless to say that the whole idea was a utopia. A worker cannot learn after his daily toil what it takes a middle class youth to learn in institutions of higher technical education. To be sure, some of the brighter workers did learn how to become trade union functionaries or plain socialist or communist politicians. So when a really revolutionary situation came up—I mean the ferment created by the Bolshevik Revolution—those of the leading syndicalists who had not in the meantime joined the Socialist Party and later the Communists, launched the slogan of *au syndicat le pouvoir* (all power to the union). A slogan which, in reality, meant *all power to the syndicalist union leaders*. This, of course, was merely a variant of Leninism which, in turn, is one of the varieties of "Socialism from Above." Speaking of the anarchists — mostly extinct outside of Spain — the revolutionists among them, like the Spanish FAI, are simply dictatorial neo-Bakuninists, that is, Leninists with a "libertarian" vocabulary; while those who stick to the post-Bakunin tradition of "pure" anarchism, are simply gradualists believing in indoctrinating their fellow-men with their humanitarian ideas — until the end of time.

Was—after Marx and Engels—Rosa Luxemburg, whom H.D. so greatly admires, a paragon of "socialism from below?" She certainly was made of better stuff than all her Marxist contemporaries, but the fact is that, in the

Marxist party of Poland of which she was the leader, she wielded despotic power absolutely unbecoming a champion of what is called "proletarian democracy." Those familiar with the Polish socialist movement know she used her authority to expel Karl Radek from her party when he disagreed with her, even though the *majority of the rank and file was with him*. It is beside the point that Radek was a louse. The fact is that Rosa believed in "socialism from below" only insofar as her followers did her bidding.

But even assuming that she was really dedicated to "socialism from below" — how come that, for all her genius, brilliance, and eloquence, what influence she had over the ultra-radical wing of German socialism, evaporated completely during the Spartacus days of 1919, when that following of hers, in total disregard of her warnings, was seized by the insensate desire to duplicate Lenin's feat and to establish a minority dictatorship, a "socialism from above," if ever there was one?

In his search for another representative of what he calls "socialism from below," H.D. points to the idealistic figure of Eugene Debs. The great orator was certainly a devoted champion of the underdog, devoid of any personal ambitions or will to power. But he was a saint rather than a revolutionary thinker. He courageously called himself a Bolshevik right after the October uprising, but at the same time he was opposed to violence; he sympathized with the valiant Wobblies (I.W.W.), but, as far as I can remember, opposed sabotage on ethical grounds, at a time when sabotage was winked at by the very moderate American Federation of Labor as one of those weapons that were always used by the underdog when he was otherwise helpless against his ruthless employers and the state-power supporting them.

Debs hoped for the workers to "fit themselves, by education, organization, and self-imposed discipline, to take control of the productive forces" — a utopian hope of course; and at the same time he put his hope in a leading militant *minority*, a noble, worker-loving elite, just like the first followers of Lenin and Trotsky, an elite of good men which, alas, in due time, always jumps on the bandwagon of the socialists "from above."

True, Hal Draper makes a distinction between the *vanguard* (H.D.'s emphasis) "from below," and the *elite* (the socialists "from above") when he says that their function is to "impel the mass-majority *to fit themselves to take power in their own name, through their own struggles*" (H.D.'s emphasis). What a pity H.D. forgets that, no matter how valiantly the uneducated underdog will *struggle*, he (the underdog) won't get *power*; he will merely assist his educated *vanguard* to get it. And the educated *vanguard*, once in possession of power, becomes a new aristocracy, just as did the followers of Lenin, Trotsky, Tito, and Mao; or as would those of Bakunin, Monatte, or the Spanish FAI, if they had had a chance. Do I have to remind H.D. of Lord Acton's saying about the corrupting influence of power? Has its truth even been disproved?

I wonder what H.D. actually means when he writes that "the point is not to deny the critical importance of minorities, but to establish a different relationship between the advanced minority and the more backward mass" — unless it is the gold old "good man" theory, of the Bevans being better men than the Bevins, the anarchist Makhnos being preferable to the dictatorial Trotskys, and the Trotskys to the Stalins. But those holding that view forget that behind every "good" leader there is always a crowd of self-seekers whose appetites will prevail over the noble intentions of the "good man."

In a way, the deeper implications of the subject under discussion were touched upon at the turn of the century by Kautsky and Lenin. In 1901 the top theoretician of German socialism had to put in their place those trade union leaders who tried to assert their "proletarian" independence from, or rather superiority to, the party leaders who were mostly intellectuals. In that polemic, Kautsky pointed out that socialist ideas had come to the working class from the bourgeois intelligentsia. In a somewhat similar situation familiar to those who have read Lenin's *What Is To Be Done?* the founder of Bolshevism said the same thing and he emphasized that, left to themselves, the manual workers never went beyond the trade unionist concept of fighting for better wages and shorter hours.

Neither Kautsky nor Lenin seem to have realized that, by making these correct statements, they were pointing to the neo-bourgeois essence of the socialist protest against capitalism. A protest which, while voiced ostensibly in behalf of the manual workers, was in reality, the expression of the dissatisfaction of the owners of education (they could be called the "knows") with the rule of the "haves," i.e., the owners of property who, except during the Dark Ages, were also owners of education. In demanding the elimination of the "haves," the "knows" have in most cases, either consciously or subconsciously, in mind their own substitution for the old ruling class, a change which is "rationalized" by them as the "emancipation of the working class ."

The self-delusion, which apparently prevented both Kautsky and Lenin from penetrating the essence of their own beliefs, was — aside from their own

166

class interests as intellectuals — based on their uncritical acceptance of the Marxist dictum that capitalism is the last possible form of exploitation. That concept precluded the idea that the non-capitalist owners of education could inaugurate a post-capitalist system of exploitation, such as was to blossom out in the Communist orbit after the elimination of the capitalists..

Hal Draper correctly points out the appeal which the privileged situation of the intellectual workers in the Communist orbit has for their less privileged fellow-intellectuals of the capitalist world. This appeal obviously accounts of the "socialism from above" of many intellectuals and self-taught ex-workers of the West. But H.D. forgets that this appeal has also a corrupting effect on all attempts at creating what he calls "socialism from below ." For an idealistic intellectual and an ambitious self-taught ex-worker will easily be tempted to identify the elevation of his own class status, implied in his becoming a member of the new "communist" Establishment, with the elevation of the working class as a whole. To be sure, there are and there will be disinterested would-be emulators of Liebknecht and Djilas, but they are fated to remain as rare and as uninfluential as their models.

H.D. has rather harsh words for those who accept the idea of the Iron Law of Oligarchy which he thinks is a "crude theory of inevitability — the inevitability of *change from above only* ." He forgets that *within that* "iron law" *changes from below* are likewise not only possible but also inevitable. All the improvements in the standard of living of the masses have been accomplished without affecting the validity of that "law." They have been brought about by the struggle of the underdog for *more and more now,* and not by the struggle for power which only his educated leaders could acquire thus perpetuating the "circulation of elites" which is identical with the idea of the "iron law of oligarchy ."

Near the end of his essay, H.D. asks himself the question "how does a people or a class become fit to rule in their own name?" He answers the question with the words: *"Only by fighting to do so"* (his emphasis). And he continues: "Only by fighting for democratic power do they educate themselves and raise themselves to the level of being able to wield that power ." H.D. forgets that the working class is not like other classes which, in the course of history, were struggling against the powers that be, classes like the bourgeoisie, the small property owners, and the intelligentsia, classes whose members were *not* illiterate or near-illiterate. The *workers,* on the other hand, are, like the slaves and the serfs of the past, a class that is deprived of the education that could enable it to exert power; and *it cannot get that education just by fighting.*

It was Kautsky, I believe, who, faced by that problem, once pointed out that the workers, just as all other classes, would rule through their *elite.* He "forgot" that the lawyers and other politicians who rule in behalf of the bourgeoisie or the lower middle classes, *belong to the same class* as those whom they represent, while the "elite" of the workers (labor leaders and labor politicians) are actually members of the middle class, and not of what is called the "proletariat."

Ever since the rise of modern industrialism, the workers have been fighting all right; they got higher wages, and their struggle occasionally *helped their educated leaders to get, or to partake in, power;* but the workers themselves remained at the bottom of the social pyramid. Did the *workers* rule in the Soviets after the Bolshevik Revolution? Their "delegates" were intellectuals and semi-intellectuals (including self-taught ex-workers, which amounts to the same thing) and it was the "knows," the Communist Party leaders and not the rank-and-file workers who got power. And thus it has remained to the present day. Did the British *workers* get power due to the fact that their leaders—Oxford men and self-taught ex-workers—are now the cream of the British Establishment? Do the American workers wield power, or will they be able to do so in the foreseeable future, because the Meanys, the Reuthers, the Dubinskys are hobnobbing with the ruling elite?

I hope my skepticism as to the manual workers, as a mass, ever becoming "fit" to rule "in their own name," and my insistence on the slogan of *more and more now* will not earn me from H.D. the accusation that I am a Gompersian defender of the capitalist status quo. I believe that *all power is evil,* that all social systems, present and future, individualist and collectivist, are bound to be systems of exploitation, and that they *all* deserve to be fought—for the sake of more comforts for the underdog and more cultural liberty for those interested in culture. I don't believe that all governments and all authority will ever disappear altogether, nor that all forms of government are equally evil. But neither do I believe that there can be such a thing as "real democracy." At best there can be a frequent change of masters who will rule "in the name of the masses" and make concessions to them, lest they be displaced "democratically" by another set of demagogues, likewise ruling "in the name of the masses ."

And the workers? Those of them who have not got it in them to become as cultured as the Reuthers or as smart as the Dubinskys, will keep on fighting for better wages and dreaming of better cars and of homes in neighborhoods not "infested" by "inferior" human breeds. For they belong to the same animal species as their bourgeois or neo-bourgeois "betters," with the only difference that they have less money and education and more prejudices. Yet I believe in helping them in their struggle for a better share of the good things of life. But I have no illusions that they will turn a new leaf of human history. For history will always remain a merciless affray in which the most ruthless, the most cunning, and the most intelligent fight among themselves for the best places on the back of the underdog.

There is no remedy against this cruel scheme of things which is as indestructible as death and other natural calamities. But its injustices can be mitigated by the permanent revolt of, and in behalf of, the suffering majority fighting for *more and more now*, and not for *power* which, at bottom, means only a change of masters.[1]

2. In Reply to Max Nomad: Hal Draper
Is Oligarchy Inevitable?

In Max Nomad's discussion of my "Two Souls of Socialism," the first two pages alone ask 17 questions about such things as Engels' opinion of the *Jungen* faction in the German social-democracy of 1890, Marx's editorship of the *Neue Rheinische Zeitung* in 1848, etc., etc. This is followed by essays on the Inevitability of Oligarchy, Luxemburg, syndicalism, Radek's expulsion, and many others—the list itself would take part of a page—and the whole *ollapodrida* takes less than seven pages to whisk off.

I cannot hope to equal this remarkable compactness, since questions like these can be asked in four lines but need forty just to be explained to the reader (let alone answered). Nomad does not waste space explaining the point of his questions to readers unlearned in the minutiae of socialist history, thus showing a faith in the erudition of the *NP* reader which contrasts refreshingly with his dim view of the ignorant masses.

On the other hand, the part of Nomad's article devoted to asserting his general view (the Iron Law) is a rather vulgarized version of that common theory—a theory which is standard equipment nowadays as much for the sophisticated political-science professors as for the cracker-barrel cynics who merely know that all-them-there-politician-fellers-are-crooks. This theory is indeed the characteristic and received political dogma of our day, as popular among many new-leftists (who avoid the danger of creating a new organizational oligarchy by the clever expedient of avoiding organization) as among apologists for the status-quo in Moscow and Peking (since, if oligarchy is inevitable anyway and "all power is evil," the choice is simply between an evil capitalist power and an evil anti-capitalist power)—and many others, all of them quite as sincere as Nomad.

To take up this overshadowing political doctrine of the age in its relatively crude Nomad version is probably unfair to it. On the other hand, I cannot altogether convince myself that *NP* readers are more interested in Engels and *Jungen*. Since the editor, exercising Power, has wisely limited this rejoinder to far less than the necessary 50 pages, I am forced into a rotten compromise (so corrupting is the exercise of power) in which many subjects will only be touched on.

The subject of "The Two Souls of Socialism," it says there, is the *meaning* of the socialist idea. Insofar as Nomad suggests a view of his own on this, it is in his sentence about "the neo-bourgeois essence of the socialist protest against capitalism" which is "voiced ostensibly in behalf of the manual workers" but is "in reality the expression of the dissatisfaction of the owners of education" (intellectuals) with the owners of property.*

This tells us what socialism means to the intellectuals who dupe the "manual workers"; but now — what is the meaning of socialism *to those "manual workers"* who are being deceived by the evil intellectuals?

Here, in the statement by him which deals directly with the question I raised of the meaning of socialism, Nomad implies that there *are* two different views about "the socialist protest against capitalism" held by these two social strata, so different that one has to dupe the other. Even if we accept only for the sake of argument that this duping must always and invariably succeed 100 percent, Nomad has obviously admitted, apparently unwittingly, that to the "workers" he is talking about, "socialism" must mean something different from the "neo-bourgeois" business of simply substituting the intelligentsia for the capitalists. What then is the other meaning?

Moreover, if the evil intelligentsia have to go to all this trouble to hoodwink the "workers" with an elaborate ideology, rituals, movement, etc., called socialism, then there must be a strong drive to be deflected and captured, and not simply one or two naive people with a utopian notion about "socialist freedom" or socialism-from-below. In point of fact, behind the ideologists whom I have described as "socialists-from-above" we find time and again *mass movements* which are not simply reflections of the leader's socialism-from-above and were not called into being by it, but which arose out of real class struggles in society with aspirations of their own.

The answer to Nomad's question, "Is there a socialism-from-below?" is to be found *first of all* not in the writings of any theoretician, not even Marx, but in the real fighting movements which arise out of the social struggle. (That, in fact, is what Marx kept repeating to all kinds of Nomads and others.) Ferdinand Lassalle was himself a thorough authoritarian, but the *workers' movement* which he partly put himself at the head of, and partly stimulated, was not simply Lassalle multiplied. Lassalleanism rode it, if you wish duped it — yes, indeed — but that which this Evil Intellectual duped has something different from Lassalleanism.

Proudhon was a thorough authoritarian — yes, indeed — but the "Proudhonist" workers of Lyons who thought he was their leader did not

---

* I pass over with regret any comment on the term "neo-bourgeois" in this connection. In any case Nomad would first have to explain what is bourgeois (neo- or paleo-) about the anti-capitalism of intellectuals who actually do go about overthrowing capitalism, even if only for their own aggrandizement.

understand just what he was getting at because *they* were getting at something else, among other reasons.

This goes on through most of the history of the socialist movement. Socialism-from-below is not represented simply by the very few outstanding thinkers whom I mentioned. On the contrary, they were what they were precisely because they viewed themselves primarily as the articulators, the generalizers, the *porte-paroles*, of an autonomous upsurge of struggle from below which could never be put in anyone's bag until it was defeated. This is the message of Luxemburg's *Mass Strike*, Marx's *Address to the Communist League* of 1850, Debs' "The Day of the People ."

The rhythm of class struggle from below goes through the whole history of the working class and the socialist movement, now quiescent, now breaking out in turbulent revolution, and various states in-between. After Nomad has got through sneering that the workers' struggles have always been defeated and swindled, all I want to know right now is this:

If my separation-out of a "socialism-from-below" is nothing but a "great delusion" as Nomad claims, how else does he account for these massive movements which have shaken society time and again in the last two centuries—not simply for "more and more" but for social transformation? He may wish to argue that any movement for socialism-from-below is always and eternally fated to be defeated and duped: very well, but it is very difficult to dupe an illusion—the movement to be duped must first exist. His all-purpose theory of the Evil Intellectuals may account for the duping, but what accounts for the movements which have to be duped?

The stormy history of the socialist struggles in various countries (however duped) could not possibly *exist* on the basis of Nomad's bitterly contemptuous picture of the working class. In a paragraph which starts with the year 1850, Nomad asserts that "the uneducated, horny-handed underdog" can *never* become fit to run society:

> Now, after a century of struggles for better wages, the enormous majority of the workers *still* constitute an ignorant mass of near-illiterate, racist-minded tabloid readers, interested in nothing but sports, crime news, and movies, and absolutely unable to understand what is really going on in this complicated world. [Emphasis added.]

Is Nomad thinking of the Russian muzhiks or of the United States? If the latter, this sounds like an approximate description of Orange County, California, and not particularly of the workers in it; in fact, it is a common pop-sociological description not only of America's suburbia but of most of the bourgeoisie too, even the non-Texan section. I do not have the space to discuss the simple-minded vulgarity of this sociological gem, but I do not have to. Because insofar as it is true that American labor and the American petty-bourgeoisie *and* its bourgeois rulers are politically and socially backward, to the same degree it is also true that there is no mass socialist movement in this benighted country. Neither from above nor from below. No need to dupe it. Nomad doesn't even have to explain the "neo-bourgeois essence" of this socialism.

But if Nomad's bitter derision of the working class has any relationship to the reality of *world* history, it would be impossible to account for the existence of mass revolutionary movements and militant revolts which had to be deceived by the "neo-bourgeois" misleaders. Nomad's acrid imprecations against the workers who failed to make the revolution can be understood subjectively without difficulty, but it makes no sense historically. I am familiar, of course, with the line that socialism belongs only to the past, but for Nomad nothing ever existed except a "great delusion."

If we look beyond the borders of Orange County, Texas, and the United States, we see a most contradictory phenomenon (my essay point out): For the first time in the history of the world, a majority of its people consider themselves "socialist" in some sense. For the first time! Yes, of course, they are duped as to what kind of "socialism" they are handed in fact — otherwise we would be basking in the delights of a new human society right now — but this duping-business always has the side that Nomad is blind too. Put it this way: for the first time in the history of the world, it has become necessary to dupe a majority of its people about socialism.

Not in the U.S., but in most of the world the question of the *meaning of socialism*, not simply in theory but in day-to-day struggle, is automatically raised high on the agenda simply by the claim that "socialism" has already been achieved or is the aim. In Britain the membership of the mass government party — consisting, one presumes from Nomad, of "an ignorant mass of near-illiterate, racist-minded tabloid-readers" etc. — is embroiled in arguments over Vietnam, nationalization, wage-freeze, and so on, not naturally on the superior level ardently desired by Nomad and me, to be sure, but merely on a level immensely higher than (say) in Marx's day. And it takes Harold Wilson to dupe them, whereas in the U.S. the workers are — well, to summarize, they are duped by an organism like George Meany. In the Communist countries, we see a new exploiting social system which has been racked by more unrest and mass revolt from below in its very first few decades than any other social system that has ever come into existence. ...

Enough of that: there is not enough space to continue. Remember, we granted for the sake of argument that all these stirrings from below are doomed eternally to defeat and deception because of the Iron Law. All we have been discussing is Nomad's question. "Is there a socialism-from-below?" and not any assurances that this amazingly ineradicable social reality can ever actually gain its aspirations. I certainly cannot offer guarantees of inevitable victory: that would be charlatanism. But when someone purports to offer guarantees — iron-clad moreover — of the reverse: that a movement which for two centuries has pressed for fruition, springing out of the ground with unceasing spontaneous motivation, is eternally never to advance to the first stage of realization, then I merely express the opinion that this is no less intellectual charlatanry — no less than the assurances of some self-styled Marxists that socialism is literally predestined because of the operation of the Historical Dialectic.

If, as Nomad reminds us, "a distinction is to be made between what a man thinks of himself and says, and what he really is and does," then there is surely nothing personal in pointing out what is obvious: a would-be ruling class always likes theories which proclaim the inevitability of its victory. Of whose victory does Nomad proclaim the inevitability? If we can assume that he does not think capitalism is eternal, then his variant of the Iron Law of Oligarchy, viz. the theory of the Inevitability of the New Class, is a theory with the same appeal as Burnham's managerial revolution or Ellul's technological autocracy. It is the theory which fits the social aspirations of the main historical alternative to socialism-from-below, that is, of the long-run enemy of working-class socialist democracy. In the same sense that Marxist theory reflects the aspirations of socialist workers, so the theory of the Inevitability of (a New Class) Oligarchy reflects a genuine social reality in a world which is seeing, not the duel pictured in the *Communist Manifesto*, but a triangular class struggle: the struggle for the world between an historically doomed capitalism, a beleaguered working class, and the "new class" of the bureaucratic-collectivist societies.

175

In the preceding lines I have just equated socialism-from-below with "working-class socialist democracy ." Let us put the spotlight on *democracy*. Nomad's case, at bottom, has nothing specially to do with socialism, from below or anywhere else. The other side of the coin of the Inevitability of Oligarchy is, of course, the theory of the Impossibility of Democracy, of democratic control-from-below.

For purely nostalgic reasons Nomad is in the habit of addressing his theories about the Impossibility of Democratic Control-from-Below to socialists, but this is only a personal idiosyncrasy. If the working masses are so "illiterate" that they are *qualitatively* different in mental caliber from even the "small property owners" of the age of bourgeois revolution (so Nomad asserts*), if they are "like the slaves and serfs of the past," if they are just "an ignorant mass" etc., then it is not socialism-from-below which is proved impossible, but democracy itself—any continuing democracy. Since the "utopian" element in socialism-from-below is not alleged to be its anti-capitalism, it can only be the ingredient of democratic control-from-below which makes it impossible. Indeed, in the bureaucratic-collectivist states, socialism-from-below *merges* conceptually with democratic control-from-below. If the former is just an empty illusion, as Nomad assures us, then the latter cannot be any less illusory.

Of course, Nomad is not one of the increasing number who have the fortitude to look this thing in the face. All he tells us is that he does not "believe that there can be such a thing as 'real democracy.'" But—

> At best there can be a frequent change of masters who will rule "in the name of the masses" and make concessions to them, lest they be displaced "democratically" by another set of demagogues, likewise ruling "in the name of the masses ."

Delightfully cynical. But it clearly a very special kind of "master" who can be displaced "democratically" (we are not told by Nomad what the quote-marks are supposed to mean) whenever the masses demand certain

---

* This assertion is so fantasmagorical, factually, that it tells us we are dealing not with a historical theory but with a cry of pain. Let Nomad undertake to show that the average Paris shopkeeper of 1789 had the equivalent of today's grade-school education. ...

concessions. And it is puzzling how this degree of power over the "masters" can be wielded by masses who are stupid, illiterate clods. In fact, if the Hungarian Revolution (say) had succeeded in installing such a government of "masters" who could be replaced at will in more-or-less democratic elections when the masses wanted different policies ("concessions"), with the obvious necessary concomitants of certain rights of organization and speech, then I trust that Nomad would not have felt called on to ridicule this development in a very witty expose on the ground that "real democracy" had not yet been established. A qualitative change would have taken place, an epoch-making stride *toward* socialism-from-below.

That is all history can be expected to do for people who are not ultimatists: make strides *toward* socialism-from-below, toward "real democracy" however defined. It is a direction, not a dogma. *It is a line of struggle,* not a finished utopia. But Nomad remains just as metaphysical a dogmatist now as when he thought he was an anarchist. He habitually proclaims things in absolutes: "history will *always* remain a merciless affray," there is *no* remedy .. ." "the Liebknechts 'are *fated* to remain' uninfluential, and, of course, '*all* power is evil. ...'"

How does he know all these flat, blown-in-the-bottle absolutes, not just about the past but about the eternal future? It takes *chutzpah.*

Nomad's belief in the sacredness of his absolutes is so naive that he can ask whether "Lord Acton's saying about the corrupting influence of power" has ever been "disproved ." The answer is no. Power corrupts. This is the beginning and end of Nomad's wisdom, but there are at least two other things about power that have never been disproved either:

(1) Lack of power corrupts too.

(2) Power not only has a "corrupting influence" but also other "influences." It does not have only a one-dimensional effect. Power sets up an inevitable *tendency* toward corruption, no doubt, but the actual outcome of any given social conjuncture does not depend on this one tendency alone.

The same game can be played with other counters. Organization corrupts. ... Civilization corrupts. ... Sex corrupts. ... Ideology corrupts. ... Yes, even education corrupts. All this is true, in the same context.

It is only as a dogmatic absolutist that Nomad accepts Acton's game uncritically. In practice, insofar as he lives in the real world of power, he ignores it. For example, trade unions cannot exist without wielding power, and they also allocate power to people called either officials or porkchoppers.

Power corrupts, and we well know that its corrupting influence is not exactly unheard-of in unions. Yet I take it that Nomad is assuming the existence of trade unions with power when he advocates—*as against the struggle for socialism*—that workers keep on fighting "for better wages," etc. No one has heard of a trade union winning better wages except to the degree it exerts power—which, as we know, corrupts. If it is to win "*more and more now,*" as Nomad advocates with emphasis, it must exert still more and more power, which inevitably must corrupt more and more. ... Nomad never explains why the wielding of ever greater (corrupting) power for *such* ends is not only permissible but laudable, to be advocated; whereas if it is proposed that, in order to make "more" possible, the capitalist class be stripped of its present power, he flies into a fury of denunciation of—the working class as a bunch of witless, illiterate dolts.

Now why *not* seek to deprive the capitalist class of its anti-social power? After all, this power corrupts too, doesn't it? "All power is evil" but apparently some power is more evil than others. All social systems are exploitive, declares Nomad, but clearly some exploitive systems like the present one, are more tolerable than others (to Nomad), even though he is really "against" all of them ... in principle.

The theory behind this differentiation is presented in this article, in the passage already partly mentioned. In it he undertakes to explain why the bourgeoisie was able to "become fit to rule in their own name" while the working class can never and will never become fit to rule. The italics in the following belong to Nomad:

> ...the working class is not like the other classes which, in the course of history, were struggling against the powers that be, classes like the bourgeoisie, the small property owners, and the intelligentsia, classes whose members were *not* illiterate or near-illiterate. The *workers*, on the other hand, are, like the slaves and serfs of the past, a class which is deprived of the education that could enable it to exert power, and *it cannot get that education just by fighting*.

Well, there is a theory about the nature of social classes through the history of the world. It is all a matter of literacy and education. We have already mentioned the illiteracy of the theory itself, but the crux is this: what Nomad seeks to prove is that *the bourgeoisie is fit to rule,* unlike the working class. He himself, you understand — we must do him justice — is against all social systems; but literacy is literacy, and at least this rotten corrupt ruling class which wields power now is *fit* to do so.

Because it is literate and educated: while we know, of course, that the Vietnamese peasants who are being exterminated by this educated ruling class are illiterate and uneducated. The bourgeoisie in Mississippi is literate and educated, therefore fit to rule, whereas the Negro masses there are even more illiterate and uneducated than the contemptible working-class canaille in the rest of the country. The German bourgeoisie which gave absolute power (which corrupts absolutely, we know from Lord Acton and Nomad) to the Nazis was literate and educated, while the mass German socialist and Communist working-class movements which fought Nazism (very badly) were just a bunch of moronic slobs, unfit to displace their masters. The Democratic and Republican parties are fit to rule, and presumably "understand what is really going on in this complicated world," being educated and all. ...

At any rate, Nomad's theory should explain why it was fit for the bourgeoisie to deprive the feudal aristocracy of power (though it is puzzling to remember that the aristocrats were better educated than the shopkeepers) and to become masters of society themselves: *that* transfer of power was fitting. It is the idea of the working class doing the same that sends him into a tear.

This leads to an unavoidable conclusion, so unavoidable that, seeing it coming on him like an express train on a single track, Nomad asks me not to accuse him of it. Out of sheer amiability, I yield to his polite request and will steadfastly refrain from accusing him of being "a Gompersian defender of the capitalist status quo ." He therefore has nothing to complain about me, but that hardly ends the matter for him. Although I am goodnatured and indulgent and have a weakness for people who declaim against "all social systems present and future," what will he say to some rude and indelicate person who merely points to the stuff he writes? After all, Gomperism came to his own mind because his "slogan of more and more now" is deliberately and literally taken over from no one else than Gompers. *Therefore* he begs not to be accused of being a "Gompersian." He is violently anti-socialist, obviously, and propounds a theory that only the bourgeoisie is fit to rule today (though we must suspect he believes that the intelligentsia may be even more fit to rule). *Therefore* he insists on not being mistaken for a "defender of the capitalist status

179

quo ." What brute could resist his plea?

All of which proves that Nomad is right – that "a distinction is to be made between what a man thinks of himself and says, and what he really is and does ."

* * *

Let us turn our attention to Max Nomad's questionnaire. The following gives terse summaries of the facts behind his questions, or else indicates where the reader can find these facts if he is interested. To make even this much possible. I confine myself to his first and longest set of questions, dealing with Marx and Engels.*

Except for one word on Nomad's Luxemburg section: It is necessary to read J.P. Nettl's new two-volume work on Luxemburg to see how far off the mark is Nomad's silly claim that "she wielded despotic power" in her Polish party. From Nettl's detailed account emerges a clear view of what was Luxemburg's fatal and basic inadequacy as a revolutionary leader, viz. her thoroughgoing *incompetence and even lack of interest* in party-organizational questions--that is, precisely in the field in which her name has been commonly used as a dead-cat to throw at "Leninism ." The organizational "boss" of the Polish SDKPL was Jogiches and only Jogiches, with whom she carried on an ambivalent personal-political relationship which she was never

---

* Except for one word on Nomad's Luxemberg section: It is necessary to read J.P. Nettl's new two-volume work on Luxemberg to see how far off the mark is Nomad's silly claim that "she wielded despotic power" in her Polish party. From Nettl's detailed account emerges a clear view of what was Luxemburg's fatal and basic inadequacy as a revolutionary leader, viz. her thoroughgoing *incompetence and even lack of interest* in party-organizational questions--that is, precisely in the field in which her name has been commonly used as a dead-cat to throw at "Leninism ." The organizational "boss" of the Polish SDKPL was Jogiches and only Jogiches, with whom she carried on an ambivalent personal-political relationship which she was never able to solve. The biggest sin of Jogiches' leadership--and the one which I usually point to, myself, in debunking the use of "Luxemburgism" against Lenin--was the expulsion of the Warsaw-Lodz opposition of 1911. Nomad mentions only the expulsion of Radek. I learn from Nettl for the first time that Luxemburg, in emigration, was an objector to the latter expulsion and at least unhappy about, or reluctant about, Jogiches' policies on the former. But in emigration she did not cease acting as the defense attorney for Jogiches in the international movement. No, Luxemburg was no "paragon" (Nomad's term): she was simply one of the greatest expositors of the meaning of socialism-from-below in terms of the ongoing social struggle. From my viewpoint, the tragedy of her failure as a revolutionary leader lies in her mistaken belief that class struggle-from-below would more or less automatically straighten out the party-organizational problem too (in the first place, in the German social-democracy, in which she never made a move to organize a left-wing political tendency, till it was too late). This was her blind side. While I regret I have no "paragons" to offer, Nomad's two paragraphs on her, in which she is simply portrayed as a despot, are nothing but defamatory.

(1) "Was Marx, during the German Revolution of 1848, a revolutionist 'from below' when ... he avoided any mention of the labor movement in his *Neue Rheinische Zeitung?*" — The brief answer is, yes. His writings in the midst of the revolution itself were brilliant examples of revolutionary appeal for militant mass action from below by the *people.*[2]

As for avoiding "any mention of the labor movement" in the paper, Nomad doesn't have his facts straight. It was only during the first month of the revolution that Marx (a socialist of some 4-5 year's standing who did not have any book on Marxism at his disposal) operated on the theory that the task of socialists in this bourgeois-democratic revolution was to act as the extreme left-wing of the Democracy. The crucial part of the story — ignored by Nomad — is that it was precisely in the course of this school of revolution that Marx learned this line was a mistake. The *NRZ's* policy, tone and contents began to change by fall of 1848: the paper began paying special attention to workers' issues and the class struggle against the bourgeoisie. In fact, it was in the *NRZ* that Marx's *Wage-Labor and Capital* first appeared as a series of leading articles! Suppressed in 1849, the last issue proclaimed in red type that "Their last word will always and everywhere be: 'The emancipation of the working class!'" The following year, Marx even wrote down, specially for Nomad, a criticism of their initial mistake, in the course of the *Address of the Communist League* of March 1850, a brilliant exposition in concentrated form of the meaning of revolution-from-below. (I have hit only the highlights, omitting the story of Marx's personal *participation* in the Cologne workers' movement even in the initial period.)

(2) Nomad's second quiddity refers to Engels' letter of April 1848, whose wording (inaccurately paraphrased by Nomad) reflected exactly the same line of the initial 1848 period that we have just discussed.

(3) Nomad points to the phrase "dictatorship of the proletariat" with a crassness which makes even Professor Henry Mayo sound sophisticated. As it happens, I have written a very long book tracing the history and meaning of Marx's use of what Nomad calls "that unsavory term," including a considerable section on the savory origin of the term itself.[3] It answers Nomad's questions in detail.

(4) The same book also answers most of the issues Nomad raises with respect to Marx's relationship to Blanqui, the "Universal Society of Revolutionary Communists," etc. Once again, Nomad doesn't have his facts straight. His description of the Society is entirely false. As for the one specific point he makes about Marx and Blanqui:

181

The leading modern authorities on Blanqui, Maurice Dommanget and Alan Spitzer, do not agree that the Blanquist movement "consisted almost exclusively of impecunious students, journalists, and other declassés ." To be sure, it was also not a "proletarian party" in the modern sense. But observe the Nomadic method: suppose that Marx, writing from London, was mistaken in accepting the general impression held of the Blanquist movement, whose class composition is even today a hard knot to unravel after decades of research: *What on earth has this to do with whether Marx was or was not a good revolutionist-from-below?*

(5) On the attitude of Marx and Engels toward self-determination, the various East European nationalities, etc.: Nomad gives no sign he understands that the crux of this problem for the two men was the issue of Pan-Slavism as a tool of Russian czarist imperialism, which they regarded as the then prime reactionary force over Europe. Their attack was specifically directed against those nationalities, or Balkanized fragments of nationalities, which were then acting as stooges for pro-czarist Pan-Slavism. Here, too, for readers who are interested in the real and knotty problems behind Nomad's reference. I freely recommend an article of mine which went into the matter in considerable detail.[4] However, Nomad's insinuation is that Marx and Engels' approach, right or wrong, was inspired by racism. This is rubbish. There is no question but that, from our contemporary viewpoint, Marx undervalued national self-determination, but what ruins Nomad's case is that this undervaluation was the result of Marx's *counterposing class conflict from below to the bourgeois-democratic aims of nationalism*, in the cases we are discussing.

(6) Nomad achieves his insinuation by throwing in Marx's reference to "niggers' (yes, niggers) ." I hope he would be less shocked if he also knew that Marx was wont to refer expansively to the fact that his daughter Laura had married a "nigger" — the "nigger" being his close comrade and friend (as well as son-in-law) Paul Lafargue, who was part Negro. What Nomad does not seem to know at all is that, decades before our very modern sensitivity to the use of ethnic labels, the word "nigger" was not necessarily a racist slur in nineteenth-century England (just as Dutchman, for German, is not necessarily so today).[5] Another detail: Marx's intimate nickname was — well, not quite "Nigger" but not far from it for those days: it was "Moor" because of his Negro-like complexion. (That I have to discuss such garbage is, in my opinion, a commentary — but not on Marx.)

(7) Nomad's small talk about the Jews is out of the same barrel. It is

certainly a fact that Marx belonged to a widespread company: that of the numerous Americans who detest Americans above all: of the many Englishmen who despise the English à la Durrell; of the Germans who denigrate all Germans à la Mann; of the anti-Irish Irishmen à la Shaw; and so on through the world. For example, suppose Marx had written this in a letter:

> I loathe Jewry and the Jews. They themselves stare at me in the street though I was born among them. Perhaps they read my hatred for them in my eyes.

Damning; but change the beginning to "Ireland and the Irish" and this is a real quotation from James Joyce's letter to his wife. The number of Irishmen who dislike the Irish is a sociological phenomenon in its own right, but that does not make them enemies of Ireland. Of this company, the Jew who dislikes Jews is one of the best publicized, with a long history, right up to the Zionists who proceeded to persecute Yiddish culture in Israel. That Marx was a Jew who had little liking for Jews is evident from a few remarks in letters.

But Marx's *politics and program* was that of unconditional support for full Jewish social and political emancipation in society, and for the integration of Jews into the larger society. Proudhon, on the contrary, advocated a pure-and-simple Hitlerite extermination of the Jews. Yet Nomad makes an amalgam of the two: what's the difference? This is a defamation. One, a Jew who dislikes Jews, fights all his life *for* equal rights for the Jews; the other advocates a *program* of government persecution of Jews in mass pogroms as well as physical extermination—and Nomad's pen equates the two, thereby graduating from mere washroom gossip to vile slander.

The innocent reader should know, by the way, that Marx's letters are full of deplorably sweeping national cusswords: not only the "lazy Mexicans" but "the lousy Yankees"; the French are usually *crapauds*, the Germans are *Straubinger*, the English—well, in short, no one escapes the cutting edge. I have no objection whatsoever if anyone wants to denounce Marx's cantankerousness—especially anyone who is himself sweet and amiable—but he should know how very general Marx's was. Besides, we were supposed to be discussing socialism-from-below.

(8) Next comes Nomad's challenge regarding the marginal notes which Marx inscribed in his copy of Bakunin's *Statism and Anarchy*. I devote the

following points to show, first, how again Nomad cannot even get the facts straight, and second, to exhibit the Nomadic method in action.

(a) Nomad gives the impression that Marx's "refutation" consisted of the remark "reverie." In fact, Marx's marginal notes comprised 15 or 16 passages, some of them quite long and interesting, plus shorter interjections.[6]

(b) The particular interjection which Nomad quotes (it read "Quelle reverie!") did *not* refer to the passage he mentions but rather to Bakunin's silly remark about "government by scientists" as the Marxist aim. Alongside the passage Nomad *is* talking about, Marx wrote a separate paragraph, and some of his other notes bore on it as well. These I have discussed in the above-mentioned book on "Marx and the Dictatorship of the Proletariat ."

(c) What Nomad actually asks is, "Did Marx attempt to refute .. ." When Marx scribbled these notes in the book margin for his own eyes, he did not know that Nomad would expect him to set down a definitive refutation. But Marx and Engels wrote a number of quite public pieces on Bakunin and anarchism; it is difficult to understand why Nomad refers only to these marginal scribbles, interesting as they are, and expects the refutation there.

(d) How does one "refute" a "prophetic prediction "?

(e) Nomad writes that "Bakunin's 'invisible dictatorship' would have amounted to the same thing" as Marx's — *would have*, he says. But as Nomad well knows, Bakunin consciously *advocated, planned, and intended* to establish a personal dictatorship by a secret elite over his "anarchist" revolution. This Nomad equates with a "prophetic prediction" that a government which is planned and intended to be a workers' democracy would *turn out* to be something else in spite of the well-intentioned aims. We know, of course, that the Iron Law requires this prophetic prediction about everyone, including Nomad; but does this really mean that a man who proposes the building of a socialist democracy is to be thrown in the same bag with a man who deliberately plots a personal dictatorship? "Beside the point," writes Nomad ...

(9) Then there's Engels and the *Jungen*. If Nomad's question means anything at all, it implies (but does not say) that Engels' attack on the *Jungen* faction was due to their "radical opposition ... to the official leadership of the German S.D. party ." This implication is a complete falsification. Engels was himself already worried by the trends in the party and soon (to quote a letter of his) he "found an opportunity to let fly at the conciliatory opportunism of the *Vorwärts* [party organ] and at the *frisch-fromm-frohlich-freie* 'growth' of the

184

filthy old mess 'into socialist society.'"

In fact, the *Jungen* tried to attach their wagon to Engels' already known concern, and to associate Engels' name with their politics. For this very reason (exactly contrary to Nomad's implication) Engels had to publicly dissociate himself, and did so. The *Jungen*, while indubitably reacting against the opportunist trends in the party, mingled an amorphous stew of anti-parliamentarism, pro-anarchism, sectarianism, monarchism, elitism, and plain confusion, without even a positive political program of their own to leaven the lot; and, incidentally, they did *not* represent a criticism from the point of view of socialism-from-below.[7]

(10) Nomad asks about the programmatic point in the *Communist Manifesto* about "centralizing all means of production in the hands of the state" — a statement which represented accurately the 1848 orthodoxy of the revolutionary-Jacobin elements in the Communist League for which Marx and Engels wrote the Manifesto. I'm afraid Nomad has put his foot into it again. He might have been more careful if he had asked himself why Marx never again repeated this formulation in the ensuing 35 years till his death. We know why, because Marx referred back to this very section of the Manifesto when he wrote the introduction to the new edition of 1872, *explaining that it was obsolete.* Why? Because —

> One thing especially was proved by the [Paris] Commune, viz, that "the working class cannot simply lay hold of the ready-made state machinery, and wield it for its own purposes ."

Thus we not only know how Marx's view of the state changed and developed, but Marx even published a prominent special warning to Max Nomad not to quote precisely the passage from the Manifesto that Nomad insists on quoting. What more could the man do?

This brings me to the end of the first section of Nomad's questionnaire, with some loose ends left but no space. The whole thing makes me think of the Rummagers League, this being the name adopted in 1922 by a splitoff from the Communist Party. They meant their name seriously, as marking their aim to "rummage the field of history and science" in order to develop the proletarian intellect. Rummaging has also been Nomad's literary vocation, but as we see, it has its limitations.

Finally, let me propose a deal with Nomad. I am more than willing to recognized one theory of inevitability—that it is an historically inevitable tendency that men will continue to fight for more and more control, no matter what new social system is won. That even under an advanced socialist democracy, at least into an indefinite future, the social struggle of the people will have to continue, and *will* continue, even if on a new level. That there will be centers of privilege to be conquered and power to be socialized, even though my crystal ball does not tell me just where the lines of struggle will be drawn. And Nomad can call the new enemy "the masters" if he wishes.

In return, all I ask of Nomad is that he stop devoting his energies to telling today's fighters for a new society nothing but "*You can't win ... you can't win ..*."

Yet, in that crystal ball—looking forward to a time when the agenda is, perhaps, the abolition of the last remnants of state compulsion—I seem to see Nomad still on the scene, repeating, "You can't win ... you can't win .. ."

I guess it's inevitable.

New Politics 1966

Chapter X:
In Defense of the "New Radicals"

There have been countless articles on the "new-radicals" and the "new-left," most of which have this in common: they do not explain whom they are talking about. It is the tale of the blind man and the elephant. The new-left is a much more shapeless phenomenon than an elephant, and the gropers come up with a wider variety of reports than the blind men.

Let's see what we are all talking about.

First: it is generally agreed that these new-radicals are to be found among student elements primarily, either on campus or in movements deriving from the campus. In good part, though not entirely, they have arisen where a line representing student movement (not *the* student movement: just student movement) intersects the line representing civil-rights movement.

Secondly: there are no new-left organizations; there are only organizations or movements in which the new-radicals form an important or even predominant tendency and affect the tone or "style" of what is done. It is misleading to speak of Students for a Democratic Society as a new-left organization; it is more heterogeneous than that; but there is no doubt that the tendency is strong in SDS. It may be that the Student Nonviolent Coordinating Committee *in the South* is a more nearly new-leftist organization--I don't know--but SNCC should not be automatically equated with the various "Friends of SNCC" groups in other parts of the country. Then there are local groups, of which the Free Speech Movement at Berkeley is the best-known example. The new-radical tendency did indeed constitute the dominant and tone-setting ingredient in the FSM, but it cannot simply be equated with the FSM. Then there are such groups as the Northern Student Movement and the Southern Student Organizing Committee, outgrowths from the impulsions given by SNCC-cum-SDS.

But thirdly: this new-radical tendency among student activists does not exist only within organizations; it also precedes organization. This was certainly true of the Berkeley FSM. As for SDS: it was originally set up as an arm of the hoary social-democratic League for Industrial Democracy, which is about as far from the new-radical style as one can get; yet it served as a convenient framework into which poured, or seeped, the new elements which were being produced at the crossroads of the student and civil-rights movements.

The new-radical weaves through these organizations and movements like the chocolate marbling in a pound-cake, intertwined irregularly with other things, sometimes mixed into shades, and forming a variable proportion of the mixture in different slices.

The rest of the pound-cake usually has two other ingredients of varying prominence. One is the pseudo-radical type I have called (in the book on Berkeley) the disaffiliates--by others called the Hippie Left--who reject society *tout court,* as well as politics. Berkeley was treated to a costumed charade on the meaning of this type in a strange interlude at its Vietnam Day Rally on October 15, when, in the course of serious political attacks on U.S. foreign policy, the novelist Ken Keasy came on, in army garb with helmet, to deride the previous speakers for discussing the Vietnam war politically and to show how it should be done. His contribution consisted essentially of repeating "Fuck it" with great emphasis, in-between playing the harmonica. The force of this prescription is that it applies both to the Vietnam war and its opponents, both to strikebreakers and to strikers, to political reactionaries and political radicals--in fact, to everybody except the disaffiliates. When this clot of *je-m'en-fichisme* organizes, it is as likely to look like Hell's Angels as like the Free Sex and Pot League.

The other ingredient, of course, is "old-leftism." This is a new radical term which means "anybody else." It is characteristic that it lumps together, as if in one political category, such disparate currents as socialists, Communists, six varieties of Stalinists and neo-stalinists, democratic socialists and reformists, revolutionary socialists and leftwingers, even ADA liberals and reform-Democrats. Just as some articles on the new-left have indiscriminately discussed the disaffiliates as if they were new-radicals (some even as *the* new-radicals), so also other articles have, with straight face, discussed (say) the unreconstructed Stalinists of the Progressive Labor group as if they were new-radicals too. Political humor can go no further. Or: a "New Left School" is set up in Los Angeles, and lo, a class on Marxism is given by Dorothy Healy, who has been the Communist Party leader in Southern California so long that sheep were still grazing in flocks on the Baldwin Hills after she had lived through six faction fights.

I do not mean to insist on purely terminological questions. Anyone who wants to use new-radical to refer to these types has a democratic right to do so; but I do not know how sense can be made that way. At any rate, in what follows, I try to define the new-radical in a more usable way.

2

These are bearers of an amorphous kind of radicalism, who start from the feeling that there is "something wrong," basically wrong, with the whole warp and woof of American society, and want to "do something about it." They reject

188

liberalism as too thoroughly integrated with the Establishment; there is "something wrong" with it, too. They are primarily activists, who want to concentrate on concrete issues ("issue politics") and who are more certain about what they are "anti" than what they are for. They think of their views as "moral choices"; their emphasis on the "moral" approach has the function of filling the vacuum left by the absence of systematic ideas. They are, above all, non-ideological radicals, that is, uncommitted to any system of ideas about the transformation of society; not only uncommitted but with a more or less strong aversion to committing themselves even when they admit the need.

For another slant on this frame of mind, consider one of the few examples I have seen of an attempt by a non-ideological radical to set down a kind of ideology about non-ideological radicalism. This courageous, if not foolhardy, effort was made by a leading FSM activist, Michael Rossman, in a Berkeley magazine. "The trademark of the new radicals," he writes, "is a primitive, moral ideology. Their activity is aimed at issues, not at political or economic goals. And the issues are moral issues: peace, Civil Rights, capital punishment." The protests do not have an ideological base, he says, "But always, if one listens, one hears the simple, naive, and stubborn cry that distinguishes the new radicals: 'This is *wrong*, it must stop!'" (*Occident*, Fall 1964-65.)

There it is, the words "primitive" and "naive," written not derogatorily but in praise. There is the *cri de coeur*, which performs the same function as stamping the foot vigorously. There is the reduction of peace, etc. to a moral issue *only*.

Behind the cry "This is *wrong!*" is an ideological vacuum; for as soon as you try to examine why it is wrong, or how you know this is wrong but not that, and above all how you choose among the various things to do without making it right, you get into "ideology," that is, more general ideas about social action and program. And then at bottom you have only "old" ideological tracks to follow to the left, because the new-radicals have not developed any new ones and do not want to.

Politics abhors an ideological vacuum. The new-radical knows, just *knows*, that racial discrimination is wrong because he has already absorbed and internalized this consensus-idea from his milieu. Just as people who "don't believe in theories" merely mean that they accept the current theories of the status quo without examination and uncritically, so also the new-radical ideological vacuum is inevitably filled with an unexamined content.

This turning of a blind eye to the need of thinking through one's ideas about social action and program, however, is not simply a defect to be decried, though I am willing to decry it. That is the easiest thing to do about it. The harder thing is to understand why it has nevertheless been a necessary link in the road to social activism for a whole stratum of youth.

It has gotten them over the "ideological hang-up." And what was that? As example, let us take a not uncommon case, that of the boy or girl growing up with parents who were among the two million or more who passed through the Communist movement or its periphery in the last decades. We are talking of those who passed through and out, either disillusioned with its prospects in this country, or indeed merely clubbed into apathy and withdrawal by the anti-Communist witchhunt, but who still retained their self-identification with "progressive" issues. Growing up in this household means absorbing indiscriminately references to Russia and to desegregation, to the Party and the unions, to the "socialist world" and to social justice for the poor—a package-deal of internalized attitudes which demands to be sorted out later.

Now then, does one have to wait to think one's way clearly through this ideological maze before being able to *act* on anything? Do you have to be clear about Russia, the Party and the "socialist world" (and who is?) before you can "do something" about desegregation or social justice or the poor? This is the "ideological hang-up." Why can't you just cut through all the bramble and say: "I don't know about all that ideology jazz, but *this* [pointing] is wrong, it must stop "?

For this you need especially an issue that can be adequately expounded by pointing, on the basis of a given internalization; and for this generation the civil-rights struggle of the Negro is such an issue. You don't need much of an ideology to feel deeply about it. "Something can be done about it" immediately, without any long-term program or perspective, and even without organization by individual action. Its solution can be cut up into innumerable small "solutions," indefinitely divisible down to getting a job for one Negro. So well fitted is this issue to "a primitive, moral ideology" that the Rossman article even admitted:

> Civil Rights forms the main thread of new radical activity. ... So
> far new radical activity has had no effect on other issues
> (perhaps it can't?), and the new radicals keep turning to the

190

Civil Rights issue for reassurance. Indeed, this is the only issue on which new radical activity has had a measurably positive effect.

This is an exaggeration, to be sure, but it highlights why so much of the new-radical current arises where the civil-rights storm hits student shores.

3

If these "primitive" and "naive" non-ideological radicals were really as devoid of ideas (ideology) as they often think they are, they would not be a distinct current, even an amorphous one. They like to call their differentness a matter of "style"--a word which is Very New-Left because it suggests without denoting: a literary style more often associated with poetry than politics. But as the attack on the new-radicals from the liberal/social-democratic right has intensified, the ideological crux of this new-leftism has been further illuminated. The new-radicals may refuse to concern themselves with ideology, but ideology does not fail to concern itself with them.

In the last two pages of my book *Berkeley: The New Student Revolt*, I argued that

> The central core of the working ideology of the typical radical activists is not defined by any one issue, but consists of a choice between two alternative modes of operation: *permeation* or *left opposition*. The former seeks to adapt to the ruling powers and infiltrate their centers of influence with the aim of (some day) getting to the very levers of decision-making--becoming a part of the Establishment in order to manipulate the reins to the left. The latter wish to stand outside the Establishment as an open opposition, achieving even short-term changes by the pressure of a bold alternative, while seeking roads to fundamental transformations.

The new-radicals choose between these two "styles," and what is characteristic is that they choose the path of anti-Establishmentarian left opposition. This is the thread that runs through the tendency as a whole. Its defenders and attackers range themselves in battle lines drawn by this pattern, whatever else they prefer to talk about.

The clash between these two political approaches has come to a head most sharply in SDS, for two reasons. First, SDS had from the beginning its own permeationist wing, led by Steve Max, Doug Ireland, and Jim Williams. In the 1964 elections this wing was given its head as leaders of the SDS's Political Education Project (PEP), on the basis of a statement, "SDS and the 1964 Elections," which was clearly "coalitionist." (In current jargon, coalitionism--or "realignment" — means the orientation toward subordinating the independent action of civil-rights or other movements to the interest of strengthening the "liberal-labor coalition" which is supporting the Johnson Consensus, and therefore orienting toward the Democratic Party as the decisive political channel for reform or progress.)

The statement, in a final section headed "Realignment," took position as follows, with a prediction which it is cruel to quote today:

> A much heralded political realignment is now taking place. We welcome it, for it means that the Democratic Party will no longer bargain with racism to elect the President, and racists will be removed from their leadership of the Congress. ... This new politics ... will make the Democratic party more consistently the liberal party of the nation.

The statement looked to the credentials challenge which the Mississippi Freedom Democratic Party was going to present at the Atlantic City party convention, and definitely chose the "realignment school" as against "the third-party school." During the elections, SDS sold buttons labeled "Part of the Way with LBJ," symptomatic of its halfway-house hunting.

Secondly, SDS's parent League for Industrial Democracy, long intellectually moribund and organizationally stagnant, has been taken over lately by a new team of relatively youthful ideologists of coalitionism and permeation, imported from the right wing of the Socialist Party, led by Michael Harrington with Tom Kahn as first lieutenant. This new LID leadership has been engaged in a gradual squeeze on the SDS.

It was not only the student arm that was at stake for the Harrington operation, which has a broader objective. It is the latest in a series of attempts over the decades to create a social-democratic wing of Establishment liberalism with a "Fabian" perspective, inoffensively socialistic in tendency and impeccably respectable in style—the "court socialist" in the palace of power. Such is the vision: so far all these attempts have come to nothing. Perhaps the last serious effort was Norman Thomas's Union for Democratic Socialism, which came into existence after the pro-Stevensonites in the Socialist Party failed to get the party to go madly for Adlai. The present effort spearheaded by Harrington also stems from the coalitionist wing of the SP but its strategy is to use the existing shell of the LID rather than set up a new name and structure. (Interestingly enough, the strategy requires these "old-leftists" to assume a non-ideological facade of their own.)

For these two reasons—the pressure of its coalitionist wing inside and the pressure of the LID—the SDS has not been able to escape a confrontation with the problem of permeationism in general and coalitionism in particular. (I am viewing coalitionism as a particular aspect of permeationism, its manifestation in the field of domestic political action.) SDS therefore had to go through what, in a radical sect, would have been frankly posed as a faction fight; but taking place in a non-ideological framework it was nothing as clear as that.

At the SDS founding convention in June, 1962, the programmatic statement ("Port Huron Statement") was clearly coalitionist in tendency, though the tendency was not flaunted. Its permeationist assumptions showed up most clearly in the section on the peace movement, as here:

> As long as the debates of the peace movement form *only a protest*, rather than an oppositionist viewpoint *within the centers of serious decision-making*, then it is neither a movement of democratic relevance, nor is it likely to have any effectiveness except in educating more outsiders to the issue. [Emphasis added.]

Of a piece is the remark that among the reasons for the peace movement's ineffectiveness is this: "that the 'peace movement' has operated almost exclusively through peripheral institutions—almost never through mainstream institutions ."

In contrast are the conclusions of the speech on "The University and the Cold War" given at the SDS conference in December, 1962 by President Paul Potter. Grappling with the same question, he points tentatively in the opposite direction:

...we must forsake the current adjustment model and begin to search for a revolutionary model which is dynamic enough to extricate us from the continually narrowing concentric circles which define the limits of change within the established political power structure. ... The Southern Student Movement in employing non-violent direct action which works outside and frequently against established channels is working on a revolutionary model.

...throughout the country students are, in small groups to be sure, beginning to look to their own resources in attempts to redefine the issues of our time... These are an interesting strain of rebels... they have chosen at least for the time being, in an important way to stand outside the organized system. They have chosen to be effective but they have shown the courage to define for themselves what is effective. But there is a grim analogue here. For in daring to be effective, in attempting to develop our own priorities independent of established priorities, in pressing to build our own institutions independent of existing institutions, we dare also to be ineffective. We risk our small influence on the existing structure in order to stand apart from it and build a new one, recognizing full well that basic changes may be impossible. It is on this point that American liberals and radicals have historically foundered—the only difference today is that civilization promises to founder with us.

A year later the SDS convention adopted a new programmatic statement, "America and the New Era," which specifically repudiated the "politics of adjustment" and dropped all "realignment" talk; in several places it even hinted at the desirability of third-party political action as against support of the New Frontier and the Democratic Party. It also included a clear statement of rejection of the permeationist approach:

...it is becoming evident that the hope for real reform lies not in alliances with established power, but with re-creation of a popular left opposition—an opposition that expresses anger when it is called for, not mild disagreement.

Over a year later, an SDS leader, in the course of *deploring* the intensity of the debate, summarized the "current infighting" between the majority and minority wings of the organization in this way:

> The biggest concern appears to be the SDS relationship to the so-called Liberal Establishment — at least it is over this that the most emotional heat and moral fervor is being generated. At one extreme are those who argue that liberalism now serves as an appendage of the corporate system, attempting to co-opt potentially radical and democratic constituencies through token programs and manipulation and stifle political conflict and real social change. This position advocates organization independent of the Establishment and primarily hostile to it, or at least engaging people in confrontation with institutions and agencies of liberalism. At the other extreme are those who seem to believe that expansion of liberalism's political base would be a positive value, that this would hasten the passage of needed social reforms, and expand the power of objectively progressive forces such as labor, Negroes, urban workers, and middle-class; consequently the job of radicals is to help defeat the enemies of liberalism (mainly on the right but also on the left) and to help enrich and radicalize its program by working within liberal coalitions. ...the anti-establishment people are primarily motivated by a profound identification with the needs of the disenfranchised and by a vision of democratic community as concretely as possible; the establishment-oriented people seem primarily moved by repugnance of the rabid right and by the possibility that radicals can win positions of respect and voice rather than vilification in this society. [Dick Flacks, in *SDS Discussion Bulletin* dated, Spring, 1964.]

To try "to capture the positions of power within existing political structures without either openly challenging their precepts or honestly involving their participants," wrote President Potter in the October 1964 Bulletin, is "both cynical and manipulative ." ("President's Report: Which Way SDS?")

Undoubtedly the experience of the civil-rights movement was of the greatest importance in pointing SDS thinking in this direction; and the tendency was hardened by Johnson's escalation of the Vietnam war. The expectation of a "realigned" Democratic Party with a liberal "new politics" by this time made embarrassing reading for all but the most doctrinaire coalitionists. The widening of the SDS's break with the Johnson Consensus and its coalition came particularly with two events: the April March on Washington against the "dirty war" in Vietnam; and the capitulation of the coalitionists on the Mississippi Free Democratic Party challenge to the Democratic Party convention in Atlantic City.

The latter issue is of special interest in our context because it brought to a head, in concrete form, the meaning of the general formulations about left-oppositionism versus permeationism. Nat Hentoff is quite right in asserting that the MFDP's rejection of the proposed compromise (a compromise which quashed MFDP's claims and gave it instead some token consolation prizes) "will be seen in retrospect to have been one of the watersheds of the new radicalism ." It was a watershed in the ideological clarification of the "new radicals" because it forced them to make a basic choice which ideological considerations alone would never have pushed them into.

The nature of the choice can be examined via the uncharacteristically obtuse rejoinder made by Harrington to Hentoff (*Partisan Review*, Summer 1965). If the MFDP had flatly stayed away from the Democratic party convention and even called on people to leave that party and join "in independent political action against *both* major parties," says Harrington, then this "would have been a defensible tactic" though mistaken. But: "When the Mississippi militants decided to go inside the convention, their strategy was no longer one of protest; it became political ... once the decision was made to organize as a *Democratic* party which would support the convention's candidate, if only to get a hearing the Movement had to ally with labor, liberal, and reform forces. Thus, the basic question was: how far would the Movement be able to move its meliorist allies ."

For Harrington there was an irrevocable and irreversible decision to work inside the walls of the Democratic Party. But such decisions are not irreversible. It is quite possible that "the Mississippi militants" set out to "go inside the convention" without examining in advance the full meaning of all possible outcomes, in the fashion which Harrington's political training had happily accustomed him. They may even have set out bravely to reform the Democratic Party, as have so many others. But the reality which confronted them shoved them brutally against the following realization: to continue to

196

pursue this inner-party course effectively meant in practice to *subordinate* their independent militancy to the party's power structure, as mediated through the labor-liberal-reform coalition which functioned as the antechamber to the Hearing Room.   Harrington is apparently arguing that the "Mississippi militants" should have thought it all through to the bitter end, in advance, and then chosen one path or the other from the beginning.   This is an extraordinarily ultimatistic approach to the self-clarification of a real movement. It is on the contrary characteristic of a grass-roots movement that it *learns* its political theses not by writing them but by acting them out, sometimes with costly experiences.

The basic question was not "how far would the Movement be able to move its meliorist allies" from *within* a coalition with these allies — a coalition in which the Movement as a minority, was a tamed captive — but rather, how best to move these "allies" and the whole Establishment political apparatus from a position of leverage *outside* the whole structure — as a left opposition to it; as a constant threat to it, rather than a prisoner of it. I am not now arguing this point but only pointing to the nature of the alternative, which does not clearly exist for Harrington.

What the MFDP compromise issue did for the "new radicals," then, was to illuminate the nature of the big choice in political approach, permeationism versus left opposition. This is what makes the question of "for or against the MFDP compromise" a litmus-paper test of radical types. The "new radical" type can effectively be defined as one which, *on a non-ideological basis*, rejects the permeationist approach to the power structure, and moves in the direction of *left opposition to it from below.*

4

In spite of the quotations I have given from SDS literature, which show a consciousness of the Great Divide in politics, I do not claim that what I have described is the *conscious* special ideology of the non-ideological radicals. I should be glad to discover that it is so more rather than less; but I am presently arguing only that it is the underlying content of the new-radicals' tendency, and also the crux of the attacks that have been made upon it by its social-democratic critics.

The two most virulent attacks have come from emplacements close to the LID leadership, both notable for two things: their open display of ill temper, and their explicit exhibition of coalitionism as the essential political objection to the new-radicals. In their own way, therefore, they confirm the picture.

One was by Tom Kahn, the new administrative secretary of the LID and, at 26, the "youth movement" of the Harrington team. His article, "Pop Journalism and Myths of the 'New' Left," was carried by *New America*, formally the organ of the Socialist Party but in practice edited as the faction bulletin of its coalitionist right wing. It is an explicit broadside against the SDS, in a tone of bitterness which, from the pen of an official of the parent organization writing in a presumably "outside" journal, would have been mystifying except as prefiguring the break between the two organizations which actually came a few months later. In the article Kahn forthrightly states the coalitionist credo. The supporters of the "coalition strategy," he writes, see this strategy:

> in the context of hastening the tendency toward fundamental
> political realignment in America. In this process, they believe,
> the Democratic Party can be transformed from an amalgam of
> New Dealers and Slave Dealers into the political instrument of
> the labor, civil rights and peace movements – and of the poor.

Surely, a Democratic Party which actually became the "political instrument" (no less) of the peace movement and the "poor" as well as of labor and the civil rights militants would put even the European socialists in the shade; and Kahn lambastes the new-radicals in the name of this dream, which has an excellent chance of coming true if Mary Poppins joins the LID.

The other article was a long blast in *Dissent* (Summer 1965) by its editor, Irving Howe. (This magazine is discussing with the LID the possibility of becoming its organ; outcome uncertain at this writing.)

Howe straightforwardly takes his stand against the new-radicals on the side of "those who look forward to creating a loose coalition of Negro, labor, liberal and church groups in order to stretch the limits of the welfare state ." The other side is described as "those who , in effect, want to 'go it alone', refusing to have anything to do with 'the Establishment,' ... a strategy of lonely assault, which must necessarily lead to shock tactics and desperation," and which "inexorably" leaves no alternative but "the separatism of the Muslims ."

There is no intelligible reason given for this theory of "inexorableness." The alternative of "independent political action against *both* major parties," which had seemed even to Harrington as "defensible" if mistaken, does not exist in Howe's inexorable world. This cartoon-version of the debate does not require discussion but it leaves no question about what Howe is exercised over.

Some other items in Howe's dossier against the new-radicals add to the effect. They are too hostile toward liberalism: for them "liberalism means Clark Kerr, not John Dewey; Max Lerner, not John Stuart Mill; Pat Brown, not George Norris ." Since the one quality which his three Good Liberals have in common is that they are dead, Howe is letting Kerr, Lerner, and Brown stand for *contemporary* liberalism ... and what more has to be proved?*

Is he really deploring overhostility to liberalism purely as a matter of historical justice? It is hard to believe so, since the coalition which he advocates to save America today is with living liberals (not one of whom he sees fit to name for the edification of the new-radicals), not with the ones that are Good and Dead.

The new-radicals, Howe complains, have "an unconsidered enmity toward something vaguely called the Establishment ." He heavily derides the use of this term, and finds no definite meaning in it. But ironically, "Establishment" is one of the few political terms which has been *formally* defined in new-left literature — specifically in the SDS's "America and the New Era ." The definition begins: "By the 'Establishment' we mean those men who have direct influence over the formulation of national domestic and foreign policies," and continues with considerable specificity. Others, including myself, would broaden or tighten up the description; but essentially it is a term pointing in the direction of whatever one thinks is the center or centers of socio-political power in this system plus the necessary agents, mouthpieces and hangers-on. Aversion to this term stems form the same source as the standard objections to the term capitalism: *it marks tenderness about the thing, not distaste for the terminology*. The crux of Howe's concern is given away in his first phrase: the *enmity* of the new-radicals to this Establishment. This is their sin.

The new-radicals, Howe writes, have "an equally unreflective belief in 'the decline of the West,'" unaware that this belief is "frequently" held by reactionaries. Again he finds little meaning in the term. Spengler aside, it is curious that he does not remind himself that some people, of all persuasions,

---

* Besides, two out or three of Howe's good and dead liberals became pro-socialist in the end. But two out of three of the living ones started by being pro-socialist and ended up as — well, examples for Howe. See?

commonly use "the West" to mean the capitalist West, in a societal sense rather than geographical. I would not undertake to say whether "the decline of capitalism" has a meaning to Howe, but it is worth considering.

This does not end Howe's dossier, but it is enough to illustrate the tendency of the most considerable effort made to give a sophisticated form to the liberal/social-democratic assault on the new-radicals. What enrages Howe is the new-radicals' far-from-vague enmity against the Establishment, including the Establishment liberals (the living ones), including the lib-lab coalition leaders who are today truckling to the Establishment. From this side too it is confirmed that this is the crux of the new-radical tendency.

The "anti-Establishmentarianism" of the new radicals leads them to a dilemma. It is an implicitly, often explicitly, revolutionary stance, and any movement which set out to implement it consistently and thoroughly would inescapably find itself acting as an extreme-left revolutionary group. At the same time, the new radicals conceive of themselves as being very "broad," quite different from the "narrow," sectarian old-leftists who failed, and as aiming at a mass membership.

This dilemma is one of the most important motors in the train of events besetting the SDS internally and externally. The contradiction is, I imagine, much less severe for SNCC, which *is* operating in a sort of revolutionary situation, that of the Negroes in the South. The contradiction did not have to be faced by the Berkeley FSM simply because it went out of existence; it is indeed behind the fact that the successor organization at Berkeley, called the Free Student Union, has never gotten off the ground. The contradiction does not have to be faced by individual new radicals active here and there, since individual activists do not have to be "broad ." Hence the dilemma has been acted out visibly mainly in SDS, the only dominantly new-radical organization which assumed general tasks analogous to those of a revolutionary party.

There is a financial side to this contradiction which I can only mention in passing, even though it is traditionally true that, with revolutionary groups, finances are usually a thoroughly *political* question. It can be put this way: how long can one finance a sort-of-revolutionary movement out of the purses of the very lib-labs whom one is opposing? A year after the MFDP watershed, the SDS was clearly heading for a break from its foster-parent; and in October a joint announcement formalized the severance of relations with the LID. The official reason given was financial: "the desire of the SDS to engage in action programs which transcend the limits imposed by law on tax-exempt

organizations" such as the LID, and the divorce was represented as "amicable
." The separation, however, will have financial consequences apart from tax-
exemption (and apart from the fact that, before October was up, the
Department of Justice had announced an investigation of "Communists" in
SDS).

The contradiction, however, is essentially political. In effect, the SDS has
been trying to reconcile revolutionism and broadness by being non-ideological
about its revolutionism. This may help to blur what you say, but there is still
the problem of what you do. Do you head for a collision with the social
powers of the Establishment? The significance of the MFDP fight and of the
April March on Washington was that these did in fact finally entail collisions,
and therefore they were milestones on the road that has led the SDS to its
present situation. But until then the SDS leadership was trying to follow a
different course, a collisionless course, in an interesting experiment, which we
have room to discuss here only as it bears on our main subject. In effect, the
SDS's attempted solution to the dilemma was not to move into head-on conflict
with the basic power structure of the system, and not to move back in retreat,
but to strike out at right angles.

This is an important meaning of the activity program which absorbed the
best energies of the SDS for the last couple of years: the organization of
"community unions" in a number of selected urban areas among the poor. The
conception behind it was that the new-radicals would bypass the
Establishment instead of bearding it, go directly to the "grassroots
constituencies" and organize them, and thus create a countervailing power
from below which could be the beginning of new social possibilities. In
practice, this meant that a task force of SDS organizers and volunteer workers
would go into a poor neighborhood, set up a community center, learn the
problems of the "native" population, work out local demands and action
programs with the constituents, and hopefully organize them to fight for these
goals themselves. The constituents were to be "the poor," "the dispossessed,"
the "slum-dwellers ." These categories were conceived to be the human
material out of which the new-left revolution would be forged.

It is no part of this article's agenda to attempt a rounded evaluation of this
program and its conceptions; the subject deserves a more serious post-mortem
than is possible here. I am interested at this point in the light the experiment
throws on the anti-Establishmentarian revolutionism of the new-radicals. I
think the outcome has confirmed that "the poor" are not organizable *as the poor*

in any stable fashion.

As Negroes, as peasants or sharecroppers, as workers, even as unemployed workers, particular groups of poor people have a positive social relationship in common. As the "poor," they have only a lack in common—lack of money—and no social movement can be held together by a no-thing. The organization of workers *qua* workers already implies an elementary social program which imposes itself on the organization even if its leaders have never heard of Marxism, socialism or even trade-unionism; it has its own social logic. But the organization of the poor *qua* poor implies no social program that can hold a movement together; what is implied is being acted out by the Poverty Program. The community in which the slum-dwellers live—the slum—does not provide a framework for socializing resentments and aspirations such as is provided by the integrating life of the factory; it atomizes. The theory was that a social force was going to be forged outside the Establishment, but the reality was the SDS organizers found themselves engaged in "sewer-socialism," Salvation Army-type uplift, missionary work to the benighted, etc.

The ideology of "community unions" is often associated with conscious rejection of another type of grassroots constituency: organized workers. Many of the new-radicals have been thoroughly imbued with the image, fostered by both the academy and Madison Avenue, of the labor movement as one monolithic, undifferentiated Fat-Cat Establishment, of no interest to radicals. They think of organized workers solely in terms of their leadership—i.e., they find themselves thinking just as bureaucratically as the leaders they reject. The concept of grassroots work which exists in the revolutionary socialist tradition—of entering the factories, organized or unorganized, as rank-and-file workers, and organizing and educating inside and outside of the union on a shop basis—is a concept which is entirely alien to the new-radicals.

Moreover, there is a disturbing relationship between two class attitudes which crop up frequently in SDS discussions. On the one hand, SDS is a very middle-class-conscious movement. On the other hand, these self-consciously middle-class elements think of themselves as "going to the people," by which they mean, going to the *unorganized* slum-proles and poor, but not to the organized workers. The analogy—only an analogy—that imposes itself on me is that of Mao Tse-tung's elite party deciding to bypass the city proletariat in favor of going to the peasants—who, precisely in the Marxist view which Mao is supposed to accept, constitute a class historically susceptible to being led *from outside and above* but incapable of effective political self-organization. For

202

the Marxists this was a reason for orienting toward the city proletariat; for the bureaucratic-collectivists, this is a reason for orienting toward that class of the poor who can be ridden most easily. When I read, in one SDS community workers' discussion article, a reference to the "poor" as our "clientele," I experienced the shock of recognition.

Pace: the SDS worries about nothing so much as the dangers of the relationship I have just described; but the new-radicals think the danger is a matter of style and awareness. I am arguing that it is built into the ideology of "organizing the poor ."

The attempt to find a course *outside the Establishment but not in collision with the Establishment* has not been successful. A question-mark is placed over a conception that has become popular among new-radicals and verges on becoming an ideological tenet: the notion of parallel or dual-power institutions as the road to revolutionary social change. According to this idea, you do not have to come into a headlong collision with the existing institutions of the Establishment; you create your own independent dual institution, and build its power up to the point where it can eventually simply supplant the other. (Once again, you do not march against the Establishment, you go off at right angles.) As was always the case with the early 19th century utopian schemes which aimed to create the Dual World on the largest scale, the outcome is and has to be elitist and anti-democratic in practice — as when a self-styled "Congress of Unrepresented People" is conceived of as actually representing the people of the United States.

At this point one is duty-bound to launch into a discussion of "participatory democracy," the SDS's most successful phrase. My difficulty is that I do not have the least idea what it means. I was confused enough when I heard it meant rejection of representative democracy, or else a "consensus" form of meeting (one of the most inherently anti-democratic devices I know, by the way). Things were worse when Staughton Lynd explained in *Dissent* that it means the dual-power institution idea, among other things. When I found out from Sid Lens, in *Liberation*, that "participative democracy" exists under Castro, Nasser, and maybe even Sukarno *more* than in the U.S., and that it does not necessarily entail free elections, I decided to go back to old-fashioned democratic democracy. I mean the "old-leftist" conception of socialist democracy in which the criterion is the degree to which people *participate* personally and unconstrainedly, from the bottom up, in political and social decision-making and in the immediate appointing and firing of decision-makers, through free organizations, assemblies, elections, trade unions, demonstrations and hell-raising.

In sum: in spite of the implicitly revolutionary significance of the new-radicals' anti-Establishmentarianism, they have so far not developed into a genuinely revolutionary tendency — not into a new kind of revolutionary tendency and not into an old one. The movement has been blurred by its unresolved need to maintain bridges to the coalitionist lib-lab wing of "mainstream" politics.* It has been blurred by its effort to avoid a collision course; by its flights into the fantasy world of dual-power institutions. *So far:* the story is not over.

6

The liberal/social-democratic attack on the new-radicals, which is most competently represented by Irving Howe's denunciation, may be powered by the politics of permeation and coalitionism, but it pays more attention to another issue: pro-Communism or anti-anti-Communism.

The middle section of Howe's article, entitled "Ideologues and Desperadoes," would seem, at least at first reading, to describe whom he means by the new-radicals. It presents cogent polemics against the following political types and no others: (1) The "remains of Stalinism," comprising the Communist Party, *National Guardian* supporters, and CP dropouts who still function on behalf of the party's "heritage ." (2) "On the far left ... a scatter of groups," not specified, who still believe in "Marxism-Leninism ." (3) "Authoritarian leftists ... like Isaac Deutscher and Paul Sweezy" who are "the true intellectual progenitors of at least part of the 'new leftism'" (and who are, of course, pro-Soviet or Maoist). (4) Black nationalists from Malcolm X and the Muslims to Leroi Jones, including kamikaze Negro militants resembling "the late 19th century Russian terrorists ." (5) Another category of "white desperadoes" of whom we are told only that one of their "central battlecries" is "alienation," and that "in effect" Howe has "already described this group"

---

* The article by Dick Flacks which we quoted previously puts the same thought honorifically: "the main thrust of the organization [SDS] has been, must and should be toward the organization of grassroots constituencies capable of exercising power independent of the establishment. But it has also been characteristic of the organization that we have been able to maintain this position, implement this strategy, and advocate a radical program while maintaining some relationship of dialogue with establishment-oriented liberal organizations and individuals--i.e., we have wanted to stay relevant to the main politics of the nation and participate in them, even as we engage in radical organization ." Or, in other words, we would like to eat our revolution and have it too.

in the previous points.

Now what is the relation of these political types to the subject of the article, the new-radicals? Are these the new-radicals? or most of them? Howe doesn't *say* so, and it would be risky to accuse him of believing it, since the first three categories are obviously "old-leftist," and black nationalism *à la* Malcolm, Muslims, or Jones is not too common among the new-radicals. Also there are phrases tucked in to the article which, properly interpreted, may mean that it is all about "a segment" of new-leftists — in which case one is never told who represents the body — and there is also a section which says flatly that "The 'new leftists' feel little attachment to Russia. ... ."

No, there is no linkage made between this section and the subject of the article: it is just there. Howe could just as well have similarly included a section on narcotics, pornography, juvenile delinquency, bad modern poetry, anarchosyndicalism, Zen-existentialism, and other ideologies and desperations, as long as he remained equally discreet in relating them to the new-radicals. It reminds me of nothing so much as the sometime method used by Clark Kerr of asserting that there were some Maoists and Castroites in the FSM — an irrefutable fact — and innocently allowing the public to infer that the FSM's complexion was thus described.

With enemies like Howe, do the pro-Communists need any friends — to evoke sympathy from new-leftists?

It is the odor of decayed radicalism which gives its characteristic effluvium to the anti-Communist pitches of men like Howe, Sidney Hook, Tom Kahn, Bob Pickus, et al. Literally since they learned to read, the radical students have been reading and hearing anti-Communist harangues from their elders, from all quarters. They may have discovered the very existence of terms like Communism and anti-Communism only in the midst of the McCarthyite period. They grew up understanding anti-Communism and witchhunting to be synonyms, like other good Americans. Many of them (or most of them) may never even have met an anti-Communist who was not also a witchhunter or an apologist of some sort for the ongoing system. This is the Standard American pattern, and the pattern itself does not change if one puts a minus sign in front of it, instead of the majority's plus sign.

The new-radicals, therefore, first found Communism to be the bogey not only of the reactionaries but also of the Establishment liberals, and finally found anti-Communism to be an overshadowing preoccupation also of a whole generation of decayed radicals, "old-leftists" of a certain type. They thereby

205

acquire a conditioned-reflex response to the phrases of anti-Communism, including all the true ones, since they find these phrases only in association with apologias for peaceful coexistence with the status quo.

Secondly: these new-radicals (I am assuming they are under thirty and were not politically conscious before the beginning of the Cold War) have never known the Communists except as enemies – or rather targets and victims – of the Establishment authorities. In this respect, for example, I am painfully conscious of the enormous gap between my own experience and theirs. Except for the tag-end of the Stalinist "Third Period" on which I came in (1932-34), but certainly from 1935 on, my own generation of revolutionary socialists learned to know the Communists as the worst anti-militant finks in the field. This was during the Popular Front period of the latter '30s when the Communists were busily "holding out the hand of friendship" to the NAM and denouncing Norman Thomas as a sectarian Trotskyite and ultra-left adventurist. At this time the student movement of the '30s was gutted and turned into a pink-tea party. (For the theory and practice of permeation and coalitionism, there is no worked-out course comparable to the writings of Earl Browder; they could be, and maybe are, a textbook for Harrington today.) The Hitler-Stalin Pact interlude, brief as it was, did not change this much since the new-found "militancy" was too transparent after Molotov announced that fascism was "a matter of taste ." Then for the rest of the Second World War, the Communist Party went all-out as a counter-insurgency corps in the labor movement, Negro movement and elsewhere, more vicious than the FBI, and as a witchhunting organization of considerable punitive power in comparison with which the present saurian-minded HUAC is a lollypop. The current identification of Communists with "far left" is nothing but a Cold War cliche.

But this is now history; and the new-radicals are Standard American enough to be indifferent to the historical view, which is inseparable from a theoretical and ideological view. History is the voice of somebody older preaching at them (a new version of the famous Ford aphorism that "History is bunk"). They prefer to make their own mistakes; that is, they prefer to repeat the mistakes of primitive radicals in the past (as they must, since they don't know what they were and don't want to find out) under the impression this course is new.

Then there is another conditioning influence: since 1953 (when our present new-radicals were teen-agers) the Standard American press, punditry and professoriat have made it an article of faith that the Soviet regime is in the process of "liberalizing," in fact converging toward our own Way of Life. If Clark Kerr can write a book with this thesis, it cannot be too monstrous for new-radicals to absorb the same outlook with a somewhat different emphasis.

Still another influence: Since the end of the war and the beginning of the irrepressible wave of national-liberation revolutions all over the world, the Standard American version (this time with a right-wing rather than a liberal cast) has been that these revolutions have mostly been controlled, tainted, or permeated by the Communists. (Where U.S. interests were deeply embroiled, even liberals went for this, as in the case of Guatemala, where social-democratic liberals like Robert Alexander and ex-Stalinist liberals like Max Lerner accepted the "anti-Communist" justification for the American-sponsored overthrow of the Arbenz regime.) As with our other cases, this identification spreads its poison both ways. For the Standard-Americans, this *taints* the liberation revolutions with Communism; for the Standard-Americans-turned-inside-out, it ennobles Communism with the glory of the liberation movements. Where the leadership of national-liberation movements *really* goes Communist or Communist-dominated, as in the case of the Vietcong or Castroism, the issue of Communism is then far overshadowed by the clear proofs of U.S. policy that it is intent on repressing national freedom in the name of anti-Communism, and not on defeating Communism for the sake of national freedom.

For all of these reasons, it is not easy for a *non-ideological* radical to perform the far-from-simple feat of combining enmity to the American Establishment with enmity to the enemy-of-this-enemy. How unreasonable it is to expect that this stance can be facilely taken can be seen by remembering the experience of the Second World War, when, finding themselves allied with the Russian regime, major magazines and newspapers, leading Hollywood dream-mongers and sober politicians glorified Stalin and his happy democracy in terms that would be printed today in the *Worker* only with embarrassment, and in comparison with which some of the queasiest new-left statements are principled documents.

But only in comparison. For all the reasons given here and perhaps some others, there is a very strong tendency among the new-radicals to "cop out" on the question of Communism. This tendency was written down most bluntly—and crudely—in a recent joint statement by Tom Hayden and Staughton Lynd in *Studies on the Left*:

> ...we refuse to be anti-communist. We insist that the term has
> lost all the specific content it once had. Instead it serves as the
> key category of abstract thought which Americans use to justify
> a foreign policy that often is no more sophisticated than rape.
> It also serves as a deterrent to building an open movement for
> change in this country, because organizations that refuse to be
> anti-communist must fight bitterly for funds and allies. Our
> feeling is that the anti-communist organizations, such as the
> trade unions, are far less democratic than the organizations,
> such as SNCC and SDS, which refuse to be anti-communist. We
> have confidence that movements can be built which are too
> strong to be "used ;" the anti-communists do not have that
> confidence.

It would be instructive to analyze these five reasons for anti-anti-
Communism in detail, but we do not have the space for this exercise. Briefly,
what stands out in this statement, *from the viewpoint of new-radicals,* is that it is
extraordinarily immoral and intellectually non-responsive.

Three short years ago, the Port Huron Statement on which SDS was
founded included a section on "Anti-Communism" which vigorously attacked
the role of the "unreasoning anti-communism" which permeates America and
"even many liberals and socialists," "takes on the character of paranoia,"
perverts democracy, etc. Clearly it did not mince words in rejecting this anti-
Communism. At the same time, it found it possible to state its *own* view on
Communism, right in this context:

> As democrats we are in basic opposition to the communist
> system. The Soviet Union, as a system, rests on the total
> suppression of organized opposition, as well as a vision of the
> future in the name of which much human life has been
> sacrificed, and numerous small and large denials of human
> dignity rationalized. The Communist Party has equated falsely
> the "triumph of true socialism" with centralized bureaucracy.
> the Soviet state lacks independent labor organizations and other
> liberties we consider basic. And despite certain reforms, the
> system remains almost totally divorced from the image officially
> promulgated by the Party. Communist parties throughout the

rest of the world are generally undemocratic in internal structure and mode of action. Moreover, in most cases they have subordinated radical programs to requirements of Soviet foreign policy. The communist movement has failed, in every sense, to achieve its stated intentions of leading a worldwide movement for human emancipation.

This passage did not say everything that should be said about Communism nor did it try to, but it was enough for the purpose. It stated why *radicals* had to reject Communism in their own way, for their own reasons, and in the name of their own vision of a better society; that is, why they had to be anti-Communist. Has this statement "lost all the specific content it once had"? Is it the "term" that has lost this content, or is it rather Hayden and Lynd who have lost something? What is now wrong with the *content* of this passage?

When this rejection of Communism appeared in the context of the Port Huron Statement's attack on American anti-Communism, did it serve to justify a foreign policy no more sophisticated than rape? Was SDS less democratic then than it is now because of it?

Hayden and Lynd's field of vision includes only one fact: the use of anti-Communist tirades as a weapon against America's cold-war rival. But in every war and in every pre-war propaganda barrage, the Establishment always tries to pose as the defender of Good and the enemy of Evil; and there usually is an Evil around to serve the purpose. In the First World War, it was Prussian militarism and Kaiserism, which was a reality: did the Haydens and Lynds of 1917 proclaim indignantly that they refused to be anti-militarist because a hypocritical government was using anti-militarism to justify rape? (On the contrary, Gene Debs went to prison for his anti-war activity while proclaiming quite accurately that he was far more hostile to Prussian militarism than Morgan's government ever cold be, and solidarized himself with the revolutionary German enemies of Prussianism like Karl Liebknecht.)

There was a peace movement in America in 1939-40 too, which faced the fact that the government was heading into the Second World War under the slogan of anti-fascism. Should it have announced that it refused to be anti-fascist or take a stand on Hitlerism, on the ground that anti-Nazism had no content other than pro-war propaganda? There was indeed one tendency which did take this line, represented most prominently by the Lindberghs; and Mrs. Lindbergh's book *The Wave of the Future* launched this notorious phrase on its career. It is not true that she was pro-fascist; she merely argued for anti-anti-fascism.

On the other side of the cold war, there are people in Russia who are hostile to their own Establishment, let's say among the students who listen to Yevtushenko's poetry readings. They hear all about capitalism as the whipping boy of their own propagandists. Should they decide that anti-capitalism has "lost all specific content" for *them* because it has been turned into a cuss-word by their own government.

It is an old story: Hayden and Lynd see anti-Communism solely in terms decided by the Establishment; they accept the same frame of reference and put a different sign in front of it. It is the Establishment's ideology they are working with; and isn't this inevitable as long as they eschew a consciously thought-out one of their own? The vacuum *is* going to be filled, one way or the other.

Their anti-anti-Communism is immoral because it asserts indifference to the fate of oppressed peoples in one third of the world. One of the greatest humanistic traditions of the world's radical movements has always been their ready responsiveness to injustice anywhere. American revolutionists eagerly solidarized themselves with Irish revolutionaries and anti-Tsarist conspirators, and in return there were demonstrations in a dozen foreign countries against the execution of Sacco and Vanzetti. Today one of the most remarkable of the arguments heard in some new-radical circles is the one which says that, since we are Americans, we must concern ourselves *only* with what is wrong with America. This is chauvinism turned inside-out. Fortunately, no one really believes in this despicable principle — when it comes to demonstrating against *apartheid* in South Africa, or against suppression of student demonstrations in Franco Spain, etc. (Presumably, however, if the U.S. were at sword's-points with the South African government, the anti-*apartheid* position would lose all of its specific content ...)

The Port Huron Statement also had this remark, in the section on "Anti-Communism":

> It would seem reasonable to expect that in America the basic
> issues of the Cold War should be rationally and fully debated,
> between persons of every opinion ... It would seem, too, that
> there should be a way for a person or an organization to oppose

210

communism *without* contributing to the common fear of associations and public actions. But these things do not happen; in stead there is finger-pointing and comical debate about the most serious of issues.

It is indisputable that rational debate on the basic issues of the Cold War is infrequent in this country, but it should be possible for radicals. Therefore (the Port Huron Statement is saying) this is added reason for the SDS to make its own "conscious, determined, though difficult, efforts in this direction ." Very good; and "there should be a way for a person or an organization to oppose communism *without* contributing" either to the Cold War or the witchhunt.

On one side of the coin is the paranoid view that Communism is a great danger in the U.S. today. Turn it over and on the other side is the Hayden-Lynd position: that to state a principled democratic stand in criticism of Communism, in proper context and proper proportion, is to condone rape.

The only alluring thing about the Hayden-Lynd theory is its convenience. It is useful if one is to coexist happily with the pro-Soviet and pro-Communist elements of various kinds who are to be found in new-radical circles. Since 1962 the SDS has lived in a state of uneasy balance, one component of which was the LID presence. The principles of political mechanics tell us that, once the counterweight of the LID is removed from the scene, there is going to be a swing in the center of equilibrium.

"We have confidence," says Hayden and Lynd, that our movement can be built "too strong to be 'used'" by the Communists. But it is not a matter of either confidence or strength, but of politics. I suspect that the proclaimed confidence is based on the same conception of "conspiratorial Communist infiltration" as forms the theoretical equipment of HUAC or the FBI. (Once again the non-ideological vacuum is filled by the Establishment.) Hayden and Lynd do not want to be "used "? Do they imagine that the devilish Communists — if the SDS were not "too strong" — would have them passing manifestos for a Soviet America or sending greetings to the various Communist fronts — I mean the ones that Hayden and Lynd know to be fronts as well as I — are not doing that either; they are content to swing energetically into all attacks on American policy while remaining stonily silent about the other side. They are, so to speak, masquerading as anti-anti-Communists. There is no great point to be made simply by "exposing" them. It is the *politics* of the position — whether genuine or fake — which has to be dealt with. Except from the conspiracy-theory slant of the HUAC-FBI mind, there is no great difference between the crypto-Communist who makes like a non-ideological radical, and the non-ideological radical who has developed his own rationale for behaving like a crypto-Communist. *Politics is primary.*

The general pattern of what is happening can be expressed in the following schema; *There is a break in the continuity of the radical tradition; the socialist movements waste away; there is no handing on of the torch. But that does not mean the end of the impulsion to revolutionary change. After the interval, radicalism sends its shoots up again, from the seed. It is a new, green, inexperienced, unknowledgeable, immature, even bumbling, and exists in a welter of question-marks and confusion. In other words, it is a new beginning. Some shoots spring up and die out; others live and flourish and give rise to the new movement at last. But the new movement is not a reduplication of the one that existed before the hiatus: it works out new forms, new phrases, new activities, even maybe new theories, which eventually merge with the old ones and change them and are changed. ...*

All this has happened before, dozens of times. A new-radicalism is one of the oldest phenomena in the history of the movement. In England there were the discontinuities that followed the growth of British reaction to the French Revolution, that followed the decline of Chartism, and the defeat of the 1848 revolutions on the Continent. In France there was the political desert that followed the bloody suppression of the Paris Commune. In America there was notably the sharp break in the fortunes of socialism made by the First World War and its aftermath.

But like everything else that has happened before, it always happens in a new way. It is far from true that the new-radicalisms always represented progress in the movement; more typically, they crystallized at some distance back, and painfully made their way to levels previously attained, albeit in new ways. All the "old-leftism" around now is the end-result, in the sere and yellow leaf, of a series of "new radicalisms ."

But there is no other way. Rosa Luxemburg once said that it is the fate of all revolutionary efforts to fail—except the last. (It seems almost tautological when you speak of what is involved.) In the same sense, it is inevitable that all generations of radicals will fail—except the last, of course, which is not yet. The pole-vaulter either clears the bar or he fails; his last successful vault is built on nothing but the failures. So there can be no doubt that "my generation" of radicals failed—like all the others. That in itself is not at all enlightening. The usefulness of the experience comes only when it is studied, so the *new* ideas are generated.

The present new-radicalism is extreme in its self-inflicted cut-off from the past, from the lessons of experience, from its own history. It suffers from a morbid fear of repeating the old. This is a gangrenous weakness—not because the old holds the Answers, but because it is only in a study and critique of the old that fruitful *new* ways can eventually be found.

The new-radicals have in their mind's-eye an image of the "old-leftist" as a graybearded fuddyduddy sternly rebuking them for departing from the hallowed ways of their ancestors. These caricatures do actually exist in life, and they truly deserve no attention. Any old radical who thinks that an American socialist movement can be reborn simply by resolutely picking up where he came in, by going back to business at the old stand, is dreaming senile dreams. The problem is *how* to work out the new.

The question-mark over the current crop of new-radicals is not whether or not they have the Answers now—they haven't, and they know it; it is not whether they now have the capacity to work out the new answers—they haven't yet, and I don't think they have any illusions about this. The question-mark is whether the course they are on is fitting them to do this job, or disabling them. That is why it is crucial that, after getting over the Ideological Hang-up, they now get over the Non-Ideological Hang-up, which has been sterilizing them. It would be the end of the road if, after rejecting the enervating coalitionism of the liberal/social-democrats, they get hung up on the musty neo-stalinism of the various theoreticians of "totalitarian socialism ."

The failure of the older generation of radicals is epitomized in that it offers the new-radicals only these two popular models, viz. the apologists for Western capitalism, or the apologists for the new bureaucratic-collectivist Establishments. In short, it offers only one or the other side of the Cold War, which enmeshes the varieties of radicalism like everything else. I am far from predicting that this present wave of new-radicals will be able to unravel its way out of this entrapment. But the help they need from older radicals is not simply a scolding but a demonstration of a revolutionary democratic politics—one which is a revolutionary alternative to the apologists for the one camp and a democratic alternative to the apologists for the other.

New Politics 1964

213

Chapter XI:
Berkeley: the Student Revolt

1. Why?

Why did the student revolt break out? Why was it able to sweep such a large part of the campus? Why did it happen at Berkeley rather than elsewhere?

Virtually every magazine article that has appeared on the subject has repeated one all-purpose analysis, which lies right at hand and has added virtue of pointing to an instant solution. A convenient summary of this analysis and its accompanying packaged remedy can be read in the following passage:

> ...some of the unrest among students is traceable to a feeling that the university is a huge corporate enterprise run by remote administrators and geared to the mass production of research and of candidates for degrees. The present situation has produced tremendous soul-searching on the whole issue of impersonality and inaccessibility. Efforts at all levels should be intensified to improve the relations between the three segments of the university community: students, faculty, and administration. The Council especially urges that faculty members and administrators take a greater personal interest in students. Discussions with individual students should be encouraged concerning both personal and university problems. Furthermore, there is need to give continuing thought and attention to improving the educational environment of both undergraduate and graduate students.

About all that is missing in this summary is a reference to Alienation.

Now the Council which made this report on December 17 was the Academic Council of the state-wide University of California, and the report was then presented by President Kerr to the Regents. The next sentence after the passage quoted said: "President Kerr himself has been a leader in this search for ways to improve the university for students."

This makes the analysis official and unanimous. It is the same as saying that John Doe caught a cold because cold "germs" got into his system. This is undoubtedly a better explanation than possession by evil spirits, but it leaves something to be desired nowadays. Since there are cold viruses in the air and in the respiratory tract all the time, the fact is not an explanation of any given cold.

Likewise, there is little that is really new in the feeling of the student that the mass university of today is an overpowering, over-towering, impersonal, alien machine in which he is nothing but a cog going through pre-programed motions—the "IBM" syndrome. Nor is it a new complaint that teaching, especially undergraduate teaching, is sacrificed to research and the publication rat race, at least at most of the major universities. Nor is Berkeley the first place where students have felt a lack of close personal relations with professors.

It is perfectly true that the mass universities have become huger than ever, but the alienation of a bewildered student in a campus of 5000 can be as thoroughgoing as in a Knowledge Factory of 25,000. One can be as completely lost in a forest of only a hundred square miles as in the High Sierra.

The correspondingly superficial remedy is the "warm bosom" solution, or "chuck 'em under the chin." Just as there is truth in the analysis, so there is virtue in the remedy, and enough of the remedial syrup can conceivably be poured to soothe the inflammations for a while. But it does not attack the roots of the problem.

There is an exact counterpart to this soothing-syrup approach: the "human-relations engineering" theory of how to counteract the alienation of the worker in the factory, with solutions ranging from elaborate paternalisms to Muzak over the public-address system. The personnel manager is taught how to be "human" in relations with the "hands," as the university administrator is urged to encourage "greater personal interest" in the thousands of "head" of students.

It is true that there was a wing of FSM activists who emphasized the issue of educational reform at the university, and some who even looked on this question as the dynamic of the movement. While it is widely and warmly agreed that the result of this new interest in university betterment was valuable, it was a by-product of the movement, not its spur. This was quickly shown by the end of the semester: when the FSM became quiescent, an effort was made to fill the vacuum with a University Reform Movement, whose sponsors even talked naively about using the sit-in tactic (that cure-all) as a means of bringing about basic changes in the system of study. This illusion evaporated in a jiffy, and the new "movement" became merely one useful interest-group among many.

The results of the two Somers surveys likewise tend to show that dissatisfaction with the quality of education given by the university played no

216

major role in motivating the fight, although the surveys do not exclude the hypothesis that such latent dissatisfaction contributed a background conditioning influence. In this connection, let us cite Professor Somers' own summary of his findings:

> We found sympathy for the demonstrators to be widespread and dispersed throughout the campus even to the extent of one third of the students approving the tactics that demonstrators had used. This support was clearly concentrated among students in certain fields – the social sciences, humanities, and physical science – but as strong among freshmen as among graduate students, and not related to the number of semesters a student had been on this campus. Nor is support particularly related to feelings of dissatisfaction with the educational functions of the university. On the contrary, we found a remarkable amount of satisfaction with courses, professors, and so on, and appreciation of the efforts made by the administration to provide top-quality education for students here. Thus, the prevailing explanation in terms of characteristics peculiar to the "Multiversity" seems to have no support. Rather, it appears that students resent being deprived of their rights to political activity, being excluded from full political citizenship, and this sentiment is especially strong among those who are emotionally involved in the civil-rights movement. Thus the material we collected suggests that the mainsprings of the rebellion are an optimistic idealism about the type of society which can be shaped by the new generation, and an unwillingness to allow the paternalism endemic to college campuses to extend its coverage to the activities necessary for the furtherance of those ideals.

The students' alienation from the university establishment was a function of their social and political involvement, not the other way around. Their discontent with the micro-society of the campus was an extension of their disillusionment with the values of the macro-society outside.

There was "something wrong" in the Multiversity. There was "something wrong" also, they felt, about the Great Society in which the Multiversity was

217

embedded, with its fraudulent non-war on poverty, its fraudulent crypto-war in Vietnam, and its fraudulent civil-rights laws in Washington — to mention only three strings whose plucking evoked a sympathetic tone from thousands of students who followed the FSM. Most of these thousands did not claim to know what was wrong, let alone what to do about it: they had no "program ." They wanted to "do something about it." (Significantly, Berkeley is also the campus with most volunteers to the Peace Corps.)

But the social malaise was still there, and no "personal relations" with professors would help. In fact, beyond a certain point closer personal acquaintance with most professors only deepened the problem, for the student was likely to find the professor insensitive, timid or cynical about the social or political ideals which he, the student, took seriously.

To put it moderately, there are few professors on the Berkeley campus who are likely to provide inspiration or encouraging understanding to a student beginning to feel a radical estrangement from the values of the American Way of Life; much fewer if we omit young professors scarcely more integrated on campus than the students themselves, and still fewer if we consider only the eminent "name" professors who had arrived in the Establishment.

Now this meaning of the students' "alienation" does not leap to the eye of the journalist who visits Berkeley for two days to do an "on the spot" quickie piece and accumulates some fast quotes in interviews. Yet, if it is easy to overlook it, it is also tempting to overstate it in reactive emphasis.

For these thousands of students are *not* finished radicals in any real political sense. At the same time, to an unexpected extent, it will be found that they do not think of themselves as "liberals" — that is, as mere liberals. Liberalism is too thoroughly integrated with the Establishment; they know there is "something wrong" with liberalism too.

The large majority of FSM activists would call themselves radicals, if forced to choose a label after strenuous objection to "labeling," but it is most commonly an amorphous kind of radicalism.*

---

* The *Graduate Political Scientists' Report* plays down the radicalism of the bulk of FSM activists as a concession to respectability but its version will not withstand analysis. Asking "Are the [sit-in] demonstrators 'a bunch of radicals'?" it answers with the following statistics: "Only 4.5% of [them] belonged to 'radical' groups (DuBois Club, Young Socialist Alliance, Young People's Socialist League, Independent Socialist Club). The others covered the full range of the political spectrum: 18.2%, liberal groups like Young Democrats; 25.6%, civil-rights organizations like NAACP and CORE; 1.2%, conservative groups; 7.3%, religious organizations. Furthermore, 57% of the students belonged to no political organization at all ."

Since the element of positive program is weak, since the estrangement from the Great Society has not yet led to a clear idea of an alternative society, the pent-up energy of dissent tends to burst out in forms that have two leading characteristics. One: concentration on concrete issues ("issue politics," in the jargon of the campus activists); and two: greater certainty on what one is against than on what one is for (what we can call "anti" politics). this is one of the natural forms of a radicalization that is in its first stages.

Hence the situation that the reservoir of radical *energies* is greater than the stream of radical beliefs.

The civil-rights issue is, of course, made-to-order for the release of such radical energies, since its elemental appeal to the sense of justice is so powerful in itself that it does not require a more explicit political program — at least at the beginning. Very soon, of course, the civil-rights fight brings the neophyte nose-up against such programmatic problems as attitude toward the Democratic Party apparatus — typified by the decision of a section of the civil-rights leadership in the 1964 election campaign to declare a moratorium on militant actions in order not to embarrass Lyndon Johnson's Great Society. In the Bay Area this typical dilemma was dramatized around Mayor John F. Shelley of San Francisco, the liberal Democrat who was elected with the eager support of student civil-rights militants, many of whom were later hauled to jail by Shelley's police for civil-rights demonstrations.

A filtering process takes place among the civil-rights enthusiasts, and a section of them (on campus, a large section) pragmatically choose to hold to their anti-establishmentarian militancy rather than yield to the housebreaking influence of the liberal politicians who advise them to be "realistic" and "practical," i.e., to stop bucking the machine.

The choice is not necessarily made as the end-conclusion of a thought-through political analysis, and therefore the militant who makes the choice tends to think of it as being merely a "moral choice ." And it *is* a moral choice,

---

It is quite true that most of the FSM radicals do not belong to any of the groups representing known radical ideologies, but that does not settle the matter. Campus CORE (but not NAACP) consists largely of radicals, not liberals; so do Slate and SNCC; there is even many a Young Democrat who conceives himself as a radical working within the liberal establishment; etc. The following statistics presented by the *G.P.S. Report* are also of interest: "Are they 'hard core demonstrators'? ... the large majority (61.2%) of those arrested had never participated in any previous demonstration; 22% had participated in only one previous demonstration; 7.0% had taken part in two; and 9.2% in three or more demonstrations ... Furthermore, the vast majority of these protestors had never been arrested before on any charge prior to the Sproul Hall sit-in. Almost all previous arrests were for earlier civil rights demonstrations ."

of course; but all moral choices in politics are also political choices; and even if the politics of the choice is not consciously evaluated, it is still implicitly there. At this point it is radical politics in an "issue" and "anti" form, even though the immediate demands may be positive enough.

The problem is more acute in the field of foreign policy and war—for instance the war in Vietnam—for here the issue is largely intractable to treatment by mere "issue politics ." The civil-rights activist can attack injustice in Mississippi or in Oakland directly and in the life; but he has no handle at hand by which to intervene as meaningfully to determine whether Washington will or will not help to precipitate a nuclear war on this planet. On the one hand, the narrow "issue" approach may lead to concentration on a single aspect, like official lying about the situation in Vietnam—for this can be handled most easily within the non-programmatic "moral choice" field of vision. On the other hand, the simple "anti" approach tends to blur the distinction between two quite different groups of people who are against Washington's war in Vietnam: those who oppose U.S. policy because they oppose all dictatorship and colonialism in Vietnam, and those who oppose U.S. policy because they are partisans of the Communist side of that war.

2. The Non-I Radicals

We are now discussing what was in fact the dominant tendency among the FSM activists and leadership and the decisive factor in making possible the Berkeley uprising. This is the amorphous radicalism which has been given various labels: the "new radicals," the "New Left," among others. I have referred to it as unprogrammatic but this is not strictly true. What is most characteristic of it is its conscious avoidance of any radical *ideology*. It is important to take a closer look at it.

These "new radicals" are non-ideological in the sense that they refuse to, or are disinclined to, generalize their ideas and positions. They fight shy of any systematization of their political and social views. They think of this approach as "pragmatic." They are inclined to substitute a moral approach—indeed, a dogmatic moral approach—for political and social analysis as much as possible. They like the description "existential" because it offers a non-political label.

I once asked an active exemplar of this trend to define what he meant by calling himself a "radical ." His answer was: "We take a position on a certain

220

issue — say, civil rights. We have a particular position on another issue, say, Vietnam. And so on. I would define radicalism as the sum total of these positions ." He was describing a kind of political induction. Obviously, this raises more questions than it answers.

First of all, why the extremely strong disinclination to generalize — that is, to move in the direction of a knit-together *theory* beyond issue-politics? At first blush, this is a strange development particularly for intellectuals, people who are involved in a whole period of life-training in the development and generalization of ideas. It is not that the non-ideological (for short, non-I) radicals question the need for generalization and theory in principle. I suggest that there are three powerful inhibitions at work.

(1) What they reject above all are "old" ideologies and radical theories, more than they reject ideology and theory itself. A new radical ideology could sweep them, but it is not even on the horizon. So to speak, there are "new radicals" but there is really no "new radicalism," in terms of program, theory or ideology.

This is above all a reaction against the failure of all previous wings of American radicalism to become mass movements. All the radical programs have "failed": there must be something wrong with them: we must do something new.

The operative word is *new*. The term "New Left" has a charisma unmatched by any other; and the vaguer it is, the more magical, since as soon as it takes on a specific content, the visage of some "old politics" is plain. The "old politics" has committed the sin of being unsuccessful: a very American sin.

A number of the non-I radicals on the Berkeley campus, and no doubt elsewhere, come from parents who went through the Communist movement; they associate "old politics" and "ideology" chiefly with the politics and ideology of the Communists. One way to reject Communist ideology without falling into the conformist rut of Establishment "anti-Communism" is to reject it not in the first place because it is Communist but because it is ideology.

(2) There is the fear that unity of action on issues would be impaired by ideological clarification. One of the distressful results of arriving at a more specific radical program is that different people are bound to disagree about what they specify. There will be disputes, hostility, factions, splits, fragmentation — in short, disunity; and is this not part of the "old politics" that failed? Therefore it seems better to act most unitedly by remaining on the

ground of "issue politics" only.

This consideration is a strong one up to a point, and indeed the FSM illustrated its limits to some extent. The FSM achieved a wide unity around an issue, but it did so only as an *ad hoc* fighting force temporarily united for that issue. It never considered itself a permanent organization or movement. By January it took the course, envisioned from the beginning, of putting itself on the shelf. (The new organization which re-formed in April under the name of the Free Student Union is quite another story.)

The FSM was essentially a United Front plus some added representation, not a membership organization. Now United Fronts are indeed the "old" form through which different ideological radicalisms achieve unity on particular issues. The FSM was illustrating the "old" pattern – in a brand-new form, as history usually does.

The FSM quite consistently, and largely deliberately, declined to do very much about drawing broad societal conclusions from what it itself was doing. On campus the main job of expounding radical interpretations of the "free speech" fight was carried by the "old" radicals – mostly the Independent Socialist Club, in a number of interpretive meetings and a culminating "Conference on the Student Revolt" in January. A good part of the FSM leadership participated in such meetings, but it would have been unwise for the FSM to try to fill this role. It could play an action role, but not an ideological role.

(3)There is the pressure of the American political climate. In almost any other country of the world, a great many of the non-I radicals would be calling themselves socialists. But in the U.S., for most of the public, socialism (not to speak of Communism) is a "dirty word ." Why get specific about "labels" which will only stand in the way?

As a matter of fact, this notion of sneaking socialism past the American public by calling it something else is one of the oldest politics there is, as old as the socialist movement itself. There is a source of reluctance here to develop even a *new* radical ideology, since any new "ism" would hardly be more congenial to the current American temper than the old.

None of the characteristics of non-I radicalism that have been described is hard and fast; it is a process rather than a standpoint. It ranges from elements just beginning to doubt the immaculateness of the American conception all the way to people who are full-blown socialists in everything except "label ."

Off at right angles to this line is another spectrum of students whose reaction against the American Establishment's party line has thrown them toward some degree of sympathy with the rival social system which disputes the world with Washington: the Communist power. It is a widely varied spectrum indeed, especially in the Bay Area, and over most of its range has little or no connection with the Communist Party. The spectrum begins with the student to whom the local Communists are simply "the enemy of the enemy," that is, other radicals opposed to the powers that be, and who literally refuses to think about the nature of Communist totalitarianism where it already has power, since such questions are divisive (dangerous thoughts). It ends with a thin scattering of the usual party-hack types who are apologists of terror against "free speech" in any country controlled by their friends.

Few of the present non-I radicals are aware that the Communist youth and student movement in its heyday was extremely skillful at setting up organizations which combined a non-ideological and even non-political facade with the implicit Communist line (*vide* American Youth for Democracy and the later years of the American Student Union). There is a long history of Communists posing as non-ideological radicals. I mention this because, as one who went through a good deal of this history, I claim to know the difference. This element was very small in the Berkeley uprising.

The non-ideological radicalism which constitutes a sort of "new Left" on the campus *is* new. It is no one's invention and no one's patsy. It showed great strength and great weaknesses in the FSM fight, but both the strengths and the weaknesses were its very own.

3. "New Left" Balance Sheet

The dominance of the new non-ideological radicals not only gave the tone of the Berkeley uprising but also accounts for its main strong points. Its advantages were at least these three, in ascending order of importance:

(1)*It made it very difficult to smear the FSM with the "Communist" label.* The point is not simply that the decisive FSM leadership and followers were *not* Communist in fact; innocence has not always stopped the ignorant or malicious from redbaiting or witch hunting. The point is that after a minimal amount of actual contact with the FSM, almost anyone close to the situation had to recognize that the "feel" was not only non-Communist but alien to any kind of Communist approach. Naturally this does not apply to those authorities on the Berkeley fight who became experts on the subject by reading the news dispatches 3000 miles away. It does apply particularly to the Berkeley faculty, and had its effect as time went on.

(2)*It accounts in part for the explosiveness of the student uprising.* This was the explosiveness of uncalculated indignation, not the slow boil of planned revolt. In many cases it was born of the first flash of discovery that the mantle of authority cloaked an unsuspected nakedness. The experienced radicals on campus did not consider this to be news; after one has become accustomed to taking a dim view of Important People, it is hard to experience a fresh movement of revulsion at every repetition of the lesson. There is first love; there is the first baptism of fire; there is the first time you realize your father has lied; and there is the first discovery of the chasm between the rhetoric of Ideals and the cynicism of Power among the pillars of society.

I talked with an FSM activist who was in the thick of the movement all through the fall semester. He was not only non-ideological but non-political, and had come in at first with the confident view that it was all merely a question of overcoming the administration's misunderstanding of what the students wanted, due to the fact that they had been antagonized by hasty clashes at the beginning. The process of rapid disillusionment was a personal shock, and the reaction was correspondingly violent. He read outright falsifications in the newspapers every day; he heard systematic distortions by the leaders of the university itself; he talked to faculty members who were bitter about what the administration was doing but declined to speak up for truth or justice; he was naively amazed at students who agreed that the administration was wrong but shrugged their shoulders and walked away from trouble. The real world did not seem to have much relationship to the ideals he had taken seriously. He had been sold ... This is the story in good part of the moral dynamism behind the impetuosity of the fight.

(3)Perhaps this is a continuation of point 2: *The FSM was able to do so much because they simply didn't know "it couldn't be done ."* They were able to win so much because they didn't know it was "impossible ." A certain amount of naivete and inexperience was as a shield and a buckler to them. After all, ideologies (by which I mean merely systems of ideas) are distillations form past experience, if they possess any validity at all; and past experience told the "old radicals" what powerful forces they faced. But lack of a radical ideology meant also lack of a systematic view of what basic social powers were at stake. It was only after it was all over that a leading Graduate Coordinating Committee student told me ruefully that he now realized the impossibility of revolution on one campus alone. If he had known more to begin with, he might have been able to do less: a plain case of "a little knowledge is a dangerous thing ." Therefore the militant wing of the FSM comprised mainly non-I radicals, and to a lesser degree those who were moved not merely by a radical but by a revolutionary socialist ideology.

These advantages were decisive ones. President Kerr has testified that he was "taken by surprise"; so was the whole campus, including the students, many of whom were just as surprised at what they found themselves forced to do. The history of revolts and revolutions tells us that this pattern is not new: the explosive irruption of new strata of inexperienced but outraged masses, while ideologically more advanced movements stand flatfooted, is a frequent phenomenon in times of crisis. Yet it always comes as something new, by its very nature; and of course these new and unawed forces are commonly non-ideological in motivation, being impelled not by theories but by intolerable conditions, not necessarily economic. In this generic sense, waves of "new radicals" are an old pattern.

The other thing that history tells us about such irruptions is their limitations, which tend to become more serious as the system recovers from the impact of the first massive assaults.

The first steps in the uprising are unitedly directed against the visible enemy, and the first demands are easy, being a direct response to the intolerable conditions. But beyond this elementary stage, the problems of perspective and program multiply, as more basic issues and powers are brought to the surface. Even to know now what the basic issues are, requires a broader and more general conception of what the fight is about — in effect, an ideology. The ruling authorities, who made decisions easier before by being flatly intransigent, now provide an enticing variety of compromises, halfway houses, promises — anything to get the headlong assault to pause, break up and mill in confusion. The non-ideological radical feels that the first pristine beauty and simplicity of the issues have faded, and moral indignation by itself does not seem to point to answers.

Even in the first stage, one of the most prominent characteristics of FSM functioning was the interminable, indecisive discussions of the leading committees at critical junctures. The picture of the FSM drawn by some in terms of sinister super-efficiency and generalship so brilliant as to put the administration to rout, is one of the most ludicrous misrepresentations in this story. Time and again, the Executive Committee and Steering Committee of

225

the movement discussed literally for days, coming finally either to no firm decision or to a decision which was negated the very next day by events so that the actual policy was improvised. At such times the policy problems of the FSM were most often solved not by its councils but by some new "atrocity" by the administration. One of the main reasons for this often paralyzing disability was the fact that there were no fixed points in any discussion: everything was always "up for grabs ." Every problem which any movement of opposition inevitably runs into had to be explored *ab ovo*: how long would it have taken Adam to learn to walk if he had had to figure out separately the proper function of every muscle, ligament, and nerve cell in the ambulatory process?

There was another problem before the non-I radicalism of the FSM, which became especially troublesome in the spring semester. This was a certain blurring of the difference between serious political and social opposition to the status quo (even if considered non-ideologically) and the nihilism of the disaffiliates.

The latter term requires an apology, but it is a significant phenomenon and needs a name. The best definition I know of is provided, by example, in the motto of Celine which is quoted admiringly in Henry Miller's "Red Notebook": *Je pisse sur tout d'un grand hauteur.* From a great height — that is, from above the real world, and outside it. The French have another word for something like it: *je m'en-fichisme;* which roughly means fuck-it-all-ism. Unlike the beats (one extreme variety of disaffiliation) the types under consideration do not "opt out of society" (the rat race) in consistent practice, only in attitudes.

Je pisse sur tout is a kind of social program, with a primitive ideology of its own, which provides a simulacrum of social radicalism, since among other things it rejects also the going social system and its authorities. But it is only a simulacrum, for it has no real social vision or even moral vision of its own. These types want to disaffiliate from society, not to transform it. They are basically hostile to the social radicals, since the latter *are* deeply concerned about and involved with society. They tend to be scornful of tactics and strategy in a social struggle, however militant, since such considerations make for further involvement; the alternative is simply to smash things up, or pull the linchpins. They propose their own version of "militant" tactics mainly to scandalize that Beast, the Public (*épater la bourgeoisie*) and not to win, for winning involves taking responsibility. Their salute is not the clenched fist but the thumb to nose. They actually achieve their personal program of disaffiliation from society only by opting out of the real world with marijuana

226

or LSD, which is their personal "revolution ."

To the historically-minded, this description may partially suggest the old Bakunin type of anarchist, but the nihilism we have here is non-ideological. What we have described applies to only a small fringe of the university community in Berkeley, but it shades into the non-ideological radical tendency on one side, and tends to have a certain coloring effect upon it. I think this was one factor, not in the FSM struggle of the fall, but in the "obscenity" row of the spring semester.

Finally, there was another limitation of non-I radicalism which was prominently manifested in the spring. It is the other side of the coin of the movement's explosiveness: lack of persistency.

The FSM itself, as an organization, was not expected to persist, as we have mentioned; we are speaking of the individual non-I activists of the FSM . When the outbreak of the Second Round called for the reorganization of the FSM, it became painfully plain that a strange thing had happened by the end of April: of the FSM Steering Committee that had led the fight during the fall, only two were still taking part in the renewed struggle. One was the DuBois Club representative—hardly non-ideological—and the other was Jack Weinberg. Virtually the entire status of non-I leaders of the FSM Steering Committee had, for one reason or another, retired from the arena, after one semester of eruption, with no adequate replacement leadership in sight. It would appear that the simple/moral drive to action is more ephemeral than the ideological, and it is not hard to understand why. All of this makes a very mixed balance sheet. The conclusion may be that both ideological radicalism and the "new radicalism" have a great deal to learn from each other.

4. The "New Radicals" and the "Old Radicals"

While the non-I radicals set the dominant tone of the FSM, their role cannot be fully understood except in relation to the programmatic radicals of the political clubs on campus which we have mentioned in the course of the story. One of the unique features of Berkeley student life is the "across-the-board" array of radical clubs representing a wide variety of left-wing viewpoints in a turbulent climate of political discussion and controversy. It is dubious whether there is any other campus in the country today that resembles it in this respect.

A membership count of these clubs would show perhaps 200-300 members in all, but their influence extends pretty strongly to another few hundred, and in more diluted form to perhaps a thousand; from this point it would shade off rapidly. This is a small minority of the campus, but it accounts for an enormously disproportionate amount of the ideological life that goes on and an even greater proportion of the political life. Previous to the FSM, it gave its tone to much of the campus far out of line with its strength.

> Berkeley students have always made more use of their political rights to meet and speak freely on campus than American students elsewhere. Every sort or extreme-left group is represented — the DuBois Club (Communist), the Young Socialist Alliance (Trotskyist), the Independent Socialist Club (Revolutionary Marxist Socialist), and the Progressive Labor Council (Maoist)... [Lipset & Seabury in the *Reporter.*]

Kerr put it this way in an interview:

> If anything in the United States today could be said to resemble the Paris left bank, it is the area around Telegraph Avenue just off campus... this disorganized, anarchist, "Left bank" crowd was able to strike a responsive chord among so many students this fall because ... a new student generation ... is now with us. The tone of a student generation is set by rather a small number of people ...

"Berkeley," wrote *Look* magazine (February 23), "is the most 'politicalized' campus in America." There is naturally a constant air of political debate going on, not only in formally organized meetings but in the pages of the *Daily Cal*, in impromptu rallies, in bull sessions on the Terrace of the cafeteria. There is a market place of political ideas, with a direct counterposition of leftish liberalism (Young Democrats) to right-wing social democrats (YPSL) to revolutionary-democratic socialists (Independent Socialist Club), as well as to the pro-Soviet tendencies (DuBois Club, Trotskyists, et al.), and shades of less programmatic radicalism in such groups as Slate and Students for Democratic Society. Nor can the civil-rights groups be left entirely out of this picture, for they owed part of their existence to the work of committed radicals. Independent Socialist influence was considerable in CORE, as was Slate and DuBois influence in the Ad Hoc Committee while that group existed.

228

It was the radical clubs, including the radical civil-rights groups like CORE and SNCC, which formed the skeleton about which the FSM fleshed itself. It is quite true that the leading committees of the FSM were to the left of the ranks throughout the fight. Most of the time this was due to the fact that no one but radicals (various kinds of radicals) were willing to take the risks and burdens of leading a militant struggle. Whenever the going got sticky, the groups further to the right — from the social-democrats and the Young Democrats to the Republicans — began to veer away, leaving the militants on a limb.

On the left the relationship between the "old radicals" and the new is symbiotic. In this exchange the former tend to be the reservoir of ideas for the latter. In point of fact, the non-ideological radicals do have the benefits of ideology at their service.

There is another kind of "radical" whose role in the situation must be mentioned: the *ex*-radicals — of the faculty.* This is an aspect of the Berkeley story that is notorious in the FSM and never mentioned in outside accounts.

The fact is that the bitterest and most virulent enemies of the FSM among the faculty were not the conservatives or rightists, and not Kerr's admirers, but rather a hard core of ex-radicals who had made their own peace with the system. This was the pattern at the December 8 meeting of the Academic Senate, where every one of the speakers for the Feuer amendment, with one exception, belonged to this category: in particular, Feuer himself, Nathan Glazer, William Petersen. In the nation's periodical press, these three have also distinguished themselves by articles of vituperation against the FSM.

The dean of this group, and the author of the most violent abuse of the student movement (in a series of articles in the *New Leader*, which is more or less the organ of reformed ex-radicals), is Professor Lewis Feuer. Long a Communist fellow traveler, Feuer has been moving right quite rapidly, especially in the last few years. In the course of his savage fulminations against the FSM, Feuer put forward a theory in explanation of the Berkeley uprising which is interesting in what it reveals.

The theory itself is very simple: the students' motivation is the Generational Conflict — young vs. old, the sons rising against the fathers. What is interesting about this theory is not what it explains about the students, for

---

* I call them a kind of "radical" on the assumption the reader has heard the old story about the New York cop who is clubbing a demonstrator outside the Russian consulate. "But, officer, I'm an anti-Communist," expostulates the victim. "I don't care *what* kind of Communist you are!" says the cop — *Bash!*

it clearly can explain little about what happened. Students are *eo ipso* young, and the authorities they oppose are always an older generation, and so every movement *must* have the aspect of a generational conflict. But the students of the Silent Generation of the fifties were also young, and so are the students on every other campus in the country however quiescent or rebellious. This is a theory which can never account for any differences among student reactions, since it is based on what is biologically common to all. The one thing Feuer's theory can never explain is why such an uprising should occur on one particular campus at a certain time.*

Yet there is a "generational conflict" behind Feuer's theory, though not so much the one he is concerned about. Conflict cuts both ways; and if there is not much evidence of any special student antagonism to the older generation as such (though plenty of evidence of distrust), one must look also at the other side of the antagonistic relationship. In Feuer's shrill diatribes against the students, some of which we have quoted, and many of which make even campus conservatives embarrassed, it is difficult to overlook the extreme emotional content. We have here a typical representative of the generation of ex-Communists who, having devoted a good part of their lives to the service of apologizing for totalitarians, are now lashing out in fury at the tragedy of their own pasts. The hatred they unleash against the radical students is a self-hatred in the first place projected against the new generation which (they think) mirrors their sad youth.

This sort of thing plays a distinctly negative role in the education of the non-I radicals, who do not see the political pathology of the case but take it as a bogeyman. ("This is what happens if you become too anti-Communist," or "This is what happens to 'old radicals.'")

"How do I know that won't happen to me?" mused one FSM leader in a bull session, as if he were talking of a disease. "You don't," I told him cheerfully. "Take the 800 [arrested sit-inners]. Ten years from now, most of them will be rising in the world and in income, living in the suburbs from Terra Linda to Atherton, raising two or three babies, voting Democratic, and wondering what on earth they were doing in Sproul Hall — trying to remember, and failing ."

He shuddered — a literal, physical shudder. "It won't happen to me; I'll remember ."

Maybe; but while it is easy to remember that one had a feeling of moral

---

* Also, the Somers spring survey has some material tending to negate the relevance of "generational conflict" as a specific motivation.

indignation, it is harder to recall the feeling. If the FSM activists were really as non-ideological as they think they are, it would be even harder. But the fact is that they do have a sort of working ideology.

The central core of the working ideology of the typical radical activists is not defined by any one issue, but consists of a choice between two alternative modes of operation: *permeation* or *left opposition*. The former seeks to adapt to the ruling powers and infiltrate their centers of influence with the aim of (some day) getting to the very levers of decision-making—becoming a part of the Establishment in order to manipulate the reins to the left. The latter wish to stand outside the Establishment as an open opposition, achieving even short-term changes by the pressure of a bold alternative, while seeking roads to fundamental transformations.

What separates the style of the radical "New Left" from liberals who may agree on many given issues, is their rejection of the permeationist method. This was, of course, at bottom the basis for the bifurcation between FSM militants and moderates too; and the difference was dramatized as in a charade when, on the very same day (November 9), the militant leadership of the FSM went into illegal opposition with a civil-disobedience policy, while a wing of the moderates went to try to make a deal with President Kerr: a symbolic split. Many of the non-I radicals are fairly conscious of what their rejection of any kind of support to the Democratic administration and their hostility to the Democratic Party as a trap for liberals. Instead of adapting to power, they talk in terms of organizing for struggle from below. This wing of Students for Democratic Society, for example, look to work among the urban poor and unemployed as their special kind of project. Leaving aside what results can be expected from this particular work, the effort exemplifies their chosen alternative. On campus, other non-I radicals, looking for a road to take that does not lead to integration with the Establishment, have been attracted to work among California's exploited farm laborers—literally at the grass roots. I cite these as examples of a groping in a certain direction, not as a program.

This also helps to explain what even some friends of the "New Left" radicals have complained about. Thus in a *Nation* article Jack Newfield writes a glowing account of "The Student Left: Revolt Without Dogma," and then chides:

> Immediate predecessors like Socialists Bayard Rustin and
> Michael Harrington are repudiated on the absurd ground that they

Socialism from Below

have "sold out to the Establishment"—Rustin because he supported the 1964 moratorium on street demonstrations and the compromise offered the Mississippi Freedom Democratic Party at the 1964 Democratic Convention, and Harrington because he is a consultant to Sargent Shriver and Walter Reuther. The new radicals also reject the Rustin-Harrington theory that social change is achieved by an institutionalized coalition of church, labor, Negro and liberal groups reforming the Democratic Party. (*The Nation,* May 10, 1965.)

To the "New Left" radicals, the point is not that people like Rustin and Harrington have "sold out" in the usual venal sense, but that they have moved to attach themselves to the pillars of power, as advisers at the left ear of authority, while the "New Left" radicals are moving in the opposite direction. The crux is not the sincerity of any individuals but the permeationist theory which is stated in Newfield's last sentence. Probably few of the new radicals would give as theoretical a form to their alternative course as the permeationists give to theirs, but there is a basic ideological element there for all that. It is not surprising that so many observers were moved to comment on the "revolutionary" feel of the FSM uprising, for we are now discussing, as a matter of fact, what has been the historical line of demarcation between revolutionary and reform currents in social movements of dissent. In fact, the new radicals are in process of rediscovering another "old politics" — the politics of left opposition to the ongoing system in the name of a new social and moral vision.

No one can say whether this is a stream of thought and action that will deepen and extend, or whether it will dry to a trickle while new social movements arise elsewhere. It has already made a significant contribution in jolting the affluent complacency of middle-class, liberal America. It has been a catalyst—a trigger, an example—unleashing FSM-like actions and movements throughout the nation. No matter what happens now, whether there are advances or setbacks ahead for this unformed movement, it is laying a groundwork for the future freedom-fighters of the United States, by training and inspiring new cadres of idealistic youth with social goals so imbued with a new moral vision as to raise basic questions over the established order of society.

From *Berkeley: The New Student Revolt* (Grove Press, 1965)

232

Chapter XII:
Free Speech and Political Struggle

What exactly does the right of "free speech" apply to?

This is a problem with a long history, but it became acute in 1967 with the wave of student demonstrations against Dow Co. and other CIA recruiters on campus. Militant anti-war demonstrations demanded that the administrations cease to provide Dow recruiters with special university facilities. The administrations replied: This would be a violation of their right to free speech; they must be accorded the same rights that you yourself demand for your anti-war agitation.

In the face of this line, leftish opinion fragmented in three different directions:

(1)Many liberals and social-democratic types fell on their face before the administration gambit; they echoed the view that the demonstrations violated the Dow recruiters' "right of free speech" and were therefore bad.

(2)Many radicals and student militants agreed with the administration contention (that the demonstrations violated Dow's free speech), but concluded that it was a good thing to violate the right to free speech in such a good cause.

(3)The third position denied that the right to free speech applied to the Dow case, and took both a principled position for the right to free speech and made a militant defense of the anti-Dow demonstrations.

It was No. 2 that was the disconcerting development in this situation. There was no surprise in finding that the same liberals and social-democrats who regularly argued that any militant anti-war action was sinister, should crank out arguments proving that the anti-Dow demonstrations were the work of the devil. But it was another thing when people who had associated themselves with the various "free speech" struggles around the country, now gave support to arguments which effectively dumped the right to free speech altogether. For this was and is the consequence of position No. 2. However put, this position boiled down to the "hierarchy of values" proposition: In our hierarchy of values, free speech is only one rung; stopping the war's barbarism is a higher value; therefore the right to free speech must give way before this value.

This line of reasoning does not dump the right to free speech simply for certain cases; it dumps free speech as a right altogether. It reduces it to something you tolerate if there isn't any "higher value" around to negate it at the moment. Moreover, by introducing the need for an ad hoc judgment in each case about the given "hierarchy of values," it also introduces the judge who is to make this decision — naturally in accordance with his own values. There is no despot or authoritarian who could not accept such a theory of "free speech" with enthusiasm — and also with justice. Dictators usually repress only those exercises of "free speech" which do in fact conflict with "higher values" which they hold.

This kind of three-way division is not new: something like it has been seen in radical circles for a few hundred years, long before Dow invented napalm. Within movements of social dissent, there has always been a strong or dominant wing of reformists and reformers, on the one hand; and, on the other, there have also been the elitist and dictatorial currents of radicalism or "revolutionism," more or less openly anti-democratic, often reflecting the aspirations of alienated intellectuals for a "dictatorship of the intelligentsia" which would permit them to impose their own "hierarchy of values" on the society they detested. Both of these have been quite distinct from the third current of revolutionary socialism-from-below.

It is quite true, then, that radicals and socialists (if we include all kinds) have never been united in support of a consistent advocacy of free speech. It is not strange that this situation is duplicated in the milieu of the contemporary New Left, where so many of the oldest and most outlived ideas of radicalism have been prolifically reinvented.

Let us try to think our way through this question.

We begin with a consideration which certainly must be granted from anyone's standpoint: it concerns the type of social situation where the right to free speech is involved — not where it is valid or invalid, but simply where it is involved or not. The question of free speech comes alive in the context of social struggles and only juridical cretins can believe that all social struggles are resolvable by any kind of speech, free or otherwise. In the last analysis, the more basic social struggles are not decided by government rules or in the courts, but by the contest of power.

The obvious case in point is a revolution, which entails an open contest for state power. The Declaration of Independence was not an exercise of the right to free speech: it was a declaration of intent to engage in a contest of power which pre-empted the field of any norms of civil peace (free speech included). It represented an appeal not to speech (democratic norms, persuasion, etc.) but to the arbitrament of force. Likewise the Russian Revolution, the German Revolution, and any other revolution. You should not claim that it is the "right to free speech" which permits you to marshal the Red Militia to seize the White House; the troops would die laughing.

This does not mean that there is no question of democracy involved in a revolutionary struggle or any other contest of power. Democracy is a wider concept than free speech. Your "right to make a revolution" — this moral right, or political right, or whatever you consider it — still demands justification and defense in terms of democratic sanctions. But this is a much bigger frame than the "free speech" question. Also: this does not mean that, once the situation has become a contest of power, there is no longer any question of free speech on your own side of the lines, within your own camp. There most certainly is. But the free-speech issue is no longer an issue as between the two sides that have broken out of the framework of civil peace.

Revolution is only the most obvious sort of case where one may decide to leave one ground and go over to another: that is, leave the ground of "free speech" and go over to the ground of the open contest of power. Of course, war is another obvious case, revolutions being only civil wars in end-form. Frenchmen who elected to help the Allied side instead of the legal Vichy government were not making a decision to which "free speech" is relevant; they were merely choosing sides in a war. In the Cold War, likewise, if you want to give American or British military secrets to the Russians, that has nothing to do with any "rights" but solely with the choosing up of sides in a contest of power.

Even in more "normal" times, there are situations, temporary and usually localized, where a group of people may decide to leave the ground of civil norms like free speech and go over to the other ground. Naturally, they must also be prepared to face the consequences. Strike struggles are always, to a small or great degree, contests of naked social power, even where there are legal forms devised to channelize and mitigate the power-confrontation. This element in a strike can produce situations very like civil war. Again we must point out, this does not mean that democratic considerations become irrelevant — not a bit; there is always the question of who are seeking power over whom, and for what social ends.

There are other types of situations outside the ground of free speech. There is the situation where the framework of civil liberties is denied by the authorities, as in the life of Negroes in the South or Northern ghettos, or by the sheriff's deputies in Delano, where direct action is taken outside the cadre of any speech. If an army unit mutinies, it is not a question of free speech. A civil-disobedience demonstration is also not an issue of free speech: the democratic function and justification for civil disobedience lie on another ground, which has been often explained.

In all these cases, it is never a matter of deciding whether the right of free speech is "negated" by some "higher value," or of dressing a list of values in a "hierarchy of values," but simply a matter of passing from one ground to a different ground, from the ground of the norms of civil peace to the ground of an open contest of power. You always face the need, of course, to justify your decision to pass from one ground to the other. You may decide to do so rightly or wrongly, democratically or not; and that decision can also be judged wise or not; but all we are concerned with here is that these situations fall outside the question of free speech.

Our subject, free speech, is an issue of the first ground, when it is a contest of views, within the framework of the existing power relations, on the basis of the existing state. With relation to such a contest of views, what do you demand of, or propose to, the governmental power?

At this point in the analysis, we may be told, by some sophisticated radicals who have heard of different kinds of states: "Hold on! What state are you talking about? Their state or ours?" if the objector styles himself a Marxist, he will say: "Are you talking about a bourgeois state or a socialist state?" or its equivalent in current New Left jargon.

There is indeed an opinion, held implicitly or explicitly, which goes like this: As long as we (the good guys) are not in power, we demand free speech and other such liberties — and we deserve them, because we are right. But wait till we get power: we are not going to be so foolish as to let you, who are wrong, make trouble and corrupt the People ...

This is not a caricature. It has been put into print by Herbert Marcuse (though not by many other sane people); I have heard it, without searching too hard, from many a young would-be radical; and of course anyone who is not naive knows that it is the unwritten program of any of the Communist Parties.

This is a view very proper to an intelligentsia aspiring to a new ruling-class dictatorship of their own; but it is alien to revolutionary Marxism. Here is a proposition: There can be no contradiction, no gulf in principle, between what we demand of this existing state, and what we propose for the society we want to replace it, a free society.

Naturally, circumstances alter cases, but since this generality applies on both sides, it cancels out and does not affect the proposition. You can legitimately consider the proposition from a moral standpoint — that is, as a moral imperative — but here I am interested not in moralizing but in political analysis. Why this proposition?

236

First of all: what we demand of this state now does constitute our real program. Secondly: the kind of movement we build now, on a certain basis, will determine our new society, not good intentions. One can, of course, build a movement on the basis of social demagogy, massive hypocrisy, concealment of real intentions—as the fascists did, as the Stalinists do—but such a movement is fitted only to install a new despotism. No movement that really aims at a free society can proceed along these lines.

It is a platitude that the right to free speech always means free speech for the fellow who disagrees, including free speech for views that you detest. Otherwise you are not talking about a right but only about what you are willing to tolerate, what you are willing to grant. We are concerned here about political rights: otherwise we are not talking about free speech at all. It is in this connection that we can use some background history on this issue.

As mentioned, this is not a new question. And the theory of the "hierarchy of values" is not a new theory. It played a very big role in this country just the day before yesterday, that is, in the era of McCarthyism of the fifties. It is widely known how ignominiously the liberals and social-democratic types collapsed before the onslaught of McCarthyism; but it is less widely understood that this collapse was not merely the result of unfortunate personal characteristics (like the existence of a vacuum where their guts should have been). There was an ideology about democratic rights that was involved—a line of justification. It was, in fact, nothing less than this so-very-new idea of the "hierarchy of values." Sidney Hook, the arch-ideologist of the capitulation to McCarthy, explained in detail (and perfectly sincerely) that he was enthusiastically for free speech, but not for every exercise of free speech when Freedom itself was threatened by indiscriminate free speech. This meant that Communists, who wanted to use free speech and other democratic rights to destroy freedom and democracy itself, could not be permitted to exercise such democratic rights. Therefore Communists could be deprived of free speech and civil liberties without impugning the "higher value" of Liberty itself. This was the basis of the liberal apologia for the witch hunt system.

This system of thought does not become a whit better when the "higher value" is taken to be something different from "democracy itself" or any other particular formulation; it is not a whit better when the "higher value" is taken to be opposition to the Vietnam war. For the methodology of the witchhunters could be combated successfully only if the argument revolved not around whether your "value" was "higher" than mine, but around the method itself, which had to be rejected at the root.

Before getting back to the method itself, however, let us fill out the picture with another version of the same problem. For the liberals capitulating before McCarthyism commonly justified themselves with another gimmick which also had a strong hold on radicals. This was the issue of "civil liberties for fascists." Not that this was the burning issue of the fifties! It had, however, been rife in the preceding two decades, and therefore acted as a methodological model.

Most radical thinking had been set in a mold shaped by an image of what had happened in the Germany of the Weimar republic: "See, Weimar Germany let the Nazis enjoy the benefits of free speech and democratic rights – and look what happened! The lesson is that a virile democracy has to crack down on totalitarians before they become a clear and present danger, not afterward when it is too late ."

The yellow liberals made liberal use of this mind-set and of this historical model, aiming it at the "Communist menace"; and the Cold War witchhunt deepened from the late forties to the middle fifties. All this was not the invention of Joe McCarthy; McCarthyism merely took advantage of it.

Here is a political exercise for the reader on this very question:

In 1949, when the witchhunt climate was deepening under President Truman, the Supreme Court took up the Terminiello case. Terminiello was a man who had made a speech in Chicago that had infuriated a good part of the audience by its unpopular views. So angry did they become that turmoil ensued, and the upshot was that the speaker was arrested for contributing to the situation (by the unpopularity of his opinions). In short, he was arrested because his opinions were so unpopular that hearers resorted to violence.

The Supreme Court decision, written by Justice William O. Douglas, supported his right to express his views. Douglas laid it down that...

> "a function of free speech under our system of government is to
> invite dispute. It may indeed best serve its high purpose when
> it induces a condition of unrest, creates dissatisfaction with
> conditions as they are, or even stirs people to anger .. ."

The case against Terminiello was thrown out, as a violation of the "clear and present danger" rule. Was this good or bad?

We must now add that this Terminiello was a fascist (a follower of G.L.K. Smith), and the unpopular sentiments which he had expressed in his speech

238

had been anti-semitic sentiments. Now—was the Supreme Court decision good or bad?

If Terminiello had to be thrown in jail for saying derogatory things about Jews, what would that mean for the right of other people, in other situations, to express derogatory opinions about other things or people? Did Communists have a right to make speeches expressing sentiments fully as objectionable as Terminiello's—for example, defending concentration camps?

The fact is that the Terminiello decision was a blow against the witchhunt, and this role is not gainsaid by the unsavory character of the individual involved; any more than the civil-libertarian character of certain more recent Supreme Court decisions on the rights of criminals and the restriction of police methods is gainsaid by the fact that the individual cases did involve criminal individuals with no claim on our own sympathy. Another fact is that it was and is not possible to distinguish, as far as the civil-liberties principle is concerned, between cases of "civil liberties for fascists" and "civil liberties for Communists ."

Here are five conceptions on this question which need emphasis:

(1)Take the above-mentioned historical analogy with the Nazis in Weimar Germany: it is wholly false. It is simply not true that the truly scandalous behavior of the courts in Weimar Germany revolved around "free speech for Nazis" cases. The judges of this very democratic republic were letting Nazi thugs go scotfree even in cases where they had been caught redhanded in murder, assault, beatings of Jews and radicals, breaking up of trade union headquarters, and similar actions. Action, not speech. If the Nazi movement had confined itself to speeches (including fascist speeches), it would never have been the danger it was. No rights to free speech had to be curtailed by a millimeter in order to have an abundance of grounds for rounding up the entire Nazi leadership years before they became even a clear and present danger. And this was not an accidental fact but inherent in the nature of the fascist movement as such: this movement never made the slightest pretext of depending on persuasion or education for power. The argument that "history tells us" that fascists have to be thrown in the pokey as soon as they express any opinions considered fascist—this argument is a phoney. In fact, just as phoney as the analogous argument of the witchhunters that the expression of Communist views must be met with policemen's clubs lest "democracy itself" be endangered.

Actions, not speech: this is the key. In contemporary America, for example, socialists are for laws making racist acts a criminal offense. If a landlord discriminates against blacks, browns, yellows, or bearded whites in renting or selling, a real democracy would crack down on him with the forces of law and order; but this has nothing to do with illegalizing his right to express any stupid or reactionary opinions on any group. (Any more than I would want to be restricted in my right to express my own opinions on the subject of Southern rednecks, liberal suburbanites, Democratic politicians, middle-class Negro businessmen, Jewish shopkeepers in Harlem, and an extensive spectrum of other types.)

(2)Of all the juridical weapons we cannot entrust to a state machine that is not ours, the worst is the right to be selective about democratic rights. Because the state will make that weapon a double-edged one; and the sharp cutting edge will be sued against the people, not against the fascists, in the long run if not the short.

Precisely if and when the state is a bourgeois state, we cannot give it our approbation in abandoning the ground of free speech; and if it is really a socialist state we do not have to. But the practical proposals we hear have to do with the former, of course. Precisely in such cases we have to stress: we do not trust this state. We do not trust it in general, and above all we cannot trust it to wield such a weapon.

(3)Although we have been using the usual phrase "civil liberties for fascists" and "civil liberties for Communists," the formulation is inaccurate. I am not interested in civil liberties for fascists or Communists. It is not their civil liberties we are concerned about; for it is certainly true that they want free speech only to help install a regime that will gag us. If this were really the issue, then there could be no two ways about it. But it is not the issue. The issue of the civil liberties of fascists and Communists is not separable from the issue of civil liberties of everybody else. It is a question of allowing no such distinctions by this state we do not trust.

In a reverse sort of way, the Communist Party found this out when it gleefully urged the government to use the reactionary Smith Act to put Trotskyists in jail, and hailed that wartime witchhunt as a triumph for progress; only to complain bitterly when, later, the ungrateful government used this same triumph for progress to put them in jail, with exactly the same right. If politics were a matter only of morality or sentiment, one might only have said "Serves them right" of the Smith Act jailings of the Communist bravos who had applauded the Smith Act jailings of Trotskyists. But there is

240

no reason for a genuine revolutionary to fall into this snake-pit. Independent Socialists campaigned against the Smith Act persecutions of the Communist Party for the sake of maintaining the rights of radical dissent in America, not for the sake of the Communist Party.

(5)Nor can we rely on this state to defend us against aspiring fascist demagogues. And is it not the height of folly to tear down the structure of what civil liberties we have, in order to encourage such an illusion? Yet this is exactly what is done when the state is asked to impugn its own free-speech standards by denying them to anyone.

The case in point that first impressed me involved, as it happens, the same G.L.K. Smith who inspired Terminiello. In 1945 fascist Smith decided to invade Los Angeles with a campaign to build his movement, and started making speeches. As organizer of our Independent Socialist movement there, I tried to get a united front going of radical organizations (and others) to organize a mass picket line against Smith. Not one could be gotten to do so, either together with us or separately—not the Communist Party, not the Socialist Workers party, nor any other. (The reasons given were the time-honored ones, such as: don't pay any attention to Smith and he'll go away, etc.) So the first picket lines against the Smith operation were organized by ourselves alone. Simultaneously, another issue arose: Smith wanted to hold a meeting in a school, and the same people who refused to participate in an action against Smith went to the Board of Education to demand that it refuse the use of the school to him. This could only be done by relying on the same ordinances that had been invented in the first place in order to deny school use to socialists and radicals!

Here was the counterposition: we were the only ones to initiate and launch militant mass action against Smith's meetings, but we refused to ask the government to dump what there was of free speech facilities in order to get at Smith. We organized people's action, but we refused to put this double-edged weapon in the hands of the government with our approbation.

(5)On this whole business, there is a fundamental difference between the reactionaries and ruling classes in general, on the one hand, and, on the other, us who are fighting for a socialist democracy.

Our aim by its very nature requires the mobilization of conscious masses. Without such conscious masses, our goal is impossible. Therefore we need the fullest democracy.

Their aim requires the straitjacketing or tranquilizing of anything like mass involvement from below. Therefore they must always want to negate or dilute or abolish democratic controls from below.

We, because of the nature of our goals, have no fear of the unlimited unleashing of democratic initiatives and drives. They, on the contrary, must always be wary of it, even when they seek to manipulate it.

And by "they" I mean not only the present ruling elites but also various aspiring elites, like the elitist intelligentsia or bureaucrats who would like to be benevolent despots in place of the capitalists.

Now we can return to the recent issue of the anti-Dow demonstrations. Was it necessary to dump the right to free speech in order to defend the anti-Dow demonstrations? I think this is nonsense, and the case against it is almost an open-and-shut one. Here are a number of considerations:

(1)The Dow recruiters did not even pretend to be coming on campus in order to present any views, opinions, or speech whatsoever. We should welcome the opportunity if they asked for university facilities to present argumentation and discussion defending what they are doing — by organizing a forum, or setting up a table to distribute their statements, or what have you. That is a question of free speech.

(2)The Dow representatives were using special facilities provided by the university not to present their opinions on the use of napalm, but to carry on their company business. That's all!

(3)Many universities — for example, at Berkeley — withdraw this privilege from companies that discriminate racially or recruit strikebreakers. Is this is a violation of the right to free speech by racist companies? The apologists cannot have it both ways. If Dow's right to use university facilities for company business lies in the ground of free speech, then these other cases lies in the ground of free speech too. Or suppose a university adopted the policy of allowing no private firm or corporation to use its premises and facilities for any company business including recruiting: this still leaves them the full possibility of setting up a headquarters near campus and advertising their presence as usual, and changes very little for them. But whatever one thinks of the desirability of such an overall policy, would it mean that the university had abolished "free speech" for corporations on campus? I do not think anyone would even claim that. The practice of allowing company recruiters on campus is defensible as a convenience for the students, but not as a right for the company.

By the way, if Dow's right to use special university facilities for recruitment of employees is a matter of free speech, then this would be so also if the Communist Party asked for special university facilities to recruit its organizers. It would be interesting to see how many universities would give the Communists this same treatment, and also how many of the liberals, who now defend Dow's "free speech," would demand such equal treatment ...

The point of arguing this liberal nonsense is only to show that defense of the anti-Dow demonstrations sets up no earthly reason to dump free speech principles – unless one has other ideological motives for doing so.

But we know, as a matter of fact, that such motives do exist. The latest case in point, in the radical milieu, is the ideological current of which Herbert Marcuse is the best known theoretician.

This current has a textbook now: Marcuse's essay in the book "A Critique of Pure Tolerance." Here, almost in so many words, Marcuse condemns freedom of speech ("tolerance" of it anyway) for those whose views are antithetical to him, and, fairly clearly, advocates an "educational dictatorship" of enlightened intellectuals like himself who know they are right and everybody else is wrong. He does this with only occasional backing-and-filling and a smidgen of Hegelianized doubletalk, but not much. (See especially his pages 109-111 and 106, but the whole essay has to be read to get the full flavor.)

What makes this almost fantastic is that this modest proposal for "intolerance" is made in the context of what is Marcuse's other ideological trademark. This is his view that there are no masses who can be mobilized for progressive struggles. "Dissent is declining," he maintains (quite wrongly, of course); and the dissenting minorities are "small and powerless ." There is nobody to fight (except a handful of intelligentsia of his own stripe). Nobody has painted a more pessimistic view of the social scene. And yet, precisely in this situation, he writes a manifesto advocating that free speech and democratic rights ("tolerance") be denied to views that you consider pernicious!

This is all the ammunition that our witchhunters need. It endorses everything Sidney Hook has ever written in justification of the witchhunt – though naturally Marcuse and Hook would use the same theory against different victims. To paraphrase the famous "It is not merely a crime but a blunder," one has to say, "This is not merely a blunder – this is bloody suicide ."

Perhaps as a result of Marcuse's influence, the SDS's Carl Davidson (New Left Notes, 13 Nov. 1967) has an extraordinarily crude formulation of this point of view. His conclusion: "it is the duty of a revolutionary not only to be intolerant of, but to actually suppress the anti-democratic activities of the dominant order ." The reason: "our critique argues" that this social order is anti-democratic. Now if someone else's critique "argues" that it is Davidson and his friends who are anti-democratic, then that someone else has just as good a case for suppressing him and his similars. Not only that, but since the "dominant order" is indeed dominant, whereas Davidson represents a small minority, there is no question of who is going to suppress whom. The very idea of an obvious minority talking about suppressing the "activities of the dominant order" is itself a give-away—if that order is indeed dominant. Among the things it gives away is that such grandiose bluster is a mark of impotence and frustration, not strength and confidence.

These elitist types—including the Marcuse types who give their reactionary views a radical cast—fear democratic liberties in their very bones. They are in the full tradition of Carlyle and Ruskin and H.G. Wells and similar theoreticians expressing the impotent aspirations of disrooted intellectuals for Platonic kingdoms of the philosopher-despot (whose visage usually has a curious resemblance to their own).

While they are impotent themselves, their real role is as apologists for less impotent would-be despots.

Revolutionary socialists propose to do the opposite. We want to push to the limit all the presuppositions and practices of the fullest democratic involvement of the greatest mass of people. To the limit: that is, all the way. No progressive social transformation is possible except insofar as the largest mass of plain people from way below in society start moving. And this movement both requires, and also helps to bring about, the fullest opening-up of society to democratic controls from below—not their further restriction. It means the breaking up of anti-democratic limitations and restrictions. It means the greater unleashing of new initiatives from below. In other words, it means the exact opposite of Marcuseism.

The issue of free speech is only one sector of this greater question; but it is nonetheless a test of politics.

Independent Socialist 1968

Chapter XIII:
Sects and "Sectism"

There is a terminological problem. "Sect" is often used as a cuss-word to mean a group one doesn't like. "Movement" is often used to describe something that does not exist in organized form; as when "the American socialist movement" is used as an abbreviation for scattered socialist elements that often do not "move" at all. We shall use these terms with more precise meanings. A sect presents itself as *the* embodiment of the socialist movement, though it is a membership organization whose boundary is set more or less rigidly by the points in its political program rather than by its relation to the social struggle. In contrast, a working-class *party* is not simply an electoral organization but rather, whether electorally engaged or not, an organization which *really is* the political arm of decisive sectors of the working class, which politically reflects (or refracts) the working class in motion as it is. A "socialist movement" sums up the mass manifestations of a socialist working class in various fields, not only the political, usually around a mass socialist party. For present purposes, the important distinction is between the sect form of organization and a form of organization common in other countries but which does not yet exist in this backward country.

This approach is basic to the paper, for essentially it deals with the question: *Is there an alternative to the sect mode of organization* which dominates the whole history of American socialism, past and present?

H.D.

NEW BEGINNINGS
About the Road to an American Socialist Movement

Since there are socialists in America but no socialist movement, it is understandable that the socialists will say, "Let us go and *form* a socialist movement ." All considerations argue for this obvious step, and there are no arguments against it: except one. This is the fact — historical fact — that no one can decide to "make" a revolution. Whatever is formed by fiat will turn out to be a sect alongside the other sects, even if it is that better kind of sect which believes in not being sectarian.

Let us make clear from the outset that we do not have the answer to the $64 question, viz., a formula or gimmick which, if only followed, will infallibly produce a party or movement out of the woodwork. We will all have to grope for some time. But we have some conceptions about the direction in which to grope, and the criteria for deciding whether developments are hopeful or hindering.

1

A socialist movement will become a possibility in this country, as it did in others, as its bases are matured by social-political conditions. If, however, it cannot be created simply by an effort of will, it is also historically true that it is not simply a matter of spontaneous generation. When the bases for a socialist movement mature, it will be difficult for it to come into being unless the nascent movement is crystallized with the help of active socialist elements. Every socialist movement has been the outcome of the fusion of spontaneity and leadership, of naturally developed elements and conscious organization.

This means that, for us American socialists today who look forward to the building of a genuine socialist movement, there is a course we can take which will further this objective and bring it nearer, which will fructify the ground on which it will arise, which will make it easier for its elements to mature from place to place. The alternative to creation-by-fiat is *not* that we passively wait for it to arise by itself without the intervention of human hands.

It follows that the course taken now by American socialists can also have the opposite effect: of turning off dispositions toward a genuine movement; of sterilizing the ground on which the seeds of the movement might germinate; of making it harder for workers to find their way to a socialist movement-in-the-making.

Unfortunately, it is this latter course which today is dominant among the sects, sectlets, and micro-sects of what passes nowadays as American socialism. The sect form of American socialist groupment today is a roadblock in the way; and the sect notions that are dominant among this groupment constitute a poison which could immobilize and abort a socialist movement even if it got started.

2

American socialism today has hit a new low in terms of sect fragmentation. There are more sects going through their gyrations at this moment than have ever existed in all previous periods in this country taken together. And the fragments are still fissioning, down to the submicroscopic level. Politically speaking, their average has dropped from the comic-opera plane to the comic-book grade. Where the esoteric sects (mainly Trotskyist splinters) of the 1930s tended toward a sort of super sophistication in Marxism and futility in practice, there is a gaggle of grouplets now (mainly Maoist-Castroite) characterized by amnesia regarding the Marxist tradition, ignorance of the socialist experience, and extreme primitivism. The road to an American socialist movement surely lies over the debris, or around the rotting off-shoots of, this fetid jungle of sects.

To be sure, we recognize that there are sects and sects: we still have with us some sects and sectlets of the "classic" type, i.e., mainly futile and fossilized, as distinct from the new crop of neo-Stalinist (Maoist-Castroite-etc.) sects that represent a more positive danger to any healthy development in the working-class movement. it is characteristic of the latter that they do not want a class movement — not because of some special organization conception but because of their basic political conceptions. Just as their "socialism" is the rule of a state despotism over a bureaucratically collectivized economy, so their organizational road to power is the formation of an elite band of Maximum Leaders which holds itself ready to bestow its own rule, at a propitious movement, on an elemental upsurge of the people. (This is new only in the sense of being a regurgitation, in new forms, of the oldest type of leftist movement, the Jacobin-putschist circles that dominated before the rise of Marxism.)

If these neo-Stalinist sects are "oriented" toward the working class — or toward the lumpenpoor, or the blacks, or the "third world," etc. — it is only in the sense that men in a hurry orient toward a pack of horses. They make clear that the historical content of "Maoism" in its different varieties is the conception of the bureaucratic revolution-from-above engineered by a band of self-appointed leaders *riding on the back of a class movement*, and bridling it; for which end, the most suitable class is one with a minimum of capacity for initiative and self-organization, such as a peasantry. These elements are — some for reasons of class makeup, enemies to the revolutionary democracy of socialism.

Hence also these elements need the sect form of organization. For them the sect is not an unfortunate necessity due to the absence of a real movement: it *is* their movement. Minuscule size may not even be a drawback; for didn't Castro "make" the revolution with only umpteen good men?* How many commissars are needed on the Long March? This indeed is part of the dynamic behind the current proliferation of sects, since they are not inhibited by the

---

* The answer, by the way, is: No, the Cuban revolution made Castro, not vice-versa. But that is another story.

prejudice that a "party" needs much of a rank and file.

3

As for the "classic" type of sects still operating: these presently divide more or less into those that stem from the Trotskyist sect tradition and those that exemplify the social-democratic pattern. (To be sure, the Trotskyist grouplets shade off at one end into the neo-Stalinist type, particularly the larger sect called the Socialist Workers "Party," whose politics has steadily moved since Trotsky's death in the direction of Stalinization.)

What characterizes the classic sect was best defined by Marx himself: it *counterposes* its sect criterion of programmatic points against the real movement of the workers in the class struggle, which may not measure up to its high demands. The touchstone of support (the *point d'honneur,"* in Marx's words) is conformity with the sect's current shibboleths — whatever they may be, including programmatic points good in themselves. The approach pointed by Marx was different: without giving up or concealing one's own programmatic politics in the slightest degree, the real Marxist looks to the lines of struggle calculated to *move decisive sectors of the class into action – into movement against the established powers of the system* (state and bourgeoisie and their agents, including their labor lieutenants inside the workers' movement). And for Marx, it is this reality of social (class) collision which will work to elevate the class's consciousness to the level of the socialist movement's program.

To move a fighting sector of the class into action against the established powers *by only a step* is more important than "a thousand programs," Marx and Engels used to reiterate, and there's no use denouncing them for deprecating programmatic politics. To the sect mind, their approach is utterly incomprehensible. For over a century now, we have seen the two touchstone; and the difference is as glaring nowadays as it ever was. The most important test has always been the relationship of the self-styled Marxist and the working class organized on the elementary economic level, i.e., the trade-union movement. (The test is all the more decisive in the United States where, unfortunately, the trade-union movement is the *only* class movement of the workers in existence.)

4

The sect-socialist* has always felt a soul-torn difficulty in the face of a trade-union movement which rejects socialism; and the dominance of sect life in the history of socialism has been accompanied by the predominance of a leftist *hostility* to trade-unionism as such.

Marx and Engels constituted the first socialist school to hold a position supporting trade-unionism as such (while critical of given policies, leaders, etc., of course). And after their time, socialist history divides mainly between the social-democratic types who supported reformist trade-unionism precisely because they were themselves reformist rather than Marxist, and the would-be revolutionary socialists who found "revolutionary" arguments for returning to the old crap of socialist anti-trade-unionism — with the addition of Marxistical rhetoric to dress up their sectist approach. Very few so-called or self-styled Marxists have understood the heart of Marx's approach to proletarian socialism: The basic strategy for building a socialist movement lies in fusing two movements — the class movement for this-or-that step which gets a decisive sector of the class into collision with the established powers of state and bourgeoisie, a collision on whatever scale possible; and the work of permeating this class movement with educational propaganda for social revolution, which integrates the two.

If this has been true in the best days of the Marxist movement to a greater or lesser extent, it took grotesque forms in the recent past of the American left, i.e., during the Sixties when the radical impulse was temporarily coming from non-worker sectors (students and some blacks not rooted in working-class life, for example).** The student New Left commonly swallowed the image of Labor dished out by the sociological brainwashers of the academy: "Big Labor" alongside Big Business etc., identification of trade-unionism with George Meany or Hoffa, implicit equation of the trade-union movement with its bureaucracy, organized workers as an ipso-facto "middle class" stratum and part of the Establishment, and the rest of the ideological garbage from the real

---

* We use this awkward term instead of "sectarian," which is usually understood to mean one who carries on certain *policies*. A term is needed for one who bases himself on sect organization, whatever the policies of the sect.

** For a more positive appreciation of the strengths and weaknesses of the New Left, see the collection *The New Left of the Sixties*, edited by M. Friedman (Independent Socialist Press, 1972).

Establishment's anti-working-class mind mills.

Even among those New Left elements — the better ones — who oriented toward going to work in factories or plants ("going to the people"), the dominant conception was that trade unions as such had to be replaced with more "radical" formations of shop organization which would somehow be outside the trade-union structure without being a dual trade union. These conceptions either remained in the realm of fantasy while making it impossible for their holders to integrate themselves into the real movement as trade-union militants, or (worse) were acted out destructively in certain places, bringing harm to the workers and discreditment to the radicals. Nowhere did the New Left impulse into the factories eventuate in a more or less well-rooted movement of militants inside the trade-union movement that could really offer opposition to the established bureaucracy: this is its indictment.

The sectist approach to the class movement showed its pointed ears in many ways that need illustration. Here are two.

Item. The student radical, heart filled with sympathy for poor workers, turns to the Farm Workers' struggle as one clearly meriting his support. Typically he does not "go to the people" by going to work in the fields like other workers; for should his special talents be buried under a clod? He goes to work "for the union," i.e., as what the union calls a student volunteer. Impressed by his own self-sacrifice on the one hand, on the other he finds that the Farm Workers scarcely measures up to his ideal of what the class struggle should look like. Pretty soon he complains that the student volunteers "have no say" in policy, i.e., he demands that powers of decision be partly shifted out of the union members' hands and into those of the alien-class visitors who have deigned to donate their time. Or, finding that the internal life and democracy of the union are far from satisfactory, he may decide that the Farm Workers do not really deserve his support. He would bestow his saving presence only on certified-pure class struggles taking place on a different planetary plane.

Item. The trade-union movement was very behindhand in producing opposition to the Vietnam war, as is well known, while antiwar feeling grew around the campuses. In student circles, the programmatic touchstone for complete opposition to the war came to be the slogan of unilateral withdrawal, which was richly justified. But finally, here and there pockets of antiwar opposition in the trade-union movement *did* start developing. Eventually a number of the more socially conscious and progressive labor leaders did screw up courage and founded the Labor Assembly for Peace in the teeth of violent denunciations by the Meany bureaucracy. These beginnings were timid in many respects, and, among other hesitancies, stated opposition to the war without specifying the slogan of unilateral withdrawal. We know of no more flagrant example of the sect mentality than the scornful attitude taken by New-Leftists toward this *beginning* of an organized anti-war opposition in the labor movement. Even in the San Francisco Bay Area, which had the most militant and most wide-open branch of the Labor Assembly for Peace and where leaders of the group if not the group itself openly spoke out for unilateral withdrawal, *not one single New-Leftist eligible* could be persuaded to taint his soul by having anything to do with a group so backward as to fall short of the unilateral-withdrawal program. The fact that this development represented the first steps of a responsible sector of the trade unions moving into collision with the established powers — this fact meant nothing to the sectists. *The only consideration they understood was their soul-saving shibboleth,* which they counterposed to the real initiation of class motion.

5

Such is the road of the sect. How to get out of that rut? There are two notions that try to remedy the ills of sectism by broadening the sect. The intention is good; the remedy impractical.

One is the proposal to abolish sectarianism by a call for the unity of all the sects. This may also be presented as a road to forming a socialist "movement." It is a piteous illusion. In practice, it may mean a spate of unity negotiations among some of the sects (a common time-killing enterprise), or even a unification or two (a drop out of the bucket). But the actual unification of all the sects is an inherent impossibility where the programmatic shibboleths on which the sects are based are politically incompatible. The product of sect unification turns out to be nothing but a somewhat larger sect, as long as the conditions for a genuine socialist movement do not obtain. The idea of an "all-inclusive" sect is a will o' the wisp.

Incompatible political programs can be held together, at least for a historical period, within the framework of a party/movement; for the cement which holds such a formation together is its role in the class struggle itself, the fact that it is the class-in-movement; what holds the antagonistic political tendencies in place is the pressure of the class enemies outside. As long as this is not the real situation of the movement, nothing else can take its place, including exhortations against "sectarianism."

The second proposal is one that aims at the same result by a different route: viz., launching a sect whose distinguishing programmatic point is that it will voluntarily eschew distinguishing programmatic points. This is to be achieved by limiting the program to some minimum socialist (or radical) basis on which "everyone" can agree, i.e., a statement of abstract socialism. If a left wing wants to push the group to a revolutionary position, like *No support to Democrats*, the minimum is exploded; in practice, therefore, the program must be reformist. The Socialist Party has wanted to be this kind of sect most of the time since it ceased to be a mass movement; and more recently the New American Movement has set out to concretize this aim in some still unclear form.

Sometimes the aim is derived by reminiscence from the different historical period (before 1917) when the Socialist Party was a congeries of different political views which were not yet consciously understood to be basically antagonistic and whose consequences had not yet been acted out. But we cannot simply pass a motion to go back to the Debs era.

As long as the life of the organization (whether or not labeled "party") is actually based on its politically distinctive ideas, rather than on the real social struggles in which it is engaged, it will not be possible to suppress the clash of programs requiring different actions in support of different forces. The key question becomes the achievement of a *mass base*, which is not just a numerical matter but a matter of class representation. Given a mass base in the social struggle, the party does not necessarily have to suppress the internal play of political conflict, since the centrifugal force of political disagreements is counterbalanced by the centripetal pressure of the class struggle. Without a mass base, a sect that calls itself a party cannot suppress the divisive effect of fundamental differences on (for example) supporting or opposing capitalist parties at home in the shape of liberal Democrats and such, or supporting or opposing the maneuvers of the "Communist" world.

6

If the road of the sect is a blind alley, what then?

The road of the sect has always been a blind alley; yet socialist movements have come into existence.

There has never been a single case of a sect which developed into, or gave rise to, a genuine socialist movement — by the only process that sects know, the process of accretion. The sect mentality typically sees the road ahead as one in which the sect (one's own sect) will grow and grow, because it has the Correct Political Program, until it becomes a large sect, then a still larger sect, eventually a small mass party, then larger, etc., until it becomes large and massy enough to impose itself as the party of the working class in fact. But in two hundred years of socialist history, this has never actually happened, in spite of innumerable attempts.

This is no proof that it will never happen in the unforeseeable future. But it is proof that *there must be some other road to the formation of a genuine socialist movement which is not the road of the sect.*

This road has been will-nigh totally forgotten in the general "sectification" of socialist circles in our period. The slightest acquaintance with Marx's view of what is to be done to build a socialist movement is enough to remind that Marx was violently and unconditionally hostile to anything resembling a sect. Not only did he never try to organize a Marxist sect, but he positively scorned those who did.

It is less easily understood that Lenin never wanted to form a sect and never did do so, and that the Bolshevik party was not the result of a sect formation that grew by accretion. When Lenin came out of exile in 1900 and went abroad to begin the struggle to permeate the existing socialist circles with the ideas of revolutionary Marxism, he never thought to et up an ideological grouplet of his own, a sect, even though the Russian socialists in exile were already divided into sects (which were already splitting, etc.).

What Lenin helped to launch was a Marxist *political center* in a non-sect form, in the form of a periodical manned by an editorial board, *Iskra*.

The political center itself educated for full revolutionary Marxism. At the same time, the party/movement it called for was an all-inclusive socialist party in which the revolutionary Marxist center would constitute *one* tendency, hopefully eventually dominant. Both sides of the picture conditioned each other: *"Before we can unite, and in order that we may unite, we must first of all firmly and definitely draw the lines of demarcation between the various groups* [tendencies]," wrote Lenin on launching *Iskra*. But the lines of demarcation were not to be drawn along sect lines, with organizational walls bounding them: this was the sect course which he did not follow.

Iskra was not merely a "literary" enterprise: this is a misunderstanding. A worker in Russia became an "Iskraist" insofar as he agreed with the political views of that political center; and as an "Iskraist" he himself became a political center for further spreading those views in the popular circles in which he worked, in his factory, in his village, in his socialist circle. One of the views spread by this political center was that the party/movement to be built should be a broad one. Lenin never gave up this conception of how to build a socialist movement at any time before the October Revolution. It was on the basis of this conception that the Leninist party actually evolved.

We do not propose either the Russian movement or Lenin's course as the model for America in the 1970s. The significance of the case is different. On the other hand, it is many of the sects that believe they are following in Lenin's footsteps in building a hard sect on the basis of a shibboleth-program. They are wrong because in this belief they have merely internalized what they have been told of the nature of "Leninism" by the anti-Bolshevik industry of the American establishment. On the other hand, the case of Lenin's road to a revolutionary party is important because he applied it uniquely. His unique course was to be serious and uncompromising about maintaining a revolutionary Marxist political center as the instrument of permeating the whole movement with its ideas, and insisting that majorities so gained be recognized by the whole movement. It was the right wing that split.

We do maintain that the alternative to the sect road which is suggested by the successes and failures of socialist history is also suggested by *generalizing* from Lenin's *Iskra* model as well as from a dozen other cases of the building of real socialist movements in various contexts and circumstances.

7

What should be done to prepare the ground for the eventual formation of a socialist movement/party in America, that is, a mass-based socialist formation which is the political expression of the working class moving toward a collision with the established powers of capitalist society?

We first address ourselves to the individual socialist who wonders what he or she should and can do other than join the sect of his choice and waste his energies in the vicissitudes of sect life:

You have the opportunity for undertaking a two-sided socialist enterprise keyed to your own circumstances. We suggest the following double-barreled liaison for you, both sides of which are necessary for the whole thing to be meaningful.

(1) Your basic contribution to the eventual formation of a socialist

movement is what you do to develop a socialist circle around you where you are now. We are thinking in the first place of your role in the work-place (factory, office, school, or whatever).

First things first: what the American working-class movement needs first of all is the crystallization of an *organized militant opposition in the trade unions*, because this is the existing class movement of the workers and the only one.

It would be a sad sectarian mistake to think of this as a "radical" or socialist opposition, even though it will inevitably be powered mostly by radicals and socialists of sorts, and also inevitably lead its militants to think in radical and socialist terms. What is needed is a broad progressive wing of the labor movement. In Marxist terms, this is adequately defined as a wing which advocates class-struggle unionism as against business unionism, whether it defines itself in "class struggle" language or not. From the point of view of the worker, there is a felt need to carry on a *militant* union fight without getting "mixed up" with socialism and reds. From the point of view of the socialist, the organization of a militant opposition to the union establishment sets up an elementary school of class-struggle socialism. One of its consequences, for example, is bound to be the politicalization of the trade-union movement: its entry into independent political action, which depends in turn on breaking up its attachment to Democratic Party politics.

This opposition movement must be a *loyal opposition*. That means: loyal to the interests of trade-unionism in the same degree that it fights the boss and the bureaucrat, whose power is not in the interests of trade-unionism. It is necessary to proclaim this today — to put it on the banner, so to speak — because the sect radicals have been so successful in discrediting themselves before conscientious trade-unionists, and confusing "radical trade-unionism" with a sect's commando raids to rip off a plant situation by a display of "militancy" even if the workers' interests are harmed, or the union work is wrecked, as long as a couple of members are recruited to the sect. The sectists who operate in unions and plants to subordinate the workers' interests to their sect-advertising adventures and sorties are enemies of the working class and of socialism, not merely "misguided radicals" who are to be chided in Marxistical editorials. They are not "adventuristic" allies of *our* camp in the class struggle; they are wreckers who cannot always be distinguished from police provocateurs. Any militant opposition movement in the trade unions which makes alliances with such elements will deserve its fate.

If you are in regular contact with a number of people — in the work-place or some other "mass" situation—whom you are trying to influence in a socialist direction, then you are doing something. What the future socialist movement needs is a network of informal socialist circles—or formal ones if you will—which have an integral relation to the real struggles people are carrying on.*

The same goes for the black movement, the women workers' movement, the student movement, etc.

You may be accustomed to the belief that only members of a sect are interested in such work. That is not so. There are innumerable cases where such cells of militancy have sprung up in work-place, office or school around people who are not even socialists, or do not know they are.

What *is* true is that membership in a sect has often been the stimulus to undertaking this role, through group pressure and guidance, and that the sect performs the service of providing reading and study materials, etc., for the circle activity. This does point to the positive side of sect work, which we cannot deny. What this means is that socialist efforts along these lines need the assistance of a *political center of some sort*, to which one can look for literature, advice and help. Moreover, there soon arises the need for separate individual and circle efforts to be linked up.

(2) But the role of a political center need not be carried by a sect.

Historically, this job has been done most often and most successfully by a paper or other publication of a socialist political center which is organized simply as an editorial board or other editorial enterprise. (*Iskra* was only one of dozens of examples of how this was done as socialist movements came into existence all over the world.) Historically, also, political centers of this sort have frequently undertaken *organizing* functions as their influence spread, the organizing being the product or by-product of the work of its agents and representatives. (*Iskra* agents were the organizing arms of the first Leninist center.) The point would be utterly lost if these enterprises were to be considered merely literary enterprises in the usual bourgeois sense. there is a continuous line which has carried such political centers from their function as

---

* Instead of the proliferation of sect-type groups, we should like to see a proliferation of open socialistic clubs, discussion circles, forums, and similar loose and unpretentious aggregations *which are formed around work-place situations* by people engaged in common work. These would be among the nuclei around which a real socialist movement could crystallize, given favorable conditions. We freely recognize that favorable conditions do not obtain now, especially since the sectists would be eager to crush such hopeful developments in their lethal embrace.

producers of "literature" to their role as centers for the stimulation of organization in one form or another.

Such political centers are operating today in this country, alongside the proliferating sects, and often quite effectively. Naturally, it is a question of political centers with widely varying political complexions, most of them distasteful to our own views and to each other's. We mention them not to celebrate their work but to exhibit alternatives to the sect road.

The *Guardian* and Sweezy's *Monthly Review* have functioned more or less as political centers emerging from a neo-Stalinist tendency of one kind or another. (Indeed, the *Guardian* is now involved with a brace of neo-Stalinist sects in talking up the formation of a Maoist "party" out of their unification.) On the right wing social-democratic side, the clique of litterateurs around *Dissent* functions as the only political center for that tendency that exists outside of George Meany's offices.

These examples differ in the amount of attention they pay, or have paid at other times, to the function of relating to their readers (followers) in the field. For our present purposes we wish only to stress that a political center does not have to be a sect. More: a political center can undertake a relationship with its followers which is not bedeviled by the rigid requirements of organizational life, its life-and-death votes, faction fights, splits, internal disputes, and ingrown rituals of imitating a miniature or micro-"mass party."

8

From the point of view of the individual socialist who wants to "do something," we would summarize our suggestion as follows: (1) Crystallize a circle of co-thinkers around you wherever you are, in the course of your activity in the arena of the social struggle that goes along with your situation. *You* are the smallest-unit political center there is.

(2) Make contact with a political center that makes sense from your own point of view, for help in literature, advice, and outside linkups, and work with it to whatever extend you find useful. But there is no reason against having this relationship with more than one political center, if they suit your own political views. Such a political center may even be a sect; but if you do not join it, it relates to you only as one political center among others. This relationship is a hang-loose relationship: if you do not have a vote in deciding its affairs, it is likewise true that it cannot tell you what to do by exerting its sect

"discipline" over your own judgment. You do not erect an organizational barrier between you as the adherent of one sect and someone else who cleaves to another sect or none. In your work, you use whatever literature you wish, whatever their source. You will use your money not for the sect's fund drives but to finance your own work. If enough take this course to break up the sect system, that would be a good thing for the future potentialities of an American socialist movement.

There is a better chance of a genuine socialist movement arising out of such a hang-loose complex of relationships than out of the fossilized world of the sects. We are *not* under the impression that a very large number of individuals are going to start tomorrow by following the course we have described above. We have been interested so far simply in illustrating the way in which socialist movements have arisen elsewhere—the only way, in broad outline. We have sketched the kind of development which provides an alternative to the sect mode of organization which is driving American socialism into the ground.

Very likely, whatever will actually happen in this country will happen somewhat differently—as usual. If the springing up of socialist circles is not happening on a mass scale, it is also true that there is no other direction visible in which the emergence of a mass socialist movement is just around the corner. All one can do is push in a direction in which one's efforts will not be wasted, no matter what the outcome. The only thing we are sure of is that the road of the sect is a dead end.

October 1973

Chapter XIV:
Marx, "Marxism" and Trade Unions

This essay is based on the edited transcript of a series of talks given in 1970 to former participants in the civil rights and anti-war movements in Berkeley who were becoming involved in the trade union movement at a time when the New Left was collapsing. Its aim was to disabuse these former student activists of the prejudices and assumptions they inevitably brought to trade union activity. It is reprinted here as an illustration of what "Socialism from Below" means in practice. [EH].

I've been asked, in connection with this talk, what there is to read on the subject of Marxism and the Trade Unions. And the answer is, perhaps surprisingly, virtually nothing. There are libraries full of weighty tomes on Marxism and Hegelianism, the Labor Theory of Value, the Application of Historical Materialism to the Epoch of Christianity and other, admittedly important, questions. But revolutions haven't been defeated, socialists haven't won or lost because of their views, mistaken or otherwise, on these important questions. Revolutions have been won or lost because of the politically conscious minority's relation, or lack of relation, to the mass of the people in motion in times of crisis. And, in particular, because of the relation of this vanguard to the trade union movement. Yet, there is almost nothing written on the subject worth reading.

As Marxists like to say, that is not accidental. At least one of the reasons for the total lack of literature on a subject which would seem to be at the very heart of the whole theory of Marxism is that, essentially, no Marxist group has ever carried on any systematic revolutionary work in trade unions.

What about the Bolsheviks? Well, Lenin was for it, but unions were illegal for most of the time in Czarist Russia and severely restricted by police control when they were legal or quasi-legal. Even so—and I can't deal with the question here—the whole problem of the involvement of the Bolsheviks in whatever trade union activity there was is important and interesting. But it is hardly the typical situation we are concerned with.

Is there anyone else? You may have heard the rumor that the German Socialist movement was Marxist in its early years, before the First World War. Did they ever carry on revolutionary Marxist work in the trade unions? In the most revolutionary days of the German socialist movement they carried on no revolutionary work in the trade unions that you could call such.

How about Rosa Luxemburg? No, her position on this question was absolutely monstrous and completely contrary to that of Marx.

Here and there in the socialist movement there have been important exceptions. Eugene Debs, for example, although of course he wasn't doing it from the point of view of an application of a revolutionary Marxist theory to trade unions, came out of a militant and objectively revolutionary struggle in the trade union. There are a couple of other examples, but nothing of any size.

We have here, then, a peculiar subject. On the one hand, by its very nature, it raises the basic question of Marxism, its relation to the labor movement. On the other hand, in a century nothing has been written on it and an account of revolutionary Marxist work in trade unions could be put in a nutshell.

Let me remind you of another fact about the trade union movement and the socialist movement. The simple idea of socialists favoring trade unions took most of a century to sink into the socialist movement. That is, before Marx there was a half century of socialism — and how many socialists do you think there were in that period who were just in favor of trade unions? The answer is — almost none. And, if we confine ourselves to those advocates of socialism who figure prominently in most historical accounts, we can drop the qualifier. The early exceptions, such as the Anglo-Irish Owenite William Thompson, are relegated to the footnotes and their pro-trade union position ignored. As it was at the time.

Think about that for a moment. England is the home of trade unionism, is it not? Capitalism arises there first and with it, trade unionism. Socialism arises in England on an anti-trade union basis. Owenism, with the exceptions mentioned above, was anti-trade union. More surprisingly, the Chartist movement, again with exceptions which have been relegated to footnotes, was anti-trade union, and that includes also the revolutionary wing of Chartism. By anti-trade union I mean a negative attitude towards the trade union movement. In general, the attitude was, "the political movement is primary and the trade unions are just a lousy reform outfit that we are really not interested in, because we're after bigger game ."

There is an historical paradox to be noted here. The Chartists were fighting for a series of political demands which they viewed as amounting to a social revolution. In fact, in hindsight, we know that all the planks of the charter which the Chartist movement was fighting for were later carried out by the bourgeoisie. The trade union movement, however, which they scorned, is still struggling — maybe not on the same level, but for the same things. Their program was not carried out by the bourgeoisie — couldn't be as a matter of fact. The difference then, between being revolutionary for one's time and being on a much more fundamental level, flows not from the revolutionary fervor of the people involved, but from something else.

It is not only a question of movements before Marx's time. Right through the 19th century you can look around anywhere and ask yourself: "just who's in favor of trade unions?" And the answer still is, with the exception of the Marxist movement, almost nobody. Only Marxism as a socialist theory was pro-trade union.

Now what I'm interested in is not only that Marx was the first prominent socialist to favor trade unions. What I want you to understand is that Marxism was and is the only kind of socialism that establishes an integral relationship between socialism – and social revolution – and trade unionism. That link does not exist for any other kind of socialism. In terms of socialist theory, Marxism is the only one which establishes an integral link between trade unionism and the social revolution; which sees the trade union movement as a revolutionary fact, even if and when the trade unions themselves are not revolutionary.

Now, of course, by the end of the 19th century the trade unions had established themselves and everybody favored them. Once something is established, it gets a favorable press. By that time that doesn't mean very much. Because trade unions fought for reforms, they were, naturally, favored by all sorts of reformist political tendencies – again, once they were established. So, around the turn of the century, it is no longer true that nobody except Marxists favors trade unions. What is still true, however, is that everybody who considers himself, or herself, a revolutionary socialist has a negative attitude towards trade unions, with the exception of Marxists, on more or less the same grounds as the Chartists. "We're revolutionaries, they're a reform organization – what have we got to do with them?"

In every country, almost every type of would-be revolutionary – except, again, Marxists – took a negative attitude towards trade unions. It took different forms. One peculiar form it took was syndicalism in France. Syndicalism was a trade union movement – wasn't it? Well, yes and no. Its revolutionary syndicalism in fact was based on a very negative attitude towards mass, reformist union movements. In Britain this sectarian attitude sterilized English socialism for a century. It divided English socialism between reformism on the one hand and sectarians, who called themselves Marxists, on the other. In America, there was the Socialist Labor Party whose hostility towards the mass movement provoked some of Marx and Engels most biting criticism. And that is saying something.

There are different ways of taking a negative attitude towards the trade union movement. For example, the SLP in DeLeon's day was not against trade unions at all. They were for revolutionary trade unions, the SLP's trade unions, which are excellent trade unions with only one defect — they don't exist. In the early years of the Communist International there was a tremendous upsurge of what Lenin polemecized against as "Left Wing Communism" — which meant in the trade union field a negative attitude towards the mass reformist trade unions.

Outside the Marxist movement there has been no revolutionary socialism which has any theoretical basis for linking its revolutionary perspective with support for the trade union movement as it actually existed. Why?

The answer is, to begin with, a very simple proposition, one which has never sunk into the Marxist movement. Only Marxism establishes a link between the trade union movement and a revolutionary perspective, because only Marxism is based on a class view of social struggle. What could be simpler than that? the class view of social struggle is the A of the ABC of Marxism. Everybody knows it and yet nobody knows it. It is very rarely used as a way of understanding the trade union movement.

It has been said, quite rightly, that Marx did not invent the class struggle theory of history. What is distinctive, is that Marxism, and it alone, basis its socialism on the class struggle. That, too, is a simple proposition which has more to it than meets the eye. Sects rival to Marxism saw socialism primarily as a set of ideas to propagandize. Marx did not.

How do you propagandize? In order to propagandize you have to find people to talk to. So you orient yourself in a particular direction. Different socialist or revolutionary sects have oriented themselves in different directions, and that is one way to differentiate between sects. For example, the Bakunin anarchists oriented themselves to the déclassé lumpen-elements, in theoretical theses as well as in practice. The Russian Socialist Revolutionaries oriented to the peasants, and the Fabians toward the middle class. Other socialist groups have oriented themselves to the intellectuals and intelligentsia, and still others to the working class. They oriented themselves in these directions because they believed that these were green fields for recruitment. Now that is one way of looking at social strata. It is not the movement of a class itself which will remake society — the class simply provides recruits for your "army." And for the purpose of recruiting your army, you orient yourself to different strata of

262

society.

There is a difference between such orientations. For example, the first socialist to decide to adopt the working class orientation was Saint-Simon. He was very clear about what he was doing. He addressed himself to the working class, saying: "My ideas are right, you adopt them and then convince your boss to do what he should in order to carry out the ideas of Saint-Simonism ."

Lasalle very consciously oriented himself to the working class because he believed the liberal bourgeoisie was hopeless. He oriented to the working class to recruit the Lassallean army. Che Guevara adopted a "class orientation" towards the Bolivian peasants; that did not mean that he thought the Bolivian peasants were going to run his movement!

This whole approach is alien to Marxism. For Marx, and for Marx alone, the significance of working class socialism was not simply that you orient to this class because you can get the most out of them, but because it is this class which, when it gets into motion, shakes the foundations of capitalist society. This is a statement about the working class which has no equivalent for those other orientations. It is an entirely different view of the class to which you orient. The aim of the Marxist movement is not to use the working class as a recruiting ground of alienated people.

Marx starts with the fact that the working class, once in motion, shakes the foundations of capitalist society, because it is moved to act by economic, not psychological, forces.

Capitalism cannot, in the long run, solve the economic problem of providing a human life for the mass of the people. You have heard that before too, but put it in proper perspective. This proposition is the basis of the class approach of Marxism. Without it you have no class approach, and cannot have one. If it is not true, there is no reason not to be a good liberal.

This is of particular relevance today because of the frequency with which one encounters, among people who consider themselves revolutionary, the idea that capitalism has shown it can solve the economic problem. Socialists, therefore, have to address themselves to other problems. Like what? The "quality of life," alienation, etc. Nowadays there is a label attached to the Marxist approach; it is "consumerism ." The term implies a contempt for those who think such things as sending your kid to school or getting a raise are important.

The basis of the trade union movement, however, is the struggle by ordinary people for a more decent life. That struggle remains still essentially economic. It is based on the fact that capitalism has not solved its economic problems. Anyone who believes otherwise must draw a couple of conclusions. One of them is that you can no longer base socialism on a class point of view. Petty-bourgeois ideologists like Marcuse or Max Nomad run down the working class because it is interested in getting the good things of life. They have nothing but contempt for such non-revolutionary aspirations. You may have noticed, however, during the ghetto riots, that the rioters, in their resentment of capitalist society, did not rush to steal Marcuse's books from the department store in order to improve their souls. As a matter of fact, they were so degenerate that they went after television sets. "Consumerism ."

Looking for "The Meaning of Life" is a possible occupation only for those strata of society for whom the economic problem *has* been solved, and who look at the problems of society from their class perspective. That is why I do not hesitate to call this position a typically petty-bourgeois ideology.

You might ask at this point: what about the *non*-economic struggles that take place in the trade union movement — struggles for "humanizing" working conditions, for example. Aren't they about the "quality of life"? Sure they are. That is why I am not putting down the phrase as such. When you talk about the "quality of life" for workers on the assembly line, however, you are talking about a question of surplus value for the capitalist. Such improvements in working conditions and the resulting improvement in "quality of life" must be paid out of some capitalist's pocket. From the capitalist's point of view, and the point of view of the capitalist system, the distinction between economic and non-economic demands does not exist. It costs money to humanize working conditions.

For the ideologists who believe that capitalism has solved the economic problem the working class has been removed as the motor force of social change. Consider, on the other hand, the reformist trade union leaders who see labor's goal as simply "more," in the sense of Gompers. They take the class struggle at its least common denominator. For 50 or 75 years now, socialists have emphasized that Gompers' slogan was pure reformism, but that the reformist leaders who use it *don't really believe it themselves*, and have been unable to carry it out consistently. Time and again, class collaborationist unions give up the struggle for more and settle for less, in order to keep the boss in business; or agree, as in World War II, to give up the strike weapon. Only a Marxist revolutionary can mean it *consistently*. The demand for more becomes revolutionary when it goes beyond the capabilities of the system to provide the

264

"more." That is the link between the fight for reforms and social revolution from a Marxist perspective. It depends on the root idea that the economic problems of the system cannot be solved within the system. The class struggle depends on this "more." All that Marx claims is that in the course of the fight for "more" out of the system—regardless of what it costs the system—the struggle becomes, in the end, a revolutionary struggle. In the end; but not in the beginning. In the beginning it means a struggle for reforms and it means organizing at a low social and political level.

The class struggle begins on a much lower level than the Marxist program itself, but the Marxist program says that this struggle is revolutionary from the beginning. The basic goal—the primary aim—is to *get the class as a whole moving.* Any such movement of the class as a whole is in itself and of itself progressive and revolutionary in its implications, because the class is. And this is true even if that class begins moving on a basis far from satisfactory to Marxists, socialists or other revolutionaries. That is the conception of class struggle held by Marx and Engels in a completely thought-out and consistent way, and by very few others.

For Marx, the First International was a working class movement because it organized workers. A socialist propaganda group is not a class organization. The problem for a socialist propaganda group, even of the best kind, is how to establish its relations with that real movement of the working class. Marx's definition of "sectarian" was a mind set which *counterposed* the socialist propaganda group to the real movement of the proletariat, because that real movement was so backward.

In this country, the trade unions are the only class organization of the proletariat. Trade unions are class organizations *par excellence* because they organize only members of a class and organize them for the sole reason that they belong to that class. The class character of any organization does not depend on its ideas; it depends on its objective role and function in society.

This movement, however, is on a level which doesn't satisfy us socialists. It therefore provides a test case. Does a class collaborationist union carry on the class struggle? Let me put it put it in its most extreme form. Take a lousy union like the Teamsters—scabbing on the Farm Workers, not very democratic, gangster ridden, racist, etc. Yet the Teamsters carry on some of the most energetic social struggles in the country.

The United States, in many respects, is the ideal country to take for these purposes. In the U.S. you have the combination of energetic, even violent,

265

struggles on behalf of "more," combined with some of the most disgusting and reactionary practices. Is a union in which the membership has practically no rights at all carrying on the class struggle? Of course it is. You have got to get clear in your mind that there is a difference between the objective meaning of a class struggle and what socialists want and fight for in the trade unions. They are not the same thing at all.

Time and again revolutionaries have been carried away by their hatred and disgust of the practices of the trade union movement—of its leadership, its bureaucracy. So we have the case of Rosa Luxemburg who, in a pamphlet entitled *The Party, the Mass Strike and the Trade Unions*, gives no discussion of the problems of trade union work. In her whole career as a revolutionary she had no connection with trade union work whatsoever. Even though, as Carl Schorske emphasized in his study of the Social Democracy, her strongest support in the party came from industrial constituencies dominated by trade union militants. When, during and after the 1905-1906 revolution, Rosa Luxemburg was faced with the development of legal trade unions in Poland, she, and her party, opposed the organization of legal mass reformist trade unions. They wanted trade unions only under party control. As her biographer says, this was no doubt her reaction to having come through a decade of fighting in Germany against the Social Democratic trade union bureaucracy, which was one of the main sources of reformism. "Why should we organize in Poland the kind of movement which is giving us so much trouble in Germany?"

To answer that question is to sum up this talk. In Poland, as in Germany, those trade unions represented the working class in movement as it was. The socialist has to choose. Either you counterpose to the real class in movement a revolutionary program (Luxemburg's approach), or you take part in the real movement in the conviction that the consistent pursuit of the movement's own goals to the end is only possible on the basis of a revolutionary program.

For the same reason that Rosa Luxemburg could not understand why it was important to build a mass, reformist union movement in Poland, she was never able to build an opposition inside the German trade union movement and party despite her great personal popularity among the rank and file.

* * *

How do we get from here to there? "Here" is society today, and "there" is the socialist society as a goal. One part of getting from here to there has been popular in the socialist movement: that part dealing with "how to make the revolution ." For some self-styled revolutionists that is all there is to the question of how to get from here to there.

Marx thought that the elementary force that led to social revolution was the tendency of working people to press beyond the limits of capitalism in their attempt to attain their goals (whether they thought that is what they were doing or not). That is why every strike is a sort of rehearsal for revolution.

That is also why every strike settlement always raises the question of the limits of capitalism. The capitalist raises it himself: "I can't afford it ." And, increasingly, the government says: "The economy can't afford it ." What they propound is the thesis of *Capital*.

The purely economic struggle does not automatically lead to revolution, but it does lead to the recognition that the economic struggle has its limits and, therefore, has to go over to a political struggle which brings it beyond the limits of capitalism — if that struggle is carried on consistently and without shrinking back from the consequences. That is a very big "if" — especially for the trade union movement — and that "if" explains why there is a need for a socialist vanguard in the union movement.

The great problem for socialist sects has been that the level the working class is operating on is always, until a very late stage, unsatisfactory to socialists. Socialist literature is full of horror stories, mostly true, describing the unsatisfactory state of the trade union movement. The great failure of the socialist movement has been the inability of the sect to bridge these two levels — the level the working class is moving on, and the level the sect is thinking on.

How do you bridge the gap? On the one hand, you have the socialists who bridge the gap by driving right across it and over to the other side, losing themselves (and their socialist ideas) in the mass movement. This has been a very popular thing to settle for, and it is one way of solving the problem personally.

On the other hand, you have the absolutely natural reaction which would make it impossible for that to happen. Avoid all temptation to lose yourself in the mass movement by having nothing to do with it.

The socialist sect guards against the first possibility by counterposing its own very fine ideas to the actual mass movement of the class — and it remains a sect.

This chronic problem becomes acute when the socialist sect arises as a congregation of intellectuals who have, to begin with, no organic connection

267

with the working class at all. This congregation has the additional problem of changing itself before it can change anything else. It is not rare for socialist groups to begin as congregations of intellectuals. Marx and Engels were very sensitive to the question. They were nervous about even admitting intellectuals to socialist groups. In the First International it was Marx who proposed and put through the rule that branches had to be at least two thirds workers.

I wonder what Marx and Engels would have thought of a Marxist sect that consisted only of intellectuals? I think it would have blown their minds. It is a grotesque political animal — a "proletarian socialist movement" without any workers but with lots of fine ideas. And it faces a serious contradiction. It can't really change until it has workers in the organization and it can't recruit and keep workers until it has changed.

The first way out of that vicious circle, historically, has been the conversion of the intellectuals into workers - the industrialization of the intellectual membership. There have been several experiments with this. As far as this country is concerned, the two best cases that I know of were the Communist Party during the CIO period and the independent socialists in World War II.

When the drive to organize the CIO started a symbiotic relationship evolved between the CP and John L. Lewis. The CP took advantage of the situation by getting their people into the early organizing drives of the CIO. In doing this, they were doing something different from two other ways of getting into the trade union movement: working in a shop or factory, or becoming one of the intellectual flunkies of the bureaucracy. They didn't do either. They went in and did not make communist speeches at CIO meetings. They went in and tolerated Lewis' dictatorship. They lived under it and it was very hard to do. But what they got was invaluable experience which they could not have gotten in any other way. They got something else — something that comes from organizing workers on the job who know that you have fought for them — moral authority. They got their credentials as militant trade unionists while they were tolerating Lewis' dictatorship. Finally, while they couldn't get up and make revolutionary speeches, they spread their influence and their ideas — a little more subtly and in some ways more effectively.

Take a contemporary example. Cesar Chavez may be a "bureaucrat," although he does not compare with Phillip Murray, John L. Lewis, or others who were better than those two. The sectarian will say: "Chavez does not let you make your own decisions. He tells the organizers what to do." But Chavez is not the problem; at any rate, he is not your problem. The best thing that

268

could happen to many radical intellectuals is to become United Farm Workers' Organizing Committee organizers even if they have to keep quiet for a while in order to gain those three other things. That is, get the "feel" of it. They don't know how to talk to workers. They won't begin as professors; they will begin as pupils. They will have to learn a few things they don't know and get some credentials in the workers' eyes. They will have to win the authority to talk. "After all, who are you to tell us what to do? Have you ever organized two workers? Are you going to tell Cesar Chavez how to organize? Why should we listen to you?" Do you see the nature of the problem?

There are a couple of problems that the student-based New Left faces today that differentiate it from its predecessors. First, there is the question of responsibility. Students are "irresponsible" literally. They are not weighed down and shackled by the obligations which most workers have. They are free in many respects. Workers are not free. We are dealing with the social and political consequences of life style. In a union, when you make proposals, you have to think them out in a new way, in a way you don't have to do in a student movement. Otherwise, you're likely to get the reputation as the kind of person who makes an irresponsible move at the drop of a hat. And you won't be listened to by people who are interested in keeping their jobs, paying off their mortgages, and supporting their husbands and wives.

What does your program mean to the lives of those responsible people whom you are trying to organize and whose lives and careers may depend on you if you are a union organizer?

Another difference between students and workers is that in a union you are dealing, for the most part, with people who have a permanent prospect of having to be workers. Students, even when they enter the workplace, always have alternatives; for the average worker there are no alternatives. This is an unbridgeable gulf that students and intellectuals can't get over. They can recognize it. They can't get over it.

What does this mean in terms of the life of the radical sect? Let me take an example from the second case that I mentioned; the case of independent socialists in World War II in which I was involved. I am not going to discuss now the actual work done by independent socialists in the movement against the no-strike pledge. I want to consider some of the problems that arose in what was, eventually, a successful attempt by a student based group to bridge the gap I mentioned. Of course, we had advantages the New Left does not have. We had a core of experienced trade unionists and more of our members had a working class family background.

From 1942 to 1946 a large part of our membership entered industry. Jobs were readily available because of the war time labor shortage. Many members, however, found it difficult to get interested in "low-level" things like explaining elementary socialism to workers to whom it is a brand new idea. They were bored. Intellectuals get bored very easily; they live in a world of ideas, and if the ideas aren't challenging enough they lose their interest. There were comrades who could listen to trade union reports and find them just a lot of mumbo-jumbo. They just weren't interesting. Others participated not just as an audience requiring entertainment or amusement, but as activists learning how to do a job. They found a good elementary talk on socialism fascinating—because they were thinking "how can I do this where I work?"

* * *

Neither the experience of the CP in the thirties nor of independent socialists in the forties should be taken as a predetermined pattern to be followed everywhere. The trade union movement, because it represents the working class as it is, varies from one situation to the next. Organizing a core of class conscious workers requires experience in the specific union situation over some period of time. This is true even for people with some trade union experience; often they will find themselves faced with a situation where their experience does not apply.

Let me give you an extreme example from my personal experience. The first union I belonged to, and of which I became president at the age of 21, was the most peculiar union local I've ever heard of. It was a real local of WPA workers. There were about 50 of us—teachers employed by the Workers Education Project—and every single one of us was some sort of Communist, Socialist or Trotskyist. I became President because I was a member of the Socialist Party and we had the largest fraction! Would anyone be so foolish as to consider this "trade union experience" as much of a guide for anything?

Granted that was a pretty weird case, but most specific situations cannot be generalized much more easily. Teachers unions, even normal ones, are different than most other unions, white collar locals are different from blue collar locals, and public employee unions like AFSCME, which organize workers with widely different skill and educational levels, differ from single industry unions like the Oil Workers.

What is more, unions differ enormously in their internal structure and the degree of internal democracy. Factional or caucus organization in the

270

Typographical Union was for many years institutionalized (within the bureaucratic shell of the union) as a two party system. There are other unions where opposition to the leadership is physically dangerous. Generalizations about trade union experience are always risky.

I am telling you all this to counteract the generalizations I am now going to make. One of the problems faced universally by socialists and radicals active in trade unions is the one raised by the example of the CP in the thirties. That is their relation to the union leadership — both the local leadership and the top leadership.

I say "union leadership," even though it is more "politically correct" to say Union Bureaucracy. This raises a terminological problem. The term "bureaucracy" has become ambiguous, especially in New Left circles. For students and the academic milieu generally, the word bureaucracy has taken on the flavor suggested by Weberian theory, where the word denotes a social institution taken in a vacuum. When you look at the union leadership there are important ramifications of the term you have to take into account.

One source of the ambiguity of the term "bureaucracy" is the fact that in common parlance it has two different meanings. On the one hand, "bureaucratic" means undemocratic. On the other hand, it refers to a type of hierarchic, structured social institution, which may be democratic or not. It is the institutional aspect, the social role and function of the union bureaucracy or officialdom as an institution — whether democratic or not — that is important.

The "horror story" approach towards the trade union leadership is absorbed by radicals, especially radicals outside the trade union movement, from two sources particularly — the press and other communications media and the academy. In both cases, in other words, from the bourgeoisie. That approach is misleadingly one-sided.

The trade union officialdom, bureaucracy, structure, whatever you want to call it, actually has a dual social function, and it is important to understand both.

One function of the union leadership is to provide the organizational leadership of *our* class. Whereas, the state bureaucracy, for example, is the organizational leadership of *their* class. For the academic sociologist, it doesn't make any difference; there's no such thing as "their class" or "our class" — there are just bureaucracies. You have the union bureaucracy, the state bureaucracy and fifteen other types of bureaucracy and one bureaucracy is pretty much like any other. They all conform to the same system. A theory which denies the

271

reality of class is, of course, one of the classic symptoms of an ideology which is defending the *existing* class structure as the natural order of things.

Let me make an analogy. If you are in a revolutionary army, you have an officer corps — whether you call them officers, marshals, commissars or whatever and whether they are elected or appointed. That's *your* officer corps; you're fighting *with* them, while at the same time you may not like them and may resent their authority. But you and they are on the same side of the barricades. In the same sense, the trade union bureaucracy is the bureaucracy of *our* class.

The other function of the union leadership is that of channel and agency for the exercise of bourgeois influence on the working class, and for bourgeois control of the working class, at the same time that it is the bureaucracy of our class. It is both at once.

This doesn't mean, of course, that at any given instant any particular section of the union leadership is acting simultaneously in both roles equally. Until a revolution breaks out, however, every union bureaucracy is going to continue to serve both functions. It cannot help but serve both functions — even if you constituted it, and it does this in continuing uneasy tension and in varying forms. This duality of the trade union leadership is not a surface phenomenon.

This view of the social role of this social stratum is inherent in Marxism and Marxism's view of the class struggle in a capitalist society, and it is peculiar to Marxism. It follows from the notion that the proletariat in motion already implies the dissolution of capitalist relations and that actual revolution is only the culmination of that process. The trade union is always an alien body in a capitalist society.

You may remember Marx's oft-quoted and pregnant remark (in the Inaugural Address) that the passage of the 10 hour workday bill in England represented a victory for "the political economy of the working class." A sectarian will say,"But the 10 hour day is only a reform that will keep the working class satisfied with capitalism ." That has always been the line, for example, of the Socialist Labor Party. And it is *half* true! When the capitalists were forced to concede and passed the 10 hour bill, the class struggle was temporarily eased. That helped keep capitalism together. The capitalists were defeated in battle and gave in — they made a concession that didn't destroy capitalism. But it was also a victory by the working class.

This duality characterizes the development of the trade union from beginning to end. At first, the capitalists fought it to the death, recognizing that legalizing trade unions meant giving up the prerogatives of ownership. Yet in most capitalist countries, trade unions have been legalized in some form or another. But that didn't mean that the capitalists gave up. Capitalism is still here. They made the best of the situation by utilizing the concession to undercut the struggle of the working class. This process started in England in the 1880's with the move from the legalization of the trade unions to the domestication of the trade unions — that is the housebreaking of the unions in order to use them to discipline the work force. And this has gone on for over a century.

That is the view from the capitalists' side. If that is the only side you see then you are looking at the trade union movement from the vantage point of the bourgeoisie. From the other side, you have to consider this. Without such discipline by the bureaucracy, the trade union movement couldn't exist under capitalism. It is true that as revolutionists, we don't like that role of the bureaucracy, because of what it disciplines the working class for. Nevertheless, until the revolution, by definition, the trade union has to exist within limits set by capitalism.

That is why it plays a dual role. On the one hand, even in the most apathetic times the class struggle is always seething down below. On the other hand, even in the most radical times (that is times of ferment which stop short of revolution), the trade unions still retain the role of disciplinarian. Neither side ever wholly disappears.

Does this disciplining serve the bourgeoisie? Of course it does. But, does it serve the bourgeoisie only? Doesn't it also serve the interests of the trade union movement? For the trade union movement to continue to exist and not shake itself to pieces that discipline is necessary. Even a militant union leadership — even you — will also have to discipline the ranks. Although you, of course, will use persuasion and democratic means — as most union leaderships do in most cases. If you think that the only form of discipline used is clubs then you are a victim of establishment brainwashing.

The important thing to understand is that the union leadership is always under two pressures and discipline is the only means of balancing them. One is the pressure from above, from the bourgeoisie and all of its institutions — political and non-political, state and non-state, especially non-state. That is a pressure from outside the working class. The other pressure is from below, from the ranks. And it is in the course of the struggle within the

273

trade union movement that the relative strengths of these two forces is measured.

That is why there is and always has been a role for radicals, militants and revolutionaries in the movement. It has been their special function to organize that other pressure against the leadership—even a good leadership. (I might add that one of the functions of horror stories is to soften up radicals and socialists. When they run into labor leaders who do *not* fit the bourgeois stereotype, it becomes much easier to play the part of radical press agent for the "good" leadership. That is another role traditionally reserved for radicals and especially ex-radicals in the trade union movement.)

The role of a socialist in the trade union does not depend on the character of the leadership. That changes, often radically, the tactics and strategy of rank and file movements. It does not eliminate the need for them.

* * *

As far as I know there are just three times in the history of the American labor movement when a left progressive opposition movement of some kind was a real force. One was in the DeLeon days, before the SLP turned to dual unionism. They were then a very powerful force in the Knights of Labor and later in the AFL.

There was a second period, just before the First World War, when the socialist bloc in the AFL—in 1911-1912—got over thirty percent of the votes for Max Hayes who ran against Samuel Gompers for the presidency of the organization.

The third episode—about which I want to say a few words—was that of the TUEL, the Trade Union Educational League, in the years 1922-23. The Trade Union Educational League was organized and launched by William Z. Foster *before* he became a member of the Communist Party. William Z. Foster had been the leader of the packinghouse workers successful organizing drive and of the 1919 steel strike, perhaps the most important of the post-World War I class struggle movements in the country. He was a first-class trade union organizer and revolutionary socialist—before he ended up in his later years, tragically, as a Stalinist hack.

Foster had been a member of the IWW and a syndicalist. He organized the TUEL in 1920 because he came to the conclusion, after a life of excellent trade union work, that the whole IWW and syndicalist attempt to build dual unions was wrong and that you had to organize a left opposition in the existing trade union movement.

When Foster launched it the TUEL was Foster and a group of militants around him. It took off when the Communist Party, at Lenin's insistence, put their weight behind it. This was the early Communist Party, in the days when its membership, and a good part of its leadership, consisted of people who were trying to be revolutionary, democratic socialists, as best they knew how.

In broad outline what happened after the Communists decided to take the approach to the trade union movement advocated by Foster was that the TUEL, in the space of a couple of years, became a national force. So much so that there was a realistic possibility of the TUEL taking over the AFL.

Whole sections of the movement, hundreds of locals, sections of national unions, and regional bodies looked to it for leadership. How could that in happen in a couple of years? There were two issues facing the labor movement which the TUEL did not invent. One was amalgamation (what today would be called industrial unionism) of the craft unions and the other was independent political action by labor. There was a tremendous amount of steam behind those two issues which the TUEL did not create.

It was not that Foster, or the relatively small Communist Party which worked with him, were such terrific organizers that in two years they were able to build from virtually nothing a movement that threatened the leadership of the AFL. What happened was that, as a result of the policy they followed, all the ferment that existed, all those currents of opposition that flowed beneath the surface of the movement, coalesced around the TUEL.

What happened after is a sad story which I'll have to go into later; for right now I want to emphasize what the TUEL did that was right. Foster began with the idea that you start with the working class as it is. Not, of course, passive elements of the working class, but those sections that are fighting now. You look to those issues which will move as large a section of the class into action. What issues? All power to the soviets? Well in 1920 large sections of the American working class looked with some sympathy on the soviet experiment but it was hardly an issue to move their fellow workers into immediate action. Amalgamation was. Unionized workers and non-organized workers who took their lead from them saw in the obsolete craft organizations that dominated the AFL an immediate obstacle. And amalgamation was an immediate demand that seemed realizable. It was a demand that allowed the TUEL to move tens of thousands into action. That movement made many of them Communists.

* * *

Unfortunately, the membership of the CP, because of their past, remained suspicious of the TUEL approach. What was that past?

If you ask yourself why the world isn't socialist today, and if you go back and try to put your finger on the crossroads in the recent history of Europe and the world where that was decided, there is no question, in my mind, where would have to point. At the end of World War I, after the Russian Revolution, revolution was sweeping through most of Europe and the key was Germany and the fate of the German Revolution. It was the defeat of the German Revolution, at the end of 1918 and 1919, which was the link in the chain that led to the defeat of the revolution throughout Europe and the subsequent development of Fascism and of Stalinism and all the other ills that have plagued the socialist and revolutionary movements – and the world – for the last several decades.

What was the problem? You can answer in two ways. When I give lectures on the German Revolution I usually emphasize that the German Revolution was defeated, not by the bourgeoisie but by the Social Democracy. However, even after you have shown that, as I think I can, you still haven't answered another question. After you have shown that the Social Democracy was the last-ditch defender of capitalism, you still have to explain why the Social Democrats' opponents on the left were unable to defeat it. Why could they in Russia and not in Germany? It was not because Karl Liebknecht had a false position on Marxian economics (which he did, by the way). It was not because Rosa Luxemburg had a wrong position on national self-determination in Poland. In fact, it wasn't because of any of the issues on which the movement has spent a great deal of time. Let me outline a tableau which illustrates the problem.

At the end of the war in 1918, the German working class was ready and eager for revolution and a socialist government. There was a potential revolutionary leadership in the Spartacus League and there was another leadership someplace else. You may not be aware of it, but at the end of the war, when the revolution that was to overthrow the Kaiser was brewing, there were two sets of revolutionary leaderships—both planning a revolution. Neither got around to it because the German people intervened and overthrew the government first.

The two revolutionary leaderships were the Spartacus League, and a group misnamed the Revolutionary Shop Stewards which had become the accepted leadership of the organized working class; in Berlin especially, but in other

276

industrial cities as well. And the basic tragedy of the German Revolution, which meant its defeat, was that there was no relation between these two groups. They not only never got together, but the Spartacists didn't have any notion that they should get together.

Luxemburg and Liebknecht thought they ought to, but the membership of the League was wildly sectarian and voted them down. When approached by the leadership of the rebellious workers Luxemburg and Liebknecht chose to stay with the sectarians of the League with whom they did not agree.

So there you had the Spartacus League, who are usually thought of as the revolutionary wing of the movement, with no contact in the factories! No contacts in the trade unions! And what do I mean by the unions? Not the bureaucracy. They were the counterrevolution by now. I mean the mass workers movement organized independently of, in opposition to, the top leadership. They were the militants, stewards, local officers, in many cases lower level functionaries, who had been the base of the left in the party before the war. They were the ones who had voted for Luxemburg and Liebknecht in party congresses. They had organized the first anti-war strikes in 1915 in protest of Liebknecht's imprisonment. And the Spartacus League had no connection with them. That was what decided the fate of the German revolution.

It took the German Communist Party two or three years, in the middle of a revolution, to straighten itself out on the elementary question of how it should relate to the trade union movement.

This tableau has been repeated time and again in the history of the socialist movement. If it is obvious at a crucial moment like this, that's because it had existed for decades in reality. And it continued to exist.

There is an obvious explanation for the sectarian character of the Spartacus League. Its membership, a small one, were largely young people who had reacted in disgust to the war. They were very inexperienced. They were not old cadre of the Social Democratic movement who had been revolutionized. They were primarily new and inexperienced — which was not their fault. And the Communist Party in Germany which grew out of this milieu continued to suffer from the same problems for years. And, as part of the process, the German Communist had to deal with tendencies which formally rejected any connection with the real workers' movement.

The problem was not confined to Germany. Throughout Europe and in the United States before World War I as a response to the growing conservatism

277

of the social democratic parties and the official trade unions, there was a whole series of attempts to devise new forms of organization which would be immune to the reformist disease.

The form this most often took was what has been called "dual unionism." A short discussion of this phenomenon is in order, but not because the proposal today enjoys any serious support. (Although, naturally, some of the New Left sects have reinvented this old idea along with 7,543 other new ideas that are a hundred years old.) In general, the experiment was so disastrous that it has gone out of favor. The "dual union" proposal is important because it illustrates in chemically pure form the anti-trade union politics that has bedeviled the socialist movement. It carries those politics out to a logical conclusion which most today are not foolhardy enough to follow.

First, we have to deal with a terminological problem. The term "dual unionism" covers a lot of territory, and distinctions have to be made. There are two types of "dual unionism" that have to be discussed completely separately.

The first and simpler one, which everyone is acquainted with, is simply a split in a union which leads to the organization of two trade unions, and the loss of trade union unity. Trade union unity is not the normal state of affairs, if you look at the world as whole. There are few countries where there are not rival union federations. There are three in France—Communist, Socialist and Catholics. On occasion, the Catholic union federation has been more militant. In the United States, after the CIO split from the AFL, there were two rival federations, often at one another's throats, for almost twenty years. It was a period when the political and economic influence of the trade unions was higher than it ever was before or has been since. Even now, within the AFL-CIO, there are all kinds of dual unions. There are three unions that organize laundry workers only one of them the Laundry Workers Union. And the rivalry between AFSCME and the SEIU for the support of government workers has often benefitted the employees they are trying to organize. England might seem to prove the exception, but there another pattern emerges. In some industries, one plant will be organized by several different unions, each with its own apparatus responsible to its own national officers. As a consequence, in some places, local committees of shop stewards have often functioned as a union "dual" to the various "official" unions.

I am not arguing here for making a fetish of trade union unity.

These cases, and others, such as the independent unions of garment workers before World War I or Deb's American Railway Union, all arose out

278

of the trade union struggle itself. These movements all spilled out of the old structure. They often had a "revolutionary" feel and their leadership was often socialist or, like Debs, became so as a result of the experience.

The other kind of "dual unionism" is something quite different. Let's call it "leftist" unionism ." (It is often called "revolutionary unionism," but that is not completely satisfactory since these experiments are often self-described as "militant" or "class-struggle" unions and do not openly profess a radical ideology.) The distinguishing feature is that the split is based on some sort of ideological notion of what trade unions ought to be. They are not the result of movement from below.

This notion of leftist unionism has been one of the great will-o'-the-wisps of the socialist movement. It has been one of the misconceptions that has gutted one promising development after another.

The United States has a rich history of its own in this field. It is one of our problems. The first case I know of was DeLeon's Socialist Trades and Labor Alliance. At its height the organization had a few tens of thousands organized. As a group inside the AFL it was a serious movement. Once it set itself up as a rival to the AFL it became a joke and petered out by the turn of the century.

The second big example is really quite different. That was the IWW. It began as movement of experienced unionists, leaders as well as rank and file, who felt that the AFL was simply incapable of organizing the unorganized. Its founding convention included not only socialists like DeLeon and Debs but also the Western Federation of Miners — a militant industrial union. They came together initially not because they shared a common ideology — they didn't have one — but out of a common frustration with the AFL.

The organization of the unskilled has often been the task of the left wing of the trade union movement without any ideological impulse. The need to organize the unorganized is obvious to any union activist without any ideology. At the same time the influx of new, enthusiastic workers with new leaders is unsettling to the incumbent leadership. They react with caution and suspicion. These two qualities are not always useful in an organizing drive where enthusiasm and audacity are required.

In the IWW, this instinctive leftism was combined with the ideological leftism of the socialist movement which was at the height of its influence on the American working class – in the AFL as well as the IWW. The ideological leftism proved to be the undoing of the IWW. Its attempt to define itself as a revolutionary union led to the inevitable conflict between the variegated

279

ideological trends in the union. The Western Federation of Miners soon left in disgust. The departure of the most significant union delegation meant that there was no longer any pressure on the ideological tendencies to restrain themselves and the IWW evolved along lines that are too familiar. In the end, one sect was left. The revolutionary syndicalist group typified by Vincent St. John.

Since this IWW was to be a revolutionary union, there could be no compromise with the capitalist system. No contracts, no stable relationship of any kind with the employer. *It* would not discipline the work force, *its* members would not become the labor lieutenants of capital. The consequence was that the IWW led a number of heroic battles at the conclusion of which it refused to accept the capitalist's surrender. It could never win a victory. In the end, the IWW usually walked away and left the workers on their own. Still unorganized.

As we know from hindsight, the ideological leftism and the drive to organize the unorganized were not bound up together logically. The mass organization of the unskilled was achieved by the CIO. In order to do it, the CIO had to split from AFL; that is it had to become a "dual union" of the first type. But it did not follow the example of the IWW.

It was this heritage of the IWW that William Z. Foster rejected when he set up the TUEL. Unfortunately, the tradition of dual unionism in the second sense was too strong in the American left. When a favorable climate for this kind of leftism arose in the international Communist movement, for reasons which had nothing to do the American labor movement, the old tradition reasserted itself.

The TUEL was turned into a dual union federation. But it was not even the kind of "dual union" the IWW had become. The Trade Union Unity League, as the TUEL was now called was very openly a front for the Communist Party often sharing the same office. The example of the TUUL is as instructive as that of the TUEL. It is an object lesson in what not to do.

The history of the TUUL, like that of the IWW, is also one of heroic trade union battles that led nowhere. On the one hand, there were tremendous forces tapped which the AFL never did and never could tap. On the other hand, these forces were confined within the CP's dual union structure and isolated from the larger movement.

When the CIO came along the CP unionists abandoned their dual union efforts and played a major role in organizing the new unions as I mentioned earlier. They did not, however, attempt to do anything like what the TUEL had done, or like what DeLeon or Max Hayes had done in the AFL. There were extraneous reasons for this that had to do with the Communist Party's changing political position, but the confusion on the fundamental issues we have been discussing played a major role too. The old pattern repeated itself. The only alternatives the CP militants could see were the sectarianism of the TUUL and burying themselves in the CIO. When the CIO, as a result of its success in organizing new workers, came up against political obstacles that could not be dealt with through pure and simple unionism there was no coherent opposition with an answer. When John L. Lewis, whose defiance of the AFL leadership had led to the CIO, found his "pure-and-simple" militancy inadequate in dealing with the Roosevelt administration's anti-labor policy, he could think of nothing else to do but vote Republican. And there was no one to tell him any different.

With the few significant exceptions I have touched on, and others which are also relegated to footnotes, the history of the relation of socialists to the trade union movement is not a happy one. But these exceptions point the way out of the blind alley the socialist movement is currently lost in.

Hal Draper 1990

Chapter XV:
Vladimir Ilyich Jefferson and Thomas Lenin

A recent book, which we will mention later, once again raises the question of the contrast between the democrat Jefferson and the communist Lenin. Let us first review some basic facts about these two political leaders, before getting to the point.

If these basic facts seem overly familiar to you bear with me patiently.

1

Everyone knows that Jefferson was the apostle of American democracy, the fountainhead of libertarianism, the champion of freedom of the spirit. He swore "eternal hostility to every form of tyranny over the mind of man ." He taught that "Error of opinion may be tolerated where reason is left free to combat it," that "The tree of liberty must be refreshed from time to time with the blood of patriots and tyrants," that among our in-alienable rights are life, liberty, and the pursuit of happiness, and other great affirmations of the philosophy of civil liberty.

2

On the other hand, it is equally well understood by almost everyone who has gone through a course on *Understanding Communism* or *Political Science 1* that Lenin was a totalitarian. You are asked to pay close attention to the following factual summary:

In the Revolution itself, Lenin applied the notorious Bolshevik maxim that civil war suspended the rule of law; that justice had to be denied to opponents of the Soviet regime; that the maintenance of state power was more important than moral values; that there could be no toleration for serious differences of political opinion on the issue of for-or-against the Soviet government; that there was no acceptable alternative to complete submission to the revolutionary cause; that there was liberty only to praise it, none to criticize it.

Early in the Revolution, the Bolsheviks passed a decree stamping as criminal the use of "disrespectful words" against the authority of the new regime or any regional soviet. Lenin was not even slightly disturbed by this obnoxious restraint on freedom. Also declared a crime was "any word," or attempt to "persuade," in behalf of the old regime. A heavy fine and five years in prison were decreed for anyone who might even wish health to the Czar or who induced anyone to express this prohibited sentiment. Such laws were passed as a useful dragnet against persons who could not be convicted of overt treasonable acts. Lenin ordered the imprisonment of all persons in the border regions against whom "legal evidence cannot be obtained" when there was "suspicion that they are disaffected from the Soviet power, and will when occasion serves, aid the enemy ." This meant prison not only on mere suspicion that a person *had* aided the enemy, but on mere suspicion that he might do so at some future time.

Lenin and his colleagues imposed a loyalty oath, in order to identify for purposes of punishment every person who, in Lenin's words, was "a traitor in thought but not in deed." Only those who swore loyalty to the Bolshevik power should enjoy the rights of citizenship, all others being "secret enemies," they agreed. Non-signers were stripped of civil rights (though forced to pay additional taxes) and could be sent to internment places (precursors of concentration camps). Red military commanders were ordered to uproot from military zones all who refused to take the oath or who were merely suspected of disaffection. Next, regional commissars were authorized to jail "any persons whatsoever, whom there may be just cause to suspect of disaffection," and many languished in jail without a hearing or even a court-martial.

In one case, that of a gang of White bandits led by Josip Filippovich, Lenin drafted a decree of attainder and outlawry — precisely what he had always bitterly denounced under the Czarist regime — and the Soviet promptly adopted it without debate. The most sinister aspect of this decree was that, deliberately in order to by-pass the regime's own laws and courts, it not only incited anyone to kill Filippovich, but it meant that any of his "associates" might be killed out of hand on the mere supposition that he shared his leader's guilt; and a man might be shot, by any vigilante, on the mere supposition that he was an "associate" of Filippovich.

Justifying this later, Lenin argued that, to be sure, such decrees had been abused under the Czar, but "what institution is insusceptible of abuse in wicked hands?"

Said Lenin: "No one doubted that society had a right to erase from the roll of its members any one who rendered his own existence inconsistent with theirs; to withdraw from him the protection of their laws, and to remove him from among them by exile, or even by death if necessary ."

Despite his denunciation of any restraints on freedom of the press, Lenin was *for* press censorship — not advance censorship, but that form of censorship which is effected by making a paper liable to prosecution for publishing anything deemed by the government to be "false facts" or "falsehoods ." Lenin subsequently made clear that the whole opposition press, in his opinion, printed virtually nothing *but* "false facts."

As for his alleged commitment to fair and open political debate: there is an interesting letter of Lenin's in which he comments on a public meeting which the opposition S-R's tried to hold in Petrograd on the Brest-Litovsk Treaty, only to be driven away with clubs and stones by a Bolshevik mob. One historian says the letter recounts the episode "with some glee," but in any case the letter certainly lacked any censure of this mob action.

Then there was the famous case of the treason trial of A. Burrev for trying to sever the Ukraine from the country. To Lenin's dismay, this trial ended in Burrev's exoneration. Yet, in a special message to the Soviet Congress, Lenin branded him a traitor; and this, admittedly, on the basis of little that constituted "formal and legal evidence," chiefly letters "often containing such a mixture of rumors, conjectures, and suspicions, as render it difficult to sift out the real facts." Having convicted Burrev publicly, Lenin then proceeded to mobilize all the resources of the state to prove the pre-conceived guilt. One of Burrev's aides had been illegally arrested by the military and brought to Moscow to stand trial for treason; this prisoner talked freely after Lenin had voluntarily assured him on his word of honor that nothing he said would be used to incriminate him. But when the aide's full confession included unshakable insistence that Burrev had *not* wanted to sever the Ukraine, Lenin proceeded to break his word and ordered him committed.

Throughout this period of agitation against Burrev, Lenin gave undeviating support to a reign of terror instituted by the Red general Vilkinovich in Kiev, on grounds of an expected invasion of the Ukraine by Burrev. The general saw traitors everywhere. "Under circumstances so imperious," Vilkinovich told the Red governor of Kiev, "extraordinary measures must be resorted to and the ordinary form of civil institutions must for a short period yield to the strong arm of military law ." His own military rule was needed, he argued, "to repress traitors and arrest the disaffected ." When the governor pleaded that he could not comply with those demands in the absence of legal authorization, Vilkinovich imposed the equivalent of martial law on his own say-so and unleashed a saturnalia of lawlessness. Prisoners were summarily arrested and shipped to Moscow

in chains. "I shall arrest," announced the general, "anyone against whom I
have positive proof of being accomplices in the machinations against the
state ." One P. V. Ogdunarsky was thus arrested but, when produced in
court, was freed on the ground that there was no evidence against him: yet
within 2 hours both he and his attorney (whose crime was to intercede for
him) were rearrested by the military and shipped to Moscow. When a Kiev
judge denounced the general's act, the judge was himself arrested. Over 60
other victims landed in jail.

Lenin's reaction to his general's conduct in Kiev was to applaud a job
well done. He persisted in this approval even after the full details of the
reign of terror were spread on the record. Vilkinovich had claimed that his
terror was justified because Burrev was approaching Kiev with an army of
6000-7000. Lenin had to explain to him that in point of fact the Burrev forces
consisted of only eighty to a hundred men; but this did not modify his
approval. On the question of the general's justification, said Lenin, "there
can be but two opinions; one, of the guilty and their accomplices; the other,
that of all honest men ."

It was in connection with the Burrev case that Lenin openly came out
with the dictum that, when the safety of the regime demanded it, "*the
universal resource is a dictator .*"

Toward the end of Lenin's career, he was already using the army and
navy of the nation mainly to harry and beleaguer the people themselves. It
was indeed in this connection that he put into so many words the famous
amoral doctrine that the end justifies the means. The Soviet Congress, he
instructed one of his ministers, "must legalize all *means* which may be
necessary to obtain its *end* ." (Emphasis is original.)

One such means was Lenin's repeated proposal to falsify a standard
history book in order to make it conform with his party line. Gumoff's great
History of Russia was the text which all students were brought up on, and
there was no immediate possibility of replacing it; it had to be used even
though it "poisoned" students with its reactionary views, which were only
reinforced by its literary charm. What to do? Fortunately, a good Bolshevik
had concocted a rewritten version of the History, a version which changed
passages wherever necessary to give the "correct" line on all issues. Lenin
proposed to publish this falsified version for student use, while presenting it
as the original Gumoff. The party-line reviser, he wrote to the head of the
publishing agency, "gives you the text of Gumoff purely and verbally, till he

comes to some misrepresentation or omission ... he then alters the text silently, makes it what truth and candor say it should be, and resumes the original text again, as soon as it becomes innocent, without having warned you of your rescue from misguidance ." This intellectual deception appealed to Lenin: "And these corrections are so cautiously introduced that you are rarely sensible of the momentary change of your guide. You go on reading true history as if Gumoff himself had given it."

But the agency head objected; and when Lenin proposed the same scheme to another agency, the second objected too. It was never actually carried out.

Need we go on? Is it not absolutely clear and irrefutable that, even if only half of all this is true, the basis for the later totalitarian system of Stalin was fully laid, that all the assumptions and patterns for it already existed in ovo in Lenin's regime? Can it possibly be denied then that Leninism gave rise to Stalinism, or at least that Leninism invited Stalinism?

3

Dear Reader—who we trust has not peeked ahead: we must now confess that this familiar-looking review of the facts is a pure fabrication. None of it is true about Lenin, even though it could appear word for word in any current book on the Horrors of Leninism without raising an eyebrow.

But it is not a fabrication out of the whole cloth. To make it a plain chronicle of historical fact, make one change; where it says "Lenin," read: *Thomas Jefferson.**

Yes, Thomas Jefferson, the apostle of democracy, liberty, etc.: the same Jefferson who swore eternal hostility to every form of tyranny over the mind of man, etc. The section above is, in fact a brief summary of parts of a recent book published by Harvard's Center for the Study of the History of Liberty

---

* And, of course, corresponding changes in the rest of the cast: for Burrev (Aaron Burr); Filippovich (Josiah Philips); Vilkinovich (General Wilkinson); Ogdunarsky (Ogden); Gumoff's History (Hume's *History of England*); Kiev (New Orleans). Translation of other terms, like "Bolsheviks" for Jefferson's party, should be clear. The strong phrases used unquoted in this section are Levy's, not mine: e.g. *sinister, intellectual deception, saturnalia of lawlessness*, etc.; for the most part the summary judgments are in Levy's own words. Quotations are straight out of Jefferson, or Wilkinson when indicated, only slightly adapted when necessary to the "Russian" context. In general, I have tried not to add a single "incriminating" word to affect the picture which Levy presents.

in America: *Jefferson and Civil Liberties: The Darker Side,* by Prof. Leonard W. Levy of Brandeis.[1]

Levy's book has a good deal more of the same; we have given only samples. In particular, we have barely touched on two detailed chapters dealing with Jefferson's means of enforcing his Embargo policy. On this a few summary sentences by Levy may do:

> On a prolonged, widespread, and systematic basis, in some places lasting nearly a year, the armed forces harried and beleaguered the citizenry. Never before or since did American history exhibit such a spectacle of derangement of normal values and perspectives. ... Under Jefferson, from the summer of 1808 until the time he left office, in March of 1799, "insurrections" were continuous throughout an entire section of the nation and the armed forces were employed on a sustained basis as if it were normal for American soldiers and sailors to enforce against American citizens their own laws. ... The result, in Henry Adams' words, was that "Personal liberties and rights of property were more directly curtailed in the United States by embargo than in Great Britain by centuries of almost continuous foreign war ."

How many times have we read that it was because Lenin was always sure he was right that he was led into totalitarian ways, since if you are sure you are right then you will be fanatical and messianic about enforcing your ideas by any means ... ? Of the man Lenin, this is a vulgar caricature; but it is Levy's repeated and evidence-filled judgment about the man Thomas Jefferson.

Jefferson's rationale, as we have indicated, was the threat of armed attack by enemies. If in peacetime Aaron Burr moved with *a hundred men* on New Orleans, this was enough to justify what Levy calls a "saturnalia of lawlessness" and a "reign of terror" by Jefferson's general. In 1777 Jefferson's plans for internment areas, arrests on suspicion, etc., were justified by the "appearance of a hostile Fleet in the Bay of the Chesapeake" (though the expected invasion did not come). But on the other hand: our stern modern moralists, uncompromising in their righteousness, are unmoved by the plea that the early Soviet regime under Lenin was beset not by a hundred men who were rumored to be approaching, but by over a dozen armies mobilized by the most powerful capitalist states in the world, invading from all sides and overrunning the revolutionary land until at one point the Soviet government controlled only an area around the capital. Poof, what of that? he was a totalitarian, wasn't he?

And likewise for Jefferson's peccadillos—poof, what of them? he was a great democrat, wasn't he? We *know* this.

So surely do we know this, in fact, that some reviewers of Levy's book seem to wonder why anyone would think the "darker side" of Jefferson even worthy of publication. That which, in the case of Lenin, is proof positive of deep-dyed totalitarianism—which one can extenuate only at the risk of being considered pro-totalitarian oneself—is for Jefferson only a series of venial slips, which do not deserve to be brought to scholarly notice; or, if noticed, they are to be explained as merely secondary blemishes on an otherwise refulgent championship of freedom. (As a matter of fact, the last is Professor Levy's own reiterated attitude.)

Now, I am not proposing that anyone "excuse" Lenin by pointing to Jefferson: "Why, even Jefferson ..." Lenin's policies and acts must be defended or attacked on their own ground. Jeffersonianism is no model for Marxists, not because it is too good but, on the contrary, because not even the best of the bourgeois-democratic paladins have ever risen to the level demanded by socialist democracy.

So I do not propose to argue from the revelations in Prof. Levy's book that Jefferson laid the basis for (say) Joe McCarthy; that, so to speak, "Jeffersonianism produces McCarthyism." Even though present-day witchhunters have far more cause than President Jefferson to believe that the system they defend is beleaguered by a fateful enemy, such a conclusion would be simply *unhistorical*. But then: I apply the same standard to the "Leninism-produces-Stalinism" dogma—even apart from the fact that Stalin's totalitarian rule could be established only after he had physically wiped out the whole generation of Lenin's Bolsheviks.

In this way, I claim to avoid the intellectual sin of doublethink.

Now, dear reader, do you?

Chapter XVI:
The Myth of Lenin's "Concept of the Party"
or
What They Did to *What Is To Be Done?*

The myth for today is an axiom of what we may call Leninology — a branch of Kremlinology that has rapidly grown in the hands of the various university Russian Institutes, doctoral programs, political journalists, et al. According to this axiom, Lenin's 1902 book *What Is To Be Done?* (for short, *WITBD*) represents the essential content of his "operational code" or "concept of the party"; all of Bolshevism and eventually Stalinism lies in ambush in its pages; it is the canonical work of "Leninism" on party organization, which in turn bears the original sin of totalitarianism. It establishes the "Leninist type of party" as an authoritarian structure controlled from the top by "professional revolutionaries" of upper-class provenance lording it over a proletarian rank and file.

My focus here will be on *WITBD* itself, and on Lenin's views and practices in the period between *WITBD* and the Russian Revolution. Issues ramifying farther into the inevitable multitude of questions will not be treated in the same detail.

The Leninological axiom under discussion is commonly reinforced from two directions. As was pointed out by the prominent Leninologist Utechin (for whom see the appended Special Note), *WITBD* is given a similar exalted position in the party schools of the Stalinist regime. In fact, Utechin's way of demonstrating the basic importance of *WITBD* is to quote the Kremlin's official *History of the Communist Party of the Soviet Union* on this point. The work, says Utechin (much like other Leninologists), "became a guide-book for his followers in matters of organization, strategy and tactics and...has been adhered to by Communists ever since. Lenin himself consistently applied these views... In *WITBD*...his argument has a general validity and has in fact been generally applied by Communists.. ."[1] In short, both the Western Leninologists and the Stalinists agree that Lenin's book was a totalitarian bible: which is not surprising but does not settle the matter.

"Lenin himself consistently applied these views": we will see how far from the truth this lies. My subject is not my own interpretation of *WITBD*, but a survey of Lenin's own opinions, recorded many times, on the question raised, viz., the place of *WITBD* in his thought. According to the myth, endlessly repeated from book to book, Lenin's "concept of the party —

(1) saw the party as consisting mainly of "intellectuals," on the basis of a theory according to which workers cannot themselves develop to socialist consciousness; rather, the socialist idea is always and inevitably imported into

the movement by bourgeois intellectuals;

(2) posited that the party is simply a band of "professional revolutionaries" as distinct from a broad working-class party;

(3) repudiated any element of spontaneity or spontaneous movement, in favor of engineered revolution only;

(4) required that the party be organized not democratically but as a bureaucratic or semimilitary hierarchy.

In point of fact, we will see that these allegations are contrary to Lenin's views as many times repeated and explained by him, beginning with *WITBD* itself. We will indeed begin with *WITBD*, where we will find something different from the myth. But even more important, it must be understood that *WITBD* was not Lenin's last word -- it was closer to being his first word. It is only the Leninologists who write as if *WITBD* were the sum-total of Lenin's writings on the issue.

We will find, for example, that Lenin protested more than once that his initial formulations in *WITBD* were being distorted and misinterpreted by opponents, after which he went on to clarify and modify. If we want to know Lenin's "concept of the party" we must look at the formulations he came to, *after* there had been discussions and attacks. There is not a single prominent Leninologist who has even mentioned this material in his exposition of *WITBD*'s original sin.

1. Socialist Consciousness and Intellectuals

Let us start with the myth which claims that, according to Lenin's views in 1902 and forever, the workers cannot come to socialist ideas of themselves, that only bourgeois intellectuals are the carriers of socialist ideas.

We will be eager to see what *WITBD* actually said on this point; but there is an introductory point to be made beforehand.

(1) It is a curious fact that no one has ever found this alleged theory anywhere else in Lenin's voluminous writings, not before and not after *WITBD*. It never appeared in Lenin again. No Leninologist has ever quoted such a theory from any other place in Lenin.

This should give pause at least. In ordinary research, a scholar would tend to conclude that, even if Lenin perhaps held this theory in 1902, he soon *abandoned* it. The scholar would at least report this interesting fact, and even perhaps try to explain it. The Leninologists do not behave in this fashion. On the contrary, they endlessly repeat that the virtually nonexistent theory (nonexistent after *WITBD*) is the crux of Leninism forever and onward -- though they never quote anything other than *WITBD*. (The explanation for the curious fact itself will emerge from the points that follow.)

(2) Did Lenin put this theory forward even in *WITBD*? Not exactly.

The fact is that Lenin had just read this theory in the most prestigious theoretical organ of Marxism of the whole international socialist movement, the *Neue Zeit*. It had been put forward in an important article by the leading Marxist authority of the International, Karl Kautsky. And this was why and how it got into *WITBD*. In *WITBD* Lenin first paraphrased Kautsky.[2] Then he quoted a long passage from Kautsky's article, almost a page long. Here is Kautsky, whom Lenin then looked up to as the master (some said the "pope") of socialist theory:

> Of course, socialism, as a doctrine, has its roots in modern economic relationships... But socialism and the class struggle arise side by side and not one out of the other; each arises under different conditions. Modern socialist consciousness can arise only on the basis of profound scientific knowledge. Indeed, modern economic science is as much a condition for socialist production as, say, modern technology, and the proletariat can create neither the one nor the other, no matter how much it may desire to do so; both arise out of the modern social process. The vehicle of science is not the proletariat, but the *bourgeois intelligentsia* [emphasis by Kautsky]: it was in the minds of individual members of this stratum that modern socialism originated, and it was they who communicated it to the more intellectually developed proletarians... Thus, socialist consciousness is something introduced into the proletarian class struggle from without and not something that arose within it spontaneously.[3]

There it is — the whole theory laid out, the devilish crux of "Leninism"; and it turns out to be the product of *Kautsky's* pen! When Lenin paraphrased it a few pages before, he began, "We have said that.. ." — that is, he tied it up immediately as the accepted view of the movement (or so he seemed to think). His summary was by no means as brash as Kautsky's formulation. But we will return to Lenin's formulation.

Why did Kautsky emphasize this view of socialist history at this time? The reason is perfectly clear: the new reformist wing of the movement, the Bernsteinian Revisionists, were arguing that all one needed was the ongoing movement of the workers, *not theory*; that the spontaneous class activity of the trade-union movement and other class movements was enough. "The movement is everything, the goal is nothing" was Bernstein's dictum, thereby seeking to shelve theoretical considerations in favor of shortsighted concentration on the day-to-day problems. Reform was the concern of today (the movement); revolution had to do with tomorrow (theory). Kautsky's generalization about the role of the "bourgeois intelligentsia" in importing socialist ideas into the raw class movement was one way, in his eyes, of undercutting the Revisionist approach. And this, of course, gave it equal appeal for other opponents of the new right wing, like Lenin.

It is no part of my subject to explain why Kautsky was misguided in this line of argument, and why his theory was based on an historical half-truth. But it is curious, at any rate, that no one has sought to prove that by launching this theory (which he never repudiated, as far as I know) *Kautsky* was laying the basis for the demon of totalitarianism.

(3) So it turns out that the crucial "Leninist" theory was really Kautsky's, as is clear enough to anyone who really reads *WITBD* instead of relying only on the Leninological summaries. Did Lenin, in *WITBD*, adopt Kautsky's theory?

Again, not exactly. Certainly he tried to get maximum mileage out of it against the right wing; this was the point of his quoting it. If it did something for Kautsky's polemic, he no doubt figured that it would do something for his. Certainly this young man Lenin was not (yet) so brash as to attack his "pope" or correct him overtly. But there was obviously a feeling of discomfort. While showing some modesty and attempting to avoid the appearance of a head-on criticism, the fact is that Lenin inserted two longish footnotes *rejecting* (or if you wish, amending) precisely what was worst about the Kautsky theory on the role of the proletariat.

The first footnote was appended right after the Kautsky passage quoted above. It was specifically formulated to undermine and weaken the theoretical content of Kautsky's position. It began: "This does not mean, of course, that the workers have no part in creating such an ideology ." But this was exactly what Kautsky did mean and say. In the guise of offering a caution, Lenin was proposing a modified view. "They [the workers] take part, however," Lenin's footnote continued, "not as workers, but as socialist theoreticians, as Proudhons and Weitlings; in other words, they take part only when they are able.. ." In short, Lenin was reminding the reader that Kautsky's sweeping statements were not even 100% true historically; he pointed to exceptions. But he went on to a more important point: once you get beyond the *original* initiation of socialist ideas, what is the role of intellectuals and workers? (More on this in the next point.)

Lenin's second footnote was not directly tied to the Kautsky article, but discussed the "spontaneity" of the socialist idea. "It is often said," Lenin began, "that the working class *spontaneously* gravitates towards socialism. This is perfectly true in the sense that socialist theory reveals the causes of the misery of the working class... and for that reason the workers are able to assimilate it so easily," but he reminded that this process itself was not subordinated to mere spontaneity. "The working class spontaneously gravitates towards socialism; nevertheless,... bourgeois ideology spontaneously imposes itself upon the working class to a still greater degree ."[4]

This second footnote was obviously written to modify and recast the Kautsky theory, without coming out and saying that the Master was wrong. There are several things that happen "spontaneously," and what will win out is not decided only by spontaneity! — so went the modification. It cannot be overemphasized that if one wants to analyze Lenin's developing views about "spontaneity" one cannot stick at this byplay in *WITBD*, but rather one must go on to examine precisely what the developing views were going to be. All that was clear at this point was that Lenin was justifiably *dissatisfied* with the formulation of Kautsky's theory, however conveniently anti-Bernstein it might have been. We will see more about his dissatisfaction.

(4) Even Kautsky's theory, as quoted in *WITBD*, was not as crass as the Leninologists make it out to be (while calling it *Lenin's* theory, to be sure). The Leninologists run two different questions together: (a) What was, historically, the *initial* role of intellectuals in the beginnings of the socialist movement, and (b) what *is* -- and above all, what should be -- the role of bourgeois intellectuals in a working-class party today.

Kautsky was not so ignorant or dull-witted as to believe (as so many Leninologists apparently do) that *if* it can be shown that intellectuals historically played a certain initiatory role, they *must* and *should* continue to play the same role now and forever. It does not follow; as the working class matured, it tended to throw off leading strings. The Leninologists do not argue this point because they do not see it is there.

As a matter of fact, in the International of 1902 no one really had any doubts about the historical facts concerning the beginnings of the movement. But what followed from those facts? Marx for one (or Marx and Engels for two) concluded, from the same facts and subsequent experiences, that the movement had to be sternly warned against the influence of bourgeois intellectuals inside the party.[5] "Precisely in Germany these are the most dangerous people," they averred. The historical facts were so many reasons to take the dangers seriously, to *combat* intellectuals' predominance as a social stratum in the movement.

(5) No one in the international movement was more forceful or frequent than Lenin in decrying and combating the spread of intellectuals' influence in the movement. This is easy to demonstrate, but I will not take the space to do so here. In any case a mere couple of well-chosen specimens would not be enough. Just to cull the most virulent passages alone would fill a book. As against this indubitable fact, let us ask a question: can anyone cite any passage in which Lenin ever advocated *increased* influence, or *predominant* influence, by intellectuals in the party?

There is no such passage, in point of fact. None is cited by the Leninologists. Their whole case on this point is hung on a deduction (of theirs) from a theory in *WITBD* which is essentially Kautsky's, it turns out. We know indeed that the typical social-democratic reformist party is very much dominated on top by intellectuals derived from the bourgeoisie. We do not typically see the leaders of these parties denouncing this state of affairs. On the other hand, Lenin's collected works are chock-full of denunciations of increased influence by intellectuals. Obviously, this does not settle the matter, but still less is it reasonable to rest virtually the whole case against Lenin, on this point, on what is *not* in Lenin's 1902 book.

In the Russian movement, the Marxist left's denunciations of intellectuals in the movement started with the founding congress of the Russian Social-Democratic Labor Party itself (the congress to which *WITBD* was directed). In fact, the Bolshevik-Menshevik split over the notorious membership rule (who could be a party member) which was directly connected with the Mensheviks' anxiety to make it easier for nonparty intellectuals to be accounted as members, while Lenin fought to make it harder. (This is hardly disputed.) The Leninological myth that, according to Lenin's "concept of the party," the

296

organization is to consist only or mainly or largely of bourgeois intellectuals — this is contrary to fact.

(6) Lastly, since it is a question of a "party concept" alleged to be peculiar to Lenin and Leninism, we should find that it is *not* true of the other Russian socialist parties -- the Mensheviks and the Socialist-Revolutionaries. But just the reverse is true. The case is most clear-cut with regard to the S-Rs, for while this party aspired to *represent* the peasants' interests and mentality, it was very far from being a party of peasants. Notoriously it was a party composed overwhelmingly of bourgeois intelligentsia. (You need only read the main scholarly work on the S-Rs, by O. H. Radkey.) The proportion of bourgeois intellectuals in the Mensheviks or supporting the Mensheviks was *greater* than in the case of the Bolsheviks, not less.

2. "Professional Revolutionaries" and Spontaneity

Let us take the second claim, that the Leninist "concept of the party" demanded that the party should consist of so-called professional revolutionaries only. This view was "deduced" from *WITBD* by opponents. As soon as the deduction and the claim appeared, Lenin denied (scores of times) that he wanted a party made up of professional revolutionaries only. The Leninologists endlessly repeat the "deduction," and do not mention that Lenin consistently and firmly repudiated it.

One of the difficulties (not Lenin's) is that there are several questions confused under this head, as usual. In the first place, the most important background fact was the condition of illegality suffered in Russia by any revolutionary party. It was not a question of some general or suprahistorical "concept of the party" offering a formula for any country at any time. *WITBD* asked what was to be done *in this autocratic czarism* in this year of 1902. Whatever views on this question are discerned in *WITBD*, it is false to ascribe them to a generalized program of organization good for any time or place.

In *WITBD* Lenin was discussing the need for a *core* of "professional revolutionaries" in the party for the sake of effective functioning -- to make sure that the history of the party was not simply one shipment of revolutionaries after another to Siberia. A good part of the Leninological myth rests on a confused definition of "professional revolutionary ." The Leninologists seem to assume that to Lenin a "professional revolutionary" meant a *full-time* party worker or functionary, devoting all his time to party activity. This is absurd from Lenin's viewpoint; it would indeed exclude workers, as the Leninologists deduce.

It can easily be shown, from Lenin's copious discussions of the professional revolutionary for years after *WITBD*, that to Lenin the term meant this: *a party activist who devoted most (preferably all) of his spare time to revolutionary work.* The professional revolutionary considers his revolutionary activity to be the center of his life (or of his life-style, if you will). He must work to earn a living, of course, but this is not his life's center. Such is the professional revolutionary type.

I have come to believe that part of the confusion stems from the important difference in the meaning of *professional* between English and most Continental languages. In French (and I think the usage in German and other languages stems directly from the French) the word *professionnel* refers simply to occupation. Whereas in English only lawyers, doctors and other recognized "professions" can be said to have "professional" activity, in French this can be said of anyone in any occupation; the reference is simply to occupational activity. Under the aegis of the English language, a "professional" revolutionary must be as full-time as a doctor or lawyer. (Of course this does not account for non-English Leninologists, and is only one factor in the confusion.)

It follows from Lenin's view that even the "core" of professional revolutionaries were not necessarily expected to be full-time party activists, which usually means functionaries. (The number of functionaries in a revolutionary group is a question with its own history, but this history is not presently ours.) The point of defining a professional revolutionary as a full-timer, a functionary, is to fake the conclusion, or "deduction": only nonworkers can make up the party elite, hence only intellectuals. This conclusion is an invention of the Leninologists, based on nothing in Lenin.

From Lenin's standpoint, professional-revolutionary workers were important to the movement for two reasons. One is obvious: the greater amount of time and activity that they could devote to the work of the movement. A professional revolutionary regarded even the hours he spent on the job as opportunities for socialist and trade-union propaganda and organization. The second aspect of the professional revolutionary type, much emphasized by Lenin, was that such a worker could be *trained* in revolutionary work, in a more meaningful way; that is, given conscious education and courses in self-development on how to operate as a revolutionary. The

298

professional revolutionary worker was, or could become, a *trained* revolutionary worker.

Lenin had no trouble understanding and acknowledging that only a "core" of the party could consist of such elements. All he argued was that the more such the party had, the more effective its work. This is a far cry from the Leninological myth.

As for the myths about the alleged "theory of spontaneity" versus "conscious organization": much of this is the result simply of failing to understand what the issues were. No one in the movement, certainly not Lenin, had any doubts about the important and positive role played by "spontaneity" -- spontaneous revolts, struggles, etc. (In many cases, when we say a certain revolt was "spontaneous," all we mean is: *we do not know* how it was organized or by whom.)

What Lenin argued against in WITBD and elsewhere was the *glorification* of spontaneity for its own sake; for what this glorification meant in actuality was a decrying of conscious organizational activity or party work or leadership. This latter attitude made sense only for anarchists, but it was also likely to be assumed by extreme reformists as a cover for opposing independent working-class organization. For the Russian "Economists" (who advocated "economic" action only) the line was that *no* revolutionary party was necessary and the Russian party should be liquidated; and in this context the glorification of "spontaneity" was simply a way of counterposing *something* to the organized political struggle by the working class.

The claim that Lenin was *hostile* to "spontaneous" struggles verges on nonsense. Whenever a Leninologist purports to quote Lenin on this subject, what he really quotes are Lenin's arguments against *relying only on spontaneity* to usher in socialism by some millennial date. Lenin advocated that the spontaneous action of the people must be integrated with the element of political leadership by trained socialist workers, and part of such training was precisely the capacity to take advantage of spontaneous struggles when they turned up. The overwhelming majority of the International would heartily agree. There was nothing specially "Leninist" about this, except Lenin's usual clarity on the point, as compared with the often hazy thinking of reformists.

3. Lenin's Party Concepts

We still have to take up Lenin's later comments on WITBD. But something of a historical introduction is necessary here.

The reader of Lenin's *WITBD* must understand that if it embodied some specially Leninist "concept of the party" *Lenin himself was entirely unaware of it* at the time. *He* thought he was putting forward a view of party and movement that was the same as that of the best parties of the International, particularly the German party under the leadership of August Bebel — only allowing for the big difference that the Russian movement faced the special problems of illegality under an autocracy.

The naive Leninologist seems to assume that when Lenin referred to "centralization" or "centralism," he was necessarily talking about some *super*centralized organizational form. But in fact the Russians (and others) who used this language often meant the same thing that the Germans had once meant when "Germany" was a geographical expression fragmented into thirty-odd states and statelets. Where there was no center at all, the demand for "centralism" was a call to establish *a* center. In 1902 there was no all-Russian party in existence at all.

A First Congress had taken place in 1898, but had led to nothing. The Russian movement consisted of isolated circles, discrete regional conglomerations, unconnected factory groups, etc. There was no center; in fact there was no "party" except as a future label. The Second Congress scheduled for 1903 was hopefully going to establish an organized all-Russian party for the first time. *This was the situation toward which Lenin directed his little book in 1902.*

The point of holding a congress was to establish a *center* at last. No "central" organization whatever existed as yet. Everyone who looked to the congress was in favor of "centralizing" the work of the now-decentralized circles operating inside Russia. This was what "centralization" meant under the circumstances. But it was ambiguous then as now.

The German party had also gone through a period of illegality, from 1878 to 1890; and during this period its practices had not been ideally democratic at all. One of the main features was the domination of practical party work in Germany, insofar as it was possible, not by the elected National Executive in exile, but by the Reichstag Fraction of deputies, who remained legal. But this Fraction had never been elected by the party; the deputies had been elected by local voters. Marx and Engels looked askance at what they considered to be the "dictatorship" of the Reichstag deputies over the party; but the arrangement was generally accepted for its practical usefulness.

300

As the Russian situation developed from 1902 to 1914, it turned out -- in hindsight -- that there *was* something distinctive about Lenin's "concept of the party," even though he was not specifically aware of it. There are two points to be made under this head, the second being more important.

(1) SECTISM OR MASS PARTY. Throughout the history of the socialist movement, there has been a tendency for socialist currents that considered themselves to have distinctive ideas to organize *as a sect*. The alternative is to operate as a current in a *class movement*.

One must distinguish clearly between these two organizational forms. The class movement is based on, and cemented by, its role in the class struggle; the sect is based on, and cemented by, its special ideas or program. The history of the socialist movement began mostly with sects (continuing the tradition of religious movements). It was only the continued development of the working class which gave rise to mass parties that sought to represent and reflect the whole class-in-movement.

The outstanding example of the class movement, as counterposed to the sect, was given by the First International, which broke down sect lines (it did not even start with socialism in its program). In the form that Marx brought about, it sought to organize the entire working-class movement in all its forms. This much of its character was continued by the Second International, except that trade unions were not affiliated. In France the fragmentation of the socialist movement into sects continued until 1905, when a united Socialist Party was formed. In Germany the Lassallean sect had been absorbed fairly quickly, in 1875. Sects still continued to operate in many countries, like the Social Democratic Federation in Britain, which claimed to represent "revolutionary" socialism.

In 1902 when Lenin wrote *WITBD*, there was a big difference between Germany and Russia (which indeed *WITBD* discussed): in Germany the revolutionary wing (or what Lenin and others considered such) was in control of the party, whereas in Russia the right wing had the dominant influence. Lenin's response to this situation was *not* to organize the revolutionary wing as a left-wing sect outside the general movement. *In fact, if we consider the whole period before 1914, Lenin never organized, or sought to organize, a "Leninist" sect.* (The theory of "revolutionary" sectification arose out of the degeneration of the Comintern to become a "principle of Leninism"; before 1917 it had been kept alive on the fringes of the Second International and in the anarchist movement.)

The course which the young Lenin took was then the normal one in the International: he sought to organize the revolutionary current as a political center of some sort inside the mass party (or what was going to be the mass party if the Second Congress was successful). Most political centers in the socialist movement, leaving aside sects, were currents established around periodical organs; this was the case in the German party, for example. When Lenin went into exile from Russia, he did *not* establish a "Leninist" sect; he went to the *Iskra* editorial board, which was not a membership group. Even after the Bolshevik-Menshevik split, and for the next several years (at least until shortly before World War I), the term "Bolsheviks" and "Mensheviks" meant a political center *inside* the mass party, the RSDLP, not a membership sect.

(2) SPLIT AND UNITY. This involved the second distinctive feature of Lenin's party concept. One can distinguish three approaches to this question, as follows.

(a) There were those who believed in *split at any cost*, that is, the revolutionary wing in a reformist party must split away at the most opportune moment, and organize its own sect. This is the characteristic theory of sectism.

(b) There were those, and they were legion, who believed in *unity at any cost*. The unity of the mass social-democratic party must never be breached; a break was the ultimate disaster. This was the mirror image of the first approach: the fetishism of unity.

This approach was the dominant one in the International, including the German party. What it meant in practice was: accommodation with the right wing, even by a *majority* left wing. If the right wing must be persuaded from splitting at any cost, then the majority left had to make concessions to it, sufficient to keep it in the party.

One of the most enlightening examples of this pattern took place in the Russian party soon after the 1903 congress, at which Lenin's wing won majority control with the support of Plekhanov. The Menshevik minority then split. Thereupon Plekhanov, under pressure, swung around and demanded that the majority of the *Iskra* editorial board be handed back to the Mensheviks, for the sake of "unity." In short: if the Mensheviks had won the majority, there is no doubt that Lenin would have stayed in as a minority; but if the left wins, the right wing picks up its marbles and quits; then for the sake of "unity" the left has to hand control back to the right... (c) Lenin's distinctive approach was this: he simply insisted that where the left won majority control of a party, it had the right and the duty to go ahead with its own policy *just as the right wing was doing everywhere*. The Bolshevik-Menshevik hostilities hardened when Lenin rejected Plekhanov's demand to reverse the outcome of the congress. This distinctive approach was: unity, yes, but not at the cost of foiling the victory of the majority. Unity, yes, but on the same democratic basis as ever: the right wing could work to win out at the next congress if it could, but it would not do to demand political concessions as a reward for *not splitting*.

One of the chapters in Lenin's life most industriously glossed over by the Leninologists is the period that followed the Second Congress and Plekhanov's about-face. One must read Volumes 6 and 7 of Lenin's *Collected Works* to see how heartsick he was in face of the break, and what continued efforts he put into healing the split with the Mensheviks on the basis of full democratic rights for all. In test after test, it was the Mensheviks who rejected unity on this basis, or on any basis that failed to give them party control in defiance of the Second Congress outcome. In fact, the first test of course had come at the congress itself, since it was the *Mensheviks* that split away because Lenin had gained a majority in the voting (after extreme right-wing elements had walked out for their own right-wing political reasons). The common claim that it was the Bolsheviks who split is one of the myths of Leninology.

All this was tested again in the period after the upheaval of the 1905 revolution, which opened up Russian political life for a while. Legal organization became possible temporarily, open elections, etc. In this situation, the question of unity of Bolsheviks and Mensheviks was again raised. But we will come back to this in Section 5.

4. Lenin After WITBD

In the first two sections we discussed what is in *WITBD* and what isn't; but, as mentioned, this is very far from exhausting the question of Lenin's attitude toward *WITBD*. Part of the Leninological myth is the claim that the "concept of the party" found in *WITBD* (whatever this is) was Lenin's permanent and abiding view, which he "consistently applied" from then on. We must therefore turn to find out what Lenin thought about *WITBD* in the ensuing years.

For one thing we will find this: that, from the time *WITBD* was published until at least the Russian Revolution of 1917, Lenin insisted that this 1902 work of his was *not* a canonical exposition of a model form of party organization, but simply an organizational plan for the given time and place. It was devised for (a) an underground movement functioning in secrecy under conditions of autocracy, and (b) a movement which had not yet succeeded even in forming a national organizing center in its own country, as had most social-democratic parties in Europe. This 1902 plan was therefore not automatically applicable to other situations — to other places in Europe, or to other periods in Russia, where there was more elbow room for political liberty. This plan was time-bound and place-specific.

In his *Letter to a Comrade on Our Organizational Tasks*, September 1902, that is, a few months after the publication of *WITBD*, Lenin explained more than once that the forms of organization needed were determined by the interests of secrecy and circumscribed by the existence of the autocracy.[6] But then, at this time his later opponents, like Martov and Plekhanov, were at one with him in viewing the ideas of *WITBD* as unexceptionable conclusions from the struggle of a serious revolutionary underground movement. It was only after a falling-out on other grounds that these opponents, and their successors, began to read into *WITBD* everything they thought was sinister in Lenin's course, including his inexplicable refusal to yield up the congress majority power to the people who had been the congress minority.

Already at the Second Congress itself, before the final split, Lenin had pleaded with critics not to take *WITBD* passages "wrenched from the context ." In doing so, the first point he had made was the one mentioned above, viz., that *WITBD* was not intended to present "principles" of party organization. The discussion on *WITBD*, he said optimistically, had clarified all the questions: "It is obvious that here an episode in the struggle against 'Economism' has been confused with a discussion of the principles of a major theoretical question (the formation of an ideology). Moreover, this episode has been presented in an absolutely false light ."[7]

He directly confronted the claim about subordinating the working-class movement to bourgeois intellectuals:

> It is claimed that Lenin says nothing about any conflicting trends, but categorically affirms that the working-class movement invariably "*tends*" to succumb to bourgeois ideology. Is that so? Have I not said that the working-class movement is drawn towards the bourgeois outlook *with the benevolent assistance* of the Schulze-Delitzsches *and others like them*? And who is meant here by "others like them"? None other than the "Economists..".

This was a further step in adding qualifications to the bare Kautsky theory, without breaking with Kautsky. He added an even more serious qualification:

> Lenin [it is claimed, says Lenin] takes no account whatever of the fact that the workers, too, have a share in the formation of an ideology. Is that so? Have I not said time and again that the shortage of fully class-conscious workers, worker-leaders, and worker-revolutionaries is, in fact, the greatest deficiency in our movement? Have I not said there that the training of such worker-revolutionaries must be our immediate task? Is there no mention there of the importance of developing a trade-union movement and creating a special trade-union literature? ... [8]

And to end this same speech, Lenin made the point which is among the most important to keep in mind about *WITBD*:

> To conclude. We all know that the "Economists" have gone to one extreme. To straighten matters out somebody had to pull in the other direction, and that is what I have done.[9]

This is the main key to what Lenin was doing in *WITBD*. Throughout his life his constant pattern was to "bend the bow" in an opposite direction in order to push back against some immediate dangerous pressure. His metaphor on these occasions was often to "turn the helm the other way" in order to compensate for the dangerous pressure. Now it happens that personally I do not sympathize with this propensity, though I admit it is natural enough. I think that a bow which is bent in various directions is apt to be bent out of shape. But it is a common enough resort by people of all political complexions, and only asks for understanding. In Lenin's case it is a fact that demands understanding, especially when he specifically explained the pattern in so many words, as he did often enough. And any Leninologist who refuses to understand it is bound to write a great deal of nonsense.

We are still at the Second Congress. On August 15 Lenin's first speech in the Rules discussion was summarized in the minutes in nine lines. Most of it was devoted to saying this:

> It should not be imagined that Party organizations must consist
> solely of professional revolutionaries. We need the most diverse
> organizations of all types, ranks and shades, beginning with
> extremely limited and secret [ones] and ending with very broad,
> free, *lose Organisationem* [loose organizations]. [10]

He could not have been more explicit in correcting any false impression
that might have been conveyed by his "bow-bending" in *WITBD*.

Lenin repeated this clarification in his second speech that day:

> Comrade Trotsky completely misunderstood the main idea of
> my book *What Is To Be Done?* when he spoke about the party not
> being a conspiratorial organization (many others too raised this
> objection). He forgot that in my book I propose a number of
> various types of organizations, from the most secret and most
> exclusive to comparatively broad and "loose" organizations. [11]

If it is charged that this was *not* clear in *WITBD*, well -- that is the function
of discussion: to clarify and modify. Lenin clarified and modified, not merely
later but right in the congress discussion.

It may be said that if *WITBD* was misunderstood by so many, there must
have been a reason. This is quite true. There was more than one reason, and
the first has been mentioned: Lenin's bow-bending. In addition there was a
will to "misunderstand," as there is still today. An objective scholar writing
today with the advantage of a longer perspective and fuller documentation
should be expected, however, to set forth and weigh Lenin's repeated attempts
to clarify and modify (qualify and recast) his views. What is typical about
contemporary Leninology is that it ignores Lenin's clarifications in favor of a
purely demonological exegesis.

Lenin, we said, was not thinking in terms of a general "concept of party
organization ." When in a 1904 article in the *Neue Zeit* Rosa Luxemburg
attacked his ideas, as set forth in his brochure *One Step Forward, Two Steps Back*
dealing with the Second Congress, Lenin wrote a reply which rather mildly
protested -- what? Not that he was right, but that he did not hold the opinions
Luxemburg ascribed to him.* This is what Lenin wrote:

---

* Luxemburg's article is commonly reprinted under the bogus title "Leninism or

Comrade Luxemburg says, for example, that my book is a clear and detailed expression of the point of view of "intransigent centralism ." Comrade Luxemburg thus supposes that I defend one system of organization against another. But actually that is not so. From the first to the last page of my book, I defend the elementary principles of any conceivable system of party organization. [12]

That is, Lenin believed that he was only working out the forms of any party that could conceivably *exist* under the given conditions in Russia.

Rosa Luxemburg further says that "according to his [Lenin's] conception, the Central Committee has the right to organize all the local Party committees ." Actually that is not so... Comrade Luxemburg says that in my view "the Central Committee is the only active nucleus of the Party ." Actually that is not so. I have never advocated any such view... Comrade Rosa Luxemburg says...that the whole controversy is over the degree of centralization. Actually that is not so. ...our controversy has principally been over whether the Central Committee and Central Organ should represent the trend of the majority of the Party Congress, or whether they should not. About this "ultra-centralist" and "purely Blanquist" demand the worthy comrade says not a word, she prefers to declaim against mechanical subordination of the part to the whole, against slavish submission, blind obedience, and other such bogeys. ...Comrade Luxemburg fathers on me the idea that all the conditions already exist in Russia for forming a large and extremely centralized workers' party. Again an error of fact... [13]

And so on. By the way, anyone who thinks that Rosa Luxemburg was a sainted angel in internal party brawls is naive. In this case, either she was retailing vicious slanders, of the sort she was familiar enough with in the Polish

---

Marxism?" -- a title which is not only a Leninological invention but distortive of Luxemburg's view. Those who are sensitive to questions of inner-party democracy, so popular with Leninologists, should note that although Luxemburg's article was a virulent attack on Lenin, the democratic editors of the *Neue Zeit* refused to print Lenin's mild reply.

movement, or else someone should demonstrate that Lenin *was* advocating the views with which she charged him. The latter has not been done.

5. Toward Party Democratization

Let us put demonology aside. It must be noted that, in the period inaugurated by the 1905 upheaval, as the situation in Russia changed and the pressure of the autocracy lightened, Lenin's "concept of the party" changed drastically, in accord with the new circumstances -- *just as we would expect if his protestations were taken seriously.*

> Already in February 1905, in a draft resolution for the Third Party Congress, Lenin wrote: "Under conditions of political freedom, our Party can and will be built entirely on the elective principle. Under the autocracy this is impracticable for the collective thousands that make up the party." [14] Writing in September 1905, he hailed the German party as "first in respect of organization, integrality and coherence" and pointed to its organizational decisions as "highly instructive to us Russians ."

> Not so long ago organizational questions occupied a disproportionate place among current problems of Party life, and to some extent this holds true of the present as well. Since the Third Congress two organizational tendencies in the Party have become fully defined. One is toward consistent centralism and consistent extension of the democratic principle in Party organizations, not for the sake of demagogy or because it sounds good but in order to put this into effect as Social-Democracy's free field of activity extends in Russia. The other tendency is toward diffusiveness of organization, "vagueness of organization..".
> [15]

In November 1905 he stressed in an article that the socialist worker "knows there is no other road to socialism save the road through democracy, through political liberty. He therefore strives to achieve democratism completely and consistently in order to attain the ultimate goal -- socialism ." [16] The same month he published an important essay, titled "The Reorganization of the

Party ." In it he called for a new party congress in order to put the whole organization "on a new basis ."

This article went to the main point directly: "The conditions in which our Party is functioning are changing radically. Freedom of assembly, of association and the press has been captured ." [17] What followed? Lenin answered: "organize in a new way" ... "new methods" ... "a new line ."

> We, the representatives of revolutionary Social-Democracy, the supporters of the "Majority" [Bolsheviks], have repeatedly said that complete democratization of the Party was impossible in conditions of secret work, and that in such conditions the "elective principle" was a mere phrase. And experience has confirmed our words. ... But we Bolsheviks have always recognized that in new conditions, when political liberties were acquired, it would be essential to adopt the elective principle. [18]

It must be kept in mind that the impracticality of open election of local leading committees under conspiratorial conditions was not a Bolshevik peculiarity; the secret police had made it as difficult for Mensheviks or S-Rs.

> Our party [wrote Lenin] has stagnated while working underground. ... The "underground" is breaking up. Forward, then, ... extend your bases, rally all the worker Social-Democrats round yourselves, incorporate them in the ranks of the Party organizations by hundreds and thousands. [19]

These were "new methods" only in Russia, of course; this was what bourgeois democratic regimes had possible in Western Europe before this. Lenin had always viewed the German Social-Democracy as a model of organization; now the Russian Social-Democrats could emulate it.

> The decision of the Central Committee...is a decisive step towards the full application of the democratic principle in Party organization. [20]

All comrades, he enjoined, must "devise *new* forms of organization" to take in an influx of workers, new forms that were "definitely much broader" than the old, "less rigid. more 'free,' more 'loose.'" "With complete freedom of association and civil liberties for the people, we should, of course, have to found Social-Democratic unions..." [21] "Each union, organization or group will immediately elect its bureau, or board, or directing committee..."[22] Furthermore, he recommended, it was now possible to bring about party unity, Bolsheviks with Mensheviks, on the basis of a broad democratic vote of the rank and file, since this could not be organized under the new conditions. [23]

All of this sea-change had to be explained to Russian workers who had never faced such conditions before. We must not be afraid, Lenin argued, of "a sudden influx of large numbers of non-Social-Democrats into the Party ." [24]

Note this remark made almost in passing: "The working class is instinctively, spontaneously Social-Democratic, and more than ten years of work put in by Social-Democracy has done a great deal to transform this spontaneity into consciousness ." [25] *It looks as if Lenin had forgotten even the existence of the Kautsky theory he had copied out and quoted in 1902!*

> The initiative of the workers themselves will now display
> itself on a scale that we, the underground and circle workers
> of yesterday, did not even dare dream of. [26]

He seized on the new conditions especially to advocate that mass recruitment of workers (possible for the first time) should swamp over the influence of intellectuals in the party work:

> At the Third Congress of the Party I suggested that there be
> about eight workers to every two intellectuals in the Party
> committees. How obsolete that suggestion seems now!
> Now we must wish for the new Party organizations to have
> one Social-Democratic intellectual to several hundred Social-
> Democratic workers. [27]

The article concluded this way, with a typical Lenin reaction: "We have 'theorized' for so long (sometimes -- why not admit it? -- to no use) in the unhealthy atmosphere of political exile, that it will really not be amiss if we now 'bend the bow' slightly, a little, just a little, 'the other way' and put

310

practice a little more in the forefront ." [28]

So now the bow bent the other way -- "slightly ."

The situation would now be quite clear even if Lenin never mentioned WITBD again. But in fact we can now turn to remarks by Lenin in which he reconsidered WITBD specifically, in the light of the new conditions and of these new concepts of party organization (new for Russia).

In November 1907 Lenin published a collection of old articles, called *Twelve Years*. Its aim was to review the thought and action of the movement over that period of time, a historical purpose. His preface to this collection was plainly addressed to the new audience generated by the revolutionary upheaval going on since 1905, an audience to whom the old disputes were now past history. Here he explained why WITBD had been included in the collection. Note in the first place that it required an explanation.

WITBD had been included (explains Lenin) because it "is frequently mentioned by the Mensheviks" and bourgeois-liberal writers; therefore he wanted to "draw the attention of the modern reader" to what was its "essential content ." His explanation began with a statement that might just as well be addressed to contemporary Leninologists:

> The basic mistake made by those who now criticize WITBD
> is to treat the pamphlet apart from its connection with the
> concrete historical situation of a definite, and now long past,
> period in the development of our Party.

This applied, he said, to those "who, many years after the pamphlet appeared, wrote about its incorrect or exaggerated ideas on the subject of an organization of professional revolutionaries ." Such criticisms were wrong "to dismiss gains which, in their time, had to be fought for, but which have long ago been consolidated and have served their purpose ." [29]

It is obvious that the reference to "exaggerated ideas" is an admission of a degree of incorrectness, even if the confession simultaneously maintains that the incorrectness was pardonable. But that had already been the sense of the "bending the bow" remarks; it was not really even new.

WITBD had done its 1902 job, and should not be treated any more as if it were a current proposal; it had been by-passed. Lenin did not apologize for it or repudiate it; this was something different. He was pigeonholing it as of historical interest only. Socialists would not repudiate the First International either, but no one would dream of bringing it back to life.

It was a far cry from a permanent "concept of the party ."

6. Last Words on WITBD

Typically Lenin argued that the "exaggeration" in *WITBD* had been necessary at the time in order to make progress in the *direction* desired, even if the exaggerations themselves were not tenable.

> To maintain today that *Iskra* exaggerated (*in 1901 and 1902!*) the idea of an organization of professional revolutionaries is like reproaching the Japanese, *after* the Russo-Japanese War, for having exaggerated the strength of Russia's armed forces, for having prior to the war exaggerated the need to prepare for fighting these forces.* To win victory the Japanese had to marshal all their forces against the probable maximum of Russian forces. ...*[Today* the idea of an organization of professional revolutionaries has *already* scored a complete victory. That victory would have been impossible if this idea had not been pushed to the *forefront* at the time, if we had not "exaggerated" so as to drive it home to people who were trying to prevent it from being realized. [30]

The claim made here that the professional-revolutionary idea had "already scored a complete victory" showed once more how little the usual Leninological version of this idea jibed with Lenin's. This "victory" included opening the party to an influx of "raw" workers who, hopefully, would swamp not only the party intellectuals but also the old experienced cadre of trained activists (professional revolutionaries). The idea that had shown its power ("scored a complete victory") was the need for a *core* of trained activists in the organization. It had nothing to do with the chimera of a party composed only or mainly of full-time functionaries. This chimera was especially grotesque in the light of Lenin's appeal for mass recruitment.

---

* It should be remembered that Lenin (along with almost the entire International) favored the victory of Japan in that war with Russia.

WITBD, continued Lenin, was merely a summary of the organizational policy of the *Iskra* group of 1901-1902, "no more and no less ."[31] That is, it was the joint policy of those (the *Iskra* group) who later divided into Mensheviks and Bolsheviks on *other* grounds. In other words, Lenin was again insisting, in still another way, that at the time he did not regard the ideas of *WITBD* as unique to himself or his tendency.*

Now, under the new conditions of legality, Lenin boasted as follows:

> Despite the split, the Social-Democratic Party earlier than any of the other parties was able to take advantage of the temporary spell of freedom to build a legal organization with an ideal democratic structure, an electoral system, and representation at congresses according to the number of organized members. You will not find this, even today, either in the Socialist-Revolutionary or the Cadet parties...[32]

Here he was talking about the party (the RSDLP) as a whole, not just the Bolshevik wing; there had been a unity congress in May. Who built the party to its present effectiveness as a democratic structure? "It was accomplished by the organization of the professional revolutionaries... glance at the delegate list of any of the groups at, say, the London congress, in order to be convinced of this.. ."[33] Note that he referred to the "delegate list," or, as he put it in the same sentence, "the central core that had worked hardest of all to build up the Party and make it what it is ." It scarcely makes sense to believe that in Lenin's view the party membership (far wider than the "delegate list" or the core) was to consist of professional revolutionaries only -- even if we stick with Lenin's

---

* Some previous statements should be mentioned too. In August 1903 Lenin had scribbled a few lines for himself, as a note on "Martov's Contradictions and Zigzags ." The second of four points was that "He [Martov] always defended *Iskra*'s ideas of organization *(What Is To Be Done?)*, but secured the incorporation of a Jaurésist [reformist] first clause in the Rules ."[32] In January 1904 Lenin published a pamphlet preface in which he challenged the Mensheviks to state their *new* concepts of organization: they have "announced...the existence of differences over questions of *organization*. Unfortunately, the editors are in no hurry to specify just what these differences are, confining themselves for the most part to hinting at things unknown ."[33] The man who wrote these words was plainly under the impression that up to this point the Mensheviks had *no* distinctive line on "concept of organization ." In March 1905, in a reply to Plekhanov, Lenin insisted that "Plekhanov's assertion that our relations cooled on account of *WITBD* is absolutely untrue ."[34] These are only a few of the many indications of this fact: at least when he published *WITBD*, and until controversy developed subsequently, Lenin thought that the book's views were the common property of the *Iskra* group.

reasonable definition.

The Kautsky theory of 1902 had long disappeared from Lenin's ken by this time; there was no indication that he even remembered its existence. At this point he was busy pointing with pride: the organizational successes of the party were due to the inherent organizational capacities of the working class.

> Without this condition an organization of professional revolutionaries would be nothing more than a plaything, an adventure, a mere signboard. *WITBD* repeatedly emphasizes this, pointing out that the organization it advocates has no meaning apart from its connection with the "genuine revolutionary class that is spontaneously rising to struggle ." ... The professional revolutionary has played his part in the history of Russian proletarian socialism. No power on earth can now undo this work... [34]

Throughout these pages, more often than we can reasonably cite, Lenin repeated the theme that the day of *WITBD* was in the past. "In the historical conditions that prevailed in Russia in 1900-1905, *no* organization other than *Iskra could have* created the Social-Democratic Labor Party we now have ." This preceded the statement that "The professional revolutionary has played his part.. ." The bitter disputes within the émigré circles characterized "a young and immature workers' movement"; "only the broadening of the Party by enlisting *proletarian* elements can help to eradicate the "circle spirit ." "And the transition to a democratically organized workers' party, proclaimed by the Bolsheviks...in November 1905, i.e., as soon as the conditions appeared for legal activity -- this transition" was a break from the "old circle ways that had outlived their day ." [35]

"Yes, 'that had outlived their day,'" Lenin repeated, "for it is not enough to condemn the old circle spirit; its significance in the special circumstances of the past period must be understood.. ." -- and so on. "The differences among the circles were over the *direction* the work was to take... The circles played their part and are now, of course, obsolete ." [36]

Next Lenin commented on Plekhanov's statement that "he differed from me in principle on the question of spontaneity and political consciousness ." [37] Once again Lenin insisted that there was no real difference involved at the time. "Plekhanov's criticism," he said, was "based on phrases torn out of context," and, he added, "on particular expressions which I had not quite adroitly or precisely formulated ." The particular criticisms by Plekhanov to which Lenin was here referring were to the pamphlet *One Step Forward, Two Steps Back*, but against them Lenin here appealed to "the general content and the whole spirit of my pamphlet *WITBD* ." All of us had agreed (he went on to say) upon the "formulation of the relation between spontaneity and political consciousness" in the draft Party program put forward by the *Iskra* group. And then Lenin made a statement which capped the whole problem:

> Nor at the Second Congress did I have any intention of elevating my own formulations, as given in *WITBD*, to "programmatic" level, constituting special principles. On the contrary, the expression I used -- and it has since been frequently quoted -- was that the Economists had gone to one extreme. *WITBD*, I said, straightens out what had been twisted by the Economists... The meaning of these words is clear enough: *WITBD* is a controversial correction of Economist distortions and it would be wrong to regard the pamphlet in any other light. [38]

It would be hard to imagine any more telling refutation of the *WITBD* myth, unless perhaps Lenin had staged a bonfire of all extant copies of *WITBD*.

There is no record that Lenin ever went back on the above-quoted statements about *WITBD*. In fact, there is no record that he was aware of a problem about it.*

---

* As far as I know, the only claim that Lenin ever came back to the subject appeared in an article which requires notice because it has occasionally been quoted. This article, published in 1938 by Max Shachtman in the theoretical organ of the American Trotskyist group, ascribed *WITBD* to the specific Russian conditions of the time and went on to say:

> That is why Lenin, in answer to a proposal to translate his brochure for the non-Russian parties, told Max Levien in 1921: "That is not desirable; the translation must at least be issued with good commentaries, which would have to be written by a Russian comrade very well acquainted with the history of the Communist Party of Russia, in order to avoid false application ." [44]

Unfortunately the article gave no source for this quotation; and while it gave a list of sources for the article as a whole, I have not been able to find this episode in any of the works listed.

Now which is "the Leninist concept of party organization" — Lenin's approach of 1905-1907, just described, or the formulations of 1902 in *WITBD*? The answer that Lenin's ghost would give, obviously, is: neither -- no "concept of the party" taken as a "principle" divorced from time and place. Lenin's ideas on party organization, like those of most others, varied depending on conditions, especially such an immense difference in conditions as that between the underground conditions in an autocracy and the conditions of relative political liberty and open organizational opportunity that characterized Russia in the 1905-1907 period.

At least one Leninologist was able to recognize this elementary idea, and as a result drew the wrathful fires of Leninological authority on his own head. Deviating from the consensus, John Plamenatz wrote this much:

> There is nothing specifically undemocratic about the opinions
> so vigorously expressed in *WITBD*. ... He never, when he wrote
> *WITBD*, intended that the "party of the proletariat" should
> drive and bully the workers, or even that it should make their
> revolution for them, and then govern Russia in their name but
> without taking the trouble to consult them.

If it were not for what happened after the Bolshevik Revolution, says Plamenatz, "We should not venture to call them [the ideas of *WITBD*] undemocratic, but merely say of them that they were advice perhaps well enough adapted to the needs of a revolutionary party active in Russia in the first decade of the twentieth century." [39]

Lenin's 1902 proposals for the Russian movement of the day may have been good or bad proposals – this discussion is pre-empted by the Leninological myth. Recognition that *WITBD* was not antidemocratic in its views still leaves open the belief (which Plamenatz for one holds) that "Leninism" took an antidemocratic turn in "what happened after the Bolshevik Revolution." The point about the Leninological myth is that it makes discussion of these developments impossible: political-historical analysis is replaced by demonology.

AMAZING STORY:
UTECHIN'S EDITION OF LENIN'S *WITBD*

The preceding essay was in part drafted in 1963 for use in a book review. The year 1963 was a great year for the Leninologists, with the publication of three biographies of Lenin, plus a relevant volume of memoirs by Angelica Balabanoff. Another event of the year was the publication of a new English translation of *WITBD*:

What Is To Be Done? Translated by S. V. and P. Utechin. Edited, with an introduction and notes, by S. V. Utechin. Oxford: Clarendon Press. 213p.

This edition was noteworthy especially because it was, I think, the first example of a major Western publisher's recognition that Lenin's writings were at least as important for the history of sociopolitical thought as, say, those of Lactantius, Leibniz, Lilburne or Luther. It was the first production, from these scholarly precincts, of a critical edition with scholarly appurtenances, annotation, etc.

The milestone was the fact that it was done at all. The nature of the edition issued was of no mean interest. The job was done by S. V. Utechin, author of *Russian Political Thought* and a *Concise Encyclopaedia* covering Russia. The present note will not discuss the views expressed by Utechin's introduction; these views were rather standard specimens of the Leninological consensus on the original sin of *WITBD* as the fountainhead of all Bolshevik deviltry. We will be concerned only with what editor Utechin did to the text of Lenin's work.

In the first place, the Utechin edition does not present the complete text. This is doubly puzzling, because (1) Lenin's brochure makes a fairly small booklet to begin with, and (2) the amount cut out by Utechin is not very great in bulk. The reason could hardly have been an overwhelming need for economy by Oxford's Clarendon Press. (The publisher could have saved more space by cutting Utechin's footnotes arguing that conditions under czarism were better than Lenin made out.) There is, of course, reason for condensed versions of notable books, but usually for inclusion in fat collections. This is a small book made smaller.

To justify publishing an incomplete version like this, Utechin refers to the "slightly abridged" version which Lenin himself published in 1907 as part of a collection titled *Twelve Years*. As compared with the original 1902 edition, Lenin here made about a dozen cuts, none of them very important, the largest being the elimination of Chapter 5, Section A. (We should recall that when this 1907 publication took place, Lenin explained to the reader of the collection that

WITBD was now mainly of historical interest.)

Utechin claims in his preface that "The 1907 version [that is, the abridged one] was used for the only English translation hitherto, that by...J. Fineberg, which has appeared both as a separate pamphlet and in various selections and collections of Lenin's works put out by Communist publishers in Moscow and outside the Soviet Union ." This is not true. The Fineberg translation was of the full 1902 text. It appeared in the old (unfinished) *Collected Works*, Volume 4, Book II, published by International Publishers of New York in 1929; and also in the paperbound edition widely read, viz., No. 4 of the Little Lenin Library. Moreover, another *full* translation of the 1902 edition was subsequently available in English in a paperbound edition put out by the Foreign Languages Publishing House of Moscow. Finally (as Utechin does mention a little later) the new multivolume *Collected Works* in English, published by FLPH, presented still another full translation in its Volume 5. These translations were not the same; and so we had three different English versions of the *unabridged* text before Utechin. The abridged version of 1907 appeared in English only in the various sets titled *Selected Works*.

In any case, the abridgment practices followed by the Communist publishing houses should hardly have been a model for the first Western scholarly edition of a Lenin work.

The second strange thing about Utechin's edition is that *he does not even present the abridged 1907 version*. His surgical operation on the body of *WITBD* only starts with the 1907 abridgment, for he accepts all but a couple of the cuts made there. Then in addition he makes thirty-two further excisions in the text, ranging in length from over a page to a line here and there. Then, from the text which is left, he cuts twenty-four of Lenin's footnotes -- some of them rather long ones and several of them quite important and interesting.

The reader may wonder why Lenin's first Western scholarly editor snips his shears around the work like that; but he may assume that all of the cuts are of unimportant passages. This is true in a few cases, especially where only an odd line has been snipped out here or there. It is odd indeed, but--

Now we come to the fantastic. Many of Utechin's excisions are of passages with considerable interest; some of the excisions are important enough to stay in the most drastically condensed edition; *and a couple of the excisions are among the most important passages in the work.*

We have already seen that one of the most-discussed sections of *WITBD* concerns the role of bourgeois intellectuals in the socialist movement, and the

theory that the working class by itself can come only to trade-unionist consciousness. I have pointed out that in reality Lenin presented this theory by
quoting it from Kautsky, and that his own paraphrase was based on Kautsky.
I have mentioned that Leninologists' discussions of *WITBD* rarely or never
mention the inconvenient fact that the demonic theory was really Kautsky's.
How does Utechin handle this problem?

Easy: he simply exercises his editorial shears and excises the whole
quotation from Kautsky *from the text of the book*.The reader of this sanitized
edition will never be confused by finding out that the very crux of Leninist
deviltry actually started with Kautsky, not Lenin.*

Fourthly: if the suppression of this crucial passage is bizarre, there are a
whole group of cuts that are no less so. Here is an enlightening example.

One of the disputed points in disquisitions on *WITBD* is the question of the
origins of Lenin's thought: does it stem mainly from the European Marxist
tradition or from the Russian revolutionary past? Utechin is a rather all-out
proponent of the latter thesis: his introduction argues that Lenin's spiritual
ancestors were Tkachev and Ogarev in particular. The Tkachev bogey is most
commonly dangled before readers, for Tkachev was a Blanquist-type
nineteenth-century revolutionary of the vulgarest sort.

The text of *WITBD*, writes Utechin in this connection, "is not particularly
enlightening on this question." It was not advisable for him to refer to the text.
For he has carefully excised from this text every passage in *WITBD* that fails to
conform with his thesis, and that he can take out without ruining the
continuity.

Take the specific case of the bogeyman Tkachev, Lenin's "real" ancestor
according to Utechin and Leninology. It would have been a kindness to
Utechin if Lenin had thrown into his writings a few enthusiastic references to
Tkachev -- say about one percent of the number of references he constantly
makes to his European Marxist models. It would have been a boon for
Leninologists if he had published just *one* kind word about his "real ancestor

---

* The rule that Leninologists do not mention Kautsky in this connection has exceptions
that prove the rule. One of the few exceptions is one of the Lenin biographies published
in 1963, namely, the one by Possony, who starts off his chapter on *WITBD* with this very
quote from Kautsky. The reason is entirely clear and revealing: as a far-out political
rightist, Possony is interested in extending the usual anti-Lenin attaint *to the whole
socialist movement, right wing included.* The other two biographies published in the same
year, by Louis Fischer and Robert Payne, do not mention Kautsky in this connection at
all. Naturally it is all a question of objective scholarship...

." But in all of the forty-five volumes of Lenin's *Collected Works* there are about five references to Tkachev's name *in toto*, and only one of these is a substantive passage expressing an opinion. This one passage bearing Lenin's view of Tkachev occurs, as it happens, in *WITBD*. And it is distinctly *hostile* to Tkachev as a protagonist of "excitative terror ." [40]

Now what does a scholarly editor do when the text fails to conform to the consensus of Leninology? *Utechin strikes out of the text the whole passage on Tkachev.*

This one and only passage in which Lenin actually expressed an attitude toward his "real ancestor" (leaving aside secondhand claims) must not be allowed to confuse the innocent reader. Not only that: in a couple of other places in the text, Utechin cuts out substantial passages in which Lenin attacks terrorism and terrorist views.

This bears only on one side of the question raised about Lenin's ancestors. As mentioned, Utechin wants to play down the extent to which Lenin based himself on the European Marxist tradition. The text of *WITBD* (the text as written by Lenin) abounds in arguments taken from this arsenal. In fact, *WITBD* contains some of the most interesting material in all of Lenin showing his reliance on the European Marxist parties as models of party organization. It is this sort of material that Utechin tends to strike out, though it is too voluminous to excise altogether.

Utechin's preface refers quite consciously to this practice of his: "omitted...are chiefly details of polemics that are of no particular relevance to the main line of argument, and examples given by Lenin from the practice of the German Social-Democracy in order to illustrate points he was making, examples which would now be more likely to obscure than to elucidate his reasoning." These passages not only "obscure" Lenin's "reasoning," they ruin Utechin's case: out they must go -- *from the text.*

For example, there is the passage Utechin throws out of Chapter 3, Section F, a eulogy of how the German Social-Democratic Party operates. It is not true that this is only an "illustration," as Utechin claims -- though he never explains why enlightening "illustrations" have to be struck out of his text. This passage is an *argument* which Lenin is making in favor of his proposals. Lenin is citing the most admired socialist party as his model. Moreover, in his account of how the admirable Germans work, he is implicitly also giving his own views on how a party *should* work, on the basis of a legality such as did not obtain in Russia. If one wants to find out Lenin's "organizational concepts," it is important (to put it mildly) to find out his views on the organizational concepts and practices of the leading

European socialist party.

There are a brace of equally interesting references to the European movement that Utechin throws out. But it is not really necessary to take the space to pile one enormity on another.

Such is this first "scholarly" edition of Lenin from a major publisher, under the auspices of an eminent Western institution of learning, to reveal the lamentable original sins of Bolshevism. If a mangle-job like this had been done on, say, John Stuart Mill by a Moscow publishing agency, we would all know exactly what to think; and Utechin would probably not be behindhand in saying it. It would be called a work of falsification. But we must not be impolite.

After all, there are few Leninologists who are in the fortunate position of being able to "prove" their interpretation of a work by pruning the text to suit the interpretation. This does not necessarily mean that Utechin performed his operation on the body of *WITBD* with conscious dishonesty. It is far more likely that he knows only one way to read Lenin: through his own specially made glasses. The leading authorities of Leninology in the Western scholarly establishment are not different in kind from their blood-brothers in the Stalinist professoriat.

1990

Chapter XVII:
James Morrison and Working-Class Feminism

According to the mythology of much feminist history, advocacy of women's rights was the doing of certain enlightened intellectuals almost exclusively—Mary Wollstonecraft, John Stuart Mill, and so on. An accompanying tenet, implicit or explicit, has it that resistance to sexism can come only from the "educated classes," while the working classes necessarily remain a hotbed of male chauvinist attitudes and practices.

It is beyond question, of course, that most sectors of *both* the upper and the lower classes have been rife with sexist prejudices. It is the counterposition that is in question. Note that this counterposition contrasts enlightened individuals of the bourgeoisie with the mass ranks of sexist proles, whose enlightened individuals are seldom mentioned.

This is methodologically invalid. One reason for this pattern is that the aforesaid enlightened individuals in the lower classes, however numerous, have not tended to write and publish books (which after all is the mode of existence of intellectuals virtually by definition). Wollstonecraft and Mill published books. The influence of the others must be sought in other activities, if it is not to be misleadingly ignored.

The name of Wollstonecraft deserves special honor precisely because *there was not even a tiny minority of her class that constituted a simulacrum of a movement for her ideas.* From her class's point of view she was a pariah; this very fact adds to her stature historically, for all her limitations. We have seen that in revolutionary France there was *no* social tendency in the upper classes that spoke up in support of Condorcet, and that Olympe de Gouges was another pariah among her kind; while in contrast the women of the sansculottes took a large measure of revolutionary equality-in-action into their own hands en masse, that is, as a whole social stratum. For a short period the Revolutionary Women could be upborne on their surging movement as a vanguard, and represent a power even in high politics.

This contrast is instructive in the following way. In practice, the women of the people in Paris were far in advance of their educated "betters" *not* in the first place because their state of consciousness and enlightenment was higher, but because their actual social situation *pushed* them to assume equality in struggle. The social struggle itself was far more enlightening than any consciousness-raising lecture could be.

Historical experience (when it is not suppressed) tells us this: that when exploited classes and sectors of society emerge into view from below, take the public stage in times of crisis and upset, there also tends to be a sharp upsurge in the social forces militating against sexism. *Under conditions of social upheaval, all social ideas have a question mark placed over them;* and the state of women's rights is no exception. *Upheaval* must be understood literally: the social ground is heaved up and exposed to the eye; it is overturned; it is this social overturn that reveals what was concealed before from the sight of historians. In "normal" times, which means nonrevolutionary times, the dominant ideas are the only ones usually heard aloud because they are the dominant ideas of society. This is why revolutions are not simply suspensions of normality but tests of what has been going on molecularly in the invisible depths of the social order.

If we assume that in normal times the vast majority (of all classes) internalize the conventional sexist patterns, then as soon as cracks start appearing in the social fabric, *in what strata of society do women's interests in sex equality begin to show up most prominently?* This, of course, is a subject on which serious work still has to be done. This chapter has only a contribution to make. It concerns the hidden history of early working-class feminism in England.

1. A Trade-Unionist in the 1830s

When William Thompson died in 1833, a period of intense working-class struggle was under way that would shortly lead to the organization of the Grand National Consolidated Trades Union, the English workingmen's first attempt at general union. It was an effort that momentarily swept even Robert Owen into the movement. Cruel exploitation in the mills and workshops was producing millionaires and misery, vast masses of capital and vast reservoirs of distress. The workers started organizing trade unions for elementary resistance.

One of the centers of trade-unionism in the early 1830s was Birmingham, where the key group was the Builders' Union. From 1831 on, it grew rapidly and was on the road to becoming a national organization. The leading voice of this workers' movement was a painter by trade who had made himself what would later be called a "worker-intellectual" (so called by intellectuals). In September 1833, with strikes breaking out everywhere, James Morrison founded *The Pioneer, or, Trades' Union Magazine.* Of the trade-union organs that sprang up, this was probably "the best of the bunch" (to quote G. D. G. Cole). It quickly grew in influence as the authentic spokesman of the embattled workers.

In view of what we are going to find out about Morrison and his *Pioneer*, it must be emphasized that it was no hole-in-the-corner operation by some pariah intellectual. On the contrary. Morrison was hip-deep in the regional life of the working-class movement. Besides being himself a member of the Painters' Union (a component of the Builders' Union), he had been active in the cooperative movement, in workers' education, and in the unstamped press agitation. Naturally he considered himself a disciple of Owenism, which had no rival in England within the framework of the New Order ideas; he had been active in swinging the Builders' Union to support Owen's ideas.

The *Pioneer* got so warm a reception regionally that in a couple of months Morrison moved his center of operations to London. Beginning in February 1834 his paper became the official organ of the newly founded "Grand National." This brought Morrison in direct conflict with Robert Owen himself, for to Owen the spirit of trade-union militancy that filled the columns of the *Pioneer* was anathema.

True, Morrison wrote sincere editorial statements *in favor* of class collaboration and peace between Masters and Operatives, as a consummation devoutly to be wished. He wanted to convince employers to make such collaboration possible by voluntarily moderating the excessive brutality of their exploitive practices. It would be easy to show that Morrison's *ideas* were not much more revolutionary than Owen's.* There is a lesson here on the relation between ideas and social struggle; for with similar ideas, formally speaking, Owen deprecated militant trade-union struggle while Morrison helped carry on such struggle, as a journalist. He transmitted journalistically the pressures that heated up the workers' life-situation.

At any rate, by the summer of 1834, Owen, whose prestige was still unchallengeable in the leading councils of the Grand National, got Morrison's *Pioneer* dropped as official organ, after Morrison had rejected the cool proposal that he simply hand over his paper to the Grand National leadership. The *Pioneer* came to an end in July. Soon the Union started to break up too. Morrison came out of this racking experience broken in health. He died suddenly in August 1835, only 33 years old.

Among the most frustrating of historical accidents are the two premature deaths we have had to record in the last pages: namely, the deaths of William Thompson and James Morrison, who both might have been able to offer a

---

* For more information on the nature of Morrison's ideas, see the Special Note appended at the end of this chapter.

healthier alternative to Owen's leadership of the new socialist movement, and who did in fact start to offer this alternative. They died soon after coming into conflict with Owen, who lived on long after his positive impetus to the movement had turned into a fetter on it.

2. The Feminism of the Class Struggle

Let us make an interim contrast.

If one judges by a typical work such as W. L. Blease's *The Emancipation of English Women*, socialist feminism did not exist. Blease is more interested in admiring such giant strides toward women's freedom as the conquest of the right to ride a horse sitting astride, i.e., the great Right to Be Bifurcated. Naturally, this achievement was relevant only to rich women. Yet, despite this bifurcation in historical concerns, it is possible to find out that *the working-class and socialist movements of the early nineteenth century were centers of the advocacy of women's equality.*

This sort of feminism arose, as it had done in France, out of a life-situation of struggle. Women workers began to organize in the first trade unions as the century got started; women demonstrators were killed, along with men, in the 1819 Peterloo massacre; women operatives in the mills formed Female Reform Societies about the same time, for electoral reform. Women went on strike along with men or by themselves; and in the trade-union movement, when resolutions and decisions were up for consideration, *they voted.* Women's suffrage began inside the working class, just as it had begun inside the sansculotterie of the French Revolution. If we compare these workingwomen with the image of "Woman" portrayed in Wollstonecraft, we might be on a different planet.

Since this working-class feminism was not a theory or ideology but an accompaniment of real life, it could and often did coexist with conservative notions about "woman's place" and about the family. In a way the case is similar to the two sides of Morrison's ideas on class struggle and class collaboration: we are not dealing with intellectuals caught in the act of cerebrating, but with ideas and attitudes under pressure that were not necessarily congruent or consistent. In the real social struggles that went on, feminism was not primarily an *ism* but a condition.

This point, as it happens, was made in his own way by G. J. Holyoake, an Owenite organizer in the 1830s, who later authored a fat history of the movement from a standpoint hostile to socialism. He testified:

> To the honour of co-operators [Owenites], they always and
> everywhere were friendly to the equal civil rights of women.
> The subject is never obtruded and is never long absent. It
> continually recurs as though women were an equal part of
> the human family and were naturally inclined in Co-
> operation.

There was no comparable state of mind about women's equality in any
other section of society. This happened not primarily because the Owenite
workingmen were Advanced Thinkers, as Wollstonecraft had been an
Advanced Thinker even among bourgeois women. It happened because the
women were in fact involved in the social movement of struggle on an equal
basis.

It did not happen because of Owen himself. Owen spent his life opposing
the social and political powers that be and, in addition, fighting against the
religious institutions of society; and this is enough courageous oppositionism
for any one person. But he never made the woman question—the special
oppression of women, and the program of women's equality—a part of his
various crusades.

However, we must add that Owen did challenge the conventional marriage
institution, with its underlying sexual prudery and its double standard. (Read,
for example, his *Lectures on the Marriages of the Priesthood of the Old Immoral
World*, 1835.) He was much concerned to plan for the emancipation of women
from household drudgery; and he attacked the family as a basically evil
institution. Thus he made it easier for elements in the Owenite movement to
go beyond his own limited views.

There is no record, in any case, that Owen ever advocated social and
political equality *now* in the field of women's rights, as William Thompson had
done in 1825 under Anna Wheeler's influence. But the more advanced ideas,
having been loosed, were rife in the movement that went by Owen's name—at
a time when histories of feminism view these ideas as virtually unknown
except among some marginal littérateurs.

To find even a marginal advocacy of something approaching
thoroughgoing support to equal rights, we must look ahead to John Stuart
Mill's *The Subjection of Women* of 1869. It is no derogation of the great

importance of this work, especially for bourgeois feminism, to reveal where the younger Mill got his ideas. Certainly not from his father, as we have seen! But he also knew the man who had attacked his father... Holyoake's history added the following to the passage quoted above:

> Mr. J. S. Mill frequented their [the Owenites'] meetings and knew their literature well, and must have listened in his youth to speculations which he subsequently illustrated to so much effect in his intrepid book, "Subjection of Women."

This passage in Holyoake's history took off from a mention of Mrs. Anna Wheeler's advocacy of women's participation in political affairs. But in fact the young Mill's youth was even better spent than Holyoake remembered. Mill tells in his *Autobiography* that he, together with a circle of young Benthamite-Utilitarian disciples whom he frequented, regarded his father's article on "Government" as "a masterpiece of political wisdom," but disagreed with its paragraph on women's rights. (A good trick, and not the product of pure logic, since this paragraph laid the basis for the rest, as we have pointed out.) He recalls that Bentham himself also disagreed, though at the time none of them ever disagreed publicly, this absence of dissent being one reason why Thompson undertook his own book.

Half a chapter away from this passage in the *Autobiography*, we learn that precisely in 1825—evidently soon after the publication of Thompson's *Appeal*—this Benthamite youth section led by the junior Mill sallied into the meetings of the Owenite society in London and engaged in a series of debates, faction against faction, over a period of some months. Mill's memoirs tell us:

> ...the principal champion on their side [the Owenites'] was
> a very estimable man, with whom I was well acquainted,
> Mr. William Thompson, of Cork, author of a book on the
> Distribution of Wealth, and of an "Appeal" in behalf of
> women against the passage relating to them in my father's
> Essay on Government.

So, over four decades before he wrote his own book on the subject, John Stuart Mill was very well acquainted indeed not only with the Thompson-Wheeler pioneer work but also with Thompson's personal conversation and

328

argumentation on the subject. Besides the debates mentioned in the *Autobiography*, there was a more personal connection; for the very estimable Thompson was not only a personal friend of Bentham's but had lived at Bentham's house for several months up to the spring of 1823. One may wonder whether the young Bethamites' disagreement with the "masterpiece of political wisdom" on women's rights *preceded or followed* Thompson's demonstrations-in-debate that it was a masterpiece of antidemocratic muddleheadedness.

Given these educational experiences of the young Mill, and the nature of his relations with the Owenites, one can perhaps assume that he must have also read what Morrison's *Pioneer* was writing on the woman question. These were writings about sex discrimination and sexism such as Mill himself could not rival even when he screwed his courage to the sticking point and published his opinions in 1869, that is, on the eve of their becoming respectable.

To this remarkable organ of trade-unionism we now turn.

3. Morrison's Pioneer

The weekly *Pioneer* lasted for only forty-four issues, from September 7, 1833 to July 5, 1834, and so the relatively large amount of material devoted to the woman question hits the reader's eye as a substantial proportion of the whole. Nor did this emphasis blossom in early issues and fade away as the paper's scope enlarged. Just the reverse: the first seven numbers had little of this material, and the subject grew in importance as the paper went along.

In February a "woman's page" was announced, described as "a page for women's rights," not as a page "of interest to women"; and this department was continued to the end. It was first entitled "A Page for the Ladies," but in April Morrison criticized this designation (as quoted below), and adopted the rubric "Woman's Page ."

Morrison's first substantial statement came in No. 8 as he greeted the formation of a women's union in Leicester. Apparently this union had had to be organized at first in secret, and he congratulates the women on how well they carried it through: "you have shewn your self-styled lords and masters, that you can keep a secret as well as they can ." He generalizes:

It is in this, as it is in everything appertaining to general improvement; for after all the boasted refinement of higher society, the working classes are the first to cast away long standing prejudices.

You will be called "blue-stockings," Morrison warns the Leicester women, but this epithet "which has been thrown at every intelligent woman who happened to have more sense than her stupid husband, has not deterred the ladies of Leicester from uniting to obtain the advancement of themselves and their kindred."

Morrison makes a criticism: the Leicester lodge consists entirely of women, with the exception of two posts occupied by men, that of "protector" (sergeant-at-arms?) and secretary. You should not make these exceptions, Morrison advises: "you are able to fulfil those duties yourselves." Again he generalizes:

> Then do, we beg of you, feel the pride of your own strength, and lose the habit of leaning so much on the judgment of the other sex. ...[We would recommend that the women of Leicester do assert their own dignity, and have a secretary of their own sex, and be self-protected. Do not let us for ever see woman looking up to man for anything which needs so small acquirement. The very habit of doing a little duty like this for themselves, will create a spirit of independence which will rise to things of greater magnitude, and when women acquire freedom their children will never more be slaves. It is much to be regretted, that you have so long succumbed to the insolent despotism of man.

This is remarkable advice, indeed amazing—for the 1830s! It is far more hostile to the mind of the contemporary society than the advocacy of this or that programmatic point, though Morrison was not behindhand on program, as we will see. He did not merely advocate equality *for* women; he advised them to take equality—and there is a great difference.

Before we go on to Morrison's main writings, a possible misunderstanding must be anticipated. I have emphasized that we are not dealing here with an isolated individual who is so far ahead of his times that he or she can be admired for uniqueness. Morrison's articles were published as the official editorial expression in an organ of a mass working-class movement. One must wonder: these editorial attacks on the "insolent despotism of man" and exhortation of women to quit listening to men as masters – these sentiments which notoriously fly in the face of the stereotype of working-class sexism – didn't they elicit indignant protest and resentment from most of Morrison's readers and subscribers, upon whom he had to rely for the paper's very existence, namely, the men?

There is no sign that this was much of a problem for the paper. The *Pioneer* solicited and published critical dissents from its worker readers; it particularly solicited dissent from its views on the woman question, and it sounded as if it had trouble getting as much of it as it wanted for discussion purposes. Morrison did print, and discuss, a dissenting critique by a master tailor, as we will see.

But where was the storm of indignation that should have greeted the *Pioneer*'s militant undermining of male supremacy in the family and everywhere else? Did editor Morrison conceal the onslaught that came in, that is, suppress its publication? There is not the least indication, direct or indirect, that anything like this happened. There were no overt or covert references to any such problem. Certainly Holyoake's memory, while not favorable to Owenism, held no such recollection. Morrison's enterprise came to grief in London, not in Birmingham; and not from lack of support by his base, but rather from the rebuff administered on top, by the Owenite leadership.

In fact, the internal evidence argues that Morrison continued to write along these lines of feminist militancy just as if he felt that this line was reason for the paper's popularity, not a source of weakness. Announcing the woman's page, he wrote congratulatingly that

> The men have done their duty in throwing to the dogs the
> barbarous prejudices that women had no right to meet in
> council, nor take a mental part in human life; and from this
> movement greater goodwill will ultimately follow than any
> other step the men have taken.

To be sure, I doubt that *all* the barbarous prejudices were thrown to the dogs; the point is that the militant profeminist viewpoint of the *Pioneer* constituted not a pariah obsession but the accepted public opinion of this workers' movement. In any other milieu in England at this time or in any other country, an editor who published this stuff in issue after issue would have been fired, stoned, or institutionalized. These facts stand on their head the whole traditional stereotype of where the class roots of profeminism lie.

Morrison wanted his woman readers to use the *Pioneer* as their own outlet; he printed a rather large number of letters from women, especially woman unionists, inspired by his own articles. He first broadcast an appeal for letters in the Leicester article quoted above. "We hope then to hear from the sisterhood: but now ladies, mind and write it yourselves.. ."

> ...we [men] do not know how to write like you; our thoughts are not your thoughts, nor our ways your ways. — A man cannot feign a woman's feelings; — he does not know her wrongs; — he wrongs her most himself. — He is the tyrant, — she the slave. — How can *he* portray *her* smothered thought, or write *her* anxious wish? Write yourselves, then, write yourselves.

A few months later, Morrison devoted a whole "Woman's Page" to this same theme, beginning with the sentence: "Ah no! we cannot write as women feel!"

The letters from women published in the *Pioneer* are often of great interest, and I scant them here with reluctance. They tell us a great deal about the women's trade-union activities that were going on. Women wrote in announcing the formation of militant women's groups, mostly trade-unionist. From Derby, scene of a bitter turnout/lockout struggle, a woman's letter appealed for the formation of a "female union": "Let the first lispings of your innocent offspring be *union! union!*" A "London Mechanic's Wife" made a point that historians should take to heart:

> Shall the idiot-like, the stupid and usurious capitalists, tell us to look to our domestic affairs, and say, "*these we understand best,*" we will retort on them, and tell them that thousands of us have *scarce any domestic affairs to look after,* when the want of employment on the one hand, or ill-requited toil on the other, have left our habitations almost destitute...

A woman's letter echoed Fourier's great thesis, perhaps without having heard it before. Arguing for the proposition that "both sexes shall enjoy an equality of rights and privileges," she added: "Certain it is, no change for the better can take place in society, unless the emancipation of women is agreed upon... [In proportion as woman is made a full sharer of the benefits of 'Union,' in such proportion will man discover his ultimate success will be hastened or retarded ."

But now let us focus on Morrison's own writings.

4. A Synthetic Essay by James Morrison

Instead of pasting together a series of excerpts from Morrison's essays and exhortations, let us ask the following question: *Suppose Morrison had edited his writings on the woman question into a pamphlet or fly sheet,* wouldn't it be one of the great landmarks in the literature of the subject? Let us imagine that he did so: selected passages to make his various points, avoided repetition, eliminated some excess verbiage, emphasized his main themes, and, of course, not bothered to show excisions and jumps with suspension points and bracketed interpolations.

In the following "synthesized" essay, every sentence and every word is Morrison's own. I have added or changed nothing; only rearranged. I have altered the language in no respect, not even in spelling or punctuation. I have interpolated no comments or interpretations of my own. Let us imagine that it is entitled —

SUBJECTION OF WORKINGWOMEN
The Views of
James Morrison

Does man think, or does woman think, that women are free, because they can go out to church or market, lecture-room, assembly-room, theatre, or ball-room at pleasure? They are as much domesticated in all these places as they are at home.

What do they hear at church? A *man* haranguing the two sexes; and though he did address himself to woman only, what does he know about woman, of whose feelings he has no experience? If woman go to market, a theatre, a ball-room, a lecture-room, these everlasting men are for ever around her. They are her teachers, her counsellors, her politicians, her pastors, her agents, her every thing.

333

In fine, the whole business of society is so evidently in the hands of man, that a queen is almost necessitated even to look upon her own footman as her superior, merely because he is a man; and man is enabled, merely by the deceitful spell of this nominal supremacy, to exercise a species of control over woman, which does not result from real superiority of intellect or morals, but, like the spiritual authority of ancient priests, from some fancied excellence, which is supposed to be peculiarly and exclusively the inheritance of the male.

Men have their public meetings, their social meetings, their newspapers, their magazines, their male speakers, and their male editors, and men with men correspond in all quarters of the world; but woman knows nothing of woman, except through the medium of man — a dense medium, which distorts her native character, and bedaubs it with the false colouring of the sex whose feelings, on a thousand delicate subjects, must be the very reverse of her own.

How can woman redeem herself from such shackles of ignorance and mental slavery? By application to man? Fool she must be, if she apply to man to get a knowledge of herself, and the interests of her own sex. Men have nothing to do with women; they are two distinct animals altogether; they have each a sphere of their own, with which the other cannot, without creating mischief, interfere. Therefore, we say, let woman look to herself; allow no male to enter her meetings, until she has obtained sufficient skill and experience to act in public, and then let her assembly rooms be thrown open.

Some women say they are free; they do not want to be redeemed. But if they be free themselves, will their freedom bestow liberty upon the rest of their sex? Yet where is the woman who can say she is free? Why are the ladies so very reluctant to go out alone? Because, by going *free*, they subject themselves to reproach. But we do not call that freedom which carries reproach along with it.

Is woman free to speak or to act as her feelings prompt her? But the laws of the land have doomed her to inferiority and political annihilation! The very being or existence of a woman is supposed to be extinct during marriage; she is called a *"femme covert"* — that is, a woman whose being is not acknowledged — an invisible woman — a species of ghost, who haunts her husband, and only becomes half solidified when he is no more.

An unmarried woman is a ghost as well. Thus, for instance, if an unmarried woman should be so unfortunate as to have a child, that child can inherit nothing, because, as the law says, "he is the son of *nobody* ." Now nothing can be more clear than this: "a woman is *nobody* ." And when she has a husband, he is her all in all; she takes his name; she becomes his property; she cannot inherit individually; she is his subject; he is her sovereign.

Think of this, till your spirits are roused to a determination to compel the law to regard you as somebodies. But how will you do this, for the law won't hear you? You have no voice, no vote, no influence on legislation. Then make a legislation for yourselves, a woman's law. We shall no longer trample upon your rights; we shall acknowledge your equality; we shall divide the kingdom with you; and, each embracing that species of employment which is suited to the sex, with no political distinctions of first or last, greater or less, we shall remove the curse which was inflicted upon woman, "Thy desires shall be unto thy husband, and he shall *rule* over thee ."

Woman is an endearing, social name; but *lady* has something shockingly aristocratic and unequal about it; it conveys the idea of superiority and control; it is the counterpart of lord. Whatever was its original meaning, it implied the same kind of inequality which is included in the counter-title "lord"; and it almost looks as if it was bestowed upon woman as a kind of soothing, flattering title, to atone for the deprivation of the real authority which the name implies. Man is the lord, without assuming the title. Woman has got the title, but wants the authority.

A tailor has been rebuking us very severely for our preposterous absurdities about the women. This unionist scouts the idea of women's rights and privileges, and of their associating together to demand them of the male, and he says, that though not a profligate himself, if his wife were to go to legislate, it would be a certain way of making him a profligate. It is out at last. This is the spirit of the male. We wanted to draw it out, in order that it might be exposed.

The working-men complain that the masters exercise authority over them; and they maintain their right to associate, and prescribe laws for their own protection. But speak of any project which shall diminish the authority of the male, or give him an equal, where once he found an inferior, and then the spirit of Toryism awakes that has long been dormant. All men are Tories by nature. Even the unionists themselves, who rail against tyrants and oppressors, have the blood of the aristocrat flowing in their veins.

Our correspondent says that according to the Bible, women must be "discreet, chaste, and keepers at home, not gadding about or busy bodies; and how can this be exemplified if they go out to *legislate*?" This is the opinion of a male unionist. It only belongs to men to *gad about* and *be busy bodies*. Women have nothing to do but to keep at home, and remain in ignorance of everything but cooking, washing, scrubbing pots, &c. Now the Bible, which has been quoted against the women by a master, may be quoted with equal authority against the men. It says, "Servants, be subject to your masters with all fear ." If our opponents quote from the master's page, let them quote from the servant's page also, or we shall do it for them.

We do not want to set women a-gadding, but to prevent their gadding and their tattling. What is it that makes woman a tattler and a busy body, but the confined sphere in which she moves? She is individualised by the narrowness of her knowledge and experience. What is it that makes a villager less liberal than an inhabitant of the city? His confinement certainly. The only way to cure women of tattling and gadding is the way by which men are cured, enlarging their views and widening their sphere of activity.

Our correspondent would have each woman subject to her own husband. He may go to a coffee-house every night. *He has a right to do this,* for he makes the money. But what is the woman doing? She is working from morning till night at house-keeping; she is bearing children; she is cooking, and washing, and cleaning. And all this for nothing; for she gets no wages. Her wages come from her husband; they are optional. If she complain, he can damn and swear. And it is high treason in women to resist such authority, and claim the privilege of a fair reward of their labour!

Good God! if we thought that the sex *woman* could patiently endure such a yoke of bondage, we should hate her most heartily! But how is she to prevent it? Why, by the very same means by which the men will prevent the tyranny of the master. Women will save themselves abundance of labour by association.

Because we advocate the cause of female associations, do we therefore advise woman to cast off her feminine character, and assume the effrontery of man? If union is to produce such a corrupting effect, then, for heaven's sake, let the men beware of it; for man and woman are one nature, and are refined or corrupted by the same means.

We assure our correspondent we are more and more convinced, that he has too much of the spirit of the *master* in him; a spirit which we are determined to resist, wherever we find it. But it is degrading to human nature to admit the superiority of one being over another, merely because the *gender* is different. What is this but aristocracy? If we admit the right of man to rule over woman, merely because he is *man*, then we may, upon the same principle, admit the

336

authority of one man to tyrannize over another, merely because he is of noble blood, *high born.*

Certainly, nothing can be more unjust than that law of public opinion and of political jurisprudence which gives a fool (merely because he is a man) a political and domestic authority over a woman, who may, in every other respect except the circumstance of sex, be his decided superior. It is a tyrant's law, and is destined, for the good of both sexes, to be for ever annulled. Now is the day of general redemption for all. Black slaves and white slaves, male slaves and female slaves, must all be freed.

We warn all our sisters against every attempt in the male to scatter women and prevent their communion. Men will attempt it under every guise—the guise of love, of modesty, of religion, of chastity; in fine, every guise under which the male contrives to woo the female. But what is the consequence of your yielding to their insinuations? Why, you see the consequences already. The practice has had a fair trial. Woman is a slave, a servant to man. We burn, we weep to see her, as she appears to us daily. We know how to cure the evil; but *man, man, and she herself, deceived by men,* resist our endeavours, and cry out, like the landowners and the clergy, against all innovations.

Man is stronger than woman by nature. What is the conclusion to be deduced? Is man therefore demonstrated superior to woman? Then, by a parity of reasoning, a black bear or a wild buffalo is superior to man. But it is by this argument of the strongest alone that the doctrine of male superiority is defended. Yet man must admit that, if superior to woman in physical strength, there is a delicacy about the female character to which the male can never attain; in fine, that there is a characteristic difference between the two sexes, so peculiar to each that the one would suffer deterioration by being invested with the character of the other.

Now the query is, which of the two characters is the most valuable? A fine artist is much more highly regarded than a sturdy artisan; but the selfish male has not yet learned to apply the principle of action to his treatment of the female. A woman's wage is not reckoned at an average more than two-thirds of a male, and we believe in reality it seldom amounts to more than a third (and wives have no wages at all). Yet, is not the produce of female labour as useful?

There are many departments of the arts which are peculiarly suited to the female hand, which is much lighter in execution; and by the skillful combination of the properties of each sex, the finest results in the department of human industry may be accomplished. But the discovery of this sexual difference of handicraft will only tend to bring the two sexes to an equality.

This is the grand conclusion to which we must finally attain — that the two sexes are each distinct in their kind; that an equal proportion of both is necessary for the perfection of social happiness, and that the industrious female is consequently well entitled to the same amount of remuneration as the industrious male.

The women have always been paid worse for their labour than the men; and, by long habit and patient acquiescence, they have been taught to regard this inequality as justice. The consequence is, that men are either obliged to work for women's wages, or lose their work. It is to prevent this diminution of wages that the male tailors have declared war against the female tailors. They do not want to deprive the women of their means of living; they would have a woman's work to be valued by the same standard as that of a man's, and equally well paid. This at least is the professed reason which the tailors give for their proposed system of exclusion. Were this to have the effect of raising the wages of the women, and still preserving to them their employment, we should give the tailors our hearty support; but where they wantonly throw out of employment a number of females, merely because they were women, we think this an encroachment on the liberties of humanity, which is too much to be tolerated.

Has woman a right to reduce the wages of man, by working for less than man? Certainly not, were women considered equal to man, and did she enjoy the same rights and privileges; but since man has doomed her to inferiority, and stamped an inferior value upon all the products of her industry, the low wages of woman are not so much the voluntary price she sets upon her labour, as the price which is fixed by the tyrannical influence of male supremacy; therefore any attempt to deprive her of labour, because she works at a reduced price, is merely punishing women for the cruel and pernicious effects of male supremacy. To make the two sexes equal, and to reward them equally, would settle the matter amicably; but any attempt to settle it otherwise will prove an act of gross tyranny.

If the principle of resistance be justifiable in the male, it cannot be reprobated in the female. If women are compelled by want to leave their homes, and give their services for money, we cannot see that any law of sound morality or legislature can put an interdict upon them. Such an interdict is a war against liberty itself, and though it may do partial good to some, the

338

general good can amount to nothing.

Arbitrary laws will never save us. The last smuggler will survive the last exciseman, and if the women be prohibited from producing wealth, they will speedily become outlaws, and raise a sexual war. If women be prevented from making clothes, binding shoes, spinning, weaving, &c., what shall they do? They must haunt the street and prowl for prey, and then be reprobated by pious magistrates and other godly censurers of public morals, who devour their own children in punishing the crimes which they themselves create.

We have to reproach women for many of our young faults. They encourage the masculine habits, as they are called, of the boys, and train them from infancy to domineer over poor little miss. Now, if women were uniformly to check this spirit of control when they have the little rogues under their immediate direction, it would encourage a respect for the sex, which in time would grow into a fixed habit; and if they treated the *seducer* with as much cruelty and bitter persecution as they do the *seduced*, they would save thousands of the sex from the horrors of prosecution.

We have little esteem for unfeeling prudes: they are the occasion of more vice than the unhappy frail ones, for they are often the cause of her abandonment. Not that we wish to lay the whole of the blame on the sex whose interests we profess to advocate, but to show that women are in some measure the perpetuators of their own slavery.

There is a nominal respect paid to the women of this country, but it is in most instances only nominal. How often have we been disgusted with the hackneyed, common-place "compliments," as they are called. The reform of these abuses must begin with the women themselves; they ought to train their little male brats to think properly of their mothers, and sisters, and aunts, and the whole of their feminine acquaintance, and to instruct the little Pollys and Sallys at the same time not to be quite so afraid of masters Jackey and Tommy.

However loudly the men may bellow out for their own liberties, they will never bestow what they obtain upon women until she demands it from her masters, as they were done for theirs; and whenever that struggle arrives, the men will be as tenacious of giving up their absurd domination as is any other power which exists of relinquishing its authority.

It is fortunate, however, that the male part of the population cannot progress in real civilization without imparting the value of independence to those whom they at present consider their inferiors. A writer on the Rights of Women observes, that marriage seems ordained exclusively for the comfort of the man. Yes, and he has taken care to make the law as well as custom support him in his tyranny; for an operative may thrash his wife with impunity, and be in little danger of punishment for his brutality. Indeed, if the law were to punish him, the poor woman would become a victim for want of the means of his support.

In making these remarks, we do not wish a thought to be entertained that we desire to set the sexes at variance with each other; we only hope that, for the mutual happiness of both, the women will endeavour to create a public opinion among themselves sufficiently strong to command fair play, and the respect and kindness which is due to them, and which they will never obtain but by their own exertions and determination. Women would be no less amiable for being more independent, and mankind would be none the worse for a little of their gruffness being rubbed off to give place to the natural rights and privileges of woman.

5. Afterword: The Male-Female Unit

When I first read Morrison's essays on his "Women's Page" in the *Pioneer*, there was one feature that became more and more puzzling as I read on. Some of this feature peers through the "Synthetic Essay" above, but a full appreciation would require reading the material in greater bulk. It is not merely the sustained vigor and even passion of his defense of women's rights; this is surprising, given our stereotyped view of the time and place, but it presents no unanswered puzzle.

The puzzle is the fact that—at least here and there, and not infrequently—the language of Morrison's "Women's Page" sounds to me as if written by a woman, that is, from a woman's slant. This is not because of any particular opinion it presents; it is, frankly, an impression, and a matter of tone. Perhaps it emanates simply from the fervency of Morrison's advocacy?

Perhaps; and in any case it is difficult to find out much about Morrison personally. There is a brief reference to him in Holyoake's history mentioned above. Holyoake remarks: "His widow was long known at the Social Institution, Salford, for activity and intelligence nearly equal to his own. She was one of the lecturers of the society ." Typically, Holyoake thereupon does not even tell us her name! Morrison would have had a pungent comment on this characteristic treatment.

We can add little more information. Her name was Frances Morrison; she was active in the Owenite movement; in 1838-1839 she was lecturing in Owenite institutions in Lancashire and the North; and she published a booklet on *The Influence of the Present Marriage System* (Manchester, 1838).

At any rate, we can see that at Morrison's side was a woman of political intelligence and a comrade, herself a speaker and writer on socialism and the woman question. It becomes easier to speculate that Frances Morrison could have participated — must have participated — in the writing and preparation of at least some of the Women's Pages in the *Pioneer*.

As in the case of William Thompson and Anna Wheeler, whom the Morrisons must have known, we have at work what the Saint-Simonians called the Male-Female Social Unit: not merely a cooperation of two individuals, but the integration in their life work of a thinking man and woman in association. At this point it is possible to get lost on the seas of speculation, well out of sight of facts; but is it too speculative to wonder if the female part of the unit was instrumental in turning the male half toward his passionate identification with the cause of women's rights?

Here is another corner to be lifted on the Hidden History, the underground life of socialist feminism.

(Unpublished 1990)

Chapter XVIII:
The Principle of Self-Emancipation
in Marx and Engels

There can be little doubt that Marx and Engels would have agreed with Lenin's nutshell definition of Marxism as "the theory and practice of the proletarian revolution." In this violently compressed formula, the key component is not the unity of theory and practice; unfortunately that has become a platitude. Nor is it "revolution"; unfortunately that has become an ambiguity. The key is the word "proletarian" — the class-character component.

But "proletarian revolution" too, very early, took on a considerable element of ambivalence, for it could be and was applied to two different patterns. In one pattern, the proletariat carries out its own liberating revolution. In the other, the proletariat is used to carry out a revolution.

The first pattern is new; the second is ancient. But Marx and Engels were the first socialist thinkers to be sensitive to the distinction. Naturally so: since they were also the first to propose that, for the first time in the history of the world, the exploited bottom stratum of workers in society was in position to impress its own class character on a new social order.

When Marx and Engels were crystallizing their views on this subject, the revolutionary potentialities of the proletariat were already being recognized here and there. It was not Marx who first discovered that the proletariat was a revolutionary class. For example, Robert Owen, disappointed at the failure of his philanthropic bourgeois to become enthusiastic about the abolition of their class, turned for help to the beginnings of the working-class and trade-union movement in England; he thought to use them, not to shift power to *that* class, but as troops to push through his own scheme, in which a philanthropic elite would "do them good." Saint-Simon, disillusioned with the failure of monarchs, bankers, scientists, etc. to understand the ineffable justice of his plans for humanity, turned, in his very last work *The New Christianity*, to the workers for the first time — appealing to them to convince their *bosses* to heed the Saint-Simonian wisdom.

1. The Larger Historical Pattern

The first socialist view of the revolutionary proletariat was to regard its revolutionary potential as an instrument in others' hands; as a battering-ram to break down the old system but not as a force fit to build a new one in its own name. These non-proletarian socialisms not only preceded Marxism, but have always been far stronger than Marxism, in the socialist movements of the world — today as yesterday.

It must be emphasized that this pattern is not something peculiar to the socialist movement, but *extends into* socialism. It extends back into all recorded history, far as human eye can read. One section of the propertied classes, beaten on top, becomes desperate enough to resort to arousing the broader masses below both contestants, and therefore sets the plebs into motion, with appropriate promises and slogans, in order to hoist itself into the seats of power.

Hence, for example, the *tyrannoi* of ancient Greece have become *tyrants* in modern languages not because they tyrannized over the masses any more than the preceding oligarchy, but because they used the masses to "tyrannize" over that oligarchy itself. The pattern is visible in the story of the Gracchi; it is commonplace in modern history. It is a key to the dynamics of class struggle and intra-class struggle throughout time.

But it is always a gamble; there is a social risk. After you have called the masses from below onto the stage of social action, how are you going to get them off and back to their holes, after they have done the job for you? These animals are dangerous: handle with care. The intoxication of a joint victory may make them forget that you are the Natural Master. They may reach out for something for themselves, or smash things up in the process.

That danger was there even in ages when the broad working masses (slaves, laboring freemen, or serfs) could not and did not have any vision of a new social order which corresponded to their own class interests; when therefore their rule could not in fact mean a reorganization of society from below, but merely chaos. When that changes, what was previously a serious danger to Order becomes a mortal danger to the social order itself.

2. The Proletarian Acheron

This is the change that takes place in history with the rise of capitalism and its shadow, the revolutionary proletariat. For the first time, there is a class below, the class on whose labor society is founded, that inherently *does* suggest a social programme for its own reorganization of society. Once set in motion (in struggle), *this* class has an historical option: it is not limited to lending its services to one ruling class (or section of a ruling class) or another; it can go into business for itself. To be sure, it can still be controlled: for it is very young, and largely unformed, and often childishly stupid, and ill-educated; but how long can this adolescent giant be kept in short pants?

344

Because of this new type of danger, the class instinct of the bourgeoisie early made it reluctant to call the working masses into civil conflict even as an ally in its own drive to gain power from the older feudal order, and, since then, made it interested mainly in ways and means of fragmenting and channeling the dangerous mass forces below.

But the case of individual ideologists and political adventurers is another matter; so also political tendencies which look in the direction of an *anti-capitalist* elite.

Hence one of the characteristic differences among the bourgeois politicians is willingness to play with this fire, to one degree or another. Marx noted this, for example, in his thumbnail sketch of the French "liberal" politician Thiers who, after serving both Louis Philippe and Bonaparte, carried out the task of massacring the Paris Commune:

> A professional "Revolutionist" in that sense, that in his eagerness ... of wielding power ... he never scrupled, when banished to the ranks of the opposition, to stir the popular passions and provoke a catastrophe to displace a rival ... The working class he reviled as *"the vile multitude.*[1]*"*

This political type had a Virgilian tag, which was well-enough known in Marx's day to be of interest now. It put the pattern in six vivid words: *Flectere si nequeo superos, Acheronta movebo*[2] — "If I cannot change the Powers above, I shall set the Lower Regions [Acheron] into motion." George Brandes' book on Lassalle tells us that the would-be workers' dictator, weighing his political course, "pondering the Achilles in his tent, mentally repeated to himself for nights and days the burden of Virgil's line ..[3] ." The motto also came to Engels' pen as he contemplated the cowardice of the French liberals of a later day:

> ...the *flectere si nequeo superos, Acheronta movebo* is not their business ... They are afraid of the proletarian Acheron.[4]

Marx developed a new, third view of the proletariat, basically hostile both to the Olympian view of the ruling class and the Acherontic view of the would-be ruler.

3. The New Principle

The classic formulation of the self-emancipation principle by Marx was written down in 1864 as the first premise of the *Rules* of the First International—in fact, as its first clause.

> CONSIDERING, That the emancipation of the working classes must be conquered by the working class themselves;
> ...[5]

And it was from this source that the phrase became famous, being repeated also by various elements who did not believe a word of it.

Later on, Engels rightly predated the conception to "the very beginning": "our notion, from the very beginning, was that 'the emancipation of the working class must be the act of the working class itself'," he wrote in a preface to the *Communist Manifesto*, slightly varying the formulation, as did Marx also in his *Critique of the Gotha Programme*.[6]

From the very beginning of Marxism, he means. But if we sketch Marx and Engels' course *before* they arrived at this keystone principle of the self-emancipation of the proletariat, we will put it into context. For it was then an unknown principle, previously almost unthinkable.* There was nobody from whom to adopt it. Marx had to invent it himself—or re-invent it. The probability is that it was Marx who straightened Engels out on the subject, in the course of their collaboration in 1845 on *The German Ideology*.

4. Engels: from Elitism to Marxism

A good biography of Engels would recount the layers of ideas through which he had to fight his way before he could even get within reaching distance of Marx's approach. There was more standing in his way than in Marx's case.

---

* As usual, there are possible exceptions. A prominent candidate is the remarkable Gerrard Winstanley ("Diggers," left wing of the English Revolution); but he was entirely unknown to the early socialists, completely forgotten. Then there was Thomas Münzer (who was therefore the subject of Engels' first serious work after the 1848 revolution); and Spartacus—"the most splendid fellow that all ancient history has to show; great general—no Garibaldi—noble character, real representative of the ancient proletariat," wrote Marx.[7] But we know too little about the last two.

We will only mention now that, first, Engels had to revolt against the authoritarian pietist Christianity of his family and home; then came his early intellectual development through the romanticism of "Young Germany," followed by infatuation with the radical-liberal Ludwig Borne. Involvement in the Young Hegelian (left-Hegelian) circle in Berlin, plus an early dash of Shelley, led to his conversion to a so-called "communism" by Moses Hess, who was then in his period of *Schwärmerei* over Proudhon's newfangled "anarchism," which he understood to be similar to his own sentimental petty-bourgeois socialism. In England in 1843, Engels was at first mainly in contact with the Owenites, for whose *New Moral World* he began his English writing, although he also made the acquaintance of emigre German communist workers like Karl Schapper. Then he went through a spell of enthusiasm over Wilhelm Weitling's allegedly "working class" communism, finally making contact with the Chartist movement.

The radical scene was what this sounds like, only more so: a hodge-podge of ideas, a mingle-mangle of movements. And, before Engels got to Chartism, every one of them was basically elitist to the core: "we" will bring salvation to the toilers, and consent to lead them where sheep may safely graze.

Let us pick up Engels toward the end of 1843: he is writing articles for the Owenite *New Moral World*, as a convert to "philosophical communism" by Hess, and as an admirer of Proudhon's anarchism. In a key article, he praises Proudhon's *What Is Property?* (1840) as the most important "communist" work published (for he is ignorant of the fact that Proudhon denounces "communism," since this enthusiasm came from Hess, who had adopted that label). The article emphasizes Proudhon's view —

> that every kind of government is alike objectionable, no matter whether it be democracy, aristocracy, or monarchy, that all govern by force; and that, in the best of all possible cases, the force of the majority oppresses the weaknesses of the minority, he comes, at last, to the conclusion: "Nous voulons l'anarchie!" What we want is anarchy; the rule of nobody, the responsibility of every one to nobody but himself.[8]

There is more of this Proudhonism in Engels' article, radical in sound and reactionary in content. The following is pure Proudhonism:

> Democracy is, as I take all forms of government to be, a contradiction in itself, an untruth, nothing but hypocrisy ... at the bottom. Political liberty is sham-liberty, the worst possible slavery; the appearance of liberty, and therefore the reality of servitude. Political equality is the same; therefore democracy, as well as every form of government, must ultimately break to pieces ... we must have either a regular slavery — that is, an undisguised despotism, or real liberty, and real equality — that is Communism.[9]

This reflects Proudhon's virulent hatred of democracy, using truths about sham-democracy to damn democracy itself, not to demand that the sham be exchanged for real democracy.

5. "Philosophical" Elitism

To this Proudhonism is attached Hess's "philosophical communism," which Engels, as a disciple of Hess in this article, considers the special glory of the German mind. Unlike the economic-minded English and the political French, the Germans became Communists *philosophically*, by reasoning upon first principles," he boasts.[10] For "the Germans are a philosophical nation" and will adopt Communism "as soon as it is founded upon sound philosophical principles." This will surely be done and so, no doubt —

> There is a greater chance in Germany for the establishment of a Communist party among the educated classes of society, than anywhere else. The Germans are a very disinterested nation; if in Germany principle comes into collision with interest, the principle will almost always silence the claims of interest. The same love of abstract principles, the same disregard of reality and self-interest, which have brought the Germans to a state of political nonentity, these very same qualities guarantee the success of a philosophical Communism in that country. It will appear very singular to Englishmen, that a party which aims at the destruction of

private property, is chiefly made up by those who have
property; and yet his is the case in Germany. We can recruit
our ranks from those classes only which have enjoyed a
pretty good education; that is, from the universities and
from the commercial class; and in neither we have not
hitherto met with any considerable difficulty.[11]

This hash, which is pure Hess, give a good idea of what some of the better
elements of the day were thinking and saying. Engels' next contribution to the
Owenite paper is especially taken from Weitling, who had also been praised
in the previous article as the leader of the "working-class" wing of German
Communism. Engels now stresses...

the chief point in which Weitling is superior to Cabet,
namely, the abolition of all government by force and by
majority, and the establishment in its stead of a mere
administration ... [and] the proposal to nominate all officers
of this administration ... not by a majority of the community
at large, but by those only who have a knowledge of the
particular kind of work the future officer has to perform;
and, one of the most important features of the plan, that the
nominators are to select the fittest person, by means of some
kind of prize essay ...[12]

All this* will give an idea of the thinking of the radical world into which
Marx came. Engels' subsequent articles for the Owenites, at the end of 1844
and beginning of 1845, became gradually more ambivalent about the relation
between communism and the classes.[13]

The turning-point comes in late 1845 — when Engels is well under way in
collaboration with Marx on *The German Ideology* — and indeed in the very first
article which Engels contributes, not to the Owenite organ, but to the left-
Chartist paper *The Northern Star*. Engels spells out the complete turn he has
made by cautioning the Chartists not to expect any revolutionary change from
the middle classes:

---

* It is amusing to find Fabianism's Bernard Shaw, in the next century, rediscovering
Weitling's idea of "civil service" examinations to select an oligarchy: Shaw's pet
suggestion on how to replace democracy.

It is from the very heart of our working people that revolutionary action in Germany will commence. It is true, there are among our middle classes a considerable number of Republicans and even Communists, and young men too, who, if a general outbreak occurred now, would be very useful in the movement, but these men are "bourgeois," profit-mongers, manufacturers by profession; and who will guarantee us that they will not be demoralized by their trade, by their social position, which forces them to live upon the toil of other people, to grow fat by being the leeches, the "exploiteurs" of the working classes?

Those who remain "proletarian in mind" will be infinitely small in numbers, he goes on: "Fortunately, we do not count on the middle classes at all.[14]"

Engels is now a Marxist.

6. Marx: The Case of the Savior-Ruler

Marx's course appears to have been less complicated. Still there are significant stages to be marked. One of the first nodal points showed him what pursuit of an academic career would mean. As it happens, it has to do with the historic opposite of the principle of Self-Emancipation, viz. the illusion of the Savior-Ruler.

A common form of this illusion has always been hope for salvation from the ascent to the throne of a new, liberal monarch. Marx went through this at an early age along with the left-Hegelian circle.

In mid-1840 the old king of Prussia was succeeded by his son, Friedrich Wilhelm IV, who as Crown Prince had excited great hope in liberal circles that he would grant constitutional reforms; for he had made certain noises about liberty and national unity.[15] It seems to be a common habit of royal heirs; the same pattern had been true a century before, when Frederick the Great had uttered similar "nice phrases ... shortly or immediately after his accession to the throne." So remarks Mehring in *The Lessing Legend*, which observes that this is "the noted liberalism of crown princes.[16]" One of the leading lights of the Young Hegelians, Bruno Bauer, seized the opportunity to pay fulsome homage to "the highest idea of our State life," the spirit of the Hohenzollerns.[17]

350

These hopes for democratization from above collapsed quickly. Bauer's prostrations before the crown earned only a kick in the face: the new king appointed an orthodox reactionary to the university post that Bauer had his eye on.[18] Next, Bauer was even ousted from his post at the University of Bonn.[19] It was at this point that it was clear to Marx that, doctorate or no, an academic career was closed to him, unless he was ready to bootlick the establishment like Academia in general.

7. Marx and Koppen

There is indirect evidence that, with the rest, Marx had been caught up in the liberal illusion about the new king.

In April 1840, looking to the new reign, Marx's best friend,[20] K.F. Koppen, also a prominent left-Hegelian though ten years older than Marx, had published a book on *Frederick the Great and His Opponents*.[21] One biographer of Marx describes the book as follows:

> Koppen honoured Frederick, "in whose spirit we swore to live and die," as the enemy of Christian-German reaction. His basic idea was that the state was embodied in its purest form in a monarchy ruled over by a monarch like Frederick, a philosopher, a free servant of the world spirit. Renewal could only come from the top ...[22]

Koppen was suggesting that the new monarch should bear the torch of the Savior-Ruler like his great predecessor. Another biographer comments:

> The fact that a man like Koppen yearned for "the spiritual resurrection" of the worst despot in Prussian history in order "to exterminate with fire and sword all those who deny us entrance into the land of promise" is sufficient to give us some idea of the peculiar environment in which these Berlin Young Hegelians lived.[23]

This is unjust: there was nothing "peculiar" about this attitude. It had been dominant for a few thousand years, and essentially it still is. Frederick may have been "the worst despot" but he was a *modernizing* despot, and this variety

351

still has mass allegiance from well-intentioned people, especially those who would like to become modernizing bureaucrats or mouthpieces for the modernizing despot. Marx's liberal friends held to the old illusion that, if only power found its way into the hands of a Good Man, he would hand down salvation from his seat of rule—and thus, incidentally, spare one all the inconveniences of having to conquer salvation for oneself in struggle against power.

Koppen's book was dedicated to "my friend Karl Heinrich Marx of Trier." There is every reason to believe that at this point Marx saw nothing "peculiar" about his friend's stance, and probably shared it.[24] In addition, the following year Marx returned the compliment with an admiring mention of Koppen's book in the planned Foreword (dated March, 1841) to his doctoral dissertation.[25]

The new king's failure to conform to the dream brought about a revulsion of feeling in liberal circles. Engels later described the result:

> Indeed, the middle classes, who had partly expected that the new King would at once grant a Constitution, proclaim the Liberty of the Press, Trial by Jury, etc., etc. In short, himself take the lead of that peaceful revolution which they wanted in order to obtain political supremacy—the middle classes had found out their error, and had turned ferociously against the King.[26]

In the Rhineland (continues Engels) this revulsion or exasperation produced the *Rheinische Zeitung* in Cologne, and made its bourgeois sponsors temporarily willing to let Young Hegelian radicals edit it—Marx becoming editor in October 1842.

This is the place to mention that the young Engels also went through his stage of disillusionment in benevolent royalty, before and after Friedrich Wilhelm IV. Just before, though not yet very radical, Engels had written a friend about his disgust with Friedrich Wilhelm III's failure to carry out his promise of a constitution:

> The same king who in 1815, beset with fear, promised his subjects in a Cabinet Order that they would get a constitution if they pulled him out of that pickle—this same

shabby, lousy, g—d—king now lets it be known ... that
nobody is going to get a constitution from him ... There is no
period richer in royal crimes than 1816-1830; nearly every
prince that reigned then deserved the death penalty ... Oh,
I could tell you delightful tales about the love that princes
bear their subjects—I expect anything good only from the
prince whose head is buzzing from the bullets of his people,
and whose palace windows are being smashed by a hail of
stones of the revolution.[27]

After the accession of the new king in 1840 and the above-mentioned
"revulsion," Engels published an essay attacking the king's political and social
views and warning that a free press and a real parliament would not be
granted by the monarch but would have to be won by the people. It closed
with a hint that Prussia was nearing its 1789.[28]

All this merely taught the liberals not to expect much from this particular
monarch; by nature, liberalism typically seeks reform by seeking the ear that
is connected to the hand that holds the levers of power. But for Marx the
lesson bit deeper. It was his last illusion in the Savior-Ruler.

8. The Servile State and Academia

Marx later summarized the whole episode in hindsight at a point (May
1843) when he was in midstream of the passage from radical democracy to
communism. The king's "liberal speeches and outpourings" did signify a
desire "to bring life into the state," if only his own variety of backward-looking
life ("old German fancies"); but when even this variety of change threatened to
open the gates to other changes, the old bureaucratic-despotic system "soon
killed these un-German activities." It was a "miscarried attempt to transcend
the philistine-state on its very own basis.[29]"

One was only mistaken for a while in considering it
important which wishes and thoughts the King would come
out with. This could not change anything in substance; the
philistine is the stuff making up the monarchy, and the
monarchy is always only the king of the philistines. He can
make neither himself nor his people into free, real men, if

both sides remain what they are.[30]

Since it was impossible for this state "to abandon its own basis and pass over to the human world of democracy," the inevitable result was—

> regression to the old fossilized servile state [*Dienerstaat*], in which the slave serves in silence and the owner of the land and the people rules as silently as possible simply through a well-trained, quietly obedient servant-staff. Neither of the two could say what they wanted—neither the former, that they wanted to become men, nor the latter that he had no use for men in his land. The only recourse, therefore, is to keep silent. *Muta pecora, prona et ventri obedientia*. [The herd is silent, submissive, and obeys its stomach.][31]

Therefore—

> The self-reliance of men—freedom—would first have to be reawakened in the hearts of these men. Only this consciousness, which vanished from the world with the Greeks and into the blue mist of heaven with Christianity, can again turn society (*Gesellschaft*) into a community (*Gemeinschaft*) of men to achieve their highest purposes, a democratic state.[32]

For Marx, the freedom of self-reliance meant not only the abandonment of the Savior-Ruler illusion, but also the decision to abandon the road of scholarship in the university world. For that road was possible only by accepting a life of silent submission to the Servile State, refraining from giving battle to ensconced power, burying one's nose in scholarly busy-work and profound thoughts, while injustice and inhumanity reigned outside the stained-glass windows.

9. Marx: The Promethean Spirit

If the course of the professional panderer to power was impossible for Marx, this was by no means simply determined by history or social forces, which do not determine this or that individual. It was demanded by Marx's total personality, combined with his intellect — the two conditioned by the times.

Marx's theories, to be sure, can be held by anyone, once developed: but the way they were developed and the form in which they were expressed were all heavily influenced by the impact of Marx's personal character. The steel core of that character has been portrayed for all time by Marx's favorite poet-dramatist (alongside Shakespeare): Aeschylus, in *Prometheus Bound*. Aeschylus does not really attempt to explain why Prometheus, insisting on serving humanity whom the new gods would destroy, refuses to bow the neck to Zeus, to Power — like everyone else and as all his well-wishers advise him to do. That is simply the fatality of his character.

It was also Marx's, and as far as anyone can tell, he seems to have been born with it, as his intelligent father early recognized. Marx himself made the connection in preparing for publication the first child of his thought, his doctoral dissertation. Although its subject was Democritus and Epicurus, in writing the Foreword Marx handed the center-stage over to Prometheus. The Foreword ends with the invocation of Prometheus' defiance to authority:

> Prometheus' admission: "In sooth all gods I hate" is (philosophy's) own admission, its own motto against all gods, heavenly and earthly, who do not acknowledge the consciousness of man as the supreme divinity. There must be no god on a level with it ...
>
> (Prometheus says:)"I shall never exchange my fetters for slavish servility.'Tis better to be chained to the rock than bound to the service of Zeus."
>
> Prometheus is the noblest of saints and martyrs in the calendar of philosophy.[33]

The defiance of the closing sentence alarmed friend Bruno Bauer as "unnecessary temerity[34]" — an unconscious echo of the very counsels of timorous prudence to Prometheus by the Leader of the Chorus.

The dissertation itself had not mentioned Prometheus, although in his workbooks for it Marx had written:

> ...as Prometheus, who stole fire from Heaven, began to build
> houses and establish himself on the earth, so philosophy
> which has extended itself into the [real] world turns against
> the apparent world.[35]

Prometheus scarcely appears again in Marx's writings,* and the above passages were never published in Marx's lifetime. But the comparison was not lost upon those who knew him. When the government closed down the *Rheinische Zeitung*, a contemporary cartoon depicted Marx as Prometheus bound to a printing-press while the royal Prussian eagle gnaws at his vitals.[38] The last issue of the paper carried an unsigned farewell poem, ending on the Promethean note.

> Our mast blew down, but we were not affrighted,
> The angry gods could never make us bend.
> Columbus too at first was scorned and slighted,
> And yet he saw the New World in the end.
> Ye friends, who cheer us till the timbers rattle
> Ye foes, who did us honour with your strife —
> We'll meet again on other fields of battle:
> If all is dead, yet courage still is life.[39]

More amusing but not less indicative is the evidence of the impression which Marx's character made on his young associates. There is a long satiric "epic," protesting against the dismissal of Bruno Bauer, which Engels wrote *before* he knew Marx personally, containing versified portraits of the prominent Young Hegelians. The passage devoted to Marx goes approximately as follows, in limping hexameters:

> Then who, with fiercesome rage, comes rushing thereupon?
> A swarthy chap from Trier, a real phenomenon.

---

* The only significant reference comes soon, in Marx's 1844 manuscripts.[36] In his *Poverty of Philosophy*, Marx has to handle Proudhon's use of Prometheus as a sort of economic Robinson Crusoe, but he does not make any Promethean analogies himself.[37] Later come only passing references of no present interest. One might wonder if Marx knew Shelley's *Prometheus Unbound* (1819), but there is no sign of it; in fact, Marx never mentioned Shelley in writing; it is Engels who was a Shelley fan from youth to old age.

He neither walks nor skips but springs up in the air,
And storms about with red-hot fury as though to tear
Down to the earth the far-hung tent of the broad sky —
His arms he stretches up to seize the winds on high.
With angry fist up-clenched, he rages without rest
As if ten thousand flaming demons him possessed.[40]

The portraits in this "epic" are frankly friendly caricatures — the young Engels was a talented cartoonist — but there is no doubt of what kind of character is being caricatured.

10. Choice and Character

And so it was history and the state of society which, in 1841, presented Marx with the choice: submit to Power, or break with Power. But it was Marx's character which made the choice a foregone conclusion.

Such a character will naturally always excite a variety of reactions. After all, many in the audience are in the position of Hephaestus, who, weeping salt tears very liberally, is the one who actually fetters the hero in chains, protesting it is against his will. "The dirty job must be done," he whines to Power, "but don't push me too hard."

More are in the position of Oceanus, who delivers himself of sage advice: "I would admonish thee to prudence ... see what are the wages of too bold a tongue. Thou hast not learned humility, nor to yield to evils .. ." He will try to negotiate peace with Zeus, but meanwhile: "Do thou keep thy peace, and restrain thy blustering speech." Others are in the position of the Leader of the Chorus, who has his own diagnosis of the hero's sins: "Care not for mortals overmuch, whilst you neglect your own profit.[41]" (In other words: get a well-paying job instead of wasting your time in the British Museum.)

Then also in the audience are the descendants of Hermes, the "lackey of Zeus," who thinks anyone who does not cringe before power is simply stark mad — the very best frame of mind for a lackey

11. Marx: The Education of the Educator

But the Promethean rejection of injustice-by-power could be only half of Marx's road to the principle of Self-Emancipation; for as we have mentioned, there have been not a few who don the mask of Prometheus in order to replace Zeus as ruler. Aeschylus himself raised the question, long before Lord Acton: *"Who could endure you in prosperity?"* It is Zeus' lackey Hermes who directs this sneer to Prometheus.

Even after the collapse of the Savior-Ruler by 1841, Marx *must* have gone through the next stage, like everyone else: hope in some kind of intellectual elite, who, their hearts bursting with sympathy for the suffering people, would sacrifice themselves in order to lead the flock into a new and better sheepfold. The amazing thing about Marx is that there is only a single, and very ambiguous, scrap of evidence of such a state of mind even transiently, dating to the beginning of 1844. This occurs at the end of the article in which Marx first arrives at the idea that it is the emancipation of the proletariat that means the emancipation of all mankind. Then there is this sentence: "The *head* of this emancipation is *philosophy*, its *heart* is the *proletariat.*[42]"

Taken by itself, this sentence is compatible with the tradition of an intellectual elite which conceives itself to be the head of the movement, with the masses making up the troops. On the other hand, this interpretation is difficult to reconcile with the whole train of thought for pages before, which it merely summarizes. Marx had already explained: "As philosophy finds its *material* weapons in philosophy," and the emancipation in question must be based "on the *theory* proclaiming that man is the highest essence of man," etc. These and many other expressions indicate that, by "philosophy," Marx literally means *theory*, and not the philosoph*ers*, that is, the intellectuals.[43]

Yet it is certain that even Engels understood this sentence in more or less the traditional elitist sense (which Engels himself still held).* And certainly it would have been an extraordinary feat if Marx had managed to skip this stage entirely.

But what is not in doubt is that the general trend of Marx's thinking went the other way "from the very beginning." As early as his pre-socialist writings in 1842 for the *Rheinische Zeitung* — in fact in his first published article, on freedom of the press — we find the following retort to a legislator who argued in the Diet that man is naturally imperfect and immature and needs educational guidance:

---

* In March 1845 Engels referred, in the Owenite paper, to the prediction of Marx's "a year ago" of the union of "the German philosophers" and the German workers, a union now "all but accomplished." He adds: "With the philosophers to think, and the working men to fight for us, will any earthly power be strong enough to resist our progress?"[44]

358

For him true education consists in keeping man swaddled in
the cradle all his life, since as soon as man learns to walk he
also learns to fall, and only through falling does he learn to
walk. But if we all remain children in swaddling-clothes,
who is to swaddle us? If we all lie in the cradle, who is to
cradle us? If we are all in jail, who will be the jailer?[45]

This extension of *Quis custodiet ipsos custodes?* is already the fundamental
answer to all the arguments, old and current, for "educational dictator-ships."
It already implies that emancipation is not a form of graduation ceremony
(getting the diploma from teacher for passing the exam.) but rather it is a
process of struggle by people *who are not yet "ready" for emancipation,* and who
can become ready for emancipation *only by launching the struggle themselves,*
before anyone considers them ready for it.*

11. Theory and Theoretician

This is the principle which Marx set down in the spring of 1845 in the third
of his Theses on Feuerbach — one of the jottings in which he attempted to clarify
a new world-outlook for himself. The crux of the Third Theses is that it asks
the question: *Who will educate the educator?*

It goes directly to the elitist concept of the role of the educated "bringer of
socialism" to the uneducated masses. Naturally Marx does not question the
matter of *fact* that it is the educated who have raised the idea of socialism
before the masses. That is how it *begins*; but it cannot be merely a one-way
relationship. When Engels published his edited version of the Theses in 1888,
he usefully concretized this meaning by introducing an example, Robert Owen,
who was not in Marx's original note.

It was Owen's type of materialism which *onesidedly*
emphasized that men are the products of their
environmental circumstances and upbringing, and which

---

* In the same article, here is how Marx refutes the opponents of a free press who imply
that only the government--i.e. themselves—are inspired by God sufficiently to be
guardians of the press: "But *English history* has quite sufficiently proved that the
assertion of divine inspiration from above begets the counter-assertion of divine
inspiration from below, and Charles I mounted the scaffold as a result of divine
inspiration from below."[46]

concluded that to change men for the better, one had to
change the environmental circumstances and upbringing.

Marx's thesis cuts straight to the heart of the difficulty in this reasoning:
who are the men who are going to operate this change? These men apparently
stand exempt from the very law they enunciate; for they, who are also the
product of their environmental conditioning, are going to act to change the
world which conditioned them. Prometheus was able to change men from the
outside, because he was himself a god; but Owen's (and Marx's) problem is
harder than his.

Who are these "educators" to be, and how do they come into being?
Owen's implied answer is very simple: they are "people like me," who just
happen to get the idea, plus others whom I convince with its inexorable logic...

Against this, Marx's thesis points out (1) that "it is essential to educate the
educator himself," and (2) that until this "educator" is himself changed
("educated"), one cannot overcome the division of society between rulers and
ruled.

> The materialist doctrine concerning the changing of
> circumstances and upbringing [*that men are products of
> circumstances and upbringing and that therefore changed men are
> products of other circumstances and changed upbringing*] forgets
> that circumstances are changed by men [*themselves*], and that
> it is essential to educate the educator himself. Hence this
> doctrine must [*necessarily have the effect to*] divide society into
> two parts, one of which is superior to society. [*For example,
> in Robert Owen.*]

The coincidence of the changing of circumstances and of human activity or
self-changing can be conceived and rationally understood only as *revolutionary
practice.**

How then are the educators to be educated, and, for that matter how do the
uneducated become educators? How does this whole two-sided process of
"self-changing" take place? Marx's answer is: *by "revolutionary practice."* One

---

* If read without the bracketed italics, this is Marx's formulation of 1845. The bracketed
italics are some of the editorial explanations introduced by Engels in his 1888 edited
version.[47]

learns to revolutionize society even as one revolutionizes oneself; one learns to revolutionize oneself by trying to revolutionize society. For the working class, it is a process in which two sides interpenetrate; a mountain-climber, making his way up a "chimney" formation, can understand it better than a metaphysician.

This, the Third Thesis, is the "philosophic" formulation by Marx of the basis of the principle of Self-Emancipation. It represents the first time in socialist thought that theory turns around to take a hard look at the theoretician.

12.. The Rejection of Humanitarian-Philanthropic Elitism

The Third Thesis entails, or leads right into, rejection of the whole humanitarian-philanthropic attitude toward the masses of people, which was typical not only of Owen and the utopians, but also of all the other pre-Marxian socialists to one degree or another. There are many reasons why the masses need protection from their friends, "but the greatest of these is charity." In the long run, a people can be held in subjection most effectively not by brute force but by gutting them of the capacity to fight for themselves.

St. Peter explained it long ago: "for charity shall cover the multitude of sins." It was explained also in Deuteronomy: "For the poor shall never cease out of the land: *therefore* I command thee, saying, Thou shalt open thine hand wide unto thy brother, to thy poor, and thy needy, in thy land." *Therefore* has been italicized here since it explains the practical reason for this holy injunction.

Marx's burst of indignation at this sociological strategy of Christianity was directed, in 1847, at a pious Prussian who sermonized that "If only those whose calling it is to develop the social principles of Christianity do so, the Communists will soon be put to silence":

> The social principles of Christianity have now had eighteen hundred years to develop and need no further development by Prussian councillors.
>
> The social principles of Christianity justified the slavery of Antiquity, glorified the serfdom of the Middle Ages, and

equally know, when necessary, how to defend the oppression of the proletariat, although they make a pitiful face over it.

The social principles of Christianity preach the necessity of a ruling and an oppressed class, and all they have for the latter is the pious wish the former will be charitable.

The social principles of Christianity transfer the councillors' adjustment of all infamies to heaven and thus justify the further existence of those infamies on earth.

The social principles of Christianity declare all vile acts of the oppressors against the oppressed to be either the just punishment of original sin and other sins or trials that the Lord in his infinite wisdom imposes on those redeemed.

The social principles of Christianity preach cowardice, self-contempt, abasement, submission, dejection, in a word all the qualities of the *canaille*; and the proletariat, not wishing to be treated as *canaille*, needs its courage, its self-reliance, its pride and its sense of independence more than its bread.

The social principles of Christianity are sneakish and the proletariat is revolutionary.

So much for the social principles of Christianity.[48]

In this passage, the authentic Promethean spirit of self-reliant defiance is transferred from the bosom of a god filled with "love of mankind" *to the proletariat itself*. Prometheus plus Spartacus equals the starting-point of Marxism.*

---

* In the same article, Marx included a powerful echo of the revulsion against the Savior-Ruler, as he attacked the pious Prussian's appeal for "a monarchy relying on the support of the people" — unaware, of course, that this was going to be, two decades later, the subject of Lassalle's pourparlers with Bismarck:
"We shall make but a few well-meaning remarks to those gentlemen who wish to save the imperilled Prussian monarchy by a *Somersault* into the people.
"Of all political elements the people is the most dangerous for a king ... But the real

13. The class character of charity

From here on, Marx's war against humanitarian-philanthropic socialism is unremitting. Engels had anticipated it partly in his earlier *Condition of the Working Class in England*, in a passage attacking the charity system—"your self-complacent, Pharisaic philanthropy" which gives the victim a hundredth part of what has been plundered from his labor:

> Charity which degrades him who gives more than him who takes; charity which treads the downtrodden still deeper in the dust, which demands that the degraded, the pariah cast out of society, shall first surrender the last that remains to him, his very claim to manhood, shall first beg for mercy before your mercy deigns to press, in the shape of an alms, the brand of degradation upon his brow.[50]

This first book of Engels, is one of those germinal works of which it can be said, as Rupert Brooke did in another connection, that "thoughts go blowing through them, are wiser than their own." By 1847 Engels was more direct. An article of his on the literature of the then prominent petty-bourgeois "True-Socialist" tendency starts with a mortal thrust at one Karl Beck's "Songs of the Poor Man"—which begins with a poem addressed to the House of Rothschild:

> The poet does not threaten the destruction of the real power of Rothschild, and the social conditions on which it is based; no, he wishes only it should be used philanthropically. He laments that the bankers are not socialistic philanthropists, not sentimental visionaries, not benefactors of humanity, but just bankers. Beck sings the praises of this cowardly, petty-bourgeois *misere*, of the "poor man," the *pauvre honteux*, with

---

people, the proletariat, the small peasants and the populace, there you have, as Hobbes said, *puer robustus, sed malitiosus,* a sturdy but knavish boy, who will not let himself be made a fool of either by thin kings or fat ones.
"This people would first and foremost force His Majesty to grant a constitution with universal suffrage, freedom of association, freedom of the press and other unpleasant things.
"And having obtained all that, it would use it to show as quickly as possible how it understands the *power* ... of the monarchy."[49]

his poor, pious, and contradictory desires, the "little man" in all his forms—not of the proud, menacing and revolutionary proletarian.[51]

About the same time, in *The Poverty of Philosophy*, Marx included a pungent page devoted to—

> the *humanitarian school*, which ...*seeks*, by way of easing its conscience, to palliate even if slightly the real contrasts; it sincerely deplores the distress of the proletariat, the unbridled competition of the bourgeois among themselves; it counsels the workers to be sober, to work hard and to have few children; it advises the bourgeois to put a reasoned ardor into production...

> The *philanthropic* school is the humanitarian school carried to perfection. It denies the necessity of antagonism; it wants to turn all men into bourgeois ... The philanthropists, then, want to retain the categories which express bourgeois relations, without the antagonism which constitutes them and is inseparable from the. They think they are seriously fighting bourgeois practice, and they are more bourgeois than the others.[52]

The *Communist Manifesto* repeats this more concisely,* under the head of the "bourgeois socialism," by which is meant bourgeois social reform; for in the pre-1848 period "*social*-ism" was still a common label simply for reformatory concern with the "social question." Besides Proudhon, who is specifically mentioned.

> To this section belong economists, philanthropists, humanitarians, improvers of the condition of the working class, organizers of charity, members of the society for the prevention of cruelty to animals, temperance fanatics, hole-and-corner reformers of every imaginable kind.[54]

---

* But note that Engels' draft for the Manifesto ("Principles of Communism") does not suggest that there is any incompatibility; it is simply not taken up. Nor does it appear in the Schapper-Wolff draft (published under the title "The Communist Credo" and ascribed by some to Engels) which preceded Engels' "Principles of Communism."[53]

And a little further, it is pointed out that utopian socialism, despite its positive "critical content, tends to degenerate into this kind of socialism too.[55] "Only from the point of view of being the most suffering class does the proletariat exist for them." And "the proletariat, as yet in its infancy, offers to them the spectacle of a class without any historical initiative or any independent political movement.[56]" In contrast, the Manifesto's message is that "The proletarian movement is the self-conscious, independent movement of the immense majority, in the interests of the immense majority.[57]"

This is the "very beginning" to which Engels later referred, although the Self-Emancipation principle had not yet received the aphoristic form under which it became famous.

14. "To Walk by Himself"

Henceforward the principle weaves through the analyses of Marx and Engels as an integral part of their thought. Here are some examples that come to hand.

During the revolutionary period that followed the *Communist Manifesto*, Marx and Engels' articles in the *Neue Rheinische Zeitung* continually appealed to action from below by the populace. In this connection Engels wrote at one point: "In Germany there are no longer any 'subjects', ever since the people became so free as to emancipate themselves on the barricades.[58]" At the beginning of another article, praising the resistance of the Poles to Prussian conquest, he relates a touching anecdote about a practical philanthropist, picked up from a biography of the priest Joseph Bonavita Blank. The holy man was frequented by birds that hovered on and about him; and the people wondered mightily to see this new St. Francis. No wonder: he had cut off the lower half of their beaks, so they could get food only from his own charitable hands. Engels comments on his parable:

> The birds, says the biographer, *loved* him as *their benefactor*.

> And the shackled, mangled, branded Poles refuse to love their Prussian benefactors![59]

The experience of the revolution was one of the reasons why Marx was sensitized to the necessity of breaking the German people from the habit of obedience to authority from above:

> For the German working class the most necessary thing of
> all is that it should cease conducting its agitation by kind
> permission of the higher authorities. A race so schooled in
> bureaucracy must go through a complete course of "self-
> help."[60]

Around the same time he embodied the same idea in a letter which we have
already quoted in the preceding chapter: "Here [in Germany] where the
worker's life is regulated from childhood on by bureaucracy and he himself
believes in the authorities, he must be taught before all else to walk by
himself.[61]"

15. The Octroyal Principle

Of course, this applied not only to the Germans. It was ever present to
Marx's mind when he discussed the phenomenon of the state-sponsored
"revolution from above" in connection with Bonapartism. In pre-Bismarck
Prussia, there were the Stein-Hardenberg reforms-from-above, designed to
rally support against Napoleon; in Russia there was the tsar's emancipation of
the serfs. Marx commented (in English):

> In both countries the social daring reform was fettered and
> limited in character because it was octroyed from the throne
> and not (instead of being) conquered by the people.[62]

"Octroyed" is a rare word in English, but deserves to be more widely used.
Its connotation—more than merely "grant" or "concede"—is precisely the
handing-down of changes from above, as against their conquest from below.
(In fact, "octroyal socialism" is a fine coinage for the opposite of the Marxist
principle of Self-Emancipation.)

In his book on the 1848 revolution in France, Marx recurs to a characteristic
metaphor of the theater (as in "theater of war"): in this case, not the contrast
between "above" and "below," but rather between the active participants on
the stage of history and the passive onlookers of the pit or the wings. On the
first stage of the revolution:

Instead of only a few factions of the bourgeoisie, all classes of French Society were suddenly hurled into the orbit of political power, forced to leave the boxes, the stalls and the gallery and to act in person upon the revolutionary stage![63]

On the peasantry who were momentarily set into motion — to give Bonaparte his election victory of 10 December 1848:

For a moment active heroes of the revolutionary drama, they could no longer be forced back into the inactive and spineless role of the chorus.[64]

This metaphor illuminates Marx's concept of the revolution from below as Self-Emancipation. Less figuratively, in another passage, Marx mentions indicia of the proletariat's immaturity:

As soon as it was risen up, a class in which the revolutionary interests of society are concentrated finds the content and the material for its revolutionary activity directly in its own situation: foes to be laid low, measures dictated by the needs of the struggle to be taken; the consequences of its own deeds drive it on ... The French working class had not attained this level; it was still incapable of accomplishing its own revolution.[65]

The proletariat was as yet incapable of carrying through a rising from below, under the self-impulsion of its own class drives.

After Bonaparte had consolidated his power, Engels remarked that he hoped the old scoundrel was *not* assassinated. For in that case the Bonapartist clique would merely make a deal with the Orleanist monarchy and go right on:

Before the workers' districts could think about it, Morny would have made his palace-revolution, and although a revolution from below would be thereby postponed only briefly, yet its basis would be a different one.[66]

16. In the First International

If the principle of Self-Emancipation had to be spelled out more formally in 1864, it was because of the problem Marx faced in drawing up the programme of the new International so as to gain the agreement of a wide variety of political views. What programmatic statement could delimit the organization as a *class movement* of the proletariat, yet avoid lining up with any of the various ideological tendencies within that class (or outside it)? The very concept of a *class programme which was not a sect programme* — not the programme of a Marxist sect either — was itself a basic Marxist concept; but for this the movement was ready. The Preamble to the *Rules* was Marx's solution, beginning with the clause on Self-Emancipation which we have already quoted.

The principle was so deceptively simple that naturally academic historians of socialism never got the point till years afterwards. Thus the eminent Belgian historian Emile de Laveleye (one of those who, Engels rightly remarked, spread nothing but "lies and legends" about the history of the International[67]) wrote in *Le Socialisme Contemporain* in 1881:

> The International also affirmed that "the emancipation of the laborers must be the work of the laborers themselves." This idea seemed an application of the principle of "self-help"; it enlisted for the new association, even in France, the sympathies of many distinguished men who little suspected how it was to be interpreted later on. This affords a new proof of the fact frequently observed, that revolutionary movements always go on increasing in violence. The originators of the movement ... are replaced by the more fanatical, who, in their turn, are pushed aside, until the final abyss is reached to which wild revolutionary logic inevitably leads.[68]

In contrast to this liberal ignoramus, the viciously reactionary historian of the International, Edmond Villetard, understood very quickly that the militants of the International were so wildly fanatical as to believe exactly what the principle of Self-Emancipation said. "No idea, without excepting perhaps their hatred of capital," he charges, "entered more passionately into their heads and hearts." He quotes one of the French militants who were arrested as Internationalists by the Bonaparte government:

> We have proclaimed sufficiently ... that we no longer wanted deliverers, that we no longer wished to serve as instruments, and that we had the pretention to have knowledge of the situation, to understand our interests as well as any one.[69]"

Once launched, the principle kept recurring in the documents of the International, whether written by Marx or others. In an official manifesto addressed to the National Labor Union of the U.S., Marx went back to the "stage" metaphor:

> On you, then, devolves the glorious task to prove to the world that now at last the working classes are bestriding the scene of history no longer as servile retainers, but as independent actors, conscious of their own responsibility ...[70]

In a manifesto denouncing the shooting of strikers in Belgium, Marx granted that the Belgian capitalist was so liberty-loving—

> that he has always indignantly repulsed any factory law encroaching upon that liberty. He shudders at the very idea that a common workman should be wicked enough to claim any higher destiny than that of enriching his master and natural superior. He wants his workman not only to remain a miserable drudge, overworked and underpaid, but, like every other slaveholder, he wants him to be a cringing, servile broken-hearted, morally prostrate, religiously humble drudge. Hence his frantic fury at strikes. With him, a strike is a blasphemy, a slave's revolt, the signal of a social cataclysm.[71]

At a General Council discussion on the Irish question, in the course of a long speech attacking English policy, Marx put it sententiously: "The old English leaven of the conqueror comes out in the [government] statement: we will grant but you must ask.[72]" In other words, the octroyal attitude of the master.

17. Do-It-Yourself Movement

Not drafted by Marx but by other members of the Council was an address calling for an independent labor press:

> Benjamin Franklin is reported to have said, "If you want a thing done, and well done, do it yourself," and this is precisely what we must do ... we must take the work of salvation into our own hands ... In order to guard against deceitful friends, we require a press of our own.[73]

The historian Royden Harrison remarks that "the influence of the International and of Marx himself upon the Land and Labor League is nowhere more clearly in evidence" than it its address, modeled after Marx's, which appealed:

> There is one, and only one, remedy. Help yourselves. Determine that you will not endure this abominable state of things any longer; act up to your determination, and it will vanish. ... We are many; our opponents are few. Then working men and women of all creeds and occupations claim your rights ... to conquer your own emancipation![74]

That combines Marx with Shelley.

Aside from manifestoes, the General Council of the international was made unaccustomedly sensitive to the question of *who* acted in their name. A small but symbolic point was worked out in the General Council meeting after it had adopted its well-known address to Abraham Lincoln, which was to be presented to the U.S. embassy. The minutes record:

> A long discussion then took place as to the mode of presenting the address and the propriety of having a M.P. with the deputation; this was strongly opposed by many members who said working men should rely on themselves

and not seek for extraneous aid.[75]

The motion that was passed limited the delegation to Council members. Marx related to Engels:

> ...*part* of the Englishmen on the Committee wanted to have the deputation introduced by a member of Parliament since it was customary. This hankering was defeated by the majority of the English and the unanimity of the Continentals, and it was declared, on the contrary, that such old English customs ought to be abolished.[76]

There were other symbolic tests. In 1865 the General Council announced it had refused the proposal of a rich English lord who had offered an annual subsidy to be the organization's "protector."[77] The question of "Tory gold" was going to be an issue of Self-Emancipation all through the century.

18. Anticipations of Future Problems

The outbreak of war in 1870 and the Paris Commune in 1871 brought the question of Self-Emancipation out of the manifestoes and into reality. Later this is reflected in Marx's analysis of the nature of the Commune state. Here we mention some smaller but anticipatory reflections.

In the "Second Address" of the International on the war, Marx already points to that fact about the newly formed Republic of liberal politicians which excites his "misgivings." It is the fact that it has been engineered from above; that Bonapartism was not *subverted* (which means overturned from below) but only replaced:

> The Republic has not subverted the throne, but only taken its place become vacant. It has been proclaimed, not as a social conquest, but as a national measure of defense.[78]

The great thing for Marx about the Commune was that it was just the opposite: the working class of Paris took over.

It is a strange fact. In spite of all the tall talk and all the immense literature, for the last sixty years, about Emancipation of Labor, no sooner do the working men anywhere take the subject into their own hands with a will, than uprises at once all the apologetic phraseology of the mouthpieces of present society ...[79]

(In fact, that very Republic of the bourgeoisie about which Marx expressed instant suspicion was the instrument for smashing the Republic of workers who took things into their own hands.)

We hear more from Marx about this in his writings on the Commune State. Here let us turn to some less familiar language, written by Marx in his first draft for *The Civil War in France*. It is a passage in which he asks: What is it that is new about this revolution? True, the workers have borne the brunt; but that has been true in all French revolutions. Then there is a second feature which is not new:

That the revolution is made in *the name* and confessedly *for* the popular masses, that is, the producing masses, is a feature this Revolution has in common with all its predecessors. The new feature is that the people, after the first rise [rising], have not disarmed themselves and surrendered their power into the hands of the Republican mountebanks of the ruling classes, that, by the constitution of the *Commune*, they have taken the actual management of their Revolution into their own hands and found at the time, in the case of success, the means to hold it in the hands of the People itself, displacing the State machinery, the governmental machinery of the ruling classes by a governmental machinery of their own. This is their ineffable crime! Workmen infringing upon the governmental privilege of the upper 10,000 and proclaiming their will to break the economical basis of that class despotism which for its own sake wielded the organized State-force of society! This is it that has thrown the respectable classes in Europe as in the United States into the paroxysms of convulsions ...[80]

There follows the statement, which was effectively expanded in the final version: "But the actual 'social' character of their Republic consists only in this, that workmen govern the Paris Commune![81]Some patronizing friends of the working class," writes Marx,* ask sympathy for the Commune because it did not undertake any (utopian) "socialist enterprises." He replies:

> These benevolent patronizers, profoundly ignorant of the real aspirations and the real movement of the working classes, forget one thing. All the socialist founders of Sects belong to a period in which the working class themselves were neither sufficiently trained and organized by the march of capitalist society itself to enter as historical agents upon the world's stage ...[83]

But (he goes on) it is no defect of the Commune that it refused to set up a Fourierist *phalanstere* or a little Icaria *a la* Cabet. What it did set up was the condition of its own emancipation, "no longer clouded in utopian fables" — for

> the government of the working class can only save France and do the national business, by working for its *own emancipation*, the conditions of that emancipation being at the same time the conditions of the regeneration of France.[84]

For Marx and Engels, there was a direct relationship between the revolutionary (literally subversive) nature of their socialism and the principle of emancipation-from-below, the principle that, as Engels wrote, "there is no concern for ... gracious patronage from above.[85]" By the same token, only a movement looking to class struggle from below could be a genuinely *proletarian* movement. For it was the proletariat that was "below —" "the lowest stratum of our present society," which "cannot stir, cannot raise itself up, without the whole superincumbent strata of official society being sprung up into the air.[86]"Marxism, as the theory and practice of the proletarian revolution, therefore also had to be the theory and practice of the self-emancipation of the proletariat. Its essential originality flows from this source.

Socialist Register

---

* Marx is here doubtlessly referring to the followers of Comte; for the English Comtists, while anti-socialist, did defend the Commune against the press slander campaign; especially Prof. Edward Beesly (who had chaired the meeting that founded the First International). In a caustic paragraph just before this, Marx had distinguished the English Comtists from the French "co-religionists," and attacked Comtism as follows: "Comte is known to the Parisian workmen as the prophet in politics of Imperialism [Bonapartism] (of personal *Dictatorship*), of capitalist rule in political economy, of hierarchy in all spheres of human action, even in the sphere of science, and as the author of a new catechism with a new pope and new saints in place of the old ones."[82] This attack did not appear in the final version, either because of respect for the courage of the *English* Comtists in defending the Commune, or because of space, or both.

Reference Notes

Introduction

1. Hal Draper, *Berkeley: The New Student Revolt*, Grove Press, New York 1965.

Chapter II

2. Written in early January 1858; published in the *NAC*, Vol. 3, pages 440-446; English original reprinted only in the Marx-Engels *Revolution in Spain* (Marxist Library, Vol. 12, New York, International Publishers, 1939; *MECW* 18:219.)

3. More about Marx's views of this period on Latin American independence from European control and intervention will be found in his 1861-62 dispatches to the *New York Tribune* and the Vienna *Presse* against intervention in Mexico. Most of these are in the Marx-Engels collection *The Civil War in the United States* (N.Y., International Pub., 1937); see also pp. 64, 201 on Haiti, Cuba and Central America. Another article, "The Mexican Imbroglio," was Marx's last in the *Tribune*, 10 March 1862. See also *MECW* 19.

4. The Spanish edition of his *Bolívar* was published in two volumes (Mexico City, 1951). The English edition (London, New York, 1952) is in one volume, less fully documented.

5. A bibliography of the anti-Madariaga literature would itself be a major enterprise, no doubt. Leaving aside periodicals and reviews, I have been able to find the following more or less serious attempts to refute Madariaga between book covers:

(i) Eleazar Lopez Contreras, *Temas de Historia Bolívariana* (Madrid, 1954); chapter "El Bolívar de Madariaga ." Misrepresents content of Madariaga's book; purely hagiographic tone; no discussion of Bolívar's authoritarianism.

(ii) Fernando Diez de Medina, *Sariri* (La Paz, 1954); chapter "Los Dos Bolívares: Refutacion a Madariaga ." A dithyramb on the Hero; no discussion of our issue.

(iii) Joaquin Gabaldon Marquez, *El Bolívar de Madariaga y Otros Bolívares* (Caracas, 1960). Mainly a literary effort in cussing out Madariaga; no discussion of our issue.

(iv) M.A. Osorio Jiménez, *Bibliografia Critica de la Detracción Bolívariana* (Caracas, 1959). The section on Madariaga's book is devoted to quoting A.F. Brice.

The next four are discussed in section 5 of this article.

(v) Vicente Lecuna, *Catàlogo de Errores y Calumnias en la Historia de Bolívar* (New York, 1956), Tomo I, last chapter "El Odio de Madariaga a Bolívar ."

(vi) Enrique de Gandia, *Bolívar y la Libertad* (Buenos Aires, 1957).

(vii) Angel Francisco Brice, *El "Bolívar" de Marx Ampliado por Madariaga* (Caracas, 1952); reprinted as first part of his *Bolívar, Libertador y Estadista* (Caracas, 1953).

(viii) Brice, *Bolívar Visto por Carlos Marx* (Caracas, 1961).

I have not been able to obtain the booklet by Vicente Donoso, *Por Qué Madariaga Difama al Libertador?* (La Paz, 1952) but the title does not promise much. The most considerable recent South American biography of Bolívar, in the opinion of some, is *El Libertador* by Augusto Mijares (Caracas, 1964); it has a few references to Madariaga on specific points, but not on our issue. While Mijares is not entirely uncritical, his foreword, entitled "Justicia," provides a handy statement of the moderate hagiographer's viewpoint: "To require that an author be objective in relating a passionate life is nonsense.... Nor am I attracted by the classical representation of Justice as a blindfolded statue holding a balance. I prefer the fighting justice of the saints and heroes ." He ends: "I declare that this work of inquiry in no way diminished my respect for the Liberator, and that I finished his biography with the same devotion with which I began it ."

Another enlightening passage is from R. C. Pardo's foreword to Brice's pamphlet (No. viii above). Explaining Brice's unique qualification, he writes: "He corrects errors and clarifies concepts, without offending anyone, and succeeds in bringing off the Liberator without blemish from this difficulty. It can be said that Brice, like a good Bolívarian, has profound faith in the Liberator and thereby fathoms the obscurest points with a minimum of fear." The point could hardly be made more clearly.

6. University of New Mexico Press, 1948. In spite of its extensive reputation, it was not translated into Spanish until 1960, and then published in Mexico (the site also of Madariaga's Spanish edition). Masur certainly cannot be charged with any sympathy for Madariaga's book; he violently attacked it in the *Hispanic American Historical Review*.

7. For these, see fn. 4.

8. Cf Madariaga, op. cit., pp. 338, 522-23, 529, 602.

Chapter III

9. Berkeley, University of California Press, 1962. (Univ. of Calif. Publications in History, vol. 72.) All quotations not otherwise ascribed are from Gregory.

10. For this aspect of the Webbs and Fabianism, barely touched on by Gregory, see Bernard Semmel's *Imperialism and Social Reform* (Cambridge, 1960), chap. 6, esp. pp. 133, 140.

Chapter IV

11. The role of the corporation in dissolving the property relations of capitalism was already explained in some detail by Marx in *Capital*, III, 516-22 (Kerr, ed.); cf. 450-59; see also Marx-Engels, *Selected Correspondence* (N.Y. ed.), p. 105, and the passage which stands at the head of this article.

12. . For an acadamese version of the comparison, see Richard Eells, *The Meaning of Modern Business* (N.Y., 1960), which invents the term "metrocorporate feudalism ."

13. See W.H. Ferry, *The Economy Under Law* (1960), published by the Center; also his *The Corporation and the Economy* (1959). The Center also published Scott Buchanan, *The War Corporation and the Republic* (1958) and Berle, *Economic Power and the Free Society* (1957).

Chapter V

14. For an explanation of why the new reformists have become so tender about private enterprise, see the end of the previous chapter, where C.A.R. Crosland is briefly touched on.

15. For a rollcall on the new programs of other social-democracies in Western Europe, see Crosland's article in *Encounter*, March, 1960.

16. *Socialist Call*, Nov.-Dec., 1958, article by Leila Seigel.

17. *The Conservative Enemy* (London, 1962), p. 67. Hereafter abbreviated CE.

18. *The Future of Socialism* (London, 1956), p. 94. Hereafter abbreviated FS.

19. FS, p. 250.

20. FS, p. 219.

21. FS, p. 521.

22. Edited by R.H.S. Crossman (London, 1952). Hereafter abbreviated NFE.

23. NFE, pp. 33, 36, 41, 55.

24. Douglas Jay's bid for recognition as a revisionist theoretician, *Socialism and the New Society* (London, 1962), also, in passing, defines capitalism as laissez-faire at one point, p. 58. (Hereafter abbreviated SNS.)

25. CE, p. 114.

26. CE, p. 55.

27. NFE, p. 43.

28. NFE, p. 57-60.

29. NFE, pp. 65-66

30. FS, p. 521.

31. References are to CE, pp. 29-33.

32. CE, p. 47-48.

33. SNS, p. 102.

Chapter III

29. There is no published material on this, but a sound treatment can be found in the unpublished Ph.. D. dissertation by George P. Rawick, *The New Deal and Youth* (University of Wisconsin, 1957). This is without doubt the only attempt at an outline history of the movement that is worth reading; it has the added advantage of including also the closely related story of the American Youth Congress as well as of the New Deal youth agencies. Also still worth reading is the 1935 book by the National Student League leader James Wechsler, *Revolt on the Campus* (New York: Cocivi-Friede, 1935) even though it deals with only the first period of the movement and of course is written entirely from the then NSL viewpoint. For this first period, it is especially good for great detail on the issues and battles of the student movement, about which I have put very little into this essay. I have leaned heavily on both Rawick and Wechsler's accounts for the factual framework.

30. Rawick, *The New Deal and Youth.*

31. *NSL Organizer*, December, 1935.

32. Bruce Bliven, *New Republic*, January 11, 1939.

33. *Young Communist League Bulletin,* University of Wisconsin, 1939.

34. Robert W. Iversen, *The Communists and the Schools* (New York: Harcourt, Brace and World, Inc., 1959).

35. Ibid.

36. Ibid.

37. Murray Kempton, *Part of Our Time,* (New York: Simon and Schuster, Inc., 1955.)

38. Ibid.

Chapter IX

39. Max Nomad (born 1881), a native of Austria, was prior to his arrival in the United States (1913), active in the anarcho-syndicalist and related movements in various European countries. He was for many years a disciple and popularizer of the Polish theorist Jan Waclaw Machajsky. For a fuller treatment of Machajsky and Nomad's debt to him see E. Haberkern "Jan Waclaw Machajsky," *Telos,* No. 71.

40. For a discussion of the political activity of Marx and Engels in 1848 see Hal Draper, *Karl Marx's Theory of Revolution, Vol. 2,* (Monthly Review Press, New York and London, 1978.) A considerable number of Marx and Engels' writings in the *Neue Rheinische Zeitung* in English translation can be found in Saul Padover, *On Revolution* in the *Karl Marx Library* series, New York :McGraw-Hill, c1971.

41. The original version of this article referred to an article by Hal Draper in *Etudes de Marxologie* (Paris), no. 6, Sept. 1962 (in English). A condensation, one-third the original size, appeared in *New Politics,* Summer 1962. This article has been superceded in Hal Draper, *Karl Marx's Theory of Revolution, Vol. 3,* (Monthly Review Press, New York.

42. A three-part article in *Labor Action* for Feb. 9, 16, 23, 1953, largely based on the then recently published Marx-Engels collection *The Russian Menace to Europe* (Free Press, 1952). Volume 5 of *Karl Marx's Theory of Revolution* contains an extensive treatment of this question.

43. By chance, while writing this, I came across the entirely innocent use of "nigger" well into the 20th century by Bernard Shaw--who, by the way, was *pro*-Negro and unusually devoid of race prejudice (cf. his *Adventures of the Black Girl etc.* and *Back to Methuselah*).

44. The fullest version is presented and translated into English by Henry Mayer in *Etudes de Marxologie,* no. 2.

45. The most detailed account of the *Jungen* is in two chapters of V.L. Lidtke's *The Politics of German and Social Democracy, 1878-1890* (unpub. thesis, U. of Calif. Berkeley, 1962), p. 419-39. There are a few pages in Carl Landauer's *European Socialism,* I:295ff. These two sources supersede the inadequate accounts in G. Mayer's biography of Engels and in Mehring's *Gesch. der deut. Socialdem.*

Chapter XV

46. Leonard W. Levy, *Jefferson and Civil Liberties: The Darker Side.;* Belknap Press of Harvard University Press, Cambridge, Mass.,1963.

Chapter XVI

47. For Utechin's book, see the beginning of the Special Note appended below.

48. Lenin: *Collected Works* (Moscow: FLPH, Progress Pub., 1960-70), 5:375. (This work is hereafter abbreviated: *CW*.)

49. *CW* 5:383f.

50. *CW* 5:386.

51. I have dealt with this subject at large in *Karl Marx's Theory of Revolution* (New York: Monthly Rev. Press, 1978), Vol. 2, Chaps. 17-18.

52. *CW* 6:235+

53. *CW* 6:490.

54. *CW* 6:490f

55. *CW* 6:491

56. *CW* 6:500.

57. *CW* 6:502.

58. *CW* 7:474

59. *CW* 7:474-76.

60. *CW* 8:196

61. *CW* 9:291.

62. *CW* 9:442.

63. *CW* 10:29.

64. *CW* 10:30.

65. *CW* 10:32.

66. *CW* 10:33.

67. *CW* 10:34.

68. *CW* 10:35.

69. *CW* 10:37f.

70. *CW* 10:31.

71. *CW* 10:32.

72. *CW* 10:36.

73. *CW* 10:36 fn.

74. *CW* 10:38f.

75. *CW* 13:101.

76. *CW* 13:102.

77. *CW* 13:102.

78. *CW* 6:522.

79. *CW* 7:132.

80. *CW* 8:245.

81. *CW* 13:103.

82. *CW* 13:103.

83. *CW* 13:104.

84. *CW* 13:104f.

85. *CW* 13:106.

86. *CW* 13:106.

87. *CW* 13:107f.

88. Shachtman, "Lenin and Rosa Luxemburg," in *The New International* (N.Y.), May 1938, p. 143.

89. John Plamenatz, *German Marxism and Russian Communism* (London: Longmans, Green, 1954), 225f.

90. *CW* 5:510f.

Chapter XVIII

91. M: First Draft of *The Civil War in France*, in *Arkhiv Marksa i Engel'sa*, v. 3 (8), 1934, p. 270. See also *MECW* 22:437. [English translations are cited, wherever possible, from the two-volume Marx-Engels *Selected Works* (Moscow, FLPH, 1955), abbreviated *ME:SW*. Untranslated German texts are cited, wherever possible, from the Marx-Engels *Werke* (Berlin, Dietz, 1961-68), abbreviated *ME:W*. In other cases, full bibliographic data are given on first appearance of a title, and abbreviated afterwards. Volume and page number are abbreviated as follows: e.g. 2: 107 = Vol. 2, page 107. In all abbreviations, M = Marx, E = Engels, and ME = Marx & Engels.] This note on sources was appended to this reference in the original article. (EH)

92. From the *Aeneid*, VII, 312.

93. George Brandes: *Ferdinand Lassalle* (N.Y., Macmillan, 1911, 108.) The Virgilian line is also used as the title-page motto for the whole book

94. Letter, Engels to Paul Lafargue. 16 Feb. 1886; in *Engels-Lafargue: Correspondence* (Moscow, FLPH, 1959, I: 338-39.)

95. *M: Provisional Rules of the Association,* in *The General Council of the First International; Minutes, 1864-66* [v. 1], 288. This remained the same in the later revisions; the 1871 version is in *ME:SW* 1: 386. See also *MECW* 20:14.

96. E: Pref. to 1888 English ed. of *Communist Manifesto,* in *ME:SW* 1:28, *M: Critique of the Gotha Program,* in *ME:SW* 2:25. *MECW* 26:512 and *MECW* 24:75.

97. Letter, Marx to Engels, 27 Feb. 1861, in *MEW* 30.160; *MECW* 41:264; on Spartacus, see also Marx's well-known "Confession" (question game) in which Spartacus and Kepler are listed as his "favorite heroes"; in D. Riazanov, ed. *Karl Marx, Man, Thinker and Revolutionist* (N.Y., International Pub., 1927), 269, 277-78; or *ME:W* 31: 597; or *MECW* 42:568.

98. E: Progress of Social Reform on the Continent." *New Moral World.* 4 and 18 Nov. 1843; in *ME: Gesamtausgabe (MEGA)* I, 2:442; *MECW* 3:399.

99. Ibid., 436; 393.

100. Ibid., 435; 393.

101. Ibid., 449; 407.

102. E: "The 'Times' on German Communism," *New Moral World,* 20 Jan. 1844, in *ME: Gesamtausgabe* 1, 2: 452; *MECW* 3:410.

103. This change can be followed through several steps in the English-language articles reprinted in *ME: Gesamtausgabe* I, vol. 4; *MECW* 4.

104. E: "The late Butchery at Leipzig – The German Working Men's Movement," *Northern Star,* 13 Sept. 1845, in *ME: Gesamtausgabe* I, 4:477; *MECW* 4:645.

105. Boris Nicolayevsky & O. Mänchen-Helfen: *Karl Marx; Man and Fighter* (Phila., Lippincott, 1936), 43.

106. Franz Mehring: *The Lessing Legend* (N.Y., Critics Group, 1938), 29.

107. Franz Mehring: *Karl Marx* (N.Y., Covici Friede, 1935), 50.

108. Mehring: *Karl Marx,* 51; Nicolayevsky, 44.

109. Nicolayevsky, 45-46.

110. Cf. Helmut Hirsch, "Karl Friedrich Koppen, der intimste Berliner Freund Marxens," *International Review for Social History* (Amsterdam), v. 1

111. Karl Friedrich Koppen: *Friedrich der Grosse und seine Widersacher* (Leipzig, 1840).

112. Nicolayevsky, 39.

113. Mehring, *Karl Marx*, 47.

114. Ibid., 49; Nicolayevsky, 39.

115. In *ME: On Religion* (Moscow, FLPH, 1957), 14; *MECW* 1:29.

116. E: *Germany: Revolution and Counter-Revolution* (N.Y., International Pub., 1933; Marxist Lib., v. 13), 22-23; *MECW* 11:17.

117. Letter, Engels to F. Gräber, 9 Dec. 1839/5 Feb. 1840; in *ME:W*; Erg. Bd. 2:443; *MECW* 2:487.

118. E: "Friedrich Wilhelm IV, König von Preussen," writ. ab. Oct. 1842; pub. 1843; in *ME:W* 1.446ff, esp. 453; *MECW* 2:360.

119. M: Second letter, dated May 1843, in the "Exchange of Letters," pub. in *Deutsch-Französischer Jahrbücher*, 1844; in *ME:W* 1:341-42; transl. largely based on M: *Writings of the Young Marx on Philosophy and Society*, ed. Easton & Guddat (Garden City, Doubleday, 1967, 209-10); *MECW* 3:140.

120. Ibid., *ME:W* 1:341; M: *Writgs. Yg. Mx.*, 208; *MECW* 3:139.

121. Ibid., *ME:W* 1:342; M: *Writgs. Yg. Mx.*, 210; *MECW* 3:140.

122. Ibid., *ME:W* 1:338-39; M: *Writgs. Yg. Mx.*, 206; *MECW* 137.

123. In *ME: On Relig.*, 15; *MECW* 1:30.

124. Mehring, *Karl Max*, 59.

125. In *ME:W* Erg. Bd. 1:215; *MECW* 1:491.

126. M: *Economic and Philosophic Manuscripts of 1844* (Moscow, FLPH, n.d.), 117.

127. M: *The Poverty of Philosophy* (Moscow, FLPH, n.d.), 98-102; *MECW* 6:157-159. There is an echo of this in M: *A Contribution to the Critique of Political Economy*, tr. N.I. Stone (Chicago, Kerr, 1904), Appendix, "Introduction," 268. (This "Introduction" is a section of the *Grundrisse der Kritik der Politischen Economie*.)

128. The cartoon may be seen in Mehring, *Karl Marx*, facing p. 296, with a detailed explanation of the verso. (Not in the later paperback ed.)

129. From the German text as given in Nicolayevsky, 60. Since the author seems to be thoroughly anonymous (cf. Auguste Cornu, *Karl Marx et Fr. Engels*, Paris, P.U.F., 1958, 2: 102), one might wonder whether this was not a last flare-up of Marx's temptation to write verse. Seven years later, when Marx's *Neue Rheinische Zeitung* was closed up in the same city in 1849, a farewell poem by Ferdinand Freiligrath was published in the final issue, naturally striking the same note.

130. The poem has a long tile, usually shortened to *Der Triumph der Glaubens*, writ. and pub. in 1842; here transl. from *ME:W* Erg. Bd. 2:301; *MECW* 2:336.

131. Most of the quotations are from the Paul Elmer More translation of *Prometheus Bound*. The first (Hephaestus) is a colloquialized adaption.

132. M: "Toward the Critique of Hegel's Philosophy of Law: Introduction," *Deutsch-Französischer Jahrbücher*, 1844; writ. end of 1843 to Jan. 1844; in *M: Writgs. Yg. Mx.*, 264; *MECW* 3:187.

133. Ibid., 260-64; 181-187.

134. M: "Communism in Germany," 2nd article, *New Moral World*, 8 March 1845; in *ME: Gesamtausgabe* I. 4:344; *MECW* 4:236.

135. M: "Debatte über Pressfreiheit [etc.]," *Rheinische Zeitung*, 5 May 1842; in *ME: W* 1:49; *MECW* 1:153.

136. Ibid.; *MECW* 1:156

137. For the two versions in English, see *ME: The German Ideology* (Moscow, Progress Pub., 1964), 646, 651-52; for the two in German, see *ME:W* 3: 5-6, 533-34; *MECW* 1:4 and 1:7. In the second paragraph of the thesis, Engels introduced two changes which we have omitted entirely, as unnecessary or misguided. He deleted the words "or self-changing," and altered "revolutionary practice" [*revolutionäre Praxis*] to "transformatory [or revolutionizing] practice" [*umwälzende Praxis*].

138. M: "The Communism of the Paper *Rheinischer Beobachter*," in *ME: On Relig.*, 82-83; transl. mod. after *ME:W* 4:200; *MECW* 6:231.

139. Ibid., 85; transl. mod. after *ME:W* 4:200; *MECW* 6:233.

140. In *ME: On Britain*, 2nd ed. (Moscow, FLPH, 1962), 315; *MECW* 4:564.

141. E: "Deutscher Sozialismus in Versen and Prosa," pub. Sept. 1847; in *ME:W* 4:207; *MECW* 6:235.

142. M: *Pov. Phil.*, 124-25; *MECW* 6:177.

143. *Der Bund der Kommunisten. Dokumente* (Berlin, Dietz, 1970) 1:470 ff.

144. In *ME:SW* 1:60; *MECW* 6:513.

145. Ibid., 63-64; 517.

146. Ibid., 62; 515.

147. Ibid., 44; 495.

148. E: "Berliner Vereinbarungsdebatten.": *Neue Rheinische Zeitung*, 7 June 1848 in *ME:W* 5:45; *MECW* 7:54.

149. E: "Die Polendebatte in Frankurt," *Neue Rhein. Zeit.*, 9 Aug. 1848; in *ME:W* 5:319; *MECW* 7:337-338.

150. Letter, Marx to Engels, 26 Sept. 1868; in *ME: Selected Correspondence* (N.Y., International Pub., 1935), 249; *MECW* 43:115.

151. Letter, Marx to J.B. Schweitzer, 13 Oct. 1868; in *ME: Selected Correspondence* (Moscow, FLPH, n.d.), 259; *MECW* 43:134.

152. M: First Draft of *Civ. War in Fr.*, 280; *MECW* 22:459.

153. M: *Class Struggles in France 1848-1850*, in *ME:SW* 1:146; *MECW* 10:54.

154. Ibid., 174; *MECW* 10:80.

155. Ibid., 148; *MECW* 10:56.

156. Letter, Engels to Marx, 17 March 1858; in *ME:W* 29:305; *MECW* 40:293.

157. Letter, Engels to W. J. Schmuilow, 7 Feb. 1893; in *ME:W* 39:24.

158. Quoted here from the English translation, *The Socialism of Today* (London, Leadenhall Pr., n.d.), 152. (Translation first pub. 1884.)

159. Edmond Villetard de Prunieres: *History of the International*, tr. by S.M. Day (New Haven, 1874), 65-66. The speaker quoted was Chalain. The original, *Histoire de l'Internationale*, was published in Paris, 1872.

160. "The International Working Men's Association to the National Labor Union of the United States," dated 12 May 1869; writ. by Marx; adopted by the Gen. Council; in *Gen. Council. F.I. 1868-70* [v. 3], 102, 321; *MECW* 21:54.

161. "The Belgian Massacres," dated 4 May 1869; manifesto writ. by Marx, approved by the Gen. Council; in ibid., 314-15; *MECW* 21:49.

162. At meeting of the General Council, 16 Nov. 1869; in ibid., 182.

163. "To the Working Men of Great Britain and Ireland," pub. Sept. 1865; in *Gen. Council, F.I. 1864-66* [v. 1.], 299.

164. R. Harrison: "The Land and Labour League," International Institute for Social History, *Bulletin*, v. 8, 1953, no. 3, 174, 195.

165. Minutes of 29 Nov. 1864, in *Gen. Council F.I. 1864-66* [v. 1], 54.

166. Letter, Marx to Engels, 2 Dec. 1864, in *ME: The Civil War in the United States* (N.Y., International Pub., 1937), 273; *MECW* 42:49.

167. Jules L. Puech: *Le Proudhonisme dans l'Association Internationale des Travailleurs* (Paris, Alcan, 1907), 103n.

168. M: "Second Address of the General Council ...," dated 9 Sept. 1870; in *ME:SW* 2:200; *MECW* 22:268.

169. *M: Civ. War in Fr.*, in *ME:SW* 2:223; *MECW* 22:235.

170. M: First Draft of *Civ. War in Fr.*, 346-48; *MECW* 22:498.

171. Ibid., 348. Cf. *Civ. War in Fr.*, in *ME:SW* 1:522; *MECW* 22:499.

172. Ibid., 346; *MECW* 22:498.

173. Ibid., 348; *MECW* 22:499.

174. Ibid., 352; *MECW* 22:500.

175. *E: Ludwig Feuerbach*, in *ME:SW* 3:376; *MECW* 26:397-398.

176. *ME: Communist Manifesto*, in *ME:SW* 1:44; *MECW* 6:495.

Bibliography

This bibliography includes all works referred to in the text, including the footnotes and references. It does *not* include references to journal articles. A note is in order on the collected and selected works of Marx, Engels and Lenin. The essays in this collection appeared over a period of some thirty years and the references and citations in the original are to the various selections and collections available in English, French and German at the time the article was originally published. The translations from passages available at the time only in foreign languages are by Hal Draper. These translations and references are left as they are in the original articles

However, since the early seventies an English translation of Lenin's collected works (referred to here by the abbreviation CW) has been available. And International Publishers has already completed the bulk of its English translation of the collected works of Marx and Engels (referred to here by the abbreviation MECW). For the reader's convenience we have, therefore, provided the relevant reference to these collections alongside the reference in the original article.

List of Collections and Their Abbreviations

Engels, Frederick and Marx, Karl. *Selected Works* (ME:SW in three volumes).
    Moscow. Progress Publishers, 1969.
Engels, Frederick and Marx, Karl. *Collected Works (MECW)*. London, Lawrence & Wishart, Ltd.;
    New York, International Publishers Co., Inc.;Moscow, Progress Publishers, 1986-.
Engels, Frederick and Marx, Karl. *Werke*. Berlin, Dietz Verlag, 1956-.
Lenin, V. I. *Collected Works (CW)*
    Moscow, Foreign Languages Publishing House (FLHP); Progress Publishers, 1963-1970.

Works by Marx

Address to the Communist League (ME:SW 1:175; MECW 10:277.)
The Civil War in France (ME:SW 3:178; MECW 22:307.)
Class Struggles in France 1848-1850 (ME:SW 1:146; MECW 10:45.)
The Communism of the Paper Rheinischer Beobachter (MEW 4:200; MECW 6:231.)
A Contribution to the Critique of Political Economy . tr. N. I. Stone, Chicago, Kerr, 1904; MECW 31.
Critique of the Gotha Program. ME:SW 3:9; MECW 24:75.
Debatte über Pressfreiheit. MEW 1:49; MECW 1:153.
Economic and Philosophical Manuscripts of 1844. Moscow, FLPH, n.d.
The Poverty of Philosophy. Moscow, FLPH, n.d.; MECW 6:105.
On Britain. 2nd ed. Moscow, FLPH, 1962.
Revolution in Spain. Marxist Library, vol. 12,
    NY, International Publishers, 1939; this material also appears in vol. 19 of *MECW.*

Der Triumph der Glaubens. MEW Erg. Bd. 2:301; *MECW* 2:336.
Towards the Critique of Hegel's Philosophy of Law . *MECW* 3:187.
Wage-Labor and Capital. ME:SW 1:142; *MECW* 9:197.

Works by Engels
Communism in Germany. MECW 4:236.
Condition of the Working Class in England. MECW 4:295.
Deutscher Sozialismus in Versen und Prosa. MEW 4:207; *MECW* 6:235.
Engels-Lafargue Correspondence. Moscow, FLPH, 1959.
Germany: Revolution and Counter Revolution. MECW 11:3.
Friedrich Wilhelm IV, König von Preussen. MEW 1.466; *MECW* 2:360.

Works by Marx & Engels
Communist Manifesto. ME:SW 1:98; *MECW* 6:477.
The German Ideology. MECW 5:19.
On Religion. Moscow, FLPH,1957.

Works by Lenin
Collected Works (Not finished). International Publishers, New York, 1929.
One Step Forward, Two Steps Back. CW 7:203.
Twelve Years. CW 13:94.
What Is To Be Done? CW 5:347.

Works by Others
Adler, Mortimer J. and Kelso, Louis O.
Capitalist Manifesto. New York, Random House,1958.
Bakunin, Mikhail, tr. C.H. Plummer, ed. F. Harrison.
Statism and Anarchy. New York, Revisionist Press, 1976.
Beale, Carleton.
Eagles of the Andes:South American Struggles for Independence. Philadelphia, Chilton Books, 1963Belaúnde, Víctor Andrés.
    Bolívar and the Political Thought. Baltimore, Johns Hopkins Press, 1938.
Bellamy, Edward.
    Looking Backward. New York, Harper, 1959.
Belloc, Hilaire.
    The Servile State.   London, Edinburgh, T.N. Foulis, 1912.
Berle, Adolph Augustus.
    Economic Power and the Free Society.   New York, Fund for the Republic, 1957.
    New Directions in the New World. New York, London, Harper & Brothers, 1940.
    Power Without Property: A New Development in American Political Economy.
        New York, Harcourt Brace, 1959.

388

Berle, August Adolphus.

The 20th Century Capitalist Revolution. New York, Harcourt Brace,1954.

Blease, W.L.

The Emancipation of English Women. London, Constable & Company, 1910.

Brandes, George.

Ferdinand Lassalle. N.Y., Macmillan, 1911.

Brice, Angel Francisco.

El *"Bolívar" de Marx Ampliado por Madariaga* Caracas, Impr. Nacional,1952.

Bolívar, Lbertador y Estadista.   Caracas, Talleres CIVA,1953.

Buber, Martin.

Paths in Utopia. New York, Macmillan, 1950.

Buchanan, Scott.

Essay in Politics. New York, Philosophical Library, 1953.

The Corporation and the Republic. New York, Fund for the Republic, 1958.

Burnham, James.

Managerial Revolution::Or What Is Happening in the World Now, London, Putnam, 1942.

L'ère des organisateurs, intro. Léon Blum.   Paris, Calmann-Lévy, 1947.

Chalmers, Douglas, A .

The Social Democratic Party of Germany:

From Working Class Movement to Modern Political Party.

New Haven, Yale University Press, 1964.

Contreras, Eleazar Lopez.

Temas de Historia Bolívariana.   Madrid, Editorial J.B., 1954.

Cornu, Auguste.

Karl Marx et Fr. Engels.   Paris, P.U.F., 1958.

Crosland, C. A. R.

Britain's Economic Problem. London, Cape, 1953.

Can Labor Win? London, Fabian Society, 1960.

The Conservative Enemy: A Program for Radical Reform for the 1960s. London, J. Cape, 1962.

The Future of Socialism. London, J. Cape, 1956.

Crossman, R.H.S.

New Fabian Essays. London, Turnstile Press, 1952.

Cunow, Heinrich.

*Partei-Zusammenbruch?*n.p.,n.d.

Dana, Charles Anderson and Ripley, George.

New American Cyclopedia (NAC). New York, D. Appleton and Company, 1858–1853.

Debs, Eugene Victor.

The Day of the People, in *Debs, His Life Writing and Speeches.* Chicago, C.H. Kerr & Co., 1910.

Deutscher, Isaac.

The Great Contest: Russia and the West. New York, Oxford University Press, 1960.

Diez de Medina, Fernando.

Sariri. LaPaz, A. Tejerina, 1954.

Djilas, Milovan.

La Nouvelle Classe Dirigeante. Paris, Plon, 1957.

Donoso, Vicente.

Por Qué Madariaga Difama al Libertador? La Paz, 1952.

Draper, Hal.

Berkeley: The New Student Revolt. New York, Grove Press, 1965.

Karl Marx's Theory of Revolution New York, Monthly Review Press, 1972-.

As We Saw the Thirties, ed. Rita James Simon.

Urbana, University of Illinois Press, 1967.

Drucker, Peter.

The New Society: The Anatomy of the Industrial Order.

New York, Harper & Row, 1962.

Easton and Gadded (ed.).

Writings of the Young Marx on Philosophy and Society.

Garden City, Doubleday, 1967.

Eels, Richard.

The Meaning of Modern Business: An Introduction to the Philosophy of Large Corporate Enterprise.

N.Y., Columbia University Press, 1960.

Förder, Herwig (editor).

Der Bund der Kommunisten: Dokumente und Materialen.

Berlin, Dietz, 1970-.

Ferry, W.H.

The Economy Under Law.

Santa Barbara, Center for the Study of Democratic Institutions, 1960.

The Corporation and the Economy.

Santa Barbara, Center for the Study of Democratic Institutions,1959.

Foster, William Z.

*Outline Political History of the Americas.*New York, International Publishers, 1951.

Gandia, Enriquede.

Bolívar y la Libertad. Buenos Aires, Editorial Oberón, 1957.

Gregory, Robert G.

Sidney Webb and East Africa Labor's Experiment with the Doctrine of Native Paramauntcy.

Berkeley, University of California Press, 1962.

Gronlund, Laurence.

The Cooperative Commonwealth. London, Sonnenschein & Co., 1896.

Institute of Marxism-Leninism of the Central Committee of the Communist Party of the Soviet Union.

The General Council of the First International,1864-1866 : the London Conference, 1865 ; Minutes.

Moscow, Progress Publishers 1974.

Harbrecht, Paul P.
> *Toward the Paraproprietal Society: An Essay on the Nature of Property in Twentieth Century America*
> New York, Twentieth Century Fund, 1960.

Iversen, Robert W.
> *The Communists and the Schools.* New York, Harcourt Brace, 1959.

Jay, Douglas.
> *Socialism in the New Society.* London, Longmans, 1962.

Jimenez, M.A. Osorio.
> *Bibliografía Crítica de la Detracción Bolívariana.* Caracas, Impr. Nacional, 1959.

Kautsky, Kautsky.
> *Sozialisten und Krieg:*
> *Ein Beitrag zur Ideengeschichte des Sozialismus von den Hussiten bis zum Völkerbund.*
> Prag, Orbis, 1937.

Kempton, Murray.
> *Part of Our Time: Some Ruins and Monuments of the Thirties.*
> New York, Simon & Schuster, 1955.

Kerr, Clark.
> *Industrialism and Industrial Man:*
> *The Problems of Labor and Management in Economic Growth.*
> Cambridge, Harvard University Press, 1960.
> *The Uses of the University.* Cambridge, Harvard University, 1963.

Keynes, J. M.
> *The End of Laissez Faire .* London, L & Virginia Woolf, 1926.

Koppen, K.F.
> *Friedrich de Grosse und seine Widersacher.* Leipzig, 1840.

Labor Party.
> *Industry and Society: Labor's Policy on Future Public Ownership.*
> London, Labor Party, 1957.

Landauer, Carl.
> *European Socialism:*
> *A History of Ideas and Movements from the Industrial Revolution to Hitler's Seizure of Power.*
> Berkeley, University of California Press, 1957.

Laveleye, Émile de.
> *The Socialism of Today.* London, Field and Tuer, 1886.

Lecuna, Vicente.
> *Catàlogo de Errores y Calumnias en la Historia de Bolívar.*
> New York, Colonial Press, 1956.

Levy, Prof. Leonard W.
> *Jefferson and Civil Liberties: The Darker Side.* Cambridge, Bellknap Press, 1963.

Lidtke, V.L.
> *The Politics of German Social Democracy. 1878-1890* (unpublished thesis).
> University of California (Berkeley, 1962.

Lindbergh, Anne Morrow.

The Wave of the Future. New York, Harcourt Brace and Company, 1940.

Luxemburg, Rosa.

The Mass Strike, the Political Party and the Trade Union.

Detroit, The Marxian Education Society, 193?.

Madariaga, Salvador de.

Bolívar. Mexico City,1951;London,New York,1952.

Man, Henri de.

Corporatisme et Socialisme. Bruxelles, Éditions «Labor», 1935.

Marquez, Joaquin Gabaldon.

El Bolívar de Madariaga y Otros Bolívares. Caracas, Ediciones Paraguachoa, 1960.

Mason, E. S.

The Corporation in Modern Society. Cambridge, Harvard University Press, 1959.

Mayo, Henry.

Introduction to Marxist Theory. New York, Oxford University Press, 1960.

Mehring, Franz.

The Lessing Legend. New York, Critics Group Press, 1938.

Geschichte der Deutschen Sozialdemocratie. Stuttgart, J. W. H. Dietz, 1909.

Mijares, Augusto.

El Libertador. Caracas, Fundación Eugenio Mendoza y Fundación Shell,1964.

Mill, John Stuart.

Autobiography. London, Longman, Green, Reader and Dyer, 1873.

The Subjection of Women. New York, Appleton and Company, 1869.

Miller, Henry.

Red Notebook. Highlands, N.C.; J. Williams, 1954.

Moch, Jules.

Confrontations:Doctrines, Déviations, Expériences et Espérances.

Paris, Gallimard,1952.

Morris, William.

News from Nowhere: Or an Epoch of Rest Being Some Chapters from a Utopian Romance.

London, Reeves & Turner, 1891.

Nicolaevsky, Boris and Mänchen-Helfen, O..

Karl Marx:Man and Fighter. Philadelphia, Lippincott, 1936.

Nomad, Max.

Apostles of Revolution. Boston; Little, Brown; 1939.

Owen, Robert.

Lectures on the Marriages of the Priesthood of the Old Immoral World Delivered in the Year 1835, Before the Passage of the New Marriage Act. Leeds, J. Hobson, 1840.

Pataud and Pouget.

Comment Nous Ferons la Revolution. Paris, Librairie Illustrée J. Tallandier, 1909.

Peusch, Jules L.

    Le Proudhonisme dans l'Association Internationale des Travailleurs.

        Paris, Alcan, 1907.

Plamenatz, John.

    German Marxism and Russian Communism. London: Longman's, Green,1954.

Ponomaryov, B.N. et. al, ed. Andrew Rothstein.

    History of the Communist Party of the Soviet Union. Moscow, FLPH, 1960.

Proudhon, J. P. (Tr. Benjamin Tucker).

    What Is Property: An Inquiry into the principle of Right and Government.

        New York, H.Fertig,1840.

Rathenau, Walther.

    In Days to Come. London, G. Allen & Unwin, Ltd., 1921.

Rawick, George P.

    The New Deal and Youth. University of Wisconsin, 1957.

Riazanov, David.

    Karl Marx, Man, Thinker and Revolutionist. N.Y., International Publishers, 1927.

Saint Simon.

    The New Christianity. London, B.D. Cousins, 1834.

Selznick, Philip.

    Leadership in Administration: A Sociological Interpretation.

        New York, Harper & Row, 1957.

Semmel, Bernard.

    Imperialism and Social Reform; English Social-Imperial Thought 1895-1914.

        Cambridge, Harvard University Press, 1960.

Shiels, Drummond.

    The Webbs and Their Work

Steinmetz, Charles P.

    America and the New Epoch. New York, London; Harper & Brothers, 1916.

Sweezy, Paul M. and Baran, Paul A.

    Monopoly Capitalism: An Essay on the American Economic and Social Order.

        New York, Monthly Review Press, 1968.

Tannenbaum, Frank.

    The Labor Movement: Its Conservative Functions and Social Consequences.

        New York, Putnam, 1921.

    A Philosophy of Labor. New York, Knopf, 1951.

Utechin, S.V. and P.

    What Is To Be Done? Translated by S. V. and P. Utechin. Edited,

                with an introduction and notes, by S. V. Utechin.

        Oxford: Clarendon Press. 213p.

    Russian Political Thought: A Concise History. New York, Praeger, 1964.

    Everyman's Concise Encyclopaedia of Russia. New York, Dutton, 1961.

Villetard, Edmond de Prunieres.
> *History of the International* (tr. S.M. Day, New Haven 1874)

Webb, Beatrice and Sidney.
> *Soviet Communism:: A New Civilization?* New York, Scribner, 1936.

Webb, Sidney.
> *Fabianism and Empire* London, G. Richards. 1900.

Wechsler, James.
> *Revolt on the Campus* New York: Cocivi-Friede, 1935

Index

399

ABOUT HAYMARKET BOOKS

Haymarket Books is a radical, independent, nonprofit book publisher based in Chicago.

Our mission is to publish books that contribute to struggles for social and economic justice. We strive to make our books a vibrant and organic part of social movements and the education and development of a critical, engaged, international left.

We take inspiration and courage from our namesakes, the Haymarket martyrs, who gave their lives fighting for a better world. Their 1886 struggle for the eight-hour day—which gave us May Day, the international workers' holiday—reminds workers around the world that ordinary people can organize and struggle for their own liberation. These struggles continue today across the globe—struggles against oppression, exploitation, poverty, and war.

Since our founding in 2001, Haymarket Books has published more than five hundred titles. Radically independent, we seek to drive a wedge into the risk-averse world of corporate book publishing. Our authors include Noam Chomsky, Arundhati Roy, Rebecca Solnit, Angela Y. Davis, Howard Zinn, Amy Goodman, Wallace Shawn, Mike Davis, Winona LaDuke, Ilan Pappé, Richard Wolff, Dave Zirin, Keeanga-Yamahtta Taylor, Nick Turse, Dahr Jamail, David Barsamian, Elizabeth Laird, Amira Hass, Mark Steel, Avi Lewis, Naomi Klein, and Neil Davidson. We are also the trade publishers of the acclaimed Historical Materialism Book Series and of Dispatch Books.